As office   same barte   into the ma   had presumed it to be a broom closet. But, apparently not, because a light was shining up from somewhere below. That narrow door must lead to a cellar of some sort.

A moment later, he heard a woman's voice coming through the same open door.

"That's Litsa!" exclaimed Byron. "She sounds scared!"

Pistol in hand, Hoch ran toward the narrow door. Only when he reached the bottom was he able to look around.

He was in a cellar, sure enough. Two lamps provided a surprising amount of light. There were five other people in the cellar. In the far corner was a man with a big nose and long dark hair. That matched the description of the missing Descartes. Standing next to him, with a knife held to the man's throat, was Konrad, the tavern's owner.

Litsa was there, too, with two women holding her by the arms. They seemed to pose no immediate danger, so Gotthilf's eyes went back to Konrad and the man he presumed to be the missing philosopher. That presumption was immediately confirmed.

"Drop the gun or Descartes gets it!" shouted Konrad. Either from intent or nervousness—most likely the latter—he jiggled the knife hard enough to open a gash in the philosopher's neck.

It was a very shallow wound. But it was enough to make Descartes gasp.

It was also enough to make up Gotthilf's mind. At this range, he was quite a good shot.

He took the proper stance, aimed the revolver between Descartes' legs, and fired.

—from "Descartes Before the Whores"
by Eric Flint

THE RING OF FIRE SERIES

To purchase any of these titles in e-book form, please go to www.baen.com.

Grantville Gazette VIII

Created by **ERIC FLINT**
Edited by **Eric Flint & Walt Boyes**

BAEN

GRANTVILLE GAZETTE VIII

Copyright © 2018 by Eric Flint

A Baen Books Original

Baen Publishing Enterprises
P.O. Box 1403
Riverdale, NY 10471
www.baen.com

ISBN: 978-1-9821-2425-0

Cover art by Tom Kidd

First printing, June 2018
First mass market printing, December 2019

Distributed by Simon & Schuster
1230 Avenue of the Americas
New York, NY 10020

Pages by Joy Freeman (www.pagesbyjoy.com)
Printed in the United States of America

10 9 8 7 6 5 4 3 2 1

To the Memory of Ruthie Carrico

Contents

Grantville Gazette VIII

Preface

Eric Flint

This is the eighth anthology of stories from the electronic magazine *The Grantville Gazette* that Baen Books has published, and the first one since Walt Boyes replaced Paula Goodlett as the editor of the magazine. (Paula had edited the *Gazette* for over eleven years and wanted to concentrate more on her own writing.)

As has proven to be true with every Baen edition of the *Gazette* since we shifted to a "best of" format beginning with the fifth volume, the number of issues from which we select stories continues to expand. *Grantville Gazette V* contained stories selected from issues 5–10, *Grantville Gazette VI* contained stories selected from issues 11–19, and *Grantville Gazette VII* contained stories selected from issues 20–30.

This eighth volume has stories which Walt and I selected from issues 31 through 45 of the electronic magazine. The reason for the expansion was the same in each case: The magazine has been so successful that we've had to scramble to catch up.

1

As of the publication of this anthology in June of 2018, the magazine is up to 77 issues. Or, to put it another way, we're *still* more than thirty issues behind the magazine with these follow-on "best of" Baen paper editions. At the rate we're going, we'll need two more anthology volumes to catch up.

Except we won't, even then. Here's the publication history of the Baen Books editions of the *Grantville Gazette*:

Volume I	November 2004
Volume II	March 2006
Volume III	December 2006
Volume IV	June 2008
Volume V	August 2009
Volume VI	January 2012
Volume VII	April 2015
Volume VIII	June 2018

That's eight volumes in twelve and a half years, or an average of about once every year and a half. And for the last four volumes, the average has been more like once every two and a half years. (Why the slowdown in the production rate? Basically, because we're producing more novels in the series and there are only so many available slots for new hardcover titles.)

So . . . by the time we catch up to Volume 77 of the electronic magazine, it'll be about five years from now, at which point we'll be up to Volume 107, thereabouts.

That assumes nothing changes, of course. Which it may—series do go belly-up from time to time. But, so far at least, the Ring of Fire series has continued to enjoy commercial success and there's no indication that'll change any time soon.

Granted, I may be whistling as I walk past a grave-yard. But cemeteries hold no fear for me. Why should they?

Because of ghosts, ghouls, wraiths, spectres and suchlike?

Be serious. We're talking about *stories* here. That's what I do for a living.

Eric Flint
November 2017

Descartes Before the Whores

Eric Flint

Magdeburg, capital of the United States of Europe
Rathaus, Office of the police chief
October 20, 1636

"I'm sorry, guys, but that's the way it is. We have to put Descartes before the whores." Bill Reilly, the city of Magdeburg's police chief, leaned back in his chair and planted his hands firmly upon his desk, in that ancient gesture of bosses that signified: *Here I sit—you can do no other.*

Gotthilf Hoch glanced at his partner, Byron Chieske. He decided that this was an issue that had enough of an up-time—what to call it? flavor? aura?—that he could reasonably keep quiet while Chieske handled it. Like Reilly, Byron was an American.

And who but Americans would get this worked up over the fate of a man whom Gotthilf had not only never heard of, but was a foreigner to boot? A foreigner twice over, in fact—born a Frenchman, and still a subject of the French crown, but one who now resided in the Netherlands. And not any of the Catholic parts of the Lowlands, either, like Brabant, even though the foreign fellow in question was himself a Catholic. No, the man had been residing in the Calvinist portions of the Netherlands since he emigrated from France back in . . .

Gotthilf searched his memory, trying to bring up that item from the briefing they'd just gotten from the police chief.

Back in 1618. Almost twenty years ago now—and the man was only in his early forties.

Typical Catholic, Gotthilf thought disdainfully. This Descartes fellow had apparently left France in order to take advantage of the free-thinking—more free-thinking, at least—attitudes in Holland, but still stubbornly refused to give up his papist heresies.

Not that many of the Lowlands' Calvinists weren't also intolerant and narrow-minded, especially the more rabid Gomarists. For that matter, although Gotthilf was a proper Lutheran, there were plenty of Lutherans who suffered from the sin of pride, so certain they were that they knew every jot and tittle of God's designs for the world. Gotthilf had thought so even before the Ring of Fire and the arrival of the Americans, whose advocacy of freedom of religion had been congenial to him.

But his partner was already protesting, so Gotthilf broke off his ruminations.

"—no way of knowing if this"—Byron rapped his fingers on one of the sheets atop Reilly's desk—"so-called ransom note is even legitimate. I mean, for Pete's sake, Bill, *look* at the thing. It's like somebody's idiot notion of what a ransom note looks like based on watching B-grade cop movies. In the *seventeenth century*?".

Chieske threw up his hands. "Is kidnapping even a recognized crime in this day and age?"

As sympathetic as he was to his partner's stance, Gotthilf's stubborn honesty forced him to state, "Yes, although it's called 'abduction.' But, Byron, whoever's behind this probably *did* get the idea—both for the crime itself as well as the ransom note—from watching up-time movies. They're not all that uncommon anymore, even here in Magdeburg, much less in Grantville—and lots of people make a visit to Grantville these days."

The police chief grunted his agreement. "He's right. One of the principal tourist attractions in Grantville are the theaters showing American movies that we had on VHS or DVDs, and even some old Betamax tapes. The last time I was there both the Criterion and the Majestic theaters were running eighteen hours a day—and they were building a new theater complex that was supposed to operate around the clock."

He leaned forward and tapped his own forefinger on the same sheet of paper that Chieske had rapped with his fingers. "Just like Gotthilf says, that's probably where the perp or perps got the idea in the first place."

Scowling, Byron stared down at the sheet. Upon it were pasted letters obviously cut from different sources. Mostly from cheap newspapers, judging by the quality of the cut-out little pieces of paper.

We got FilOsoFer Des cArtE SenD

It went on like that: *We got filosofer Des Carte send 50,000 dollars or he sleeps with the fishes instructions will follow.*

"'Sleeps with the fishes,'" snorted Chieske. "One thing's for sure—somebody watched *The Godfather.*"

He reached back his long arms, planted his hands on the armrests of his chair, and eased himself down. Once seated, he gave the police chief a look that came very close to an outright glare.

"I still don't see why whatever happened to this Descartes guy is more important than three missing women."

"For Chrissake, Byron, we're talking about whores."

"No, Bill, we're not. We're talking about *people.*"

Not for the first time, Gotthilf was glad that Byron was his partner rather than Reilly. He respected the American police chief's experience and abilities, but he didn't much like the man.

Reilly had the grace to look embarrassed for a moment. But it was a brief moment. Within seconds, he was back to scowling. "My point wasn't that whores aren't people—which you know damn good and well—but that whores disappear all the time for a hundred reasons."

He slumped a little in his chair and shook his head. "Look, I got no choice," he said. He pointed to the ceiling above him with his forefinger. "I got pressure coming down—big time—from on high."

"From who?" Byron asked.

"The princess."

"Kristina? What does she care?—and, anyway, she's only nine years old. How much clout can she have?"

Reilly's scowl deepened. "Which part of the word 'princess' are you having the most trouble with, Byron?

How about the phrases 'sole heir to the throne' and 'future empress of the USE'? Those give you trouble too?"

He slapped the desk with the palm of his hand. "Look—it's settled. Descartes before the whores." He lifted the hand and made a shooing gesture with it. "So off you go. See if you can find out who's got him and where they're holding him. I don't think we're dealing with mastermind arch-criminals, here. This is more likely the work of Elmer Fudd than Fu Manchu."

Gotthilf didn't understand the specific American references that Reilly was using, but the gist of it was clear enough. He thought the police chief was probably right, too.

Chieske rose. "You'll let us know when those 'instructions' come in, I assume."

Reilly nodded.

Fifteen seconds later, Gotthilf and Byron were moving down the corridor outside, headed for the entrance to the municipal building.

Magdeburg, capital of the United States of Europe
Royal Palace
October 20, 1636

"I killed him, Caroline! The encyclopedia says so!"

Caroline Platzer glanced at the window of Princess Kristina's room in the royal palace. (Bill Reilly's finger-pointing at the ceiling of his office had been purely symbolic. Magdeburg's municipal building was several blocks away from the royal palace.)

Perhaps fortunately, the room had no view of the Elbe. By this point, Caroline was ready to dunk her charge in the river.

She wouldn't actually *drown* Kristina, of course. Just . . . give her a good soaking. The child could be a burden, sometimes.

"You did *not* kill René Descartes," Caroline said firmly. "He died of pneumonia."

"It was my fault! I made him attend me early in the morning—in Sweden! Where it gets cold in the winter. Don't tell me I didn't, Caroline! It's in the encyclopedia! I can read, you know. Four languages! Almost five, now."

The princess wasn't boasting. The girl was almost frighteningly precocious.

"For pity's sake, Kristina, that all happened decades from now—and in another universe. You haven't done anything to Descartes in *this* one."

Kristina's expression was mulish. "Well . . . maybe not. But I still feel responsible for him. And now he's been abducted! Right here in Magdeburg! We have to do something! As I said to the police chief!"

And hadn't Bill Reilly been thrilled to get that royal attention, thought Caroline. She didn't particularly care for the police chief, but at the moment he had her sympathy.

Kristina had been in an agitated mood for weeks now, ever since her betrothed had left to join her father fighting the Ottomans besieging Linz. She'd become very attached to Ulrik and emotionally dependent on the Danish prince she'd be marrying in a few years.

Well, more than a few. It'd be seven or eight years before she was old enough to have a wedding.

"We have to do something!" Kristina repeated. She charged for the door leading—eventually; the palace was large and, in places, labyrinthine—to the street.

Caroline followed, not *quite* running. Thinking thoughts of princesses tossed into rivers.

Magdeburg, capital of the United States of Europe
Ratskeller
October 20, 1636

"I insist!" said Elisabeth von Schwarzenfels, waving a chapbook under Byron Chieske's nose. "I must bring Descartes before the Horus!"

The American policeman looked up at her, frowning. "Before the . . . *what*?"

"The Horus! The eye of Horus!" Von Schwarzenfels rotated the chapbook in her left hand so that Chieske could see the cover. With the forefinger of the other hand, she imperiously jabbed at the illustration across the top. It was an eye of Horus . . . sort of. Allowing for the pronounced suggestion that this particular Horus was a Peeping Tom.

Byron groaned. Not at the illustration but at the sight of the chapbook's title.

THE NATIONAL OBSERVER
Enquiring minds want to know!

"Oh, for God's sake," he said, lapsing into the blasphemy that he usually avoided in deference to seventeenth-century mores. "*That* rag."

"It's a matter of freedom of the press!" said the young woman.

Elisabeth von Schwarzenfels was dressed in a satin-tabbed bodice with full sleeves, dyed gold and lavender and trimmed with silver braid, along with a matching petticoat. Her bodice was laced up with a coral ribbon over a stomacher, with a matching ribbon set in a V-shape at her front waist and tied in a bow to one side. A ribbon and a string of pearls decorated her auburn hair.

In short, she had the appearance of exactly what she was—a member of the German upper nobility, the Hochadel, but one whose family was not especially wealthy. The clothing was well-designed and well-made, but not extraordinarily expensive.

Gotthilf busied himself with quaffing from his stein of beer. He was seated on the other side of the table from his partner. After finishing their discussion with Reilly, the two of them had repaired to the tavern in the basement of the city hall to discuss the case of Descartes in a more congenial setting. Von Schwarzenfels had tracked them down there less than forty-five minutes after they'd left the police chief's office. How she'd managed to do that was a mystery to Gotthilf.

Perhaps an even bigger mystery to the level-headed policeman was the woman's evident devotion to a profession that would seem quite unsuitable to such a one as she. Not only had Elisabeth von Schwarzenfels chosen to become a journalist, but one who devoted most of her time to writing for a magazine which, in the short time since it had been launched, had already become disreputable. *The National Observer* was what the up-timers called a "scandal sheet" or just the pithier term "rag" that his partner had used.

"Freedom of the press!" Elisabeth repeated. "I insist on reporting on your progress in apprehending the scoundrels who abducted one of Europe's most famous philosophers."

Gotthilf laughed and gestured to an empty chair. "Litsa, have a seat and join us for a beer. I'm getting a crick in my neck from looking up at you. And stop pretending. You never heard of Descartes any more than we did—until he got taken a short time ago. He's not famous *now*."

Von Schwarzenfels looked stubborn. "Well, he *will* be famous, Gotthilf. I know! I asked Melissa Mailey. She said this Descartes fellow will be—already was, in the world she came from—one of the most famous thinkers of all time."

Chieske looked over at his partner. Hoch shrugged. "I've known Litsa for a while, Byron. If we don't let her come along, she'll just follow us and be an even bigger nuisance."

Privately, although he wasn't about to say it out loud, Gotthilf thought Litsa might even be of help to them. He'd been on friendly terms with the young noblewoman since she got back to Magdeburg from a recent adventure. One thing he'd learned about her was that when she got interested in a subject she would pursue it indefatigably—and she seemed to have a genuine knack for getting information out of people. The articles she wrote for *The National Observer* had quite a bit of real substance to them.

Her prose was terrible, though. Really, really terrible.

Magdeburg, capital of the United States of Europe
Rathaus, police headquarters
October 21, 1636

"Descartes before the—" Hoarse from her overly long and passionate peroration to Magdeburg's mayor

Otto Gericke on the necessity to save one of history's greatest philosophers, Melissa Mailey broke off from her current—equally passionate if not (yet) as overly long—peroration to the two policemen who'd been assigned to the case.

Cough, cough. "Sorry," she said. "Before the publication of his *Discourse on the Method*—that happened in the year 1637, in the universe I came from—Descartes was an obscure figure to most people. So it's not at all surprising that neither of you had heard of him. In this universe..."

She frowned, searching her memory for what she remembered about Descartes—most of which came from her perusal of the encyclopedias in Magdeburg's city library that morning. The course she'd taken on the history of philosophy in college was a long ways back.

"I'm not sure what'll happen in this universe." She gave Byron Chieske and Gotthilf Hoch a stern look. "Assuming that Descartes isn't just murdered outright, as his kidnappers are threatening to do."

"We'll do our best to prevent that," said Byron. He was trying to be reassuring, but to Melissa he just sounded stolid.

She sighed and ran fingers through her hair. It was completely gray now—and a dull and dismal shade of gray at that, to her mind. That caused Melissa some never-admitted-aloud but genuine distress. The discreet and demure up-time hair-coloring she'd used since her mid-forties and for a while after the Ring of Fire had all vanished some time ago. And Melissa simply didn't have the temperament to use the more garish types of hair-coloring available in the seventeenth century.

"Anyway," she continued, "the main thing he'd been

working on was a work called *Treatise on the World,* but he hid that away after Galileo was condemned because he'd pretty much supported Galileo's astronomical views."

Gotthilf frowned. "But Galileo *wasn't*—"

"Wasn't condemned," Melissa finished for him. "No, he wasn't—in *this* universe. That's mostly because of Larry Mazzare," she added, with a great deal of home-town pride. "So, who knows? He might wind up publishing *Treatise on the World,* after all."

The stern look returned. "Assuming you manage to keep him from being killed."

"We'll do our best," said Byron stolidly.

Once Melissa had left, Byron shook his head. "I'd still rather be looking for those missing girls. This case..." He shook his head again. "I got no idea where to even start."

Elisabeth von Schwarzenfels, who'd charged off the afternoon of the day before after receiving a tip, came charging into the office where Byron and Gotthilf had invited Melissa Mailey to provide them with some background.

"Someone saw him!" she exclaimed. She was practically bouncing with excitement. "Just two days ago! Descartes before the Horace!"

"The Horace?" Gotthilf and Byron glanced at each other.

"What would a philosopher be doing in *that* dive?" Chieske wondered.

Gotthilf shrugged. "Maybe he's fond of bad music and worse women."

"Or was looking for chewing tobacco," Byron said, followed by a snort of derision. The Horace was a tavern to the west of Magdeburg's Neustadt, about a mile from the Navy Yard. The owner fancied a décor that included imitations of up-time mementos, one of the most prominent of which was a "Mail Pouch" advertisement next to the entrance.

"You will never find a more wretched hive of scum and villainy," said Elisabeth.

Chieske rolled his eyes. "Give me a break."

"I *like* that movie," protested Elisabeth.

Magdeburg, capital of the United States of Europe
Inside Horace Tavern, Greater Magdeburg
October 21, 1636

Elisabeth looked around the central room of the tavern, scrutinizing the patrons. At this time of the day, there were only four of them. All three who were awake were clearly inebriated. Presumably, the man who was slumped back in his chair, his eyes closed and snoring, was drunk also.

"These are not the philosophers we're looking for," she pronounced.

Byron grimaced. Gotthilf smiled. He'd been quite taken by the *Star Wars* film himself, enough to have watched it twice.

The tavern keeper behind the counter along one side of the room—what up-timers would have called "the bar"—just looked puzzled. The man wasn't the owner of the establishment, just an employee, and from what Gotthilf had been able to determine he seemed not much better informed of the world around him than the yeast in the beer he served.

"When is Eberhart going to return, then?" asked

Chieske. He'd given up trying to discover the owner's whereabouts, since the tavern keeper's only response to that question—which the up-time policeman had now asked three times—was a sullen shrug.

The tavern keeper shrugged again. Sullenly.

Gotthilf continued his examination of the Horace's interior décor. This was the fourth—no, fifth—time he'd come into the establishment and he was looking for anything that might have changed since the last time he was here. There was no particular reason for doing so; he was just trying to pass the time while his partner continued his fruitless interrogation of the man behind the counter.

Next to the entrance was the Mail Pouch advertisement that had been there the first time Gotthilf had entered the Horace. That had been...eight months ago?

Somewhere around that time. To the right of that was an octagonal up-time stop sign, whose red color was starting to fade or—more likely—was a down-time replica that had never been a bright red to begin with.

To the right of the sign was an up-time television set, perched on a ledge. Gotthilf had no doubt that was genuine, since no one would have bothered to make an imitation TV set that was obviously old, decrepit and non-functioning.

The rest of the décor on the wall behind the counter was of no great note. Neither was the billiards table nearby, which was down-time made but of the American "pool" design.

More interesting was the large sign hanging on the wall facing the entrance. In Fraktur script, it read:

Nunc est Bibendum
Nunc Pede libero pulsanda Tellus

The Latin translated roughly as "Now we must drink, and stamp the ground with a free foot." It was a quote from one of the *Odes* of the ancient Roman poet Horace, after whom the tavern was named.

How the tavern's owner Konrad Eberhart, who knew no Latin and had never been known to set foot inside a church of any denomination since his arrival in Magdeburg, had come across those *Odes* was a mystery. As was, for that matter, everything else about the man. Gotthilf thought the likelihood that "Konrad Eberhart" was his real name was about the same as the likelihood that he was a former ballet dancer. Which, given his stubby legs and impressive girth, Gotthilf placed somewhere between "fat chance" and "hell freezes over."

Gotthilf tried to think of any reason a philosopher would have come to such an establishment. Besides alcoholic beverages of poor quality and the company of prostitutes who were no better, he couldn't think of any. Either this Descartes fellow was very short of funds or he just had a taste for lowlife—what his up-time partner sometimes called "slumming."

Neither seemed very likely to Gotthilf, especially the first reason. A man who could support himself without doing any visible labor wouldn't presumably be so short of money that he'd have to make do with the entertainment available at the Horace.

On the other hand, what did Gotthilf Hoch know about philosophers? Being honest, not much of anything.

"Let's go," said Byron, who'd finally given up trying to get any useful information from the bartender.

☆   ☆   ☆

When he advanced his two (very tentative) hypotheses to Chieske, after they'd left the tavern, the American policeman shook his head.

"I think it's probably even simpler than that. We still haven't found out where Descartes was staying."

"The Horace doesn't have any rooms to let," protested Gotthilf. "At least, I saw no sign of any."

"Neither did I. But he might have been staying in the vicinity and just happened to be walking by the Horace when Litsa's informant spotted him."

Gotthilf came to an abrupt halt and slapped his forehead. "Ah! Stupid! Of course—I assumed he was going into the place. But he could have just been passing in front of it."

He looked around. This part of Greater Magdeburg wasn't a slum, but that was mostly because like almost all parts of the city the construction was too new to have started decaying. Still, it was several steps down from the sort of neighborhood Gotthilf would have expected to find one of the world's greatest minds choosing to reside in.

Byron, who'd also come to a halt, gave a little shrug. "Who knows?" He started walking toward the Rathaus again. "Let's see if we can track down Melissa. She might know something she doesn't even realize she knows."

Indeed, so it proved.

"Interesting," she mused. "One thing I learned from the study I just did of what information we have on Descartes is that he was an odd duck in all sorts of ways. One of them is—a philosopher! Go figure!— he never owned very many books. Apparently he didn't like to read much. Another is that he moved constantly. From town to town, and from lodging to lodging. So it's quite possible that he'd taken a room somewhere in the vicinity of the Horace. And there's one other thing!"

Triumphantly: "I'm pretty sure I know why Descartes came to Magdeburg in the first place. That was another unsolved mystery, wasn't it?"

Gotthilf wouldn't have labeled that question a "mystery," himself. After all, lots of people came to Magdeburg every day for all sorts of reasons. Still, it was true that they hadn't yet uncovered Descartes' reason.

"Somebody with his description went to the hospital three days ago and tried to get an interview with James."

Byron looked puzzled. "With Dr. Nichols? Why? Did the guy say he was sick? And did your husband agree to see him?"

Gotthilf had to struggle not to laugh, seeing the prim and disapproving expression on Melissa's face. In point of fact, she and Dr. James Nichols were not married, although they had been living together and enjoying conjugal relations almost since the Ring of Fire. Apparently—no down-timer could ever make any sense of it—Mailey found a source of pride in the fact that she and Nichols were flouting convention.

There was a witty little saying that had spread widely in the years since the Ring of Fire: *All Americans are weird some of the time, and some Americans are weird all of the time.* Melissa, if not her paramour, was generally considered to be pretty far over to the *weird-all-of-the-time* end of that spectrum, at least by those who found her political and social views rather abhorrent.

Melissa shook her head. "James didn't see him for the simple reason that he's not in town. He went to Dresden for a few days, to help them set up the operation of their new hospital. But I'm willing to bet the reason Descartes wanted to see him wasn't because Descartes himself was feeling ill. I checked with the people who saw the fellow and they said he didn't seem sick."

"So why'd he want to see Dr. Nichols?" asked Byron.

"I think it was because Descartes must have read a biography of himself somewhere and learned that his daughter Francine is—well, she's not sick now. But in the universe we came from, she died—would die, will die; you parse the grammar any way you want—about four years from now. The girl is a year old. She's 'scheduled' to die in 1640, from scarlet fever. Of course, that'll never happen because of the butterfly effect. But who's to say she won't die even earlier, from some other disease? Child mortality's horrible in this day and age. Still is, even with the medical knowledge we up-timers brought with us."

Byron grunted. "So. You're saying Descartes showed up here in Magdeburg hoping...for what, exactly? If his daughter's not sick yet, what's Dr. Nichols supposed to do?"

Melissa shrugged. "I imagine Descartes wanted James to agree to treat his daughter if and when she does get sick—which she's almost bound to, these days. Especially if she's not living in Magdeburg or Grantville or someplace that has a decent sewage system. Which, so far as I know, is not true of any city or town in the Netherlands outside of maybe the royal palace in Brussels."

The stern look of almost-reproof came back. "Presumably, that's still what Descartes wants—if he hasn't been murdered yet."

"We're doing our best, Ms. Mailey," Chieske said stolidly.

Magdeburg, capital of the United States of Europe
Rathaus, police headquarters
October 22, 1636

The young man who was escorted into the office shared by Gotthilf and Byron looked to be in his early twenties. From various subtleties in his dress and demeanor he was clearly a down-timer, although he had an expensive-looking up-time camera suspended around his neck by a strap.

"Yes?" asked Byron. "What can we do for you?"

"And what's your name?" added Gotthilf. The man looked familiar to him, but he couldn't remember when and where he might have encountered him.

The youngster looked uncertain. "Well, I'm here because... ah, I'm Anton Fuchs."

The name refreshed Gotthilf's memory. "Ah, yes," he said. "You work with Litsa sometimes. For *The National Observer.*"

"For *Simplicissimus* too," Fuchs said, naming the other magazine Elisabeth von Schwarzenfels wrote for. He tapped the camera hanging from his neck. "I'm the freelance photographer Litsa usually hires when she needs one."

"So what pictures is she having you take now?"

That came from Byron, who didn't sound particularly interested.

Fuchs shook his head. "No, it was something else, this time. She told me she was planning to return to that tavern she visited with you yesterday. The Horse, I think it was."

"The Horace," Gotthilf corrected him. "Whatever for? And when was this?"

"She said she thought there was something suspicious about the place. And it was last night. She said she wanted to wait until it was dark so the barkeep wouldn't recognize her if he was still there when she went back. She also said she was planning to disguise herself as a whore."

"Oh, for God's sake!" exclaimed Byron, once again forgetting to avoid blasphemy.

Years of Lutheran discipline kept Gotthilf from blaspheming himself, but he had no trouble understanding his partner's exasperation.

Elisabeth von Schwarzenfels? "Disguised" *as a whore?*

The notion was preposterous. The young noblewoman had absolutely no idea how a prostitute of that station in life would speak or act. Gotthilf doubted if she could pull off being disguised as a high-class courtesan, for that matter. She had the wrong personality, to put it mildly—and Gotthilf had never seen the slightest indication that Litsa could behave in any other manner than the one that came to her naturally. Which could be summed up in the word . . .

Brash? Impetuous? Headstrong? All of them would do.

"Reckless," muttered Chieske.

Yes, that word too. Gotthilf rose to his feet. "So why

are you here?" he asked Fuchs. "I presume she hired you to serve as her watchdog."

The young photographer nodded, looking very worried now. "Yes. She said if she hadn't returned in the morning I should come here and tell you."

Gotthilf and Byron exchanged glances. For a moment, Chieske looked utterly exasperated. But he, too, rose to his feet—and took his Colt .45 pistol out of the desk drawer where he kept it when he was working in the office.

Gotthilf touched the holster at his own hip, reflexively making sure that his own weapon was there. That was done purely out of now-ingrained habit, though. The down-time-made H&K .44 seven-shot revolver that he favored was quite heavy—heavy enough that he could sense its presence even sitting down.

"Let's go," Byron said grimly. "Let's just hope the silly girl hasn't gotten herself in a real bind."

He and Gotthilf headed for the street entrance, with Fuchs trailing behind. Gotthilf thought about ordering the photographer to stay behind, since he had no weapon other than his camera. But . . . who could say? He might prove to be of some use.

Magdeburg, capital of the United States of Europe
The Horace, a tavern in Greater Magdeburg
October 22, 1636

Seeing no reason to dally, the two policemen charged into the Horace as soon as they arrived. Gotthilf went first, with his revolver drawn and in his hand.

Quickly, he glanced around to see if there was any kind of threat visible.

Nothing. The barkeeper from the day before was nowhere to be seen. The only people in the tavern this early in the morning—the sun had risen some time earlier, but they were still closer to dawn than noon—were a drunk collapsed over a table and a would-be troubadour leaning against the bar plucking away at a double-necked lute. A woman perched on the bar had her arms around him and was exclaiming some sort of appreciative noises.

No one else was to be seen. Gotthilf started to relax until his eyes returned to the woman sitting on the bar. She was fairly young and fairly attractive, but what really registered on him—nagged at him, rather—was that . . .

What was it about her?

Of course. She fit the description of one of the prostitutes who had gone missing earlier that week.

As Gotthilf grappled with that thought, trying to figure out what if anything it might signify, two other phenomena made their appearance.

First, the bartender—the same man they'd encountered the day before—came into the main room of the Horace through a door so narrow that Gotthilf had presumed it to be the entrance to a broom closet.

But, apparently not, because a light was shining up from somewhere below. That narrow door must lead to a cellar of some sort.

A moment later, the second phenomenon made its presence apparent.

That was a woman's voice coming through the same open door. Litsa's voice, to be precise—which was quite a distinctive one. And while Gotthilf couldn't make out the words she was yelling, they clearly expressed such sentiments as . . .

Outrage. Indignation. Displeasure.

"That's Litsa!" exclaimed Byron. "She sounds scared!"

Yes, that word too.

The young woman squawked with fear and threw herself off the bar so violently that she sent the troubadour-not-ready-for-prime-time sprawling on the floor. She then raced for a door in a corner on the wall opposite the entrance the two policemen had come through, flung it open, and ran into what appeared to be an alley beyond.

The barkeeper issued a squawk of his own and ran after her.

Out of reflex, Gotthilf almost chased them, but there was still Von Schwarzenfels to look after. So, he ran toward the narrow door leading down to the cellar, his pistol still in hand.

The guilty would just have to flee where no man pursued. Perhaps they could track down the prostitute and the bartender later.

He had to jump over the prone body of the lute-player to get to the door. Judging from the noises behind him, Byron had tried make the same leap and failed. It sounded as if Gotthilf's tall up-time partner had sprawled across the tavern floor himself.

But Hoch had no time to worry about that now. He was through the door and pounding down a set of equally narrow stairs. The risers were pitched so steeply that he had to concentrate entirely on not falling.

Only when he reached the bottom was he able to look around.

He was in a cellar, sure enough. Two lamps provided a surprising amount of light. Gotthilf didn't take the time to check, but he assumed they were the new up-time-designed lamps called "Coleman."

The key thing was that he could see quite clearly.

There were five other people in the cellar. In the far corner was a man he didn't know, with a big nose and long dark hair. That matched the description of Descartes. Standing next to him, with a knife held to the big-nosed, dark-haired man's throat, was a fellow Gotthilf recognized as the Horace's owner. That was the man who called himself Konrad Eberhart. He was just as stubby-legged and paunchy as Gotthilf remembered.

Since Eberhart was only armed with a knife rather than a gun, Gotthilf took the time to glance into another corner of the cellar.

Litsa was there. Two women were holding her by the arms. At a guess, going by the descriptions he and Byron had gotten, those were the other two missing prostitutes.

They seemed to pose no immediate danger, however, so Gotthilf's eyes went back to Eberhart and the man he presumed to be the missing philosopher.

The tavern's owner immediately confirmed his presumption.

"Drop the gun or Descartes gets it!" shouted Eberhart. Either from intent or nervousness—most likely the latter—he jiggled the knife hard enough to open a gash in the philosopher's neck.

It was a very shallow wound, not in the least bit fatal and not even one that bled badly. But it was enough to make Descartes gasp.

It was also enough to make up Gotthilf's mind. As agitated as he so clearly was, Eberhart was just as likely to kill his victim by accident as by design.

Nothing for it, then—and at this range, Gotthilf was quite a good shot.

He took the proper stance, aimed the revolver between Descartes' legs, and fired.

In the cramped, enclosed space, the noise was deafening. More than loud enough to drown out Descartes' cry of fear and Eberhart's shriek of pain.

Which would turn to agony, once the shock wore off. The heavy .44 bullet had passed between the philosopher's spread-apart legs and struck Eberhart's left knee. The poor bastard would be a cripple the rest of his life—which might be a short one, depending on how Magdeburg's judiciary gauged the severity of the newfangled crime of "kidnapping."

That one shot had ended the standoff, though. Eberhart had collapsed, flinging the knife away somewhere. He was now only half-conscious.

Gotthilf turned to the three women. Casually, he waggled his revolver back and forth a couple of times.

"Do I need to keep shooting?" he asked.

Hastily, the two women holding Litsa let her go. She shook her arms, took a step forward, and then suddenly spun around and struck one of the women on the face hard enough to knock her down.

The other woman backed up, but Litsa didn't do more than scowl at her.

Moving toward Gotthilf, Litsa pointed behind her to the woman she'd struck. "That one's name is Gisela. The other one's Cloris. They're two of the missing prostitutes you were worried about—ha! And for no reason! They're nothing but criminals themselves. Kidnapperesses. They're the ones who Eberhart hired to guard Descartes."

She looked up at the stairs to the tavern above. Byron was starting to come down them now. "There's a third one, too," Litsa went on. "I think her name's Brenda but I'm not sure. She was here last night but I don't know where she is now."

The one named Gisela started to rise. Seeing that, Litsa hissed, strode over, and gave her a kick to the ribs.

Gisela went down again, clutching her side.

"How's it feel, you bitch?" shrilled Litsa. Turning back to Gotthilf, Litsa said angrily, "She *kicked* me! Three times!"

She then glared at Cloris, who was by now backed against the wall. "And that one hit me!" But she didn't do anything more than glare.

Byron reached the cellar floor. "Sorry," he said to Gotthilf. "I fell." He looked around. "But you seem to have handled everything fine."

He looked at Descartes, who was ashen-faced but otherwise seemed in good health.

"You're the philosopher, right? Are you okay?"

Descartes just stared at him. So busy cogitating over the fact that he still existed that he was at a momentary loss for words, Gotthilf presumed.

Magdeburg, capital of the United States of Europe
Home of Melissa Mailey and James Nichols
October 25, 1636

James Nichols handed Melissa one of the two cups of coffee he'd just made. War with the Ottoman Empire and disruption of trade routes be damned. As the premier doctor of Europe—probably the whole world, in fact—Nichols was rich enough to afford as much coffee as he and his not-exactly-a-wife wanted.

His conjugal duties of the morning fulfilled, James resumed his place alongside Melissa in their bed. He had the subtly self-satisfied expression of a man who's spent the night before fulfilling other conjugal duties. Melissa would have teased him about it, but, truth to tell, she was feeling pretty self-satisfied herself. It had been a nice reunion.

Even if James had been gone for less than a week. He'd just returned to Magdeburg the night before.

"So how'd it finally settle out?" he asked her. Melissa had only given him a brief sketch the night before of what she had taken to calling *l'affaire Descartes*.

"Well, first off, you've got a new patient. Three of 'em, in fact."

Blowing on his coffee to cool it down, Nichols frowned. The expression signified puzzlement, not protest. "Three . . . There's the girl—what's her name? Francine?—and Descartes himself, I assume. Who's the third one?"

"Well, no. That's what we thought. But it turns out we did the same thing that we make fun of down-timers for all the time. We assumed that history didn't change at the Ring of Fire."

James made a face. "What do you mean? I thought he was 'having his way' with the servants in Amsterdam." The casual readiness of seventeenth-century men of means to take sexual advantage of their servants was something up-timers disapproved of strongly—even if plenty of American men had been (and still were) guilty of sexual harassment themselves.

Seeing the expression, Melissa shook her head.

"It's a little more complicated, in this case, from what I read about Descartes. In the original history, apparently he took care of the woman for years, even after the child died of scarlet fever. But the key is the tryst with the servant happened after we arrived. So it didn't. We assumed it did. Butterflies bite the smarty-pants up-timers in the ass."

James blew on the coffee again. "Fine. René Descartes is a paragon of virtue, at least by seventeenth-century standards. And he didn't diddle the serving girl. So who are my three patients?"

Melissa pulled her knees up to her chin and patted the bed beside her. "It turns out that Descartes was way ahead of us. He has been living in Paris, got married, and caused enough trouble to get practically assassinated and driven into seclusion since the Ring of Fire."

James sat on the edge of the bed. "Busy guy. But who are the patients?"

"Basically the same, with the addition of Descartes himself. He was actually rather badly injured in an assassination attempt, and he has some tendon damage in his hand. But he still has a wife and daughter. So he is worried about the same scarlet fever thing happening again. Or some other disease."

"What else came out of the dickering? And who did the negotiations, anyway? I can't imagine Kristina making more than a complete mess of it."

"Who do you think? Caroline Platzer, of course. She got Descartes to agree to Kristina's desire—okay, let's be honest and call it a petulant royal demand—that Descartes become one of her tutors. The girl says she's trying to make amends for—I love this part—the fact that she killed him in another universe, but the truth is I think she just likes the idea of having a famous philosopher as a tutor."

James chuckled. "He *isn't* famous. In this universe, that is." After a moment, he added, "Yet, anyway."

Again, he blew on the cup. Unlike Melissa, who'd already started drinking hers, the doctor preferred his coffee almost lukewarm. "But why'd he agree? It can't just be the medical angle. The truth is that he doesn't need me to be anything more than an occasional consultant. Possibly some minor surgery, most likely just some physical therapy, depending on his injuries. Which is just as well, since I need to get back to the siege at Linz soon. So do you, for that matter."

"Well, first off, Caroline pointed out to him all the medical advantages he'd gain if he resettled himself and his daughter—and his wife—here in Magdeburg."

Melissa set down her cup on the table next to her side of the bed and started counting off her fingers. "First, decent sewage. Second—he really liked this part, since *cogito ergo sum* can be done sitting on the can as well as anywhere else—decent plumbing. Third, the best hospital in the world."

"One of 'em, anyway," James qualified. "In some respects, the ones in Jena and Grantville are just as good or better, and there's a lot to be said for the new hospital in Bamberg."

Melissa made a tongue-clucking sound. "Thankfully, Caroline's a better negotiator than you'll ever be. According to her version, Magdeburg's hospital is *way* better than any other one. And finally—"

She counted off the fourth finger. "Caroline got Kristina to agree—and it's in writing, not just verbal—that her lessons with Descartes won't ever start before noon. Oh, yeah, and she also pointed out"—here Melissa counted off the last finger—"that the royal palace here in Magdeburg, quite unlike the one in Sweden, also has decent heating so it doesn't get cold in the winter. Not enough to induce pneumonia, at any rate."

"Actually, cold by itself is not really a major factor when it comes to contracting—"

"*As I said*," Melissa overrode James' qualification, "thankfully, Caroline did the negotiating, not you."

James decided his coffee had cooled off enough, so he took a sip. As he did so, Melissa went on to say: "But, just as you guessed, there's more to it than just the medical angle. There are also what you might call the political and doctrinal issues."

Nichols raised an eyebrow. "Meaning..."

"Meaning that Descartes is still a Catholic even if he's not what you'd call an orthodox one. That's the reason that he suppressed years of his work in the universe we came from, after the church condemned Galileo."

"But—"

"The church didn't condemn Galileo in *this* universe, thanks largely to the fact that Larry Mazzare defended Galileo at his trial." Melissa looked very smug, right then. "That would be the same Larry Mazzare, Caroline pointed out to Descartes, who is now the Cardinal-Protector of the USE."

"Not according to Cardinal Borja," said James. "And the pope who appointed Larry to that position got murdered a little while ago."

"Pfah. Descartes' unorthodoxy stretches plenty far enough that he's got no use at all for Borja and his pack of thugs. He's an adherent of the Urbanite faction in the church. And he very much liked the idea of having Mazzare as the one overseeing his work from a doctrinal angle. He's already started talking to printers about publishing his new work. He builds on all of the philosophy of the last three hundred years, and is supposedly taking it in new directions . He is calling it *Le Nouveau Monde*."

She chuckled again.

"What do you find so amusing?"

"To me, the funniest part about the whole thing is the photograph that Kristina insisted on having taken after the negotiations were done. Litsa's freelancer photographer did it, and Kristina's planning to have it framed and hung up in the palace. Fuchs is really a good photographer, I'm told, and I figure that framed photo is bound to wind up eventually on the wall of a museum somewhere."

"You're probably right. But so what?"

Melissa grinned. "The picture shows Kristina perched atop her favorite horse with Descartes—looking none too pleased about it, let me tell you—standing in front of the critter and holding the reins."

"I still don't—oh." James grinned also.

"Exactly. I'm sure Kristina's planning to title it something like 'The Princess and the Philosopher.' And that'll stick, in German or Amideutsch. But in English?"

James laughed out loud. "It'll be *Descartes Before the Horse*. What else?"

Historically Well Preserved

Virginia DeMarce

Grantville, July 1635

"I arrived in February," Robert Herrick said politely.

Mistress Sophie Thomas, her eyes fixed on the refreshment table, walked between him and Mistress Alannie Clark, bearing a tray of sandwiches and coffee.

He sent a mental prayer of thanks in the general direction of the deity for this timely interruption of the conversation and looked down at the cup of coffee in his hand. He loathed coffee. He loathed the custom of congregating over coffee and pastries for an hour of what amounted to ecclesiastical baby-kissing after the services. He hated baby-kissing, literal or metaphorical, political or ecclesiastical. A bachelor, almost forty-five years old, he was quite content with that status. The fragments of poems that constantly fluttered around in his mind were often addressed to mistresses, but his Julia and Anthea, his Amaryllis and Corinna, even when he was acquainted with their models, were purely imaginary creatures who, clad in diaphanous draperies, danced barefoot through the sparkling diamonds of May's dew-studded grass.

It was very satisfactory of them to remain imaginary. Real women—the "fellowship room" on the ground floor of the church, under the sanctuary, was, at the moment, occupied by too many of them—weren't sufficiently... ethereal. His glance swept the room at floor level. They were more likely to wear sturdy shoes and trudge through slush in January or mud in July.

If he had been able to hibernate in the libraries, as he had originally planned when he began this journey... Still, he had learned some things of use. He would eventually become a published author—in another fifteen years or so. That was some consolation for not being a published author as of the present *anno Domini*. But Grantville was an expensive place to live, even if one lived simply.

He glanced around and then shoved the cup of coffee behind one of the curtains on the windows. Services were held above, accessed by a rather attractive flight of double, curving stairs that were almost modern in their design.

Modern by the standards of Europe in 1635, that was.

The city historian had explained the design to him. The founder of the parish had been all too aware of the proclivity of the creek that ran through Grantville to flood more or less regularly, so he had insisted that all the more expensive aspects of the building be placed as high as possible, well out of the reach of muddy waters.

Mistress Thomas said something to Mistress Clark. As soon as her attention turned away from him, he ducked quickly behind a portable flagpole on which the USE flag was mounted before another overly zealous member of the Daughters of the King Ladies' Society could thrust a replacement cup of coffee into his hand.

This time, he remembered to avoid the huge hole in the floor. There had been an unfortunate incident one Sunday when he forgot about it. The vestry had determined to install a temporary railing, but so far hadn't located a carpenter who was willing to work for what they were willing to pay. The historian told him that it had been excavated during a period of time when the building had been rented by a heterodox body called the Church of Christ that practiced the baptism of adults by total immersion. When there had been a proper carved white marble font still in place upstairs! Anabaptists! Generally speaking, heretics had no common sense at all, even aside from their theological idiosyncrasies.

Babies! Kissing babies! He winced. One had only to look at Mistress Riddle's granddaughter to realize that she would shortly be inflicting a quite unavoidable christening party upon him.

Surely, in a world absent the effects of original sin, it would have been possible for a poet to earn a living without becoming a clergyman.

Eve had a lot to answer for.

At least, the up-timers were so focused on time and time schedules that after weekday Morning Prayer, they had the good grace to depart at once—if they came at all, which most of them did not. Weekday Vespers services usually consisted of himself and Mr. and Mrs. Thomas Price Riddle, with their granddaughter assisting the old man. On Sunday, however, a person couldn't get St. Alfred's parishioners out through the doors with a shovel, as Mistress Thomas remarked with appalling good cheer every time he brought the topic up. They stayed and they ate.

Mistress Clark, undeterred by the reprovisioning of the refreshment table and the flagpole, zeroed in on him again. "So, you came in February. So what?"

Herrick raised an eyebrow. "I agreed to provide this church with regular services and sermons for a space of six months in return for my board and room while using the libraries."

"And?"

"I still plan to leave next month." Mentally, he inserted a thankful, *Praise to the Lord, the Almighty, the King of Creation*. The content of the up-time hymnals was one of the few ameliorating aspects of his stay in the up-time city. He had dropped suggestions here and there among the members of the parish that one of the hymnals would be a welcome, much-appreciated, farewell present. He should also mention to the bishop, when he got home, that a praise service dedicated to the memory, if that was the right word under the circumstances, of one Miss Catherine Winkworth, now-never-to-exist, once-upon-a-time-nineteenth-century, zealous-and-indefatigable, translator of German religious lyrics into English, might not come amiss.

He shook his head to collect his wandering thoughts.

Mistress Clark, although she had only been acquired into the parish "by marriage" as the up-timers put it, bade fair to become a most formidable organizer. "Has anyone done anything to get a replacement for you?"

"I've written to Archbishop Laud," Mistress Veleda Riddle said, manifesting from the other side of the flagpole. "Again, as I've said plenty of times before, I really want a bishop, but a person would think that now he's in exile, living off the charity of Fernando and Maria Anna in the Netherlands, he'd have at least one impoverished chaplain around who would be happy enough to come to Grantville for a while. He's *very* slow at answering his correspondence."

Herrick smiled politely.

If he were an archbishop, he would delay replying to letters from Mistress Riddle, too.

"I'm to the point that I don't care if someone is a *Durchlaucht* or an *Erlaucht* or just a plain, ordinary, everyday lout." The pen flew out of Mallory Parker's fingers and across the room.

Mary Kat Riddle caught it. "Hey, be careful. These calligraphy pens are expensive."

"You don't even have the excuse that we went to high school together for drafting me into this. I'm five whole years older. I was out before you were in."

Mary Kat laid the pen gently on the desk, next to a stack of best-quality cream-colored paper with matching envelopes. "The only excuse that I needed was that I saw you were in town for a week to visit your sisters." She grinned. "I did at least overlap in high school with Nina and Chelsea, if that counts."

Mallory leaned back. "Not to mention that I'm Methodist. We're Methodist. All of us Parker girls are Methodist. Why me, O Lord? Why not Nina and Chelsea?" She picked up the compilation of titles and appropriate forms of address that Mary Kat had borrowed from the chancery in Rudolstadt and slammed it shut. "Nor am I into diplomatic protocol."

"You'd better learn to be, since Anton wants to get promoted."

Mallory sighed and shifted uncomfortably in the swivel chair. Before she married the Rudolstadt city council's clerk, he had omitted to mention that he had ambitions to rise higher. Much higher. He had an application in with Ed Piazza's office in Bamberg. And one with the office of the secretary of state in Magdeburg.

If he got either job, she would have to quit her job teaching English in Jena.

But since she was pregnant anyway . . .

"Open the book, Mal," Mary Kat said. "Chelsea and Nina aren't on vacation. You are. Grandma's on the warpath about raising funds to renovate Grantville's dilapidated little Episcopalian church. Every envelope gets a letter; every recipient gets the proper form of address. *Most illustrious*, just plain *Illustrious*, or not illustrious at all. Or a plain, ordinary, everyday lout, if he also happens to be a rich lout. They're addressed as 'Herr.'"

"I can't see that there's a desperate deadline. Seems to me that it would be easier if you all just gave up and joined the Methodists. They call us 'Methodist Episcopal' after all—or, at least, they used to, before we turned into 'United Methodist.' Will you even be having services once the temp she found goes back wherever he came from?"

"Who knows? We may be back to lay readers and prayer services. That's what we did before he came." Mary Kat, considerably more pregnant than Mallory, stood up and rubbed her lower back. "To work, minion. There are roofs to be re-shingled, cracked stained glass windows to be repaired, fresh leading for the windows to be obtained, water-damaged woodwork to be replaced, floors to be refinished, organs to be built, and therefore money to be found." She grimaced. "Not to mention grimy old asphalt siding to be removed and replaced with something more attractive, I hope."

"And your grandmother to appease."

"That, too. Be sure to hold out the letter you address to Archbishop Laud in Brussels. Grandma wants to put a personal cover letter in the envelope with it."

"Where's a squire when ye need one?" Thomas Welford paused on the bridge at the three-way intersection, looking along the street to where Grantville's St. Alfred the Great Episcopal Church perched at the very end, four blocks away, as far from the creek as a building could be sited without running into a shale hillside.

Richard Tomkins nodded solemnly. "Yep. Where's a squire when ye need one?"

Ordinarily, Welford and Tomkins would not have taken it upon themselves to call upon the wife of a respected barrister.

Of course, back home in Herefordshire, they would just have been very insignificant members of the parish. The squire would have worried about things like this. Or the local gentry who served as trustees of the parish endowment. Or the vicar, who was likely the squire's younger brother. Or the rural dean, who was probably the nearest baron's younger brother. Or the bishop, who might well be the nearest earl's ex-tutor.

If they had never become soldiers, they could have spent their Sunday mornings until the day they died figuring out ways to skip services in the village church without being disciplined for it by their betters.

In Grantville . . . well, there weren't very many adherents of the Church of England.

They could have taken this as a license to skip church for the indefinite, nearly infinite, future, without the risk of incurring any discipline at all, since Grantville's authorities didn't care in the least whether or not they conformed to the established communion.

Instead, somehow, they had ended up feeling...sort of fond of the town's tottering little parish. Responsible for the well-being of this remote outpost of the Anglican Communion, as the up-timers called it. While it wasn't home, it was as close to home as a lad from Herefordshire was likely to find in Grantville. One of Thomas' passionate defenses of the establishment had recently gotten him into a brawl with a Scots Presbyterian at the Thuringen Gardens. It hadn't been the first time and probably wouldn't be the last time.

He shook his head, which still had a lump from the fight. "There's a downside to this up-time idea that all men are created equal. It appears to require the created to do a lot of work that they could otherwise have left to their betters."

Tomkins nodded. "That's us, now, me lad. Equal and stuck with it."

"Mr. Martin Riddle could have been more cooperative. Even if he is now of a different religious persuasion, he's still the lady's grandson. It would have been more *appropriate* for him to approach her. What did we get for our pains?"

"He laughed until he choked and said, 'Time to belly up to the bar, boys.'"

Veleda Riddle pursed her lips.

Tompkins sort of liked it when the old lady did that. When she pushed her mouth out, it made her look even more like the sheep named Ewegenia on the Brillo pamphlets. Helped a man forget that she was the wife of a highly respected barrister.

"It came to me this morning while I was shaving, missus," Welford said. "It just came down and landed on top of my head, like the tongues of fire at Pentecost, or something. I really like that front window in the church, by the way, now that the carpenters have pulled off those old sheets of plywood that were hiding it."

"Are you sure it wasn't caused by that blow to your head?" Herrick asked.

He found a vestry board that included two common ex-mercenaries to be a very distressing phenomenon. Of course, they were doing well—far better than two sons of common farm laborers ought to be doing, if anybody in Grantville had requested his opinion on the matter, which nobody had. The parish had held a celebration—small and discreet in a time of public mourning—when Tomkins, after the anti-vaccination riot of the previous March, had been appointed "Head of Security" at the firm manufacturing the vaccine. The man had not only learned his letters but also obtained the famous "GED." During the process, he had developed an annoying mannerism of pulling his spectacles from the pocket in his doublet, carefully placing the hooked ends of the frames behind his ears, picking up the agenda of the vestry board meeting, and saying, "Humph."

The spectacles were a product of the "vision screening" to which all GED candidates in Grantville were subjected and were also the reason that the man had finally been able to learn his letters. He was all too prone to wax eloquent in regard to the epiphany the Lord granted to him when the "apprentice optometrist" handling the machines announced cheerfully, "No, you're not a dunce, whatever they told you twenty years ago. You're just farsighted. Go to McNally and get this prescription filled before you start classes."

Welford had learned to read and write, but did not yet have the "GED." One of the up-timers in the parish was tutoring him in first-year algebra, which appeared to be the sticking point. He was one of the night watchmen at the vaccine firm, but had a promise of heading a squad at the Leahy Medical Center once the GED was in hand. The commander was holding the position for him.

Why, just to command a squad of guardsmen, did the man need to know even first-year algebra? By the time the rowdy brawler—he just could not seem to *pass up* a fracas in his free time—*passed* this course, if he ever did, he would know more higher mathematics than most professors at Oxford and have no use for it at all. The up-timers' view of the necessary components of education for what some of their books called the "working class" verged upon the insane. Why didn't they just call a peasant a peasant and a laborer a laborer? It was as if, in their minds, academics and gentry did no work. Requiring the "GED candidates" to learn to swim might make some sense, but why algebra?

Herrick looked at Welford closely. Why him? Surely there must be a more appropriate candidate for promotion in this city. Hadn't Saint Paul said something applicable? No. He was thinking of "neither a borrower nor a lender be," and that was from Polonius, not

from Paul; from Will Shakespeare's *Hamlet*, not the
Bible. Still, one could surely derive "neither a brawler
nor a . . . some word starting with the letter 'l' . . . be"
from Paul's admonitions on the necessary qualities of
a bishop. Or a member of a vestry board. Couldn't
one? His mind drifted toward the composition of a
satirical epigram. What word would work that began
with "l"? He had heard Mistress Riddle's grandson
use the term "limp noodle" in conversation, but that
lacked a certain poetic ambiance. Moreover, no one
had been willing to provide him with a precise defini-
tion. It didn't scan, either.

It hadn't been so bad when he arrived. The vestry
board had been headed by the chief justice of the
SoTF Supreme Court. But then, after the election,
Mr. Charles Riddle had moved to Bamberg. If the
admiral and his wife were only here . . . but they were
in Magdeburg, so he might as well wish for the moon.
The Holcombs were in Magdeburg. Almost every
up-time Episcopalian of any social distinction was . . .
somewhere else.

Which left a seven-person vestry board consisting
of . . . Mistress Riddle. He could think of her, if he
tried hard enough, as a representative of her husband,
who was becoming increasingly feeble. Mistress Wendy
Thomas, from the Technical College faculty. She had
been divorced, but the first husband had been left
up-time, thank goodness, so he could consider her a
widow. But remarried, now, to a Lutheran, which was
a most undesirable state of affairs. Mr. Kitt—thank
the Lord for Mr. Kitt. Mistress Christie Penzey from
the high school faculty, also divorced, but with her
husband thankfully left up-time, so another honorary

widow. Mr. Edgerton, also from the high school faculty but, alas, like Thomas Riddle, far from young. And two rather crude ex-mercenaries.

Rather crude? He took a mental red pen to his composition. *Very crude.*

A vestry board on which there were women? Almost as many women as men? Herrick shuddered. If Mistress Thomas could be induced to resign in favor of her brother, who was also an academic, husband of the overenthusiastic coffee purveyor...Yes, that might work. That left the problem of Mistress Penzey. Who else was there who might replace her? Mr. Clark, perhaps, though he was young for such a responsible position and away so much of the time...

Well, he was going back to England, so it wasn't his problem anymore. Herrick dragged his attention back to the conversation.

"We've been to that village in Gloucestershire once," Tomkins said more practically. "With the cowpox people. So we know how to get there. And how to get back with a group of people in tow, if Vicar Barneby is willing to come with us, which is more to the point. If we leave now, we can get there before winter. If we leave now, we can get back with them before winter, and then St. Alfred's won't have to depend on visiting priests who come to see the libraries and are willing to hold services for a while, but spend more time in their homilies reciting poetry than they do quoting the Bible."

He gave Herrick a rather fishy eye. "Not that you haven't improved the way we speak," he added grudgingly. "We know many more words now than we did a few months ago, not to speak of a few years ago.

Not that most of them come in handy for anything practical."

Mistress Riddle raised her eyebrows. "What makes you think that Mr. Barneby would be willing to come?"

"Uh," Welford said. "Well."

That was the problem with sudden inspirations. It was hard to explain why you thought they would work.

One of the problems, anyway.

"Vicar Barneby seemed like a very fine man," Tomkins said. "His wife seemed to be a very good lady. They have five children. If they bring their servants, too . . ." He beamed. "It would practically double the size of the regular attendance at our services."

"That's not," Welford grumped, "why the idea came to me." The eye he gave Herrick was more evil than fishy. "One thing, though, Vicar. You stay put until we get back. No haring off for greener pastures 'til we find someone to take your place."

"We should write Vicar Barneby . . ." Veleda started.

"What's the point?" Tomkins asked. "We can get there as fast as a letter can. Just write it and we'll take it with us. Anyway, even if a letter might get there first if you sent it as far as Amsterdam by air post, there's no point in giving Barneby and his wife time to think up reasons to refuse. That's not the result we want. It's a lot harder to say 'no' to someone's face."

Herrick smiled suddenly. "Mistress Riddle."

"Yes?"

He looked at Welford and Tomkins. "May I suggest that we bring in front of the vestry a proposal to divert enough of the funds now on hand for the purposes of renovation to send . . ." He paused. ". . . to send *these gentlemen themselves* as far as Brussels by *air post*. It would save considerable time, so perhaps I would be able to depart as scheduled."

Tomkins turned white.

"But the building..." Veleda sputtered.

Tomkins looked at her hopefully.

"Ah," Herrick said piously.

He'd heard Mary Kat call it his "stained glass voice." She had loaned him a very irreverent book with the title *How to Become a Bishop Without Being Religious*. Irreverent, and it dealt with Methodist heretics, but still, the sheer practicality of many of its recommendations had been... eerily accurate... such as the advantages that a young clergyman derived from marrying a girl who wanted to marry a minister and the even greater advantages that came with marrying a girl who had an impressive dowry... ideally, by marrying one who combined both qualities.

"Ah," he said again. He looked at the ceiling. "But is it not more important to ensure that the flock is fed with the Word of God than to worry about their having a well-fenced pasture?"

She frowned.

"Anyway," he said briskly, "we can send a round-robin letter to the absent parishioners who are prospering—prospering very well—in their diaspora, explaining the situation and requesting a special contribution to replenish the fund."

Slowly, she nodded. "We should send them via Brussels, though, not Amsterdam. That way, they can speak directly to Archbishop Laud about the parish's concerns."

Welford turned as white as Tomkins.

Where was a squire when ye really needed him?

Brussels, The Low Countries, late July 1635

William Laud had only himself to blame. He had *asked* his secretary to locate, sort by date of arrival, annotate, and deliver to his desk a compilation of all the requests he had received from Mistress Veleda Riddle of Grantville, State of Thuringia-Franconia, since their arrival in Brussels.

This would not be complete, of course, but under the circumstances of his departure from the Tower of London, no one could blame him for having left the earlier ones behind in the archdiocesan archives in Westminster.

He tapped his fingers on the desk.

Thomas Wentworth did not have to display *quite* such a level of hilarity over the idea that a building no older than Grantville's St. Alfred the Great Episcopal Church (constructed in 1897 and thus barely more than a century old at the time of the Ring of Fire) might merit funds for something called historical preservation.

His secretary—William Dell had made his own dramatic escape from London in order to join his employer in exile—was responding with even more hilarity in regard to the enclosed pamphlet (illegally liberated from the Grantville City Hall's archives; please be so kind as to return it) describing the up-time National Trust for Historic Preservation and another (illegally liberated from the Grantville City Hall's archives, but we have quite a few copies, so you can keep it) describing the up-time West Virginia State Historic Preservation Office.

These pamphlets asserted that any building over

fifty years old counted as historical up-time. Mistress Riddle derived from these an extensive argument that in a properly organized world, St. Alfred's should be eligible for federal matching funds, if only it had any funds on hand for the federal government to match.

"I believe," Wentworth commented, "that to the best of my knowledge, the parliament of the United States of Europe has had more urgent calls on its time than the maintenance of historical buildings. If the up-timers are so solicitous of historically significant structures, why did they blow up the Wartburg?"

"I believe," Dell said, "upon the basis of several close readings of the material..." He cleared his throat. "I believe that it was their general propensity to blow up historically significant buildings that led to the passage of this legislation. Can you even imagine a world in which structures were replaced so quickly that one that endured a half-century was considered to have attained a significant age?"

Laud picked up another broadsheet. "What is a 'New Deal' and why is it important that they have a mural from it in their post office? For that matter, what is a 'Preserve America mini-grant'?" He handed it over to Thomas.

Wentworth looked at the illustration dubiously. The shiny paper was of marvelous hardness and astounding whiteness; the colors of the reproduction were superb. Why had anyone gone to the trouble? "The muralist, presumably, was a local amateur," he commented. Frowning, he looked at it again. "What are these mechanical devices pictured in it?"

"I have no idea," Dell answered. "But I am quite certain that we barely have enough money to pay next month's rent on our quarters here in Brussels and certainly not enough to repair this Mistress Riddle's church building. Shall I draft a refusal? Polite of course, with a recommendation that she would do better to seek a wealthier patron?"

Laud nodded. "That's the first pile. Now as to the second...she wants a bishop?"

"If we didn't need our diplomatic contacts here in the Low Countries," Wentworth commented, "we could always move to Grantville ourselves and provide her with one slightly tattered Archbishop of Canterbury for her greater convenience."

"When she first presented her request, the main reason was that she perceived a need for there to be someone on the continent who could ordain clergy. For now—although, I most sincerely hope, not for long—that is scarcely an issue, since I am on the continent and can perform any needed ordinations myself. Still, *because* I hope that our sojourn will not be long, there is some merit to the request. Grantville by itself certainly isn't large enough to deserve a bishop, but it might be feasible to appoint a bishop to cover the entire Anglican diaspora in the United States of Europe."

"*In partibus infidelium*, I presume," Wentworth commented sardonically.

Near Gloucester, England, July 1635 ·

William Barneby drew up his horse, handed the reins to his groom (who was also the family's gardener, general man-of-all-work, and footman). Dick Badger fell well into the category of "jack of all trades and master of none," or, at least, not quite master of any, but he was willing, cheerful, and strong, which made up for a lot of other lacks. Will the Younger hopped off the sturdy Welsh pony they had borrowed from Squire Albright for this expedition to the cathedral town.

Grace came out and kissed them both, the younger children trailing in her wake. "Is it good news? Is he accepted?"

Her voice was a little anxious. They were far from wealthy. If Young Will, with his angelic voice, could become a chorister at the cathedral, his education would be assured and they could husband their resources for the schooling of Benedict who, alackaday, croaked like a bullfrog, even at the age of eight.

"Accepted," Barneby said. "But . . ." He looked around. Dick had a lot of gossips at the village tavern and the girls might chatter with their friends when they went to take lessons with the governess that Squire Albright employed for his daughters. They would mean no harm, but Mistress Warren was inclined to repeat all that she heard. "Later." He nodded toward the house.

Grace turned and led the way into the hall. The stone-built vicarage was old-fashioned. It had stood for well over two centuries and might well have sufficed for a celibate papist vicar before the reforms of King Henry. She wished she had a modern parlor into which she could welcome her friends without having everyone else passing through on errands. The four chambers were not adequate, although Dick slept over the stable and Betty in the loft. William had taken one for his study; they shared one, the boys shared one, and the girls shared one. If guests came to stay, she and William had to give up their chamber for the sake of hospitality and sleep on cots in the hall. The kitchen, cellar, and brewhouse were in a separate building and she should not complain, because apart from Squire Albright's manor house, it was certainly the largest and most comfortable in the village.

With a nod, Barneby dispatched Dick to the stables. With another nod, Grace dispatched Betty to the kitchen. She told Young Will to change and take the other children out to the kitchen garden to weed, since weeding was a task never done.

"Accepted." Barneby resumed the conversation they had started outside.

"But?"

"But I am not certain that I want him there. The bishop..."

"What has Godfrey Goodman done now?"

"His tendencies toward papistry are becoming more and more pronounced. Not in superficial things such as Archbishop Laud encouraged, such as the vestments and music. Those are, ultimately, adiaphoral, which is what the Puritans fail to understand. Goodman is deviating from the Thirty-Nine Articles in matters of doctrine and faith. While I am far from counting myself as a Puritan and like an afternoon of bowls and archery after the Sunday service as well as any man..."

Grace nodded. "There is such a thing as a proper balance. A good, sturdy, Anglican faith is what England needs. But where else can we place him? Gloucester is near enough that he could come home regularly. Worcester? The King's School is there for the choristers and Thomas Tomkins is a truly outstanding musician."

Barneby shook his head in the negative. "With all

due respect to Thomas Tomkins, there is the matter of the bishop. I will place no son of mine under a man who may well have committed bigamy."

Grace smiled. Bishop Thornborough's tangled matrimonial history, with a divorce case of scandalous proportions in York while he was dean of the cathedral there and his taking a second wife in Ireland while he was bishop of Limerick there with the first still alive in England, had provided the ladies of the region's gentry with much entertainment, even if it all happened thirty years in the past and the man had married and buried a third wife since then—he being her third husband as well. It was all as fresh as ever in the recollection of Squire Albright's widowed mother. Her eyes would gleam as she recited, "And then the second wife was accused of providing the poisons that the Countess of Somerset used to poison Sir Thomas Overbury, and..."

But . . . She pulled her thoughts together. "You're quite right. In any case, he is much too inclined to tolerate the Puritans. Bishop Thornborough enjoys saying that he has outlived several men who expected to succeed him in his see. If the old man isn't careful, he will find that he has outlived his diocese and will see his cathedral vandalized, his choir abolished, and the organ torn to pieces by fanatics before he dies. So not Worcester. But, where?"

Barneby stood up. "God will find a way, Grace. And I have a sermon to prepare." He kissed her absently and headed for the small chamber where he kept his books safely away from a rambunctious household full of small children.

She watched him until he closed the door and then started to see how the children were doing in the garden. But instead of starting down the path, she leaned against the gate, watching them.

God was causing life to contain so many repetitions of "but" since the appearance of the visitors from Grantville who had come looking for cowpox and departed with vials of horse pox two years earlier. She would never have thought that the pamphlets about such things as clean water would cause such concern. It was not because anyone objected to clean water. Even in rural England, there were proverbs that presumed a reasonable level of cleanliness.

> In the morning when ye rise
> Wash your hands, and cleanse your eyes,
> Next be sure ye have a care,
> To disperse the water farre.
> For as farre as that doth light,
> So farre keepes the evil spright.

But that was sheer superstition. There were no sprites, no fairies, elves, brownies, or gnomes to be kept away by tossing a pan of water or attracted by serving a saucer of milk.

Both the bishop's officials and king's, from the lord lieutenant down to Squire Albright as the local justice of the peace, had taken undue interest in the pamphlets brought by the *vaccine* hunters. So far, all was well, but if they tried to place Will at a cathedral farther away than Gloucester, where they were still comfortably secure because the persons in authority knew them well, it would bring down more attention, probably from strangers, very possibly with less favorable outcomes.

They would have to do something. But what? Go someplace. But where?

But when? The answer to that was, soon.

But who would have them? But how would they get there?

She didn't even have to ask herself—But why?

The pamphlets came from Grantville, after all. The men who now controlled the king, since Her Majesty's much-grieved death and His Majesty's unfortunate injury, did not care for items and ideas that came from Grantville.

Everyone in the vicarage, right down to Betty— everyone who had met the travelers, even poor little Peter and his father who had been called in and interviewed—was . . . What did the pamphlets say about smallpox? Contagious. What did they call unclean water? Contaminated.

What did Grantville's pamphlets say about the source of contamination?

Find it and eliminate it.

It was only a matter of time before someone, somewhere, drew the logical conclusion from that recommendation.

Brussels, August 1635

". . . two members of the vestry board of St. Alfred the Great Episcopal Church in Grantville," Dell said as he escorted the two men into Archbishop Laud's overly small study.

In the course of the next hour, Welford and Tomkins gave the three men gathered there a rather shocking introduction to new-time Episcopalianism, in Grantville of the here and now, as viewed from the hop fields and orchards of Herefordshire and the battlefields of the continent. Somehow, the communications from Mistress Riddle had omitted to mention that she actually served on the vestry board, as did other women from the up-time.

Laud had assumed that she stood to the parish in the role of a prominent benefactor, which was, of course, quite acceptable. He had never heard of a parish that was loath to accept benefactions from wealthy women.

But for a woman to be not a patroness of the church, but one of its administrators . . . ?

"St. Alfred's was built originally by a nineteenth-century coal baron who immigrated to the United States of America from Cornwall, with his own private funds," Tomkins said.

"I thought that the up-timers did not have barons."

"It's just what Herrick would call a figure of speech," Welford answered. "They didn't have titles of nobility. It just means that he was rich as hell."

"Like a squire," Tomkins added helpfully.

"Rich as hell and made his money from coal mines. Most of the rich-as-hell people who used to live in Grantville did. They also had 'railroad barons.' The up-timers, I mean. 'Cattle barons.' Umm . . . Any others?"

"Not that I can think of." Welford grinned. "His wife, they say, was very pious. The coal baron's wife, I mean. Now, there's come to be something else on my mind, most respectfully speaking, that Mistress Riddle has not directed me to say."

A concerned look crossed Tompkins' face. This

had not been planned in advance. Welford's sudden inspirations were becoming worrisome.

"About schools . . ."

A half hour later, Welford waved his hand. "The way the Dutchies do it, you know."

The handwave was broad enough that it clearly encompassed not only the Netherlanders—Dutch in civilized English—but the ramshackle Germans—*Deutsch*, as they called themselves.

"How?" Wentworth asked with some curiosity.

"Well, they do it with a school in every parish—just enough schooling that the children learn their letters and numbers." Tomkins frowned. "That won't work in England. The parishes are too big, and quite a few of them are in the wrong spots. There are churches where people used to live a long time ago, way back in history, and no churches where a lot of people live now."

Welford grinned, "'Follow the money,' as they say in the detective stories. If it has an endowment, then it has a clergyman. If not, not. Ye gentlemen and lords"—he nodded at Wentworth— "aren't likely to send your younger sons into a position that won't support them in the style they want."

Wentworth squirmed uneasily.

"Ye need more sons of poor men going to the universities and becoming clergy," Welford plowed on. "Ye need more scholarships, more grammar schools such as young King Edward of lamented memory founded. Had he only lived . . ."

"So what do you suggest?"

"A school in every village. Make the parents send their children, girls as well as boys. *How* ye make them do it, I can't tell ye. Among the Dutchies"—Tomkins waved again—"'tis the city councils and gentry that force the farmers to send their sons and daughters. In England, 'tis the gentry who want to keep us unlearned. Ye've got to make the squires make the farmers do it until it's just a...custom, like it is in the Germanies. Once that's done, we can discuss the building of more grammar schools."

"Daughters!" Laud sputtered.

"Daughters." Welford grinned maliciously. "Ye should visit Grantville, Your Excellency. Mistress Riddle is not alone. There are many more like her. Many more to follow in her footsteps. Mistress Clark, for one." The grin reached his ears and his hairline. "Ye should meet the lady I hope to wed once this task is done."

"Lady?" Wentworth quirked his mouth.

"In Grantville, they're all ladies unless they don't act like ladies." Welford paused. "It's not like back home."

"What is Mistress Riddle like?" Laud asked.

"Past eighty years old, they say," Tomkins began.

Laud's expression brightened at the thought that this nemesis might not continue to harass him for many more years. His cheer did not survive the next comments.

"But a lady of good health and great energy. She is, as they say there, very well preserved."

Tomkins nodded. "Much better preserved than St. Alfred's. Of course, she was not so neglected during her middle years, nor allowed to fall into decay."

Laud sighed and picked up the funding request. The purpose of the audience he had granted to the two unlikely vestrymen was to discuss that—not these other, most unsettling, concepts.

Grantville, August 1635

"...a reasonable number of contributions for the renovation project as a result of the last set of letters," Veleda reported with satisfaction. She beamed at Vicar Herrick, Christie Penzey, Wendy Thomas, and Marshall Kitt. "Now about the christening..."

Herrick did not wince. Mistress Riddle's granddaughter had produced a son the previous evening. By the wonders of radio, the child's father, off in the Rhineland, had determined the infant's name, to include that of both grandfathers.

Nasty continental influence, that. It was one thing for these Germans to baptize babies with double and triple names, but in England, they received one. One. John, Richard, or Henry. Agnes, Alice, or Joan. One Christian name was quite enough. The Grantville up-timers were a mongrel lot of foreigners, of course. How could a pack of immigrants from everywhere between Norway and the western coast of Africa regard themselves as being descended from a set of English colonies?

Mistress Hawkins, the French teacher, had told him a "colonialist joke," about up-time children from Algiers and Morocco, in the midst of the twentieth century, sitting in their schoolrooms and reciting, *"Nos ancêtres les Gaulois,"* the first line of their introductory history textbook.

It wasn't that funny.

Nevertheless. He would pass young Charles Roger Utt across the font on Sunday morning with all the courtesy he could muster.

Mistress Mary Kat wanted to ask her friend Mallory Parker, the wife of the Rudolstadt city clerk, to stand as the godmother, but the woman was a heretic. How could one ask a heretic to vow before God to see to the religious training of a child in a different faith than her own should he lose his parents?

The Clarks would be godparents. The christening would occur in proper form.

Which would be followed by food.

And by coffee. The inevitable coffee. Why not sack?

He wondered how well Tomkins and Welford were succeeding in Gloucestershire.

The father, a heretic, wasn't present at the christening party. He was assisting with an effort to contain the spread of black plague, somewhere in the Rhineland. The grandparents weren't at the christening party. They were in Bamberg, that being the new capital of the State of Thuringia-Franconia. The great-grandparents were present, with one uncle, also a heretic, and his family. The father's sister had moved to Magdeburg, taking her children, to join her husband, whom Herrick had never met. She, too, in any case, was a heretic.

What would it be like for the child to have such a small body of relatives?

Herrick had been not even three when his father cast himself from an upstairs window and died of the fall. Not that the event had made much difference to him at the time, since he was still placed out to nurse and far too young to understand the rapid legal maneuvers by which his uncles managed to avoid a verdict of suicide and the consequent confiscation of his property as a self-murderer. His mother had taken his sister and the baby to live with one of her sisters and then remarried, but he had scarcely been lonely. When he was old enough, he and his brothers grew up in his Uncle

William's house. With eleven cousins. Plus the cousins provided by his other ten Herrick aunts and uncles. Plus the relatives on the Stone side—all of the Soames and all of the Campions. In a London townhouse. An ample townhouse, by London standards. A chaotic pit of hell by any other. His tiny room at Oxford had come none too soon to save his sanity. A man could live far more content amid a few good friends, whom one saw when one chose, than amid a seething mass of relatives.

Or a seething mass of parishioners. One of the up-timers had quoted a proverb to him. "You can choose your friends, but you can't choose your relatives."

You couldn't choose your parishioners, either.

There was Mudge, back in Dean Prior.

> *Mudge every morning to the postern comes,*
> *His teeth all out, to rinse and wash his gums.*

Horne, back in Dean Prior.

> *Horne sells to others teeth, but has not one*
> *To grace his own gums . . .*

Personally, he had a toothache today. He would set up an appointment with the dentist tomorrow. It wouldn't be long before he left Grantville, so indulging himself in a prudent amount of up-time tooth repair shouldn't be postponed.

Just why was he planning to return to Dean Prior? Oh, yes. The income that supported him.

The infant's great grandfather pulled himself upright with his walker and raised one hand to propose a toast. How many more weddings and christenings would he have to attend before he died? The population of Dean Prior was about four hundred persons, total. Of those, perhaps half were children or elderly. Two hundred persons made one hundred couples. Couples or potential couples, since some adults were currently unmarried. Say, sixty married couples. Weddings, perhaps two to four a year. Those always had parties. Baptisms, perhaps twenty per year. Funerals with wakes, perhaps ten in a normal non-plague year. One of the few good things that could be said of plague, perhaps, was that there were no wakes for those who died of plague. The up-time encyclopedias said that he would live almost forty more years...

How many toasts did that make?

How many of those toasts would be proposed by Mudge?

He raised his own glass to wish young Charles Roger Utt a prosperous future.

Gloucestershire, August 1635

"They're back," Peter said, catching himself with one hand on the doorpost of the vicarage kitchen.

Betty looked up from the hearth. The urchin was panting. His face was flushed, his bare feet were muddy. It was raining—again—so his hair was drooping over his ears.

"Who?"

"The cowpox hunters. Not all of them. Just the two Herefordshire men. I saw them in the village."

"If you saw them, then so did everyone else. Not everyone, maybe. But everyone who saw them will have run off by now to tell the rest."

"I need to go on and tell Pa."

She handed him a mutton turnover. "Run by Squire Albright's first and make sure you tell him directly. I'll go in and let the vicar know."

He swallowed two bites before he turned around.

Betty let the vicar's lady know. Mistress Barneby could handle telling the vicar.

Richard Tomkins looked at the group gathered in the vicarage orchard.

There wasn't room for them all in the house.

Barneby had said that he didn't want to use the church. Not for this discussion. It didn't feel right.

Tomkins and Welford presented the offer from the Grantville parish, with a cover letter signed by Archbishop Laud himself.

If, the squire pointed out, he was still an archbishop.

"He is in the eyes of God," Tomkins said. "He was consecrated. A king can't undo that. He can take away the temporalities of his see, but he can't take away that God's made him into a prophet. Like Elisha. Or was that Elijah? Jezebel could persecute him, but he was still a prophet of God."

"Not to mention," a voice called from the back of the little crowd, "that God sent Harry Lefferts to save him from the Tower. With fireworks as bright, from all I've heard, as any lightning that Elijah called down on the priest of Baal. Who, it sounds like to me, are on their way here. Or, probably, first to Gloucester and then to here."

"That's what it amounts to," Squire Albright said. He rubbed his hands together, not around and around as if he were wringing out wash, but briskly up and down, as if he was dusting them off. "I can do some things—a few things—to slow down any circuit riders they send out from London. But I can't stop them from coming, nor persuade them what to think after they've come. I'm sorry, Barneby, but since these men"—he waved at Tomkins and Welford—"have returned, it's all too likely that they'll reach the conclusion that you've been corresponding with the enemy all along. They'll be bringing soldiers with them, since that's the finding they expect to make, even before they start to hear the evidence."

"How can we prove that we haven't? We've had nothing to do with the Grantvillers all this time and didn't know that Tomkins and Welford were coming again."

"Ye can't," Welford interjected. "Something I learned in the GED classes. Algebra and such-like. Ye can't prove a negative."

Barneby opened his mouth.

"S'true," Tomkins said. "That's why to make a case in court, there, you have to have enough evidence to persuade the jury that the criminal did it. They figure that even if he didn't do it, there's no way a man can *prove* he's innocent. He can claim an alibi, but unless he was singing a hymn in plain sight of the judge, in which case he wouldn't be charged, well . . . everyone knows that friends will lie for each other. I don't think that a 'reasonable doubt' plea will work with Boyle's lackeys."

"Before they came . . ." Grace Barneby also waved a hand at Tomkins and Welford. "Before they came, already, I was asking myself when. I didn't finish it even in my mind to ask when we would leave, but when we would do—whatever had to be done. I was asking myself where we would go—when the time came to do whatever it was. Who would be willing to receive us. How we would get there, how we would live. I thought about the Netherlands. If King Charles hadn't sold the American colonies to the French, I would have thought about Massachusetts."

Barneby stared at her.

"You don't have time, Mr. Barneby," she said. She might call him William in private, even term him 'my dearest and most darling Willikin' in enthusiastic moments when they were alone, but it would be disrespectful of his office to do so in front of other people.

"You don't have time to think out into the distance. You have to think about the work you do, while you're doing it. Sermons don't write themselves and you have to pay attention to getting the right verses in place and such. Putting up plum preserves from morning to evening on a long summer day leaves a person's mind emptier. Open to considering different possibilities."

Barneby nodded slowly. He had never put up plum preserves, but he had picked plums often enough as a boy. Plums, apples, pears, damsons. It did leave the mind free to consider other things. Things such as, in his case, getting a scholarship like his older brother Henry and doing something other than spending the remainder of his mortal days picking fruit in the orchards.

He looked around. If they left, he would miss the benefits of those carefully preserved plums.

God had placed the parable of the rich fool in the twelfth chapter of the book of Luke just for men who harbored such thoughts. How often had he preached on it? Perhaps an abundance of plum preserves in the pantry was not quite the same as having "no room where to bestow my fruits," but it represented an excessive attachment to material things, nonetheless. And Squire Albright was clearly warning that if he now chose to remain here, take his ease, "eat, drink, and be merry," he was all too likely that the king's men, if not God directly, would ensure that, "this night thy soul shall be required of thee: then whose shall those things be, which thou hast provided?" And he would be that fool.

Not just on his own behalf, but for Grace and the children. It was unlikely they would receive mercy.

Everyone had heard of the treatment meted out to Oliver Cromwell's family. Cromwell was just a simple country squire himself when that happened. Not a powerful threat to the Stuarts in any way.

"So is he that layeth up treasure for himself, and is not rich toward God."

He nodded decisively.

"I accept your offer, gentlemen. And given that we have no royal license to remove ourselves out of the kingdom, it would probably be prudent for us to leave as soon as possible."

"I'm coming with ye," Betty said.

Dick Badger stepped up next to her. "Aye."

"Us," Peter's father said. He nodded at Welford. "If the likes of him can study as deeply as any university man, if Tomkins there can learn the law, why not my sons, too?"

By the time the village sorted itself out, Welford was griping that they hadn't expected to be moving half the neighborhood, and there was no way that everyone and their gear would fit onto the little boat that had brought the pair of them into Bristol.

"My cousin," the vicar said suddenly. "My mother's nephew. If he isn't in port when we get to Bristol—he's married to a Dutch woman and goes back and forth along the coast, so he probably won't be—there will be captains who know him enough to trust that we will pay. He has two half-brothers on his mother's side who are fishermen and three half-sisters who are married to seamen as well."

Squire Albright smiled a little sourly. "God will provide, eh, Vicar? Ye go and leave me here with the mess."

"Come along," Grace suggested.

"Nay. It should not be that bad. In any case, as my uncle who did so well for himself in the cloth trade in Worcester used to say each time that his brother-in-law sailed off for the Levant, 'Someone has to stay home to mind the store.'"

Grantville, August 1635

It was a memorial service, Herrick told himself firmly.

He was not conducting a Christian funeral for a heretic whom he had never met.

He was bringing comfort to Mistress Riddle's granddaughter, whose husband had died in the service of his country.

Mary Kathryn Riddle was a faithful member of the Anglican Communion.

She was also the widow of Derek Utt, the deceased.

The up-timers were taking with entirely unsuitable enthusiasm to the foreign continental custom by which women did not, as they should, assume their husband's name at marriage.

It had been a perfectly legal, valid, and sacramental marriage while it lasted, though.

He had checked.

With the up-timers, he had learned, it never did to take anything for granted.

They were using the church building that belonged to the Methodist heretics, because so many people wished to attend.

That was better, in all truth. It made it even more a memorial and less a service of Christian burial.

There were other memorial services for the man, elsewhere, being conducted simultaneously. The one in Bamberg was being conducted by a layman, Mistress Riddle's son, the chief justice of the supreme court of the state of Thuringia-Franconia. By the dead man's father-in-law.

There was no ordained Anglican minister in Bamberg.

The one in Magdeburg was being conducted by a Methodist heretic, also a layman.

There was no ordained Anglican minister in Magdeburg.

He looked across the chancel.

The organist was Roman Catholic, and female.

He gritted his teeth. It's a memorial service, he told himself again.

Men had been called upon to do worse things than this in the service of the Church of England since the days of the eighth King Henry.

English Channel, August 1635

The waves were choppy.

Richard Tomkins was cheerfully not seasick.

William Barneby was quite the reverse. Seasick and wretched. He had sailed with his cousin at times, but never out of sight of the coast. Never on a fishing boat permeated by the odor of cod oil.

Grace's brother, Augustine Ashmead, who had appeared on the dock in Bristol as if this journey had been planned well in advance, held Barneby's head.

"S'alright, Vicar," Welford assured him. "Tomkins is fine now, but just wait until we get on board the plane. You should have seen him between Grantville and Brussels."

"Plane?" If it had been possible, Barneby would have turned greener.

"Just you and your household. The rest of these hangers-on will have to find their own way beyond Amsterdam, no matter how deeply Ashmead here is convinced that the Grantville high school needs a teacher of classical Greek and it is his destiny to supply that need."

Ashmead cocked his head. "If we take a boat all the way, up the Rhine and then as far as possible up the Main and the Kinzig, I understand we should arrive in time for the start of the fall semester."

"You understand from whom?"

"Why, that would be telling."

Grantville, late August 1635

Robert Herrick turned around to wave goodbye.

At this point, it couldn't hurt to be polite just once more. He had survived the farewell pulled pork barbecue, not without some stomach pains resulting from the sauce. He was on the trolley. The trolley would take him to the train. The train would take him some distance before he had to rent a horse which he would ride until he could get upon a boat, which would get him as close as possible to Brussels.

He would rather have gone by way of Amsterdam, but the vestry board had given him a sheaf of papers, a number of verbal remonstrances to be delivered to Archbishop Laud, and a little extra money in addition to the much desired, possibly even much coveted, up-time hymnal about which he had dropped so many hints. Discreet hints, he hoped. So.

Symbolically, he should shake the dust of Grantville from his sandals.

Practically, he was wearing a pair of very well-made and highly polished Calagna & Bauer boots, so the gesture didn't seem very appropriate.

Veleda Riddle waved in return. Then she took William Barneby by the elbow and said, "I've scheduled a vestry board meeting at 4:00 P.M., so we'll have plenty of light in the fellowship room. We've been having some problems with the wiring at St. Alfred's, so the electricity is turned off for the time being. I don't want to risk having the whole building burn down after all the work we've done. That will affect the overall estimates in the restoration budget, of course."

She shoved a packet into his hands. "You'll have just enough time to familiarize yourself with it before the meeting."

The plane from Amsterdam, called the "Monster"—and monstrous it truly was, a modern leviathan—had encountered some delays. By the time it got into Grantville, Tomkins and Welford had hurried him to the trolley station barely in time to see his predecessor's departing face.

He had no idea where Grace and the children were.

He had no idea when he would find out.

Two women hurried onto the platform. One threw her arms around Tomkins. The other threw her arms around Welford.

"Ah," Tomkins said. "Our fiancées, Vicar. Meet Misty and Jessica. They will be in need of instruction. Misty is Welford's. Misty Zeppi. She's a beautician. Her family's Italian, or they were before they came to America. She's a Roman Catholic. She's divorced. Jessica's mine. She's never belonged to any church, so you'll have to start by baptizing her."

Barneby made a slightly strangled sound.

"She's a drill sergeant," Tomkins announced proudly. "At least, she used to be. Now she's adjutant of the SoTF forces training battalion."

Barneby recovered and greeted both of them.

"Aye," Tomkins continued, squaring his shoulders with obvious pride. "Her name is Jessica Hollering and she deserves the name. She can yell louder than any drill sergeant I ever met while I was in the army. We'll be back for the vestry meeting."

The four of them vanished.

"What," Barneby asked Mistress Riddle, "is a 'beautician'?"

Drill sergeant was a concept well within his grasp.

A massively tall and blond young man came dashing up to Mistress Riddle and, without waiting for introductions, shook Barneby's hand. "Hi, I'm Dane."

"You are Danish? Like the late King James' queen?"

"No, not a Dane. Dane. That's my name. I get that question a lot these days. Dad's assigned me to show you around. He's on the vestry board. My wife Jailyn's getting your wife and kids organized at the house we rented for you. If you don't like it, we'll look for something else, but Herrick was perching in one of the Riddles' guest rooms and we figured that wouldn't work for a family."

Barneby arrived promptly at four o'clock, courtesy of the carillon in the tower of what he did not yet recognize as the middle school. In the interval, he had recovered his family and been presented with a colored map of the town and surrounding area.

"What," he had asked Dane, "is a Chamber of Commerce? Or, at least, why is it donating expensive maps to newcomers rather than engaging in commerce?"

There were several people in the room. The man of middle years, by elimination, had to be Dane's father. There was an elderly man. In addition to Mistress Riddle, there were two other women.

Tomkins and Welford grinned broadly.

"We may have left a few things out of the letter we took along when we went to fetch you," Tomkins said.

It occurred to Barneby that in his brief glimpse of Herrick as the trolley bore him away from Grantville, his predecessor had been smiling as broadly as the two Herefordshire men were at this very moment.

Brussels, late August 1635

Robert Herrick swallowed hard.

The exiled archbishop of Canterbury forged onward, leaving no opportunity for interruptions or objections. "Truly, I think our friend Wentworth's suggestion in regard to this is inspired, since you have the necessary diplomatic background from your time as chaplain on the Duke of Buckingham's 1628 expedition, not to mention that you already have experience in dealing with the up-timers. They, in turn, should welcome you as a choice because your father was a working goldsmith rather than a noble lord. You were apprenticed to the trade yourself, under your uncle, and did not go up to Cambridge until the age that most students are preparing to leave, but nonetheless, you are university educated and have spent several years in a parish. Your brother's contacts will be important in the merchant community on the northern coastal cities—not to mention the Cavrianis. Yet, since your uncle has been knighted, you will be acceptable to the majority of those Englishmen of gentle birth who are serving the king of Sweden, as well."

William Laud leaned back and smiled. "Just be grateful that I am not assigning the remainder of the European continent to your jurisdiction as well. Thomas suggested it, but that would involve a truly immense amount of travel."

Herrick blanched. Yes, he had pastoral experience, and not only in Grantville. During the last few years before he came to the continent again, stuck away in a country parish in "loathed Devonshire" in the diocese of Exeter, he had longed for London. He had not, however, longed to become rector of a London parish, discussing roof repairs with a vestry board. He had longed to move once more in the city's sophisticated literary circles, among the other writers who considered themselves to be the "Sons of Ben." Writing the occasional scathing epigram about one's somnolent and inattentive parishioners was nowhere nearly as satisfactory.

"Grantville..." he began tentatively. There were salons in Grantville. Interesting visitors.

"Magdeburg," Wentworth said firmly.

Herrick closed his mouth. Magdeburg might not be so bad. It surely couldn't rain more there than it did on the edge of Dartmoor, "the dull confines of the drooping West," and the capital of the United States of Europe would certainly have fewer sheep than Devonshire. There was some hope that in Magdeburg he could create a parish board whose members included Admiral Simpson...whose wife was a patron of the arts...and...he wouldn't have to worry about tenants on the glebe farm. There wouldn't even be a glebe farm. No, perhaps it would not be so bad.

Even though it was certain that the men who now controlled the king would not allow the export of his other annual forty pounds of income that came as interest on his inheritance. They hadn't allowed it when he left, which was why he had taken the parlous little support offered by St. Alfred's. They were unlikely to change their minds. Some groveling sycophant of the Royal Almoner...

What about churchwardens? Was there a building available? One would scarcely need them if there was no church fabric for them to maintain. Overseers of the poor? Who cared for the poor in Magdeburg? In Grantville, it had not been the responsibility of the parish...in any case, he was not gifting Laud with the hymnal, now. It would hold a place of honor as the first item in his new cathedral library.

When his mind came back to the conversation, Laud was saying, "Of course, there is no endowment to support such an office, but I will attempt to raise funds to at least match the income you have been drawing from the parish of Dean Prior, since it will be necessary for you to resign that living. Or, perhaps, not necessary. Since you received it in the king's gift, Charles may very well simply take it back once he finds out that you have accepted an appointment from me."

Match the measly little income from Dean Prior? Forty pounds per year? Forty pounds disposable, at least—there were obligations such as the curate's salary that nibbled away at the gross. For a bishop? Had the archbishop ever stopped to think just why he had found himself taking that temporary appointment at St. Alfred the Great to support his months in Grantville?

"What about Greene, my curate?"

"He who does most of the work?" Wentworth smirked. "Fills out the church registers, signs them, sends them to the bishop every year? At least you are not being as difficult as the famous bishop of Hippo whose would-be flock had to drag him into the cathedral by his heels to get him consecrated, while he screamed and tried to get a saving grasp on each pillar he passed as his head and shoulders bumped along on the floor. When we speak of a vocation, that's what I perceive as a genuine matter of being called into the service of the Lord as opposed to volunteering."

Laud frowned. "Behave yourself, Thomas." He turned his eyes back to Herrick. "I will do what I can do see that he is not deprived. Perhaps your friend Weekes can undertake something on his behalf, since he is a Devonshire man."

Laud, or perhaps Dell, seemed to have prepared an answer for every objection that Herrick could raise.

And as if that was not bad enough...

The archbishop's eyes twinkled. "Now. Next. One of the biblical qualifications for a bishop is that he be the husband of one wife (1 Timothy 3:2), which implies that you should acquire a suitable wife with more than deliberate speed."

Herrick countered that this passage was normally interpreted by Protestants to mean that the bishop should not be a polygamist, rather than as require- ment that a bishop be married—omitting altogether the papists' twisted view that it meant that a bishop should be married to the church, and thus celibate in regard to earthly marital ties.

"Be practical, Herrick," Wentworth answered. "A bishop needs a wife in order to deal with all of the social obligations that are attendant upon the office, particularly since your new headquarters will be in Magdeburg and your role will include a lot of..." He paused. "How did Harry Lefferts describe it? A lot of *schmoozing* with important figures in the USE government as well as coaxing your parishioners into contributing the money to build a church and, perhaps, subsidize whatever income that William can provide for you. Indeed, 1 Timothy 3:2 requires that a bishop not only be 'vigilant, sober, of good behavior' but also 'given to hospitality' as well as 'apt to teach.'"

If the issue was practical rather than theological... "Elizabeth, my widowed sister-in-law? She and her children have been with me for a half-dozen years," Herrick ventured hopefully.

"Adequate for a rural parish, but not the same— though, of course, should they wish to join your household again, they would doubtless be welcomed in Magdeburg." Laud nodded solemnly. "Herrick, you need to marry, with dispatch. Luckily, we have a couple of suitable candidates available right here in Brussels, clerical widows, both of them. Quite pious."

He smiled mischievously. "One, Mistress Carey, is some years older than yourself. She not only has a substantial independent income, which her connections in the Huygens and Crommelin families managed to get out of England and into the Netherlands, but is also in excellent health. As I understand they say in Grantville, she is very well preserved."

Herrick flinched.

To add insult to injury, the archbishop turned around and asked his secretary to bring them a pot of coffee.

Where was a glass of good sherry when a man could really use it?

Bank On It

Griffin Barber

"There, the Genevans killed my father. Hung him by the neck, like a common house-breaker. Even left him there to rot, refused to return his remains to my mother," the Savoyard said, looking ahead at the gate.

"Didn't know that, seigneur," Gervais said, using his breathless state as excuse not to use the younger man's name, which was one of those horrid Italian tongue-twisters Gervais preferred to not even think about, let alone speak aloud. The muddy track was something of a climb from the river, and Gervais had always liked his food and drink better than keeping pace with horses.

"Of course you don't. Why would you, a commoner—" the rider freed one foot from the stirrup and nudged Gervais on the shoulder, "and foreigner to boot—have any inkling of events thirty years and more in the past?"

"Don't know, that's sure," Gervais panted, stumbling under the touch.

Boot back in stirrup, the nobleman went on, "The duke refused to pay ransom for my father or his men.

The very men he ordered into the attack. I hear they even celebrate it."

"What?"

The mounted man reined in to look down on Gervais. "Hanging my father, dolt."

"Ah," Gervais answered, carefully stepping clear as the horse, irritated at being reined in, tried to stamp his foot flat.

"You don't care, Gervais?" the Savoyard asked, leaning down to pat the massive shoulder of his stallion. Not to correct it for attacking Gervais, but because it was upset.

At a safe distance, the Frenchman bent over to catch his breath and gain a moment to think through his answer. Knowing the noble for an impatient sort, he gasped, "Church tells us it's not for the low folk to concern ourselves with the doings of those above us."

"You quote well the words of priests," the Savoyard said, flicking the tail of his long coat free of the last of the morning's rain and revealing the rapier at his hip. "Best be careful with such pious talk. We enter a nest of heretics who will not find your simple views suit their palate. It wasn't so long ago the Calvinists were executing good Catholics for resisting their heresy. Keep your mouth shut, or you will find I shut it for you."

Still trying to catch his breath, Gervais bowed his head, "As you say."

The nobleman edged the mean-spirited horse closer, crowding the older man, "Not good enough, Gervais."

Unable to remain bent over lest he get tumbled to the ground, Gervais stumbled upright, raised a hand. "I will not let slip who we are."

"Good," the nobleman said. "Need I remind you further that neither of us need distraction from our appointed tasks?"

"No, no." Gervais said, unable to keep the edge of anger from his voice.

He felt the younger man's eyes on him before the other went on, "It's not me that holds your child hostage, thief. You would do well to remember that."

Keeping his eyes down, Gervais nodded, "I do. Just don't see how my work will benefit them that have my Monique. What's more—" he hoped to tease some information from the Savoyard, "I don't understand why they wish to put you at risk, too."

The noble sniffed, pretending disdain. Gervais still heard the bitterness of the reply. "You don't need to understand. Just do as the bishop told you and we might both come away from this with what we desire."

"Yes, seigneur."

"Are you ready, then?"

"Yes."

The rider kneed the stallion into motion, apparently satisfied.

They did not speak again in the hundred steps it took to reach the gatehouse.

A pair of guards wearing the red and gold livery of Geneva stepped forward to bar the way, pikes shouldered. The elder of the two, a largish man with the scars of some pox, looked them over before addressing the mounted man: "Who wishes to enter Geneva?"

Silently thanking God he easily understood the man, Gervais stepped forward and gestured at the Savoyard with a flourish, "The envoy of Duke Amadeus, first of his name: Seigneur Vicario of Turin, here to see the council and leadership of the city on behalf of the duke."

The guard bowed slightly. "*Bienvenue*, then, to the duke's envoy. The council is expecting you. There is stabling to be had just inside the gates, or you can head up the hill to the Cheval Blanc. The sign is of a white horse prancing in the paddock, the place across the square from our cathedral. Lodgings have been arranged for you there."

Gervais dutifully translated the guard's words. Vicario grunted and kneed his horse through the gate. The clatter of hooves echoed loudly in the gatehouse, making the Savoyard's stallion rear slightly. Vicario quickly reined the foul-tempered beast in. Say what you will about his manners and mind, the Savoyard was a capable hand with a horse.

Gervais shot a glance at the militiaman as he broke into a trot to catch up. Based on the curled lip climbing the older guard's face, Gervais was fairly certain the envoy had not gained a friend at the gates.

They came across few people as they followed the narrow road climbing from the gate to the cathedral. Gervais considered remarking on their absence, but decided to save his breath and concentrate on his footing for the climb. The Savoyard wasn't likely to appreciate his observations, regardless.

Despite his exertions and the weight of leaden legs, Gervais eventually gained the plaza laid out before the cathedral. The cathedral itself was very impressive, though lacking the ornament Gervais was used to. He'd heard Calvin and his cronies had stripped the cathedral of its ornament to pay for the city's defenses, but seeing the graceful building so bare was sobering.

The White Horse was a set of squat buildings just where the guardsman said they would be. Turning toward it, he found the Savoyard already halfway across the square.

Again it struck Gervais there were too few people about for what had turned into a pleasantly sunny afternoon. He'd heard the Calvinists were opposed to all things pleasurable, and he'd seen none of the taverns and knocking-shops he was used to in a city this size.

A young man came out of one of the buildings in the courtyard of the inn, obviously intent on stabling the Savoyard's horse. The youth said something to Vicario, who looked over his shoulder, then turned in his saddle. The distance wasn't so great that Gervais missed the way the noble's lips thinned when he discovered Gervais so far behind.

"I'll handle it, seigneur," Gervais called out.

"Damn right you will," the noble snarled, dismounting.

The Cheval Blanc wasn't so busy that Bertram had become used to hearing Clément calling out to customers entering the courtyard. He still managed to at least partially ignore the local's patter and remained focused on the report he was preparing for his superiors in Grantville.

He nearly ruined the letter when a stream of angry-sounding Italian rent the air outside his window. First, because Italian *always* sounded to him like the speaker was cursing God. Second, because he'd been warned to watch for whomever the duke of Savoy sent to represent his interests at the council, and third:

the duke's representative was the only one who had yet to arrive.

Still seated at the tiny escritoire he'd purchased from the university provost, Bertram pushed the shutters wide in hopes of getting a look. Too late, he caught the merest glimpse of a dark-haired man in a fine coat stalking into the inn. He gave up trying to pierce the shadowed doorway and examined those he could see.

Clément held the bridle of a large, powerful horse while a pot-bellied, red-faced man of middle years worked at the leather thongs lacing saddlebags in place.

The stablehand, unusually glib for a Genevan, said something Bertram couldn't hear. The older man's laughter was easy to catch, but his reply was too quiet for Bertram to overhear. Whatever it was, both men chuckled, sharing a moment as working men do when commiserating over the behavior of bad employers.

Even though he couldn't hear what was said, Bertram was encouraged by the exchange. First, the stablehand spoke nothing but the local French-Provençal, so Bertram was reassured that he might at least communicate with the fat man. Second, if the noble's use of Italian was any sign, the Savoyard might not understand the local tongue. Such ignorance could play in Bertram's favor.

Assuming he'd have more to report once he'd observed the newcomer, Bertram put down his pen and corked the ink pot. He carefully slid the unfinished report into the escritoire and positioned both pen and pot where any disturbance would be readily apparent. Satisfied things were as secure as he could make them without raising undue suspicion, he stood.

His stomach growled, lending wings to his feet as he descended the stair. Geneva's strict adherence to the Calvinist faith might preclude houses of ill repute or even quality drinking establishments, but there was absolutely nothing wrong with the food prepared at the Cheval Blanc.

Gervais slung the saddlebags over his shoulder and smiled across the horse's back, "Thanks, I needed the laugh. I'd like to buy you a drink, when you've time."

"I'll take you up o— Ah, good afternoon, Monsieur Weiman," Clément said, looking past Gervais.

"Good day, Clément. See you for supper?"

Gervais turned to see who was speaking, saw a slight man of about Clément's years walking across the courtyard. He was dressed well, though not so well Gervais could peg him a noble—or even rich—man.

"Lamb tonight, just the way you like it." Clément sniffed. "Though why you should like such spices is beyond me."

"Blame it on my misspent youth."

Weiman had a faint accent, but one Gervais couldn't place. He certainly didn't *sound* as German as his name.

"I will, Monsieur Weiman," the stablehand said with a grin.

Weiman chuckled, nodded at Gervais, and stepped into the inn.

"Who is that?" Gervais asked.

Clément hiked a thumb at the door, "Monsieur Bertram Weiman?"

Gervais nodded.

"He's been here near a month now. Like your master, come to observe or take part in the council deliberations. Supposed to be some kind of steward for an eastern princeling of the Germanies, he says. Educated, but a good sort, even so."

Gervais shared a chuckle at the follies of the over-educated, then asked, "Not the place where all the strangeness started?"

"No, someplace farther east," The stablehand shrugged. "I think."

"Ah." Gervais picked up the Savoyard's saddle bags.

"Go on, I'll be in after I've seen to your master's horse. I doubt there'll be another needs my service tonight."

"There anyone I should speak to about food?"

"My aunt Nadine will see to it."

Gervais nodded, making a point to remember the familial relation to avoid complications that might arise from a little slap and tickle with any of the women here.

"Gervais! Get in here and explain to this woman what I want!" Vicario called.

"Coming, seigneur." With a long-suffering glance at Clément, Gervais suited actions to words and walked from the courtyard.

The taproom was well-lit and quite clean, surprising Gervais, who was used to the smells of stale beer and old piss in most public houses he frequented. Here, all he could smell was the mouthwatering odor of roast lamb.

Vicario was standing before a matronly woman at the hearth, lips twisted in his habitual scowl.

Gervais hurried over, "Yes, seigneur?"

"Tell this woman I want a bath prepared, and a meal sent to my rooms."

Gervais translated, adding courtesy where Vicario refused to.

The lady looked relieved as Gervais spoke up but shrugged helplessly, "So very sorry, seigneur, but there is only the one room set aside for you, and it will take some time to get water drawn and heated. We have no baths in the rooms, you will have to come down."

Gervais repeated her words in Italian, knowing the noble wouldn't accept her apology with grace. *Is it too much to ask, Dear Lord, that you make this noble shit to mind his manners? Just enough that he doesn't get everyone looking at us as the villains before I've done the job?*

"And the meal? I trust that won't be too much to ask?" Vicario snapped. From his expression, you would be forgiven for thinking the man robbed of his birthright rather than slightly inconvenienced.

With what he'd learned outside the gates, Gervais had begun to lay the blame for Vicario's lack of courtesies on the absence of a fatherly example growing up at court, but the man's constant petulance made each offense harder and harder to excuse. Some people, nobles especially, were simply incapable of courtesy.

Then again, the bishop was similarly highborn, full of courtesies, and far more dangerous than the Savoyard.

"No, seigneur, the food will be along in just a short while," the woman said. She waved, prompting a younger, slightly more pudgy version of the stablehand to come to her. "My son will take you to your room, seigneur."

The boy grinned, "It's in the garret. I love the garret," he raised a hand above his head, "the roof is right *there*."

Crushed by the thought of another climb, Gervais stifled a groan, saving his breath for the stairs. He decided not to translate the boy's words for Vicario, if only to save himself the effort of editing the noble's rude response.

Vicario and the boy quickly left him behind, the glory of youthful vigor outpacing weight of wisdom and old legs. As Gervais prepared to climb the third flight, the boy passed him going down, muttering something foul.

Breathless again, Gervais made the attic.

Vicario was sitting, and gave Gervais no time to catch his breath before pointing at his high riding boots, "Get these off."

Gervais, still fighting for air, stumbled over and started to pull on the offending boot.

"Get the weight of that massive gut of yours into it."

Wishing he was pulling the man's leg from its socket, the better to beat him with, Gervais managed to pull the boots free.

"There..." Vicario sighed, wriggling his toes.

Gervais leaned against the wall, doing his best to catch his breath and ignore the smell coming off the noble's stockings. He didn't even want to look at the bed he knew he would not be allowed to rest in.

After a moment he sensed Vicario watching him. He glanced at the younger man.

"No wonder you were caught, thief."

Gervais leaned over, sucking wind. Eventually he replied, as respectfully as he could given the circumstances, "While it helps when running, wind is not—" another breath, "everything."

Vicario snorted, disbelieving or mildly entertained, Gervais could not say.

"So, what do you think of the latecomer, young Bertram?" the minister asked.

"Outspoken." Bertram answered, moving his piece. His opponent's next move would prove the turning point beyond which there would be no saving the game.

"Ha! Your gift for understatement is almost as good as those Englishmen of my acquaintance."

Bertram smiled though he did not find the observation funny. Best to keep the local happy, however. *All the development taking place back home needs funding, and the family coffers can carry only so much debt . . .* He hid a grin. *And when, exactly, did I start thinking of Grantville as home?*

Concentrate: you have to lose without appearing to throw the game, he thought, eyeing his host.

Gregoire Sauveterre was a power on the ruling council, and the reason Bertram had been sent to Geneva. Gordon Partow, an up-timer studying for his ordination as a Calvinist minister, had reported Sauveterre's interest in the USE's banking system last year. Knowledge of the financial practices used in the USE were not, precisely, state secrets, but they were a powerful attractant for rulers of states whose coffers had never recovered from the Reformation and Counter-Reformation. Knowing how successful the banking enterprises would be in those states that would eventually comprise the Swiss Confederacy was reassurance to the USE leadership, who recognized the need for strong financial allies. Better still if the people of the Confederacy could acquire other means to support themselves than taking service as mercenaries in the armies of the USE's enemies.

Prime Minister Stearns and his advisors decided informal and discreet contact would be best, what with Cardinal Richelieu's close interest in everything Grantville and the USE did. So Bertram had been dispatched with several useful books and a stern admonition to remain in the background unless it looked as if the venture would fail completely.

He glanced across at his opponent's contented smile. Failure did not seem likely, given how Sauveterre said things stood with the council.

He sighed. Sauveterre's continuing contentment was another reason Bertram moved his queen instead of taking the knight and setting up his victory in three moves. However cooperative the man was, Bertram still didn't like having all of his information passed, and therefore filtered, by the one source. It was a weakness he would have seen remedied if he'd had more resources. As things stood, Sauveterre had to be kept happy.

Sauveterre apparently had no such concerns, and took merciless advantage of the opening offered, placing Bertram's king in check.

The younger man pulled at his lip as if suddenly vexed, "Has the council considered the man was sent here to ruin the talks?"

"He seems to be doing that, regardless of his patron's intent."

Bertram nodded, moved his rook to remove the threatening piece. "I can't believe the duke would wish to sustain such poor relations when, by agreement, he would first gain an ally aligned with the Confederacy of Helvetian States, and second, gain considerable financial assets. With so many of his holdings under quarantine to prevent spreading the plague, you'd think he needs coin for his coffers."

"You presuppose two things: One, that the duke is his own man. Two, that either the duke or the seigneur possess the sense to know where their own best interests lie."

No, I don't. Pretending surprise, he asked, "Whose man is Seigneur Vicario, then?"

The minister again placed Bertram's king in check, "The bishop of Geneva."

Genuine surprise lifted Bertram's brows, "But why?"

A shrug. "The bishop is not the man of God his predecessor was. Lacking that fine man's holiness, he hasn't even managed to maintain the flock Francis managed to return to Rome's shadow, let alone reclaim the seat better men than he managed to lose."

Bertram cocked his head, mildly surprised a leading Calvinist would speak so highly of a Catholic bishop, even one dead many years. "But how does the bishop gain the allegiance of one of the duke's men? So many of them are Huguenots who fled to Savoy for protection after Saint Bartholomew's Day."

The elder stroked his beard, nodding approval. "You know the history of our struggle, young man. Not all Lutherans do."

Sorry, you're the only Christian in the room, putz.

Unaware of Bertram's inner monologue, Gregoire continued. "But even back then there were more than a few nobles already in Savoy and the French Piedmont who would have sided with both Rome *and* the Spanish, had they not seen which way the wind was blowing."

Bertram nodded, mind racing. "But how did you learn who was behind the man?"

A shrug and a movement of the man's beard that Bertram took for a smile. "A little bird told me disparate facts. Like a mosaic, they but needed placement in the proper mortar to make a picture."

"And may I know the facts you learned?" Bertram asked with a smile, putting his king on its side, ceding the game.

The older man leaned forward, eyes glinting in the candlelight. "Just one. The man with him, the fat servant?"

Bertram nodded. "Yes."

"He was being held for the ecclesiastic court in Annecy three months ago. A thief. Apparently quite accomplished. He made off with the lion's share of the bishop's personal portable wealth. He was caught only because his daughter made the mistake of telling her love she was leaving town, never to return. The bishop's men caught him on the road as a result."

"And what was the sentence?"

"That's just it. There was no judgment entered. He disappeared from both prison and rolls."

"So the servant is the bishop's creature, does it necessarily follow the seigneur is, as well?"

"Perhaps not without other information I possess that you, alas, do not," the minister said, picking up the pieces and beginning to reset the board.

"Another game, perhaps?" Bertram asked, knowing that to press at the wrong time would do his cause no service.

The minister shushed him, glancing at the door. "You know we followers of Calvin don't play games nor dance. Such is unseemly in God's eyes."

"Oh, of course. Perhaps, as the ancients called such things, more 'exercises of state'?"

The minister strangled a laugh. "Yes!"

And you'll tell me all I need know by night's end.

"Exercises of state indeed..." The older man chuckled, hands busy on the board, finishing the setup.

"So, how went the council today?"

Vicario's lips twisted in a snarl. "I made better progress than you, I suspect."

"So sorry, I was but trying to make conversation."

"Are we now a married couple, to be making small talk?"

"No, seigneur."

"Then leave me to my work."

"Yes, seigneur."

It was Vicario who couldn't maintain the silence he claimed to desire: "What progress have *you* made?"

"All is ready. It is only the timing of the thing that remains."

Vicario's mouth dropped open. "In less than a week, you have it arranged?"

"You needn't look so surprised, seigneur." He couldn't keep all the sarcasm from his voice as he went on, "We are about God's business, after all."

"I hope your bitterness will not cause undue haste."

"I won't have my daughter in Annecy any longer than she has to be."

The younger man snapped his mouth closed, clearly wishing to find fault with Gervais' answer. He shook his head after a moment. "Tell me how it's to be done, then."

"Do you really need to know? I would rather not say."

Vicario's lips thinned. "Just tell me."

Gervais nodded, "Once you have chosen the day, I will wait till the services are done and the cathedral empties for the night."

"Where will you wait?"

"The crypt."

Vicario's brows rose. "You have no difficulty with disturbing the dead?"

Gervais looked away. "The bishop promises absolution for my actions on his behalf, and a full pardon for me and mine for my earlier, earthly crimes."

"And what of after?"

"Everything will be as I was ordered to make it before I return here."

The noble didn't appear to recognize the careful response for what it was. "And if they catch you?"

"They will not."

Vicario tossed his head. "I'm sure our friend the bishop would tell you that such pride surely went before your fall."

"That he did. But I argued then, and still do, that it was my daughter's love that led to my capture, not my sins."

The noble's smile was dark, and held nothing of humor. "And yet, despite your thoughts on the matter, here you are."

"Yes. Here I am. When great men feel their interests lie counter to those of the common man's, there is little the common man can offer except compliance."

"You sometimes speak like a man of learning, thief."

"I had some schooling as a child, seigneur." *More than you, I wager.*

"Ah, some priest take an interest in you?" Vicario made the very idea sound lecherous.

"Something like that," Gervais said. He managed to avoid further conversation by leaving the room, ostensibly to collect the seigneur's meal.

And where have you been? Bertram thought, watching Seigneur Vicario's thief enter the Cheval Blanc from the courtyard. The commons was quiet this early. Bertram himself had only just taken his place, having been driven from sleep when the innkeep's boy began his daily molestation of the chickens. Not that he minded; he had hens of his own to check the laying of, one having just entered the inn.

The Savoyard's man seemed far too sober for someone who'd been out all night, even if the Genevans were inclined to tolerate such debauchery as an all-night bender.

Catching the Frenchman's eye, Bertram gestured with his drink. "Come share a cup with me. I do not like to eat alone."

The fat man stopped, gave a tired smile, and changed direction, joining Bertram at his table.

Taking note of the man's fatigued stride, Bertram poured the man a cup of weak beer that passed for part of breakfast here and gestured at the bread and cheese set out for him by their hostess. "Break your fast, Monsieur . . . ?"

The man hesitated. "Gervais, sir."

Bertram pushed the bench across from him back with one foot, repeating the gesture.

Gervais sat heavily and took a piece of cheese. "My thanks, sir."

Bertram noticed a whitish smear of something—dust or chalk—on the sleeve of the arm that reached for the cheese. *Now, I wonder where that came from?* Filing the observation away, he smiled and shook his head. "I'm no noble, Gervais."

A flashing grin. "All the same, very noble of you."

Bertram chuckled at the wry humor. "Not so noble a motive. I'm starved for conversation this early."

Gervais yawned. "Afraid I'm not yet fully able to feed your need. I'm hardly awake myself."

"And what had you out all hours, the soft touch of a young and pretty thing I hope?" Bertram asked, quirking an eyebrow.

The Frenchman snorted. "While it is young, the seigneur's horse is all hard muscle, hoof and bone. He has me watching the damn thing all night. You would think the big brute was his lover, the way he insists it be lavished with care."

Bertram smiled and took another drink to cover his thoughts. *And that, as the up-timers would put it, is absolute bullshit. And not very good fieldcraft, telling two absolutely different cover stories so close in time and space. If you're working for Richelieu, he's not getting full value for his coin. Clément already told me the tale of the young woman you told him you would be visiting nightly. Then again, he clearly sees me as some kind of noble—more like Seigneur Vicario than a burgher or peasant he could rely on to share certain attitudes.*

Swallowing. "An indifferent horseman myself, I do see the prudence in protecting one's investment. Such horses do not come cheap."

"That's a fact." The man nodded. "And what is it that you do, being an indifferent horseman?"

"I am here to study at the university and, coincidentally, report back on how things are proceeding with the current matter under consideration by the council."

"Oh?"

"Yes, while my father might labor under the belief that I'm wasting my time getting a foreign education," Bertram said, "the Austrian lordling my father collects the rents for is somewhat different from his peers—and my father—in that he actually looks forward in time, rather than backward, when planning for the future."

At last the cathedral grew silent and descended into darkness.

Why on God's green earth did you ever agree to do this? Gervais asked himself.

The same answer he'd had for months now was graven in his mind's eye: Monique, thin and dirty, eyes tearing in the light of the bailiff's torch, begging forgiveness of *him*, of all people.

Now, after all the waiting, you haven't time for this. Matins will start soon.

Pulling a slow match from his pocket and using the attached striker to light it, he used its dim glow to find the small bullseye lantern he'd hidden in the crypt on an earlier excursion. The lantern quickly caught.

Reaching under his heavy tunic, he unbuckled his belly. Catching the weight in both hands, he lowered it to the steps and checked the seal. Satisfied, he shuttered the lantern until only the air holes were emitting light, and picked it and the bladder up.

Holding the heavy weight before him, he followed it up the narrow stair.

Gervais walked across the cavernous apse of the cathedral, passing the chair and pulpit that had been enshrined by Calvin's followers to approach the altar.

He inspected the work of the last few nights. Finding all was as it should be, he raised his eyes heavenward and said a brief prayer. He knelt behind the altar and put the bladder between his knees. He carefully unwound the lead wire that prevented the stopper from popping out should he bump against something in his guise as kettle-bellied servant.

Gervais carefully wound a third of the wire around his finger, then folded the remaining metal to form a stand. Setting his handiwork aside, he eased the stopper from the large mouth of the bladder and looked inside. The vial was not immediately visible. He gently tilted the bladder to one side, careful not to spill the contents. It took a moment, but the end of a glass vial slid into view. He reached in and carefully withdrew it. Placing the vial in the stand, he replaced the stopper and set the bladder aside. Sweating, he pulled a chamois from his belt-line and wiped his hands. The slaked lime wasn't only caustic, it reacted strongly to water, something he planned to take advantage of, in due time. For now, though, it had to be kept absolutely dry if he was to keep to the timetable.

Opening his right shirtsleeve and pulling it up, he revealed what appeared to be a long bracelet of copper. He unwound the hollow metal tube from his arm, careful not to pinch the relatively soft metal. Inserting one end into the acorn atop the lantern, he carefully worked to open that end into a wider funnel-shape.

Pulling the hand drill and soft mallet from their slots inside the leather and taking a deep breath to steady his nerves, Gervais set to work on the third and last hole, praying this would be the last night he'd require.

"We shall pray upon our path and render our decision Monday," the elder said, a roll of thunder punctuating the statement. Spring thunderstorms were not common, but suited the mood in the council chamber well.

Bertram barely stopped a sigh of relief passing his lips. Such would not be proper, given he was present only as an observer, with supposedly little at stake. He needn't have bothered, as those he shared the gallery with began to whisper among themselves, providing plenty of cover noise.

"And?" Vicario asked, lips pulled into the probably unconscious and certainly habitual sneer Bertram had grown to detest over the last weeks.

The elder spokesman frowned, "I do not understand the question."

"Very well, I will make it explicit. Why the wait?"

"Because the council needs to confer and pray upon the matter, as I said."

"I do not see why. The duke has pledged a portion of his treasury to back the formation of the bank, has he not?"

Several councilors nodded, but the elder shook his head. "And that is good, but we, the *free* people of Geneva, are somewhat wary of the promises of Catholic princes."

The remark caused murmurs among the watchers

sharing the gallery with him, but Bertram ignored them, kept his eyes on the Savoyard. *Not so undiplomatic as it might seem, given the elder probably wanted to come right out and say "Savoyard Princes."*

The seigneur's sneer became a toothy grin. "Well then, I suppose we wait for greed to overcome distrust."

Several of the councilors muttered darkly. *They don't appreciate being reminded how precarious their financial situation is, and even less how much they need the duke to do as he's promised.*

The elder councilor, red-faced and clearly reaching the end of his diplomatic rope, nodded curtly and rose to his feet, signaling an end to the session.

Most everyone followed suit, though Seigneur Vicario remained, putting his boots up on the council table. The councilors chose to ignore the man's disrespectful posturing, filing out through the side door.

The audience slowly left, the day's session causing quite a few animated conversations to linger in the air. Bertram waited, watching the Savoyard from the shadows.

Why should he be so entirely pleased with himself? Frustrates me no end I can't see what either of his patrons might win from his disrespect.

Realizing his presence would be noted if he stayed much longer, he left. The wind was up, and the skies weeping. Pulling the collar of his coat up, he walked up the hill toward the cathedral and his lodgings. He pulled at his lip the entire way, as if by pulling flesh he could pull the Savoyard's thoughts from behind the sneer.

He had no more answers by the time the White Horse came into view.

"Bonjour, Monsieur Weimer," Jean, the proprietor's son, called from the shelter of the porch.

"And to you, Jean," Bertram returned absently, turning for his quarters and the hope of dry clothes.

Lightning flashed almost directly overhead, followed closely by a rolling crash of thunder so loud it made Bertram jump despite knowing it was coming.

A horse screamed in the stable, the humanlike sound followed closely by the heavy, thudding blows of hooves on wood.

"Whoa, Ezio!" Clément's strained voice carried across the court.

A second man shouted, "Watch it!" an instant before a splintering crash.

Bertram charged into the stable to lend a hand.

He paused at the door, taking in the scene: Seigneur Vicario's stallion was thrashing, hind hoof run cleanly through the wooden gate of its stall. Clément, hands up, was trying to both calm the horse and climb over from the stall next door. Seigneur Vicario's servant was bent over, either trying to immobilize the horse's hoof or free it, Bertram couldn't tell.

Unsure how to help, Bertram hesitated.

Clément dropped into the stall with the horse.

Screaming, the stallion thrashed again, kicking at the panel holding his leg in its splintered maw. The powerful kick crunched through the weakened wood and into Gervais, tossing him across the stable like an angry child's discarded doll. The man fetched up against the far wall, coming to rest upright with his back to it.

Clément worked to calm the stallion as it backed most of the way out of its stall, snorting and stamping.

As soon as it appeared even half safe, Bertram rushed to the stricken man. He knelt, trying to remember everything about first aid they'd taught him in Grantville.

Gervais looked unconscious, but his graying head wasn't at the odd angle that might indicate a broken neck. The head didn't appear to have any wounds or large swellings, a good sign. Bertram pushed fingers into the neck, found a strong pulse, nodded in satisfaction. He next put his fingers under the man's nose over the mouth, felt warm breath. Consciously ignoring the damp stain spreading from the man's belly, he checked the collarbone and ribs. They felt sound. He moved on to the belly, which was damp with a clear liquid he forced himself to ignore. The abdomen felt...odd.

Odd, not good. If he's ruptured something internal, there's nothing to be done. But this... Trying not to think on what he was about to see and just *do*, Bertram lifted the man's tunic to take a look.

What, upon God's green...leather?

Gervais came to in a puddle. Not the first time, but he couldn't remember the last time. Come to think of it, he hadn't got drunk since Rochelle died. *Not drunk, then.*

A horse whicker brought him a little closer to the now. Memory surged. *Damn, the belly burst!*

He moved too quickly, threw up in the straw.

A friendly pat on his shoulder. "Well now, Gervais, just who the blazes are you?"

Gervais—slowly—turned his head to look at Bertram, swallowed. "No one special." It looked like they were alone in the stable.

A smile greeted that claim. "Come now, I find that hard to believe. A man who can disappear from the bishop's prison and reappear in the company of another of the bishop's foils is no common thief."

"So you know who I am, then?"

A shrug. "Does one ever truly know the heart of another?"

Gervais smiled weakly, liking the younger man, even in his deceit.

Don't. Liking him won't make silencing him easier. Find out how much time you have. "Where's Clément?"

"Sent away, so we might speak freely."

"Talk?"

"First, I don't believe we have been honestly introduced. I am Bertram Weimar. Second, I am here on behalf of the USE, and the USE is very much interested in the success of the bank. Third, I don't think you want to be here, working with the Savoyard."

Gervais grinned through his pain. "Was I supposed to believe that tale about Austrian nobles? As to that last, I would give a fine Gallic shrug, but I hurt too much."

A genuine chuckle, then: "What hold does the bishop have over you?"

"Why?"

Earnest brown eyes watched him closely. "Because I might be able to help in exchange for whatever you can tell me of the bishop's plans."

He doesn't know what else was in the bladder, doesn't know what I've been up to...

"I can see you are thinking. Care to share?"

Gervais chuckled, regretting it immediately. His belly, the real one, hurt like ... well, like he'd been kicked by a horse. He used the pain to stall a bit, thinking hard.

You can't pretend you are some kind of killer, even if you weren't just knocked out by that bastard Vicario's stupid stallion. This young man is offering help, and you always knew the bishop is not likely to keep his word and release Monique until he's got full revenge for my thieving, if ever. Not to mention all the miraculous things you've heard about the Americans and USE.

But now, if Bertram puts a stop to things, the bishop is sure to kill her.

He looked hard at the younger man. *All right, you think you can help. Let's see what you're willing to offer for the information. Might be we can both get what we want.*

"Your people, can they really help?"

"I can't promise success, certainly not without knowing more, but as you have probably heard regarding events in England and elsewhere, we are not without resources." He paused a moment before going on in a slight rush, "Resources we might not be willing to expend unless you show some value for our investment."

It was the brutal honesty of the second half of the young man's answer that convinced Gervais. "The bishop did take exception to my breaking into his vault and appropriating his treasures. So much so that he now holds my daughter as surety against my continuing cooperation."

"I see," Bertram said, eyes darkening. "Not the man of God his predecessor was, indeed."

"What?"

The younger man shrugged. "Just something I was told a few nights ago," he said. "On to more important matters. Do you know where she's being held?"

"The old prison, Annecy."

Bertram pulled at his lower lip with the fingers of one hand. "That could be a problem."

Gervais snorted, regretted it as his lower ribs protested. When he could speak again, "I should say so. It's probably the most secure dungeon in Savoy."

"Do you know a way in?"

"Only the way I was brought in, as a prisoner."

"Is Duke Amadeus aware of what you were sent here to do?"

Gervais slowly shook his head, which protested by pounding. "Not that I know of. But then, his mightiness the Bishop Jean-François de Sales doesn't include me in his private political plots. He is a most unkind prince of the church in that regard."

Bertram grinned but stuck to the point. "The De Sales family hasn't been on great terms with the duke since the death of the last bishop, some in-house squabble for power."

"I wouldn't know," Gervais replied. He decided to offer something he'd already considered. "But I don't think what I was sent to do was meant to please the duke in any way."

"Oh? Why is that?"

"You understand why I might hesitate to tell all, don't you?"

"Right." Bertram pulled at his lower lip. "This is harder than I was led to believe."

"What?"

"Turning an asset."

"What?"

"Never mind. Suffice to say I thought it would be easier to get your cooperation."

Gervais would have snorted but stopped at the last

moment, knowing it would hurt. "Perhaps some of Vicario's history will help convince you I want to help?"

Bertram nodded, gesturing him to proceed.

"His father was one of the Savoyards executed by the Genevans after the attack the locals call *L'Escalade*."

"How does that help clear up matters with the duke?"

"Nobles are supposed to look out for one another. The old duke refused to admit he was behind the attack and forbade the nobles of his realm from raising ransoms for those captured in the failed attack. Vicario doesn't seem to like anyone, but he harbors a special hate in that little black heart of his for the House of Savoy for that failure *and* the Genevans for killing his father."

Bertram's brows rose. "Well now, there's a powerful motive." He went back to pulling his lip.

Gervais let him be, began rubbing his temples in a vain attempt to relieve the pain behind them.

"What can you tell me?"

"The plot is already in motion. The duke will not be happy with the result, nor will the council. I doubt Vicario will be pleased either, if he wasn't already ordered to kill me once events ripen."

"Will anyone be hurt?"

"Not by what I've done, no."

"But they might be harmed by the reactions of those affected?"

Gervais slowly nodded. "Almost certainly."

"How much time do I have?"

"Sunday morning."

That rocked the younger man back on his heels. "Can you put a stop to what you've done?" he asked after another bout of lip-pulling.

"No, though I can minimize the damage, given time and—" he couldn't finish. The words wouldn't come.

"And assurances your daughter is safe?" Bertram said, understanding.

Gervais nodded, thinking the younger man was just telling him what he wanted to hear. He couldn't quite keep the bitterness from leaking past his lips, "If it's not too much to ask."

Bertram grinned again. "I'll give it some thought while I ride."

"Wait, ride?"

"I can't very well free her from here, can I?"

"Just like that, you'll set her free?"

"I'll try, yes."

"How?"

"I have an idea."

"The cardinal is put out with the situation, Bishop de Sales, very put out," Bertram said, dripping muddy water on the palace marble as he rose from kissing the bishop's ring. The receiving chamber was small, but dressed in too much cold stone for petitioners to gain any comfort from proximity to the bishop. When he'd presented his story at the palace, the bishop had immediately agreed to meet him.

"Oh?" the current Bishop de Sales answered, too mildly for Bertram.

Push on, keeping him on the back foot is your best chance.

"Yes. He believed your people under control, yet hears the duke is about to enter into a pact with the Genevans and you have managed to muddy the waters with your own agenda."

A moue of distaste. "Hears, does he?"

"Hears; and is most displeased by it."

"And where was his displeasure when I petitioned him regarding recovering the seat of my holy office?"

Bertram bowed slightly, but didn't back down in the face of the powerful churchman's anger. "I am sorry, Lord Bishop, I was sent with Cardinal Richelieu's questions, not his answers."

With obvious distaste, De Sales took the hint and swallowed his pride, just as Bertram hoped he would. "And what would the cardinal wish of his humble servant?"

"He asks that you put a stop to your plot in Geneva and provide me with the daughter of the man you thought to make your agent."

"Thought to—" The bishop stopped, shook his head in disbelief, "His Red Eminence *is* well informed."

Bertram cocked an eyebrow, glad of the rainwater that hid the nervous sweat he felt oozing from every pore. "You, perhaps, thought he should be otherwise?"

"No, of course not."

"You might consider how the thief managed to get his hands on your treasures so easily, and recall remarks made by his confidant and advisor on the use of one poison to counteract another at the Diet of Regensburg?"

The bishop looked lost, which was exactly where Bertram wanted him, "Poison! What?"

Bertram leaned close and dropped his voice, forcing the churchman to lean forward in his seat to hear. "His Eminence has been known to use pretexts to get things wanted by his friends and allies. Even when those friends are, themselves, unaware of his hand in the act."

"What are you saying?" the bishop whispered.

"I would not presume to knowledge of such a great man's thoughts, but I believe the cardinal had plans for your treasury. Something about stringing several causes together to get first the duke and then the pope to move on your behalf in the matter of recovering the seat of your office. He, therefore, employed the Frenchman toward this end. Now, learning of your... repurposing of his tool, His Eminence would like to ask for it back before you break something delicate."

"He— I?" The man's eyes were darting, searching for something to latch onto in the confused and entirely imaginary sea Bertram had thrown him into. "Nonsense!"

Bertram's bow was immediate and deep. "I apologize, Lord Bishop, I meant no offense against the cardinal's good name by giving voice to my thoughts. It is merely fatigue and your good reputation as a valued ally to His Eminence that led me into error. I will restrict myself to his requirements and cease to comment on them from now on."

"Indeed!" the bishop said, but the heat was gone.

I have you, Bertram thought, recognizing defeat in the eyes of the man across from him.

It was all Bertram could do not to sag with relief; hoping Cardinal Richelieu intimidated the starch from the collars of his allies was not the same as *knowing* how they would react when placed under stress. If De Sales felt even a fraction of the unease that had the acid churning in his gut, Bertram had conveyed exactly the right misinformation.

"Again, my apologies, Lord Bishop." Bertram paused, waiting for permission to continue.

The bishop waved a hand, giving him leave to speak. "His Eminence would like the girl given to me. Now. Oh, and I will need mounts for the both of us, mine was blown in my rush to retrieve the situation."

"And the cardinal will reward me?"

The proper response was a difficult pass between the mountains of too general and too vague. "I don't know, precisely, but I'll be sure to report your quick compliance, when I get it."

Bertram is not back. The thought would not leave Gervais, hadn't left him since last night. Hadn't left while he packed the seigneur's things for a quick escape. Wouldn't leave while he sat watching his idle hands, long finished with the few things Seigneur de Turin traveled with. Sighing, Gervais made his way down the stair.

Vicario was already sitting down to eat in the common room. As Gervais entered, the Savoyard slapped his rapier down on the trestle, denting the fine finish with the basket.

"Break your fast, Gervais?" Nadine offered, trying to ignore the nobleman.

Bertram is not back! he wanted to scream at her. "Please."

Gervais noted the quiet of the room as the matron served him. The stablehand had already eaten and left. Clément had been making himself scarce since Friday, avoiding both Vicario and his servant at Bertram's request. He had little appetite, but ate anyway, fortifying himself against whatever the day might hold.

The bell tolled, calling the faithful to Sunday service.

Bertram is not back.

Vicario rose to his feet, a smile, dark but genuine, teasing the edges of his mouth.

Gervais wanted to kill him. Slowly. With a dull blade.

"He's not going to services, is he?" Nadine asked as the Savoyard stepped out into the Sunday sun.

"I think he might."

Her blue eyes widened. "Why? He's no friend to our faith."

"No, that he is not," Gervais said with a sigh.

"The men say he's just here to provoke ill will."

"Bank on it, madam," Gervais muttered, rising to follow.

"What?"

"Nothing. My thanks for your fine hospitality. I do believe we'll be leaving soon, and I'd rather not have the Savoyard screaming in my ear because I slowed his progress by taking the time to thank you."

She giggled behind a hand. "He would, wouldn't he!"

He nodded, a tiny part of him noticing what a fine woman she was.

"Gervais!" Vicario shouted from the court, shattering the Sunday quiet and Nadine's good humor.

"As he's doing already," Gervais murmured before taking his leave.

The day seemed to promise warm embraces, morning sun already drying the ground it touched.

"Everything prepared?" Vicario asked, tapping his riding gloves against one leg.

Bertram is not back.

"All that can be, seigneur."

"Well then, let's go to church, shall we?" He turned.

"I don't think it a good idea, seigneur," Gervais said.

"Just as I don't care what you think, thief," the noble said without turning to face him.

Gervais ground his teeth and followed.

"If your incompetence hasn't caused you to fail our patron, today should be the first step in seeing your daughter freed. Though I should think she'll be better off with the bishop than with a penniless thief."

Consciously removing his hand from the handle of the small knife at his belt, Gervais fumed silently, the stress eating at his stomach. *Bertram is not back; he and my daughter are probably dead! I'll be damned if I let this ball of horse dung treat me like I'm not worthy of even the tiniest courtesy! I swear I'll kill him the next time he opens that sneering hole in insult.*

Struggling for calm, he looked for distraction. Gervais had often, since coming to the city, noticed how few people were on the streets at any given time. Sunday services were the exception, with a great number of families making their way toward the massive structure. Even so, the crowd made less noise than similar ones anywhere else he'd been. Even the children were sober and quiet here.

The clopping of horse's hooves drew his eye to the far side of the square. He squinted. A pair of riders, one in front of the other. Maddeningly, he couldn't discern details. They were riding toward the cathedral. He climbed the porch to get a better view.

He glanced back, looking for the Savoyard. Vicario was already in the portico of the cathedral. Gervais prayed he'd keep going.

Gervais stopped, staring at the horseman in the lead. Saw him wave.

Bertram.

Monique!

Gervais leapt down the stairs, charging across the square at the horses.

Bertram reined in a moment before Monique did. "Are we late?" he asked.

He didn't hear, all of his attention on the only thing in the world: Monique. She looked pale and thin, but otherwise healthy.

"Papa?" she asked, tears welling in her eyes as she reached for him.

Crying himself, Gervais could only nod. He helped her from the saddle and folded her in a hug, crushing her to him.

Bertram cleared his throat. "We'd have been here sooner, but Monique made a run for it as soon as we cleared the gates of Annecy. I had the devil's own time catching her. She didn't believe I was there on your behalf."

Gervais smiled up at the younger man, his voice thick. "My thanks, Bertram."

"You are most welcome, but there is the small matter of payment for my services," he answered, sliding from the saddle with a sigh of relief.

"Payment, Papa? You have no money."

He snorted. "That's so, but Bertram isn't after money." He looked back at the crowd, most of whom had already entered the cathedral. "I don't think there's anything to be done, Bertram. The altar will crack into three pieces during services today."

"What?"

"Slaked lime paste stuffed in holes I carved out these last few weeks. Should be done expanding in the next hour or so, and crack the altar in three pieces. It should even resemble a lightning bolt."

"Jesus Christ."

"I think he's little involved. This is a sacrilege of a sort I doubt he would approve of."

"Wh—?" Gervais could see the wheels turning behind Bertram's wide-shot eyes.

"And it won't look like anyone did a thing. Have you any idea how hard it was to get a good color match for an altar I hadn't even seen?" Gervais continued with a touch of pride.

"Damn."

Relief still winging through his heart, Gervais grinned. "Yes, I probably am damned, despite the bishop's promises to the contrary."

"How?"

"Lots of practice. The bishop still owns the quarry that provided the stone here."

"Be honest, Papa. It's the same technique you used to crack the bishop's vault."

He nodded.

Bertram was a smart man, and ran through the possibilities quite quickly. He shook his head. "So the bishop wants the deal to fall through and at the same time embarrass or possibly even cause a crisis of faith amongst the Calvinists?"

Gervais nodded again.

Monique tutted. "Oh, Papa, this sounds even worse than when you sold that relic to th—"

"Monique, please. Let Bertram think."

"No way to stop the reaction?"

"No, none that I know of."

The man began pulling at his lip. "Out of interest,

how were you going to limit the damage if I got back earlier?"

"I was going to scale the building last night and drop some stone on the altar." The older man shrugged, "Not perfect, but the best I could come up with."

"Not bad, but not something we can use just now."

"What's the plan, then?"

"Let me think."

"We have an hour or so. No rush."

"Now who is preventing him thinking, Papa?"

Bertram was pulling his lip, still undecided, when he spied Vicario stalking from the cathedral, face purple and every movement stiff with anger. "Don't look now, but here comes the Savoyard. My, he looks unhappy."

The sound of quite a hubbub carried from the cathedral behind him.

"That doesn't sound good," Monique said.

"No, it doesn't," her father agreed.

"Stay where you are, bastard!" Vicario shouted, pointing at Gervais. He covered the distance nearly as fast as Gervais had. Behind him, several people shot from the cathedral, heading in different directions.

Not panicked. More like runners sent for something.

"Wonder what has him so angry?"

"I think we might find out," Bertram answered, drawing his horse pistol from the scabbard and cocking it fully. Not at all certain he would avoid being arrested if he had to use it, Bertram kept the weapon concealed behind his leg.

"You scum!" Vicario shouted, drawing close, "You had to know!"

"What?" Gervais answered, pushing his daughter

to stand on the other side of her horse from the enraged Savoyard.

"Don't pretend you didn't know they had such treasures! But God has prevented your infamy! You'll have no benefit of your vile scheming!" the Savoyard screeched.

The horses shied away from the noise, revealing Monique. The Savoyard finally had a look at her. Actually looked, rather than seeing her as merely an obstacle between himself and Gervais. "And there is the proof of your infamy! You made some deal to have your daughter freed!" Vicario's face twisted, naked steel flashed in the rising sun. He lunged.

Bertram, too slow, raised the heavy pistol. He pulled the trigger, dropping the hammer to ignite the powder in the pan. Vicario de Turin buried a handspan of his rapier in Gervais' guts, expression twisted with hate just as Bertram's pistol roared and bucked. Dirty white smoke connected his barrel to the nobleman for an instant before the Savoyard fell atop Gervais, skull pulped by more than an ounce of lead.

Bertram, never having killed a man before, stared at the corpse, blood rushing in his ears and the taste of copper and sulfur in his mouth.

Monique entered his field of view, crawling to her father. "Papa?"

Her father shoved the corpse from him. "Damn, but that stings."

"Papa?"

"I'm all right, Monique. Cut, but not so deep I'm like to die."

Several men were eyeing him from the cathedral, eyes hard. Slowly it dawned on him they were considering rushing him. Shaken, Bertram dropped the pistol to the flagstones.

He knelt, tried to speak, couldn't find his voice. He swallowed, tried again. "That belly has saved your life twice now, Gervais."

"Yes. Yes it has. I don't think I'll wear it again, all the same."

Clément approached from the cathedral, a group of burghers on his heels.

"Clément, he went mad, tried to run Gervais through."

"We saw." The men behind the stablehand nodded, murmuring among themselves.

"What did he see inside that so enraged him?"

Clément's smile was broad, "God answered our prayers!"

"Amen," the men behind the local chorused.

Bertram and Gervais shared a look.

Clément laughed at their expressions. "It's true! The altar, it broke just as we were entering. But inside, inside there's a great blessing in our time of need."

Gervais didn't seem to understand any more than Bertram. "Huh?"

"We don't need the duke's money anymore."

"What?" Bertram asked.

"There was a great store of treasure hidden within the altar! The minister, he said it's hoarded coin from the days of the Catholic bishops!"

It was too much. Bertram began to chuckle, then to laugh. If there is one thing you can bank on in life, it's that God plays the very best of jokes.

Jacob's Ladder

John Zeek

Martin Meurer was hanging by his fingers from the eaves, with his feet braced over the shuttered window below, when the shutters crashed open. Martin had a good view—too good a view—of the bald spot on the head of the man who leaned out of the window. Martin silently wished... *Don't look up. Look at the church. Look at the street: Look at the house across the street, but don't look up...*

Martin's wish was granted as the man's head withdrew into the room below and the shutters were pulled closed. But he waited. Sure enough, four long heartbeats later, the shutters crashed open again. "Watchmen, call the watch! I've been robbed!" The man's voice echoed in the empty street.

Martin waited until the head withdrew a second time and he could hear the clatter of steps through the still-open shutters. Only then did he pull himself onto the roof and make his escape. Three roofs and an alley away, he was finally able to stop. Braced against a chimney, he examined his new possession.

Who would have expected a table in the middle of a dark room? Who would have expected the owner to awaken so fast? He had grabbed the first thing that came to hand, stuffed it in his pouch and bolted for the window. Now he had time to see what he had. A cup, too small to be called a goblet. It was a metal cup. Silver, he hoped. Silver would buy food for a week, and a new jacket. With winter coming on he could use a new jacket. Not bad for his first try at house creeping. Not bad at all.

Martin's breath froze when a voice came out of the chimney's shadow. "Young Meurer, you'll make a fair creeper, if you survive. You take too many chances."

Martin braced himself to run, but where? The owner of the voice blocked his escape route. Still the man was just talking, and on the roof at night, he had to be a thief. Another thief, he reminded himself. "Well, I got a nice silver cup. Not bad for an hour's work."

"It's pewter. Where would a tanner get a silver cup? And even if it is silver, which I doubt, was it worth your life?"

Martin moved a bit to the right to try to get a look at the voice's face. "Who are you to ask that question? You're a creeper like me."

The owner of the voice moved his face into the moonlight. "Not quite like you, Young Meurer, and I am not a creeper." Martin recognized Jorg Hennel, spokesman for the Committee of Correspondence in Suhl. "What would happen if you were caught by Watchman Meusser? As easy as I caught you, even an oaf could manage to find you."

With no place to go, Martin answered. "Meusser

would break through any roof he tried to walk, but if he caught me it would mean the cells."

Hennel chuckled. "The cells at night and working for the city collecting offal during the day. After you were branded. You do remember they brand thieves on the forehead? No one likes thieves. Now, here's the real question. What will my fellow committee members do when they catch you? You know that you made your escape over Gary Reardon's roof? He is protected by the Committee of Correspondence."

Martin was surprised. He hadn't known Reardon lived in this part of town. "Turn me over to the watch?" he asked hopefully. He knew he was caught. Hennel hadn't touched him, but he was caught.

Hennel laughed. "Yes, they would turn you over to the watch . . . after they dropped you off the roof." Hennel made a whistling sound followed with a slap to his knee. "*Splat*. Two broken legs, you'd have to crawl the rest of your life."

Hennel got to his feet. "It's cold. Follow me, or leave town. Your choice, but your nights creeping roofs in Suhl are done. Only one warning is given, this is yours."

Hennel moved off, over the peak of the roof away from Martin's planned route. Martin took a moment to think. *If an old man like Hennel has caught me, I must be past it. Maybe I should look for another line of work.* He moved to follow the committee man.

Two roofs to the west he caught up to Hennel. "Where are we going?"

"To church. Careful here," was the brief answer as Hennel swung down to catch the edge of a protruding window. Then, using the exposed wooden corner beams, he climbed down to the street where he waited for Martin. *He has to be joking. Church? Where are the handholds?*

When Martin finally succeeded in joining him in the dark street, Hennel led the way to the side door of a small church. "In you go, Young Meurer. Drop your cup in the poor box. If it's silver, it will feed the poor for a week."

Martin was stunned. The man was serious. *A church? Putting the cup in the poor box?*

Hennel marked his hesitation. "You're not a good enough thief to put it back. And you can't start a new life with stolen property. Of course, you could go out the front door and head for the city gate. It will be open in an hour."

Martin shook his head. Hennel was crazy. But he walked into the church and found the poor box. He thought about running but ended up leaving the cup. His curiosity was aroused. What was Hennel going to do?

When he exited through the side door, he found Hennel sitting on the steps. The man nodded. "Martin, join me in a late supper, my treat. We'll talk about your future."

After a quick meal in a nearby tavern, Martin was even more curious. Hennel had refused to talk about anything besides the food.

Finally they were standing outside and Hennel appeared lost in watching the sun rise over the city gate in the distance. "Herr Hennel?" It never hurt to be polite. "What do I do now?"

Hennel pointed as he answered. "There is the

north gate. You could be out and on your way to some other city. Not many opportunities for creepers in villages. Or you could ask yourself why you want to become a thief?"

"Because I'm poor and the rich have what I want. And I'm too healthy to be a successful beggar," Martin answered.

"Yet I found you stealing from a poor man. That tanner was just a journeyman; I would bet that cup was his prize possession. So you were making his life worse. And a pewter cup wouldn't bring enough to pay for the meal you just ate."

Martin thought. "The rich have better latches on their shutters, Herr Hennel. They're harder to steal from." He couldn't tell Hennel that the tanner was his third try tonight.

Hennel laughed. "And better locks on their doors, and bars on their windows and dogs! Don't forget the dogs."

Martin realized that Hennel knew what he was talking about. The man had to have been a thief some time in his life—from his clothing, a successful thief. *Was he a man to watch and copy?*

"Herr Hennel..."

The older man waved his hand. "Jorg, call me Jorg. I'm not a gentleman you can impress and trick with your manners."

"Jorg, what did you mean when you said my future? I am not going to leave Suhl; I was born here and have never gone out of the city. If you won't let me be a thief, what is this future? This new life?"

Jorg smiled, the first real smile Martin had seen on his face. "Ah, Martin, that is the question."

Jorg reached into his belt pouch. When his hand emerged it held two coins and a pamphlet. "Here is something I want you to read, and enough to live on for two days. I expect to see you here on Friday morning and we'll talk." He walked off and Martin looked at the title of the pamphlet. *Common Sense* by Thomas Paine.

Sunrise Friday morning found Martin pacing in front of the tavern. *Where was Jorg? Had he forgotten? Was it all an elaborate joke?* Martin was tempted by the unattended handcart resting in the street across from the tavern. Its owner had just gone in the tavern carrying two hams. There had to be more hams in the cart. A quick snatch and he would have breakfast. *Jorg had been clear, no more stealing from the poor. Does a butcher count as poor?* Besides, there were too many people in the street. *No, I am no longer a thief.*

Reading Jorg's pamphlet hadn't answered his question about his future. In fact it had raised more questions. *What was this "Natural Liberty"? The man who wrote it had to be mad. All Englishmen were mad. But the descriptions of kings and nobles rang true. Why had Jorg given it to him?*

He was lost in contemplation when Jorg tapped him on the shoulder. "You're early. Come with me."

When he turned, Jorg was already walking down the street. Walking and waving his arm. Soon three young men came out of the shadows. When the three greeted Jorg, Martin was glad he had not indulged himself by lifting a ham.

Jorg was soon passing out strips of paper and stacks of pamphlets.

"Here you go. Five *Common Sense* and ten of the new ones from Jena. You're working the landing, unloading barges.

"Friedrich, head over to the bolt factory. They're looking for a sweeper, full time. Tell Herr Reardon I sent you. Here are twenty of the new pamphlets; get them to the machinists.

"Günter, I found you an all day one, loading hides for Josef Boyer, the butcher, and unloading the hides at Schwengfeld's tannery. Take twenty of the new pamphlets to pass out in the street. I'm sorry I couldn't find you anything cleaner."

Martin realized that Jorg had found work for these men and was sending them out to spread Committee of Correspondence pamphlets. And taking their reports.

"Casper Amberger raised the wages of his journeymen. Do you think the other gun makers will follow?"

"Your friend Hatfield is hiring more *Jaegers*, and is looking for two more men for driver training. Think you could put in a good word for Heinrich Bohl?"

"Bauer, the printer, has printed thirty-five copies of that book; the one written by the Frenchman, Arouet. The one you had us read."

Soon the three men were gone, only to be replaced by four more. The same scene was repeated five more times as men came and went.

Finally the men stopped coming. Jorg waved Martin over. "That's a good start to the morning. Let's go have breakfast. We have a busy day ahead of us."

"Jorg, I read that pamphlet and I have some questions."

"No more politics until after we eat; definitely none at our meal."

Martin was curious. What did Hennel have in mind? Why did he need a skilled thief? No. A skilled almost-thief. "What are we going to be doing? I hope it involves getting some money. My pouch is empty."

"Well, first we'll eat. Then we'll see about making some money," Jorg answered as they walked down the street.

They were soon in the more prosperous part of the city. The buildings weren't as run down and the taverns had brightly painted signs. Jorg pointed to a busy tavern. "How about the Laughing Boar for breakfast? Since it's next to a bakery, they should have fresh bread."

Martin was taken aback. "Jorg, it's also next to the city watch headquarters. There are always watchmen stopping in."

"So? Have you forgotten that you're no longer a would-be thief? The watch has better things to do than to chase honest men."

Martin was unsure. *The watchman might not know I am not a thief. Besides they do chase beggars.* But he followed Jorg into the tavern.

Jorg surprised him by walking directly to the table where a watchman was seated. And not just any watchman. Martin recognized Captain Johan Frey, the commander of the watch.

Jorg seated himself on an unoccupied bench and waved for Martin to take a seat beside him. "Good morning, Captain Frey. I hope you are enjoying your well-earned breakfast. I'd like to introduce Meurer, my new associate."

Martin could see that Captain Frey was studying his face. Was the man memorizing his looks, or just thinking? Finally he responded. "Hello, Martin. You look better than when I last saw you in the market. I see you lost your limp. Given up begging, have you?"

Before Martin could stumble through an answer, Jorg commented. "Martin has decided that there was no future in being a beggar and is too honest to be a thief."

The captain smiled. "So now he is another of your projects, Jorg?"

Jorg shrugged. "He shows promise. What I wanted to ask you was if you were done with that book I loaned you? I want Martin to read it."

Martin could feel the captain's eyes still studying him. Then the watch commander nodded, "Certainly I'm finished with it. It's over in the watch office. I think Watchman Weiss is reading it, though."

Jorg said, "No, let him finish it. I'll get another copy. Tell Weiss to pass that copy on. Now breakfast. How is the porridge this morning?"

Breakfast with the commander of the watch! Martin couldn't believe it, but it happened. The man even paid for Jorg and Martin!

Jorg's rule about no politics while eating held throughout the meal. The only conversation was about Martin's life. What was there to tell? His mother had been a prostitute. She died and left him an orphan who never knew his father. Passed from relative to relative and some who weren't relatives. Small for his age, so there was no hope for work as a day laborer. Money for an apprenticeship hadn't even been a dream. His one try at being a cutpurse had failed. The roofs had been his way out of boredom. Then they had looked like his future. Now he was a failed thief.

But Jorg kept asking questions. It was a long meal; Martin wondered if he should go find Captain Frey and confess so he could be arrested.

Finally it was over. Jorg shoved his bowl away and nibbled a last crust of bread. "Now, Martin, ask your questions."

Martin laid the pamphlet on the table. "What does it mean? What are you working for?"

Jorg looked at him directly. "I am working for a dream, a dream of a perfect world. A world I don't expect to see, but one I see coming."

He touched Martin's shoulder. "I see a world where a poor man has the same standing before the law as a king. But in our world, the poor man is in chains of laws made by kings and nobles. I am working to make my dream become real: a world where all men are equal."

Martin picked up the pamphlet, "Is that what Paine meant by 'Natural Liberty'?"

"Of course. You notice that Paine said one honest man is worth more to society and in the sight of God, than all the crowned ruffians that ever lived. He could have been talking about our German nobles."

Martin thought for a moment. "You want to replace the nobles?"

"Not the good ones. Some nobles are even members of the committees. Not many, true. Most are more interested in their privileges than the lives of the people."

"So that is why you don't want me to steal from the poor?"

"Martin, I don't want you to steal from anyone, rich or poor. If you could steal from anyone's house in Suhl, who would it be?"

Martin thought. Who was the richest man in the city? "Rudolph Amberger. He's a councilman and rich."

Jorg smiled. "But he employs twenty-five apprentices and journeymen, not counting the teamsters and carters in his trade caravans. So, you would still be stealing from the poor. Besides, Amberger is working to improve conditions. He did favor allowing all residents, not just citizens, to vote in city elections. He lost, but he was in favor."

Jorg stood up. "Come on. We can talk while we walk. We're going to see Anton Bauer, the printer, and we can't be late."

"For more pamphlets?"

"That too, but mostly we need to earn some eating money. Anton's journeyman has left to open his own shop and the apprentices are too small to work the press. So you are going to help unload paper for the shop and I am going to apply some muscle to the press handle. Three days of meals if we get there on time."

The work wasn't the hardest thing Martin had ever done. Try hand-walking a house's eaves three stories above the street! But it did stretch muscles he didn't know he had. The pay wasn't the three days' meals that Jorg had promised either, only two, but the printer had given him his first real book. Jorg had said it was worth reading.

Besides, he had seen the inside of a print shop for the first time. He wondered if fourteen was too old to become an apprentice printer. Who would take him? How would he pay the fee?

Martin stopped and studied the title of the book

again. *The Social Contract or Principles of Political Right*, written by some Frenchman named Jean-Jacques Rousseau.

Maybe there were some answers in it.

Two weeks later

Martin sat on the roof peak over the attic room where Jorg was meeting with his fellow committee members. The sun was just setting behind the house across the street. He was no longer running the roofs as a thief, but he still did his best thinking high above the stink and noise of the street. The ideas from the books and pamphlets he had been given to read were going round and round in his head. The Rousseau book had pride of place in his collection, but it was hard reading; someday he would finish it.

The idea that all men are by nature equally free and have certain inherent rights was easy to understand. All the writers said that. Of course, putting it into practice would be a problem. No noble or wealthy burgher was going to give up their privileges or even believe that the poor were equal to them in the courts. And the concept that all power comes from the people was foreign to those same nobles. They thought God had given them their place in society. The very idea that the common people, even people like him, could have a voice in choosing a government would give them fits.

The voices from the room below caught Martin's attention. Jorg's meeting was breaking up. Martin's thoughts were pulled away from politics and back to his condition. Soon he and Jorg would go to dinner.

Martin was hungry; he had spent the day in the hard physical labor of unloading charcoal at Johann Will's gun works. Working at a gun shop had been interesting, despite the labor involved. Between trips to the wagon for charcoal, Will had shown him how a master shaped metal and how to hammer rough parts into a finished weapon. Martin thought maybe he might like to become a gun maker instead of a printer.

As he swung down from the roof peak to the window of Jorg's room, all the political ideas were brought crashing back by a comment made by one of the departing committee members and Jorg's answer. The member asked, "But do we have the right to change the government? Not can we? We know we have the power, but do we have the right?"

Jorg's answer was straight and to the point. "Heinrich, we are agreed that government is instituted for the common benefit and security of the people. If the acts of the government are contrary to that purpose, the people have the right to reform, alter or abolish it. So, yes, I think we have the right."

Heinrich seemed satisfied as he left, but Martin's head was suddenly full of all the political arguments he had overheard in the past weeks. All the ideas from the books and pamphlets were there and Martin decided they were worth working for. But were they worth fighting for? He knew it would come to fighting, the news from other parts of Germany were full of the events of Operation Kristallnacht. No, the so-called leaders of society wouldn't give up their privileges without a fight.

Jorg turned toward him and asked, "Martin, ready for dinner?"

Martin was more than ready, but this was more important. "Jorg, what does it take to join the Committee of Correspondence? Not just follow you around as a hanger-on, but to be a real member? I think I want to join."

Jorg smiled an odd smile and stated, "Nothing and everything. No amount of money can buy your way into our trust and fellowship, but you will give everything to our cause if you become a member. Some Americans in a future that never will be said it best. Our lives, our fortunes and our sacred honor. You know we can still lose and if we do we will be hunted down like all people in a city hunt rats. Think hard, Martin, before you ask to join."

"But . . ."

"Plus, you are younger than most of our members like for a recruit. So, no, I will not suggest you as a full member."

Martin was not too disappointed; he had never expected to be accepted as a full member. But there had to be a way. He spoke formally. "Herr Hennel, I wish to apply for the position as your apprentice. I have been your shadow for the past month and I am ready for more duties."

Bibelgesellschaft

Bjorn Hasseler

"He *kommen*...he comes...no, he goes..."

Katharina Meisnerin tried not to fidget while Friedrich struggled with the translation.

Dr. Green took pity on him, sort of. "Friedrich, parse that word, please."

"Aorist tense...passive voice...indicative..."

"Are you sure about that?"

"Uh, no."

Katharina watched Dr. Green very carefully. "No" was usually the safe answer when he asked that question, but every once in a while it was a trap, just to see if a student had any confidence in his answer.

"Then what is it?"

Friedrich hemmed and hawed before finally admitting, "I don't know."

"Anyone?"

Katharina made sure to be studying her book intently. If she so much as twitched, she was going to get called on.

"Katharina?"

Alas, sitting still didn't always work. "It's a participle," she answered.

"Correct. Friedrich, continue."

Friedrich contemplated the participle for about ten seconds and ventured, "Second person, singular, from *poreuomai*, translated 'going.'"

"Do participles have person?"

No! Katharina thought loudly in Friedrich's direction. *Case, gender, and number . . .*

"What is a participle?" Dr. Green looked around the room. "Katharina?"

"A participle is a verbal noun."

"What do nouns have instead of person?"

"Gender?" Friedrich guessed.

"And?"

"Number."

"And?"

"Case?"

"Yes. So what is this?"

"Masculine, singular . . . nominative."

"Correct," Dr. Green said. "However . . ."

The bell rang. *Thank you, God*, Katharina prayed.

"However it is not passive, but deponent," Dr. Green finished quickly. "For homework parse the rest of the verbs including participles in verses eighteen to twenty."

Katharina started gathering up her books, hurrying to get to last period gym class on time.

"Katharina," Dr. Green called.

"Yes?"

"We've received a letter. I'll read it at the *Bibel-gesellschaft* meeting."

"Thank you." Katharina practically floated down the

hallway. Dr. Green knew she disliked gym class, so he'd timed his news to give her a distraction.

Forty minutes later, Katharina had to admit that basketball wasn't actually cruel and unusual punishment. It just seemed that way because she could be doing something *productive* with her time. The gym teacher finally dismissed them, and she headed for the locker room.

"You know, Kat, you could be a good player if you'd just put in some extra practice. You could stay after tonight and practice with the team."

Katharina recognized a recruiting pitch when she heard one. "No thanks, Kelli. I have a *Bibelgesellschaft* meeting. Dr. Green told us we've received a letter."

Kelli Fritz rolled her eyes. "It's a *letter*. What's the big deal?"

"But it could be about a manuscript." Katharina tried to rein in her excitement. She'd occasionally been told that it scared people.

"I don't understand why your Bible society is looking for old Bibles. We've got perfectly good German and English Bibles. Now if you were making a new one in one of the Native American languages, that'd make sense. Or Turkish. Even Amideutsch."

Katharina shook her head. "Amideutsch isn't fixed yet. There's no need for an Amideutsch Bible, anyway. Almost everyone who can read it could read Hochdeutsch or English. As far as Turkish and the Native American languages, Alicia and Nona need to find native speakers to do the translation."

"The Abrabanels?" Kelli prompted.

"Kelli, why would the Abrabanels be interested in

translating the New Testament? And they read the Old Testament in Hebrew, anyway."

"But a couple of them came to one of your meetings," Kelli recalled.

"We had some questions about the Hebrew in a few Old Testament passages," Katharina told her. Which was entirely true. The Abrabanels had also passed along that they thought a Bible translation in any of the Native American languages would be an excellent idea, and that a relative who worked for the government had assured them that even if any such Bibles had to be given to Cardinal Richelieu for transport to the New World, that would be okay. But that wasn't something Katharina intended to repeat.

So she redirected the conversation slightly. "In the meantime, those German and English Bibles you mentioned are not 'perfectly good.' They're good, but we can look at the Greek and Hebrew manuscripts and make the German and the English Bibles better."

"How can you make the English better?" Amy Fodor chimed in. "Back up-time, we had the Dead Sea Scrolls and everything."

"Shh!" Katharina looked around quickly before deciding that the girls' locker room probably didn't contain any Turkish spies. "We do *not* want the Turks finding out about those."

"Sorry. But what else is left for you to do?"

"What's left?" Katharina was aghast. "Even you up-timers didn't have an up-to-date Majority Text in English. Just finding the manuscripts that you had but didn't collate will take at least a century!"

"So where are you going to look for them?" Kelli asked.

"We've made some inquiries, and we're going to Jena this spring to see if the theological faculty will help us." Then realism set in, and Katharina added, "Or at least write letters of recommendation for us. And Dr. Green has a letter. Why don't you come hear what it's about?"

"I can't. Practice. Let me know about it tomorrow, okay?" Kelli was equally adept at dodging a recruiting pitch.

"Okay."

The last bell rang, and Katharina hurried toward the set of classrooms everyone had started calling "the language wing." She met up with her friend Barbara on the way.

Dr. Green was tidying up after his other class, and Horst Felke was already there. He pointedly looked up at the clock. Katharina just smiled. She knew she and Barbara were on time. Getting there before she did mattered to Horst. He seemed to think it scored points for him in his ongoing competition with her.

Katharina was honest enough to admit that she really enjoyed outscoring Horst on a test. He usually beat her in math and science. She usually beat him in history. They were evenly matched in the languages, where they dueled for top of the class. But Katharina didn't see the *Bibelgesellschaft* as an arena for competition. If Horst figured out something before she did, so be it. She was more concerned with getting as much information as possible accurately organized and set out for use by...whoever could use it. The *Bibelgesellschaft* was nondenominational.

It had gotten its start over a misunderstanding. Horst and a couple of his friends had accused the

Anabaptists of not believing in the Trinity. And then, knowing Anabaptists wouldn't fight back, they'd punched her brother Georg. Henry Sims and Gena Kroll had immediately flattened Horst and his friends. Herr Principal Saluzzo had assigned all concerned to go talk to both Father Larry Mazzare and Dr. Al Green. They'd quickly found out that their disagreement stemmed from differing biblical texts in 1 John 5:7–8. Both Mazzare and Green had insisted that this was not a doctrinal issue, and Katharina and Horst had grudgingly agreed to work together to find the best readings.

So the young Anabaptist woman didn't bat an eye when two Jesuits entered the classroom. Their presence wasn't a problem for her. Figuring out what to call them had been. "Do not call anyone on earth your father." Horst had pointed out that Matthew 23 also said not to be called teacher, either. A heated discussion had broken out between the Bible society's Catholics and Protestants. Katharina's brother Georg had calmly observed that the verse seemed to be about religious authority, and that since honor was due to whom honor was due, it was acceptable to address a school teacher as a teacher. Since Johannes Grunwald, SJ, had been one of the Latin teachers, the students had addressed him as Magister Grunwald. And they did the same for Johannes Olearius and the other Latin teachers. And since Athanasius Kircher had written books and was regarded as an authority on any number of subjects, it would probably be acceptable to address him as Magister Kircher. In fact, Kircher was reasonably famous, and Katharina was pleasantly surprised that the *Bibelgesellschaft* was one thing with which he made an effort to stay up-to-date. To be honest, she was also more than a little surprised that her normally quiet brother had so quickly thought of a solution that everyone could live with. It also meant that Al Green was Dr. Green to all the students, even if most of their parents knew him as Brother Green.

Horst's fellow Catholics Mattheus Beimler and Johann Speiss arrived next. Mattheus was an old Grantville hand who attended Calvert High. He was sixteen and headed for university as soon as he graduated. The BGS was only one of his wide array of interests. He took after Magister Kircher in that regard. He might become a priest someday, but he was equally likely to become a lawyer or scientist. Johann was, in the up-time phrase, tall, dark, and handsome. He attended the new Jesuit collegium in Grantville rather than Calvert High and had his heart set on being a priest, much to the dismay of many a young lady in Grantville.

A couple of Lutherans were right behind them. Markus Fratscher and Guenther Kempf were headed into the pastorate and wanted a good working relationship between the BGS and the University of Jena since that was where they hoped to attend. At least, Guenther hoped to attend there. He was also a member of the Young Crown Loyalists club and was determined to attend university in the USE. Markus, on the other hand, was Lutheran to the exclusion of anything else. He made no secret that he'd rather attend the University of Wittenberg, but Jena would do if the war got in the way.

Alicia Rice and Nona Dobbs wandered in. Alicia was a Methodist. Nona was Baptist. They were not just interested in missions but in going themselves. That was something that had never even occurred to Katharina. Part of up-time missions had been Bible translation, so here they were. It was hard for Katharina to tell how realistic their plans were. She sometimes thought that their idea of taking the Gospel to the Native Americans was romanticized to the point of impracticability. On the other hand, Dr. Green's books indicated that stranger things had happened in the other timeline.

"If everyone would take a moment to pray?" Dr. Green requested. They did so, silently. It was another compromise that the Bible society had arrived at. Green's prayers alternated between long and boring and long and exciting enough to make the Catholic and Lutheran students uncomfortable.

"Is there any correspondence to report?" Dr. Green asked with a twinkle in his eye.

"Yes," Magister Kircher spoke up. "We've received a communication from Rome."

Katharina sat up straight. This was unexpected.

Kircher continued. "Most of it dealt with other matters but there was a postscript acknowledging 'the up-timers' concern for the uncial manuscript of the Holy Scriptures known to them as Codex Vaticanus B, and 02. We find the Gregory System fascinating. Please send a complete inventory of the Gregory manuscripts and their locations. The Father-General has promised assistance in tracking them down.'"

In spite of her own astonishment, Katharina noticed a number of reactions ranging from Horst's look of triumph to Dr. Green's firm "Well, that's not going to happen" to an awestruck "Father-General Vitelleschi?" from one of the Catholic students.

"We must, of course, follow our vow of obedience," Athanasius Kircher said mildly.

Katharina was devoutly thankful that Kircher was

an even-tempered man. Obviously he had to follow his orders. Equally obviously, Dr. Green didn't want *any* one group—Catholic or Protestant—controlling access to the biblical manuscripts or having exclusive knowledge of where to find them. Then she realized something.

"You *have* to do it, don't you?" she asked Kircher.

"Yes. Of course."

Katharina grinned. "Brilliantly done."

"I have no idea what you're talking about," Athanasius Kircher protested.

"Sure you don't." Katharina was certain that American sarcasm was fully warranted. "The University of Jena really has no option now but to join us. It's that or be left behind."

"What do you mean?" Guenther asked quickly.

"The Catholic Church is *going* to get a list of manuscripts," she explained. "If the Lutherans want one, too..."

"You arranged for that letter!" Markus accused Kircher.

"I've also received a letter. Two letters, actually," Dr. Green stated. He slipped it in so smoothly that Katharina was convinced that he had probably aided and abetted Kircher's stratagem. "The first may not be of interest to you. It's from Moïse Amyraut. You may have heard of him as Amyrald. He was the father of four-point Calvinism in the old timeline—and this timeline, too. He has some fascinating ideas about the two calls, the general and specific calls to salvation."

Dr. Green caught himself before the BGS zoned out completely. He was getting better at that, Katharina noted.

"But I'll save that for Sunday school," Dr. Green said. "The other letter, the one you're interested in, is from Archbishop Ussher." Before anyone groaned he added, "He relayed information to us from Patrick Young."

Katharina sat bolt upright. Patrick Young! The Royal Librarian of England! That meant...

"Patrick Young is studying Codex Alexandrinus, which was given to Charles I by Patriarch Cyril of Constantinople seven years ago. He specifically checked 1 Timothy 3:16 for us..." Dr. Green read from the letter. "'I have examined the First Letter to Timothy, chapter three, verse sixteen. The reading is theta sigma, which as you know is an abbreviation of Theos. I must confess I am intensely curious as to why you sought this reading of this particular manuscript, and I beg that you furnish an explanation at your earliest convenience. I have the honor to be, et cetera.'"

"Woo-hoo!" Katharina shouted.

Everyone in the room stared at her. Dr. Green and Magister Kircher were clearly amused.

Katharina watched her friend Marta approaching the table with her lunch tray, and she realized Marta looked distinctly unhappy. Marta dropped into a chair and before Katharina could ask what was wrong, she blurted, "Katharina, I can't go to Jena."

"Why not?" Katharina asked quickly.

"My parents say the BGS is not trusting God for protection."

"*What*? Last month they said it was too dangerous, so Dr. Green hired guards."

"I know. But Father visited Brother Altmann last evening and came back saying we are not trusting God."

"It's not your fault, Marta," Katharina reassured her. "Brother Altmann has always been the most cautious of the elders." Then a thought struck her. "Does that mean Joseph can't go either?"

Marta nodded unhappily then said, "Katharina, what are we going to do?"

Katharina thought. "We could ask Dr. Green to talk to your parents."

Marta shook her head. "No, that's part of the problem. Brother Altmann mistrusts Dr. Green, and my parents are very influenced by Brother Altmann."

Katharina sighed.

Two days later, Alicia Rice interrupted Katharina in the hallway before school started. "Kat, I can't go to Jena."

"How come?"

"My mom thinks it's dangerous."

Katharina frowned. "Dangerous for down-time Anabaptists or Catholics, maybe. Dangerous for up-timers? Jena? Who would dare?"

"I know, I know! But Mom was talking to Reverend Mary Ellen, and they decided it could be dangerous. Mom worries a lot, with my brother Adam in the National Guard."

"This is a lot less dangerous than the National Guard," Katharina pointed out. "We might get street corner speakers criticizing sectarians and Catholics. But they might not even notice us."

"Hey, it's not my idea. I *want* to go to Jena."

"I'm sorry, Alicia. I know you do."

"I explained that the guards are really for you Anabaptists and for the Catholics because the BGS is going to a Lutheran town. Nobody in Jena is going to attack an up-timer. Especially at the university. The students pretty much *are* the CoC, right?"

Katharina nodded.

Katharina was quiet for the whole bus ride home. She dropped her books on the table and didn't even make an attempt to start reading something before Mother decided there was enough time to work in the garden before dinner.

The hills weren't really conducive to agriculture but there was enough room for a big vegetable garden. It followed the usual practice of two paths forming a cross in the middle but the land had been a hillside so Father and Georg had built a terrace on the uphill side of one of the walks. Mother was very... not *proud*, because Brethren weren't supposed to be proud... but very *pleased* with the garden. The terrace meant that she—and Katharina—had an easier time reaching the plants on the upper level.

Before coming to Grantville, the Meisnerins had had little more than a kale yard. Now they had a proper garden. There was still a quarter of kale, but there was also a quarter of up-time lettuce and spinach. The third quarter was peas, up-time peas, and up-time string beans, and the fourth was everything else. They even had a border of herbs.

There were a lot of potatoes and onions farther down the hill. Someone—Katharina wasn't sure about the details—was paying a subsidy for potatoes that got used to grow more potatoes. The Freedom Arches was paying more but had agreed not to take more than a certain percentage. But they would happily take onions, too. The soil of the farm being what it was, potatoes and onions helped the Meisnerins get by.

Katharina thought things through while she pulled weeds. She had been counting on Joseph to do the talking for the Anabaptists in the BGS. He was one of the young Anabaptist men that Joe Jenkins thought might make a decent preacher someday. Horst and maybe Mattheus would speak for the Catholics, and probably both Markus and Guenther for the Lutherans. Her brother Georg was the only other Anabaptist boy in the BGS. Georg was involved mostly to humor her. Which meant she'd probably have to do the talking for the Anabaptists. Barbara wouldn't want to. *Speaking in public isn't a problem for me*, Katharina told herself a little firmly.

Several days later, Nona's parents were talking with Alicia's parents and the *Bibelgesellschaft* trip to Jena came up. By the end of the conversation, it was deemed to be too dangerous for Nona as well.

Finally the day arrived. Katharina was up before dawn, eager to be off to the University of Jena. Plus she got to the hot water before Georg did. She was showered, dressed, and halfway down the stairs to breakfast before she realized she'd heard no indication of Georg stirring.

"Hurry up, Georg!" she called. She thought she heard a "Mmrrff" in return.

"We'll be late!"

She heard his voice through his bedroom door. "Kat, we can't leave until everyone's there at eight of the clock. Is it even dawn yet?"

"Yes. Well, almost."

"Then it's only five and a half of the clock. I'll be down by six and a half."

Katharina and Georg's mother were already in the midst of cooking a big breakfast before they left. That wouldn't have been possible when they'd first moved to Grantville, but electrical lines had reached the Mennonite and Anabaptist settlements in the hills last year. There had been some discussion over whether they should follow the precedent of the up-time Amish and not use electricity. But there had also been the counterexample of the Mennonites using complex water pumps. Katharina hadn't cared about the technical details. What was important was the elders had accepted the power lines and hot water. Joe Jenkins' statement that electricity wasn't theology had clinched the matter, in Katharina's opinion.

"Get up, Georg!" Mother ordered. "You need a good breakfast. You'll need your strength."

Katharina smothered a grin. Georg just needed to drive the wagon. He had no intention of speaking to the professors at the University of Jena. In fact, he was mostly just going along to keep an eye on her. She sighed. She was seventeen years old and was one of eight students going. Plus there were the two pastors. Plus Pastor Green had hired bodyguards, just for a trip to Jena. They could have gotten there quickly by train, but Mother felt that was too extravagant. The elders had agreed. If it was extravagant or comfortable, there was a good chance it was sinful. When reported back to the *Bibelgesellschaft*, this had caused Pastor Green to mutter about spirit/matter dualism. Katharina was fairly sure he'd been muttering about Plato being in for a warm afterlife, too. The Lutheran members of the *Bibelgesellschaft* had taken it in stride, however, and even assured Katharina that even up-timers tended to think like this, and that one of them had even told them about a man up-time who had made up stories about a town with both Lutherans and Catholics and gently poked fun at their tendency to equate fun and comfort with sin.

In addition to making Garrison Keillor something of a hero to the *Bibelgesellschaft*, the decision that the train was too extravagant had resulted in the elders suggesting a wagon. After all, they didn't want the *Bibelgesellschaft* to walk to Jena as if they were refugees. That utterly contradicted their reasoning against the train, in Katharina's opinion, but since the elders had decided to make one of the community wagons available, she had decided not to point that out.

Pastor Green had been delighted. He said that their bodyguards had horses and could ride along. And that they could all meet at Neustatter's European Security Services. That way they wouldn't be leaving from any of the churches, and couldn't be accused of being under the thumb of any one denomination. Sometimes being non-denominational was a pain in the neck, Katharina reflected.

After Katharina and Georg had been fed more than was strictly necessary, Georg had hitched the horses to the wagon. Father and Mother had hugged them both and provided a litany of warnings. They'd promised to send a telegraph message home from Jena.

Georg stopped the wagon a little way down the road to pick up Barbara. There they received more warnings. But finally they were off. Georg was in no hurry, and neither were the horses. They heard church bells ring seven times as they skirted Grantville. Katharina fidgeted all the way. Finally Georg pulled up in front of Neustatter's European Security Services.

Sure enough, Horst Felke was already there, Katharina noted, as was Dr. Green. By the time Georg had tied the near horse to a hitching post, and helped the girls down from the wagon, Magister Kircher was coming down the road. The Jesuit scholar was wearing his clerical robes and a backpack.

After a round of good mornings, Dr. Green nodded toward the door. Katharina followed Magister Kircher and Horst inside. The office was small, with a Franklin stove in the back, just like the one Father had put in at home. There were two men seated in chairs by the stove, and a young woman at a desk to the left of the door.

All three of them rose instantly. One of the men had a commanding presence, and Katharina guessed this must be Herr Neustatter. He was fairly tall for a down-timer with broad shoulders and the look of someone who spent a lot of time outdoors. He had scary eyes, Katharina decided, the kind that appeared to know everything. Plus he was wearing a gun belt. It wasn't the neat, official kind that the *Polizei* wore, either, but a rough leather belt that dipped down on one hip. The holster held an up-time pistol, nearly as large as down-time pistols.

"*Guten morgen*, Magister Kircher, Magister Green." He examined Horst and Katharina for a moment. "And Master Felke and Miss Meisnerin, if I'm not mistaken." He shook hands with all of them. "I'm Edgar Neustatter. I will be commanding your escort today."

He had a pronounced accent, Katharina noted. Bavarian, or perhaps Austrian.

"I don't recall mentioning the names of any of the students," Al Green commented.

"You didn't," Neustatter confirmed. He continued in German. "I am training my men in investigation. I sent one of my team leaders to Calvert High." He gestured toward the blond young man next to him. "May I introduce Hjalmar Schaub? I assure you, he is older than he looks. Hjalmar has been in the field just as long as I have, since 1626."

Herr Neustatter was definitely unsettling, Katharina decided. Not only had he referred to Calvert High the way the students did, but he had also clearly anticipated what Pastor Green was about to say. Hjalmar Schaub looked really young. And he'd been checking up on them. That was...disturbing. She stole a glance at Pastor Green. He seemed to feel the same way.

"I apologize for seeming to investigate you," Neustatter said smoothly, "but sometimes my clients aren't aware of something that affects their safety. As a security consultant, I dislike surprises."

"Did we surprise you with any safety concerns?" Athanasius Kircher asked. The Jesuit scholar hadn't blinked an eye at Neustatter's explanation.

Neustatter gave them a wry grin. "I have learned more about church politics than I ever wanted to know. I understand enough to know that your BGS would like to find the most accurate Greek Bible so that you can make better translations."

That was a remarkably succinct explanation, Katharina thought. *It usually takes much longer than that to explain the BGS to a pastor. And where did he find out that we started calling the* Bibelgesellschaft *BGS among ourselves?* Then she realized that as soon as Neustatter had gotten down to business, the Austrian accent had vanished.

Neustatter was still speaking. "I also understand that collaboration between people from several different churches alarms the more extreme members of all of those churches. Which is why you came to us, yes? Hjalmar, would you assemble your team out front?"

After he left, Neustatter indicated the woman at the desk. "May I introduce Miss Astrid Schäubin. Miss Meisnerin, you and Miss Kellarmännin will be her principals."

Katharina shot Neustatter a surprised look and examined Miss Schäubin. Long, blonde hair was swept forward over one shoulder and curled inward perfectly at the ends. Her blouse was the latest Grantville fashion, a more or less up-time style made of heavier down-time fabric. She wore riding skorts and leather boots. And a gun belt, although hers was the neat black *Polizei* type. Katharina wasn't sure what to think of her. She couldn't help feeling dubious about a woman in what was essentially a mercenary company.

Neustatter was *very* perceptive. "She's quite good." He didn't sound offended.

"I'm sorry, Miss Schäubin," Katharina apologized. "I've never met a lady soldier before."

Astrid surprised her in return. "I've never met a lady theologian before."

Katharina smiled. "Fair enough. But that's not really what I am."

"Me, either," Astrid noted. "As Herr Neustatter said, you and Miss Kellarmännin are my principals."

"Does it bother the men?" Katharina asked before she could stop herself. "That you're a bodyguard?"

"Sometimes. It worries my brother, and some of the men have their doubts."

"Me, too. Being in the *Bibelgesellschaft*, I mean. Some people don't take us seriously. Come meet Barbara. She's outside."

The two of them left, still comparing notes in being a woman in what was usually a man's job.

Neustatter looked at Green and Kircher. "That worked out nicely."

Once outside, Katharina saw that the rest of the *Bibelgesellschaft* members who were going to Jena had arrived.

"Barbara!" Katharina called. "This is Miss Astrid Schäubin. She is our bodyguard."

"Miss Kellarmännin."

Barbara giggled. "I'm not anyone important. Only teachers call me Fräulein. I'm Barbara."

That was undoubtedly a good idea, Katharina thought. "And I'm Katharina."

"Then you must call me Astrid."

"I don't think I've met anyone named Astrid before," Barbara said.

"It's Danish. My family settled in Holstein long ago. We lived there before the men went off to war."

"Did you go with them?"

"No, after they first came to Grantville they came back and got their families. We all came to Grantville then."

Katharina waited for the rest of the story, but evidently that was everything Astrid intended to say on the matter.

Hjalmar reappeared with two other men. One of them was a big man. He had a smile on his face, which was a good thing, Katharina thought, or else he would look really intimidating. The other man was... average in all respects. Katharina tried to study him carefully, because she thought she'd probably forget and mistake him for a passerby. Neustatter introduced them as Karl Recker and Otto Brenner respectively. Georg had loaded everyone's luggage already, so they climbed aboard the wagon. Kircher and Green seated themselves on the bench next to Georg, while the students sat on the benches along the sides of the wagon. Katharina was right behind Georg with Barbara next to her and then Markus and Guenther. Johann and Mattheus were across from them on the right side.

So much for interdenominationalism, Katharina noted.

Neustatter and his team each had horses. Hjalmar and Neustatter rode ahead of the wagon while Karl, Otto, and Astrid brought up the rear. There was enough other traffic on the road that outriders would just get in the way.

Georg half-turned his head. "So what do you think of your bodyguard, Katharina?"

"She's... interesting," Katharina said quietly. "She's the only woman who works for Neustatter. It's kind of like being a girl in the *Bibelgesellschaft*, I think."

"She is the team leader's sister, yes?"

"Schaub, Schäubin," Katharina pointed out. "Of course."

"Some women have been following the up-time custom of taking their husband's names," Georg said mildly. "But since they have the same chin and jawline, I assumed they are brother and sister."

Katharina got a sly look in her eye. "I didn't realize her jawline was so interesting."

"Facial recognition was part of the forensics class," Georg said. "I like to keep in practice."

Katharina sniffed. Georg had gotten bored during all the extra evenings she'd been working on *Bibelgesellschaft* matters and taken an elective. She was still thinking of a comeback when Georg warned, "Hold on. There's a slope ahead at the Ring Wall."

Katharina felt the wagon slow almost to a stop. "You don't have to be quite so cautious, Georg," she teased.

"It's not that," Georg said. "There are men blocking the road."

Katharina looked past Georg and saw about a dozen men drawn up across the road to Jena. They were passing one wagon through while a couple others had pulled off to the side of the road.

"That's . . ." Pastor Green began.

"Yes, it is," Father Kircher agreed.

Neustatter and Hjalmar had already turned their horses. Hjalmar spurred to a gallop as soon as he reached level ground. Neustatter's horse ambled back to the wagon, giving every sign of being bored.

"It seems there will be a slight delay," Neustatter drawled.

"Who are those men?" Horst demanded. "They have no right to block the road!"

"I believe I mentioned extreme factions in each of the churches," Neustatter reminded him.

"But we've accounted for Catholic, Lutheran, Methodist, Disciples of Christ, Baptist, and Anabaptist," Green protested.

"Ah, but if I'm not mistaken, Master Fratscher

and Master Kempf are from Pastor Kastenmeyer's Lutherans. The men in the road are from Pastor Holz's Lutheran church. That is the church my men and I belong to as well."

Katharina's heart sank. Pastor Pancratz Holz was just as much a bigot as Ferdinand of Austria or Maximilian of Bavaria. If their bodyguards were part of his congregation, there was no way they'd reach Jena.

"Did you know about this, Neustatter?" Al Green demanded.

"I had my suspicions," Neustatter acknowledged. "I suspect that Pastor Holz assumes he can block the road because the place he is doing it is outside West Virginia County. It is outside Chief Richards' jurisdiction."

"It seems Holz has outthought us," Kircher said.

"Not entirely," Neustatter said. "I sent Hjalmar to find an SoTF marshal. This is within the marshals' jurisdiction."

Katharina's jaw dropped.

Neustatter noticed, of course. "Don't worry, Miss Meisnerin," he said. "I'll get you to Jena."

"I suppose we ought to see what they want," Pastor Green said. "Georg, keep hold of the reins."

Kircher climbed down from the wagon to let Green out. Some of the men in the road started shouting at them as soon as they realized Kircher was wearing his clerical robes.

Neustatter turned to one of his men. "Karl!" The two of them spurred forward on either side of Green and Kircher.

"If you gentlemen are almost done with the road, we'd like to pass through to Jena," Green said mildly.

"You heretics will not be going to Jena."

"Why is that?" Neustatter demanded.

"Because they are *heretics*, Herr Neustatter," Pastor Pancratz Holz explained. "They want to change the Bible."

"What I gather, Pastor," Neustatter drawled, "is they're wanting the University of Jena's help in finding old Bibles."

"They're trying to change the Scripture! I've read their books. They questioned *everything* about the Bible up-time!"

"No, we're not!" Al Green burst out. "I'm no liberal! And I'm not a higher critic, either." He proceeded to call the wrath of God down on a couple individuals named Graf and Wellhausen and then loudly pointed out that the *Bibelgesellschaft* had freedom of assembly, and if they wanted to assemble in Jena, they would, thank you very much. Pastor Pancratz Holz retorted that his congregation also had freedom of assembly, and if they wanted to assemble on the road to Jena, they would, thank you very much.

Back at the wagon, Katharina asked, "What's happening?"

"The Lutheran pastor is shouting," Georg reported. "And Pastor Green is shouting back. And they all look confused and angry." He sighed. "And now the Lutherans are shouting again."

Katharina saw the first projectile. She expected Pastor Green and Magister Kircher to run for it.

Instead, Neustatter's horse plunged into the group of men, who scattered in all directions. Neustatter wheeled the horse around and pursued a couple who hadn't scrambled quite far enough for his liking. The other guard circled in the opposite direction, forcing the men on the left away from the road.

"Take the wagon forward!" Astrid shouted to Georg.

Georg looked at her, looked at the disturbance ahead, looked back at Astrid, and flicked the reins.

"Is it safe?" Katharina asked.

Astrid brought her horse alongside the wagon. "I'll watch this side. Otto will watch the other side. Keep moving."

Georg looked rather startled but complied. When he reached Kircher and Green, he slowed not quite to a complete stop, and the two clerics scrambled onto the wagon.

"Holz is rallying his men," Kircher pointed out.

Sure enough, the mob was coming back together farther down the road, minus a handful of men whom Neustatter and Karl had driven far to the side of the road. Neustatter turned back toward the road and nudged his horse to a canter. A couple seconds later, Karl did the same.

Astrid Schäubin wished her pastor weren't trying to forcibly prevent her clients from traveling to Jena. Pastor Holz did have a point—their clients were mostly heretics, Catholics and Anabaptists. On the other hand, their clients had a point, too—they were bound for a Lutheran university to present their case as to why denominations that disagreed with each other should work together to examine and preserve ancient copies of the Scriptures.

One man pitched a stone at Neustatter as her boss cantered toward the men in the road. It went wide. Neustatter kept coming. Astrid saw the men edging backwards, and then they broke. Neustatter and Karl scattered them again.

Georg kept the wagon rumbling steadily forward. Holz was determined, but he and his men had to run to keep pace with the wagon. Neustatter and Karl were able to keep them away from the wagon. They were growing more and more frustrated but fortunately there wasn't much available to throw at the horsemen.

One man made a run at the wagon, and Neustatter wheeled his horse around to head him off. Twenty yards from the wagon he lashed out with a boot and sent the man sprawling. Neustatter gestured at Astrid to take it from there while he turned back toward Holz—just in time to find another man making a break toward the wagon. He stopped that one, too. The third one was on his way in when everyone heard a siren.

A Grantville Police Department cruiser rolled up behind the wagon. One officer got out but the driver stayed in the vehicle.

"This isn't Grantville!" Holz shouted. "You have no jurisdiction here!"

The officer passed the wagon. "Brother Green. Father Kircher."

"He's not Grantville police," Georg observed.

"That's Marshal Thomas. The marshals work throughout Thuringia-Franconia," Astrid answered.

Up ahead, Marshal Harley Thomas was explaining that fact to Pancratz Holz.

"You cannot give orders here! This is Schwarzburg!"

"And I'm a SoTF marshal. We have jurisdiction throughout the entire state. Pastor Holz, it's illegal to interfere with other people's right to assemble peaceably."

"But it won't be peaceably! They're going to Jena to try to destroy the Scriptures!"

Harley Thomas sighed. It looked like it could be a long morning.

"There's only one of you."

The marshal stepped up in Holz's face. "Yeah. But it looks like you only brought one riot with you, Holz. So get out of the way. Now."

The situation wasn't improved by Neustatter laughing out loud at that point. But Holz very grudgingly got his men out of the road.

They did make a few threats as the wagon rolled by.

"Any Lutheran who consorts with you heretics is risking excommunication!"

Green looked over his shoulder and said, "I'll be sure to warn Johann Gerhard."

Katharina surveyed the party. Markus and Guenther were on edge. Astrid seemed a bit upset, too. Well, that made sense. They were all Lutheran. Holz could make trouble for them. So was Neustatter, although he didn't seem to care. He was enthusiastically shaking hands with the marshal. Then he beckoned Astrid's brother Hjalmar and waved the wagon on. Katharina looked around and saw Karl riding ahead and Otto on the other side of the wagon. They didn't seem worried, either, but she didn't know them well enough to really tell.

About ten minutes later, Neustatter rode up beside Astrid. Katharina strained to hear their conversation.

"Miss Schäubin, I've sent Hjalmar back to Grantville to talk to the other men and their families. And to keep an eye on Pastor Holz. I know he wanted be along on your second mission, but someone needs to brief Ditmar's team. The men won't care. We all had to pretend to be Catholics in Wallenstein's army. But Stefan and Wolfram's families have been Lutherans all their lives."

"We could all just go to St. Martin-in-the-Fields," Astrid pointed out. "It's Philippist but it would do until the new Flacian church on the Badenburg Road opens."

Katharina eyed the two Lutheran members of the *Bibelgesellschaft*. They were both obviously listening, too. Markus looked very satisfied, Guenther less so.

"Excuse me," she ventured. "I haven't studied much about the Flacian-Philippist dispute, but you obviously have strong feelings about it."

Neustatter shrugged. "Flacians follow Luther more closely. It pi...annoys the Catholics more. Uh, begging your pardon, Father Kircher."

"Our pastor in Holstein was Flacian," Astrid added.

"And our pastor in Holstein was Flacian," Neustatter agreed.

Astrid knew what she ought to say. She opened her mouth and...nothing happened. She tried again. "Um..."

"Yes, of course," Neustatter agreed. "If Miss Schäubin and the others want to go somewhere else or all go to different churches, that's quite all right. Well, no, it probably isn't, but they're *allowed* to. Miss Meisnerin." He touched the brim of his hat and rode off to join Karl in front of the wagon.

After Astrid had recovered, she ventured, "Does he do that often?"

"Read your mind?" Astrid asked. "Yes."

"Doesn't that bother you?"

"I'm the secretary. It's quite helpful, actually."

☆   ☆   ☆

The rest of the journey to Jena was uneventful. They hired rooms at an inn and then walked to the university where they were met by the superintendent, Dr. Johann Major. Neustatter and his team stood back while Dr. Green made the introductions.

"I'm pleased to meet you, Dr. Green. I really should have seen to that before now. Master Kircher."

Major was accompanied by a couple students, Hans and Christoph, and within a few minutes, he had neatly split off Green and Kircher to go meet a colleague. Neustatter fell in behind them.

Katharina was hoping that Markus, Guenther, Mattheus, Johann, and Georg would lapse into theological shoptalk with the two students. But she found to her surprise that she, Barbara, and Astrid were the center of attention.

"Are you from St. Martin's?"

"No." It would have been amusing but Katharina was suddenly rather concerned about being an Anabaptist in Jena.

"Flacian, then."

"No."

"Then?"

"You know the *Bibelgesellschaft* contains students from several denominations?"

"Yes."

"I'm Anabaptist."

Christoph deflated. Hans turned to Barbara. "And you?"

"Anabaptist."

He looked to Astrid. "And you are?"

"Armed." She patted her holster.

"You are . . . you are . . ." Christoph stammered.

"A mercenary," Hans finished.

"I work for Neustatter's European Security Services. So does Karl over there."

Heads swiveled. "Well, yes, obviously," Christoph agreed. "But bodyguards? Here?"

"There was an anti-Catholic riot here last year," Astrid reminded them. "Go ahead. I'll watch the flank."

They got the grand tour of the University of Jena, ending up at a display of books.

"*Alchemia*?" Georg asked.

"By Andreas Libavius. He was a student here in the arts and medical curricula," Christoph explained. "He died in 1616. But it's the first systematic chemistry book. These are all books by university faculty or students."

Katharina glanced over the titles. *Methodus tractandarum controversiarum theologicarum.*

"That's one of Dr. Himmel's books. And *Passionale Academicum*, right next to it."

There was one in English. *Sixe Bookes of Politickes or Civil Doctrine, Done into English by William Jones.*

"Oh, Justus Lipsius was a professor here for a while. He converted from Catholicism. Then when he got hired at Leiden he converted to Calvinism. They say he was really a Stoic all along. But a lot of influential men speak well of these books—Richelieu, Olivares, Maximilian."

"Perhaps those aren't the best possible endorsements," Guenther remarked.

"And these?" Katharina asked.

"*Loci communes theologici* and *Meditationes sacrae* are Dr. Gerhard's books," Markus answered. "Some of us *are* Lutheran."

"And this is a draft of the first section of *Confessio Catholica*," Christoph announced proudly. "Dr. Gerhard is demonstrating the Catholicness of the Augsburg Confession from Catholic sources."

"Oh, please," Johann Speiss protested. Mattheus just rolled his eyes.

"A draft?" Katharina put in quickly.

"Yes. He has just started it. It probably won't be published for a few years. The book display is to show some visiting students. They're here from Latin schools and from some other universities. It's some sort of up-time idea. They call it 'recruiting.' As if a university were an army."

As if on cue, a number of other students entered the hall. Introductions were made all around, and shoptalk broke out. Katharina edged back out of the crowd and tried to locate Barbara but found herself talking to a student from the University of Erfurt.

They shook hands. "Johannes Musaeus."

"Katharina Meisnerin."

"You are . . ."

"Not a student here, no. I'm with the *Bibelgesellschaft* in Grantville . . ."

After the tour, they rejoined Kircher and Green. They had a couple hours on their own before a formal dinner with the theology faculty. Katharina was sure she would never be able to keep all the names straight, but she made sure she knew who the three Johannes were: Johannes Gerhard, considered the number three Lutheran theologian ever, after Luther and Chemnitz; Johann Major, the superintendent who had welcomed them; and Johannes Himmel, who had written a couple of the books on the display table.

Katharina had him pegged as the strictest of the three. Blessedly she didn't have to do anything but make occasional conversation and eat.

After the dinner, the BGS went back to the inn. Neustatter and his team fell in around them as they left the building.

"You didn't get to eat!" Katharina realized.

"We'll eat at the inn," Astrid said.

"That's not fair."

"I would rather be able to just eat than worry about etiquette and professors. What did you have?"

Katharina recited high-class but quite traditional fare.

Astrid smiled. "The main reasons we picked this inn are because we trust the innkeeper, and it is safe. It also has a well-deserved reputation for cheap food. But that's okay—I like stew and fries."

When they reached the inn, most of the BGS elected to stay up for a while. Neustatter pulled Astrid aside.

"Miss Schäubin, you and Otto go ahead and eat."

"But you..."

"Will eat later. You've got first watch."

Astrid discovered that being on watch was boring. After an hour, she upgraded that to really boring. Finally a door swung open and Neustatter ambled out, looking ridiculously chipper.

"*Guten morgen*, Miss Schäubin." His eyes twinkled. "Get some sleep."

The BGS met the University of Jena theology faculty mid-morning in a large room. Hans told them it was used for disputations and really large lectures. The BGS students looked around nervously as various U Jena students filtered in. Athanasius Kircher didn't seem the least bit uncomfortable, Katharina noted. He just shrugged off his backpack and started methodically arranging everything he thought he might need. Dr. Green was doing much the same thing.

"This looks like one of those newfangled tiered lecture halls," he muttered to Katharina. "Minus all the computers and AV, of course. No matter—we have everything we need."

Once everyone was settled, Johann Gerhard gestured to Albert Green. "Doctor, would you care to begin?"

"Thank you, Dr. Gerhard. We all want to know what the original text of the Holy Scriptures is. As printed editions become more common and more numerous, it has become apparent that there are a great many differences between manuscripts. By AD 2000 up-time, significant progress has been made in categorizing these differences into manuscript families. Some of that information came through the Ring of Fire with us, but much of it will have to be recreated.

"We all know we disagree on a number of theological issues. Dr. Gerhard, you have one set of beliefs. Pastor Kastenmeyer has another. Father Kircher here has yet another. And I have a fourth. What we found up-time was that when it came to correctly assessing what the original biblical text is, these differences largely didn't matter. Yes, occasionally, we are going to find textual variations that favor your position over mine or mine over yours. But our differences are almost all caused by two other reasons: first, differences in *interpretation* rather than differences in *text* and second, whether we regard Church traditions as authoritative or only Scripture as authoritative. Or as Brother Chaulker and his new converts believe,

Scripture and new tradition, which they believe to be an ongoing ministry of the Holy Spirit. I happen to disagree with them but I raise the issue to point out differences with the Pentecostals are also a matter of authority and interpretation."

"If I may, Dr. Green?" The question came from Dr. Johannes Himmel. Green nodded. "If our differences are matters of authority and interpretation, why make the effort to reconstruct the original text?"

Al Green paused for a second, then said, "For me, textual criticism is a means of confirming the inerrancy of the Bible and a tool for apologetics. Uh, that is a tool for defending the faith. I'm sorry, I don't remember if the term 'apologetics' was, uh, is used in this time period or not."

"From what we have read in your encyclopediae, your up-time denominations struggled with secularism," Himmel observed.

"Yes," Green agreed.

"Do you expect the same struggle in this world?" Himmel asked. Katharina noted that he and all the Jena professors were watching Green very closely.

"Yes," Green answered again. "First, because we brought secular ideas with us through the Ring of Fire. Second, because I really can't conceive of a future where we don't have to struggle against secularism. Which is weird since I *know* it's going to be different than up-time."

"Can you give us an example of how collecting and classifying biblical texts will help against secularism?"

"Certainly. Up-time in the late 1800s and 1900s there were people who asserted that the Gospels weren't written until a couple hundred years AD."

"That's preposterous!"

"Obviously. But it was largely a matter of faith until certain papyri manuscripts were analyzed. The Bodmer papyrus that we called P66 has the text of the Gospels—Luke and John anyway—and was written about AD 150."

"I take it that no one in your time thought the original documents survived. Or even the first set of copies," Johann Gerhard said slowly. "So then they would have acknowledged that the Gospels were written in the first century. Or several copies before AD 150."

He figured that out right quick, Katharina reflected. *Of course, he is the top Lutheran theologian alive today.*

"If they're willing to accept evidence at all," Gerhard added. "I have noticed that once one has staked his reputation on something, one becomes surprisingly inured to arguments that would be readily convincing to another."

Green chuckled. "Yes. We all claim that it is only others who attempt to remake reality as they would have it."

"So in the end it is still a matter of faith," Gerhard finished.

"Has to be."

Katharina watched Dr. Gerhard nod slowly, like her father did when he had considered and decided on a course of action.

"So studying the biblical manuscripts will likely result in some proof texts," Dr. Himmel summarized. "But why should we join with you to do this?"

"We will get more done, faster, if we work together."

"I don't think we should work with sectarians and Anabaptists."

Katharina tensed. They were expecting this, though, and had decided how to handle it.

Al Green grinned. "You don't think we're saved. Well, fair enough. I'm not entirely convinced about you all, either."

There were gasps throughout the room, and a couple people sprayed their drinks.

Green's eyes twinkled. "I think we both have concerns about our brother Athanasius here. And he about us, no doubt. As for me, I'm more than a little concerned that seventeenth-century Lutheranism seems to value adherence to a body of doctrine more than adherence to Christ. And I can only assume that you in turn are quite concerned that I'm not under any ecclesiastical authority outside of my own church's board of elders."

Katharina briefly wondered if they were going to lose Dr. Himmel to apoplexy. But Dr. Green seemed to have gauged Dr. Gerhard just right.

"That is, indeed, chief among my concerns," Gerhard answered.

He's actually just a little bit amused, Katharina realized. Her eyes cut sideways. *And Magister Kircher is struggling to keep a straight face.*

Dr. Johann Major spoke up for the first time. "Doctrinal differences would seem to be a good reason for each of us to pursue our own studies."

Al Green sat down. "Horst?"

Horst stood up and confidently faced the three Johannes. "There is a danger in each of us going his own way. Once it becomes known that we all value manuscripts of the Holy Scriptures, they could become one more prize to fight over in this war. The Calvinists in Basel hold Codex Bezae, which I freely admit is a manuscript that has some readings that appeal to me as a Catholic.

"Suppose I wished to consult Codex Bezae before publishing an edition. The Calvinists may or may not grant me access—especially if they had reason to suspect that I might find readings that supported teachings of the Catholic Church. Or suppose that you reverend doctors came to believe that manuscript B is the most accurate. Since this codex is housed in the Vatican Library, would it not be a temptation for us Catholics to impede a purely Lutheran effort? Let us argue theology and attempt to convert one another in our free time, but let us work together on the text for the benefit of all."

Good job, Horst, Katharina thought.

"A bold request, young man," Dr. Major said. "How was it done in the other world, the up-time?"

Green gestured toward her. "Katharina."

Katharina rose and addressed the faculty. Dr. Himmel's face was pinched. Dr. Major was a little startled. She concentrated on Dr. Gerhard.

"Up-time a very large majority of textual scholars favored a group of manuscripts called the Alexandrian text or the Critical Text. Eberhard Nestle published an edition in 1897, and it went through many revisions. Kurt and Barbara Aland were the primary editors in the late 1900s, and it was known as the Nestle-Aland edition." She picked up a small blue volume from the desk. "There is one twenty-fifth edition, four twenty-sixth editions, and one twenty-seventh edition in Grantville. The other members of the editorial board were Johannes Karavidopoulos, who we believe was

Orthodox; Carlo Martini, who we believe was Catholic; and Bruce Metzger, who was probably Presbyterian. The United Bible Society used the same basic text, and there are two copies of their third edition in Grantville." Katharina held up a red volume.

"There was a smaller group of scholars who favored a group of manuscripts called the Byzantine text or Majority Text because most manuscripts were classified in this group. All of our printed editions in our world are Byzantine, including the Complutensian Polyglot, Erasmus' edition, Stephanus' editions, and the one the Elzevir brothers published last year. They used the phrase *Textus Receptus* which up-time became synonymous with a particular strand of the Byzantine text. There are two Majority Texts in Grantville. This is one of them. Hodges and Farstad." This volume was white with a stylized Bible on the front. "The other, Robinson and Pierpont, exists only on Dr. Green's computer."

Katharina smiled. "Horst is Catholic. I am Anabaptist. When we discuss the text, sometimes, that matters. More often we disagree because Horst favors the Alexandrian text, and I favor the Byzantine text."

Dr. Himmel spoke up. "Fräulein, what role would you and the other young women have in this enterprise?"

Katharina took a deep breath. "Dr. Himmel, we have no intention of preaching. In Romans 16:1, Paul mentions Phoebe. She probably delivered the Epistle to the Romans for him. Let us help deliver the manuscripts." Katharina held her breath.

"If we were to join the *Bibelgesellschaft*, what needs to be done?" Gerhard asked.

Katharina exhaled slowly. That question was a really positive sign.

"Markus?" Dr. Green prompted. They were counting on the Lutherans in the BGS to clinch the deal.

"Manuscripts need to be identified and their variant readings catalogued. This had not been completed up-time, and we just don't have most of their records. It is likely that we won't be able to positively match some manuscripts with their up-time designations, so a new numbering system will be needed. And most of all, we need patience. Instead of using strong chemicals on Codex Ephraemi Rescriptus like they did up-time, we should wait until the technology exists to read it safely. There are other manuscripts which could be in danger if their locations become widely known. Examining others will require delicate negotiations. Ideally, whomever we send should speak for as large a part of Christianity as possible. Guenther?"

Guenther quickly took Markus' place. "While we welcome all those interested in preserving the Scriptures, there are some people we would really like to be involved. We believe that the University of Jena has the prestige to approach these men.

"Patrick Young, the Royal Librarian of England. Already he has examined Codex Alexandrinus for us and cleared up a reading that was disputed up-time.

"Bonaventure and Abraham Elzevir. Katharina mentioned the Greek text they published last year. And we will eventually need a publisher.

"Father Gavril, the Orthodox priest in Grantville. We will need full cooperation with the Orthodox.

"The heads of two monasteries: the Lavra on Mount Athos in Greece and St. Catherine's in Sinai.

"And we're going to need Calvinists involved, too."

"The duke of Brunswick-Wolfenbüttel. Actually,

we're not sure which duke. But one of the dukes of Wolfenbüttel this century has—will—would have collected a huge library including biblical manuscripts.

"Hugo Grotius."

"You dream large," Gerhard noted. "Still, that may be easier than you think."

"Moïse Amyraut."

"He's being tried for heresy, isn't he?"

"He was acquitted up-time," Dr. Green spoke up. "Even though they stacked the jury against him. And this time he has up-time Reformed writings to help. I saw to it."

Guenther resumed his list. "A man named Seidel would have brought manuscripts from the east sometime this century. We have no further information. We don't even know if he is alive."

"It would probably be good if the other Lutheran universities were involved as well," Guenther concluded.

"That could also be delicate," Dr. Gerhard observed. "I think we would like to confer. If you would excuse us?"

"Of course."

Dr. Green nodded to the *Bibelgesellschaft*, and they began gathering their things. Johannes Musaeus joined them, as he was also not a student at the University of Jena.

Once outside, Johannes spoke up. "That was a good presentation. I was not sure what to expect, but now I hope the faculty works with you."

"Thank you."

"If they accept, I definitely need to attend here. If you'll have me, I'd like to join your *Bibelgesellschaft*."

"Welcome aboard." Markus was the first to shake

his hand. "We can always use more Lutherans. Flacian, I assume?"

"Yes. Definitely."

They settled down into shoptalk. After about an hour, Katharina got up and started pacing. She was distracting herself with how many paces long the building was when Georg joined her.

"Relax, Kat."

"I can't. What if they don't want to work with us?"

"I think they will."

The morning dragged on. Katharina paced and prayed. Some of the others had started discussing sending a delegation for food when the door finally opened. Dr. Gerhard came out. The *Bibelgesellschaft* converged.

"One question, please," Gerhard asked. "Magister Kircher, you did not say anything." The Lutheran theologian studied the Catholic theologian for several seconds. "Rome wants information on the manuscripts, doesn't it?"

"Yes, of course."

"Have you been ordered to send it?"

"Yes. Dr. Gerhard, I would much prefer not to race you to the manuscripts. Rome wants the information. I have no directives concerning anyone else having the information as well."

"But we would have to work with Catholics."

"And I would have to work with Lutherans." Kircher grinned. "I am willing to make that sacrifice. But I would very much like to study some Sahidic manuscripts."

Katharina held her breath.

"Magister Kircher," Gerhard said, "I think I would

also prefer not to race you to the manuscripts. I might not get as many as I'd like." He glanced at Dr. Green. "You two have made this work so far?"

"Well, we're both pretty busy," Dr. Green answered. "It mostly works because the students make it work."

Dr. Gerhard smiled. "I expect that will continue. Very well, ladies and gentlemen, the University of Jena theology faculty will join the *Bibelgesellschaft*."

The students erupted in cheers. Katharina hugged Georg and then sought out Horst and extended her hand. Horst had a big grin on his face as they shook hands.

She could just barely hear Dr. Gerhard. "If all of you would come back inside?" He waved Kircher and Green through the door. "We're going to need some Calvinists. I think we should start with the University of Basel..."

The Heirloom

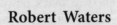

Robert Waters

March 1626, Darmstadt, Germany

Nina Weiss watched the soldiers assemble in the *Schlossplatz* from a safe place behind her father's crates and barrels. Not soldiers really, but boys, many of whom were not much older than she. Children playing at war, with their pikes and muskets and arrogant ways. She huffed and shook her head. Somewhere amidst that youthful rabble was her Stefan, cleanly shaven, fresh clothes, a bandolier of powder charges across his chest, and his uncle's old gun, the one that couldn't shoot straight, strapped to his back. She squinted to see him better, but the light of early spring blocked her view. She pushed up on tiptoes, put her hand over her eyes, and craned her neck.

A strong arm grabbed her waist from behind and a powerful hand covered her mouth. She tried to scream as the assailant pulled her off her feet and pushed her against the side of her father's shop. She struggled, but the weight of the man and the strength of his hold could not be broken. She kicked toward his crotch but only grazed the inside of his thigh.

"Ouch!" the man said, letting her go and pushing her away.

"Stefan?"

She turned. Before her stood the young man, a large mischievous smile across his face. Locks of light-brown hair fell out of a small dark cap fixed to his head. He smelled of black powder.

"You fool!" she said, beating his chest gently. "Don't *ever* do that again."

Stefan Thalberg pulled her close and they kissed, much longer than she expected in the light of day. Stefan was not one to show his affection in public. She did not resist, however, taking him close to feel his warmth one last time. He picked at the lacings on the front of her dress. She smacked his hand away. "No, no. You get no more of that," she said, "until we're married."

Stefan pulled away and shook his head. "How will that happen? Your father doesn't like me."

"Well, can you blame him? What can the lowly son of a silversmith offer the daughter of a great merchant like my father?"

They both laughed, but the seriousness of the moment returned. "Don't go, Stefan. You don't have to go. No one is making you go."

"I have to," he said, straightening his shirt and bandolier. "Wallenstein needs men."

"Wallenstein is inexperienced. Mansfeld will destroy him."

"My," said Stefan, putting his fists on his hips, "don't you know a lot today."

"My father talks and I am capable of listening."

Stefan grabbed her arms and pulled her close. "Yes, you are. So listen to me now, sweet. Wallenstein marches for God, and when this war is over, we must be on the right side of it. The winning side."

Nina stared into Stefan's deep brown eyes. There was a devout Catholic behind those eyes, though you would not know it to look at him. He seemed so secular, so simple in a way. His smooth skin, his pleasant eyes. Nina had fallen in love with those boyish eyes at first glance. But now they seemed more serious, adult, distant and anxious. Her father would never see what she saw in those eyes; he would never allow her to marry this Catholic boy...no matter what.

But it was too late for that now.

She pulled away and tried to hide the tears. "Then go. Go meet your friends and march off to Wallenstein."

They stood there for a long moment, saying nothing. Then Stefan reached into his pocket and pulled out a small package. He held it to her. "I want you to have this."

"What is it?" she asked, taking it from his hand.

"Something I made for you."

She held it up to the light. It was a medallion, perfectly shaped and smooth, pure shining silver, with the image of Mary holding the baby Jesus and looking at a cross in the sky. It was beautiful. She smiled. "Did you do the etching?"

Stefan looked embarrassed. "Well, no. I had Uncle help me with that. But I shaped and polished it for you. And I did the inscription on the back." He reached for her hand and turned it over. "See what it says? Whenever you feel lonely or afraid, whenever you have doubt, I want you to look at that and remember me. That is my promise to you, and when I return, we will marry, no matter what your father or mine will say. I promise."

He kissed her hands. They hugged and he kissed her forehead. "Goodbye," he whispered, then turned and walked away.

Nina watched him go from the safety of her crates and barrels. He disappeared into the crowd of soldiers. "Goodbye, Stefan," she said. "I will be waiting for you." She reached down and held the medallion tightly against her belly.

"We will be waiting for you."

August 1635, Grantville

Ella Lou Rice sat quietly in her living room. She had removed her black veil and had finished the cup of tea that her son, Clyde, had given her. Now she was alone, while somewhere in the house, Clyde and his wife Bettina were saying thank you to the last well-wishers that had stopped by after John's funeral. She smiled at the memory. It was a pleasant funeral, and all things considered, a reasonable one given the nature of their situation. Many World War II vets had attended, and one even blew "Taps," though it sounded a bit flat. Someone had brought an American flag and had draped the coffin with it, then presented it to her in the standard fold. It had not been the planned funeral that she and her husband had discussed, but what could they do? The Ring of Fire had left few options.

The original plan had been to bury John at Arlington

Cemetery, surrounded by his children, all six of them, with grandkids in tow. A twenty-one-gun salute, while somewhere in the distance a trumpeter would blow the notes that would carry John's sweet soul into the afterlife. But only Clyde had come through the Ring of Fire that day. Molly and her children were visiting her husband's family in Michigan, and the rest were scattered from Kansas to Georgia. If Ella Lou believed in a God with any true vigor, she might have counted her blessings, giving thanks that most of her children had been left up-time in a more "civilized" environment. But as she studied an old portrait of her husband, one taken outside of Boston right before his deployment, she could feel nothing but anger and regret. She ran her fingers over his face and whispered, "You should have been buried with all your children there. Now they will never know what happened to their daddy."

She felt the tears return and slammed the picture down on the coffee table. The tea cup rattled, dropped to the wooden floor, and shattered.

"Are you okay, Mama?" Clyde asked as he walked in.

Ella Lou raised her head, wiped her tears away, and nodded. She smiled at her son's concerned expression. Clyde was a good boy, if not a little preoccupied with business most of the time. The Ring of Fire had affected him as much as it had his mother and father, though he rarely spoke of it. He was quiet and very professional. The third of the bunch, after John Junior and Molly, but he had always been the most serious of all of them, given over to entrepreneurial pursuits, or, as his father might say, "pipe dreams." At the time of the event he had owned a storage business and had tried to maintain it, but around every corner, he saw another opportunity, another way to make money. He had gone into partnership with a down-timer from Jena and had given the management of the storage facility to him in order to pursue other, more lucrative, business ventures. Clyde was not rich, but he wasn't poor either. *I should at least be thankful for that*, Ella Lou thought.

"I'm fine, Honcho," she said, using Clyde's nickname. "I just wish your brothers and sisters were here to say goodbye to your father. He would have liked that."

Clyde nodded and scooped up the broken tea cup. "Yes." He held up the pieces and smiled. "You're rough on these cups, Mama. This is the third you've broken since we've been here."

"The first wasn't my fault," she said. "It was that damned Ring of Fire that broke it. I was drinking tea at the time, and your father was napping. A big flash happened, and I thought I was having a heart attack. I dropped the cup and yelled to John. Once we realized that I wasn't having an attack, we knew something bigger, something more serious, had happened. We didn't realize what exactly *had* happened until many days later."

Ella Lou rose slowly and walked over to a glass cabinet that contained a few porcelain frogs, a couple Hummel figurines, and a small cedar box. She opened the cabinet, took the box out, then returned to the couch. Clyde helped her sit down.

She placed the box onto the coffee table and opened it. On a small piece of velvet lay two medals. Ella Lou reached in and drew out John's Purple Heart.

"We were terrified," she continued. "We tried calling you all but couldn't get through. The lines weren't working. Then you showed up and we were glad you were safe, but we kept trying to call the others...with no luck, of course. John just paced back and forth all day, and with his arthritis no less. We thought maybe it was some kind of dream, that we'd wake up and everything would be back to normal. But weeks went by and it didn't right itself, this so-called cosmic event that people were beginning to assign to divine providence." Ella Lou huffed and shook her head. "Divine, my ass. No God in heaven—if there is one and I'm not so sure there is—would ever do such a terrible thing to His children. If there is a devil, this is his doing."

Clyde laughed. "They don't call it the Ring of Fire for nothing. But we can't do anything about it, so we might as well—"

"I want to go home, Clyde!" Ella Lou said, interrupting her son. "I want to go home. I hate it here! I hate this goddamned place. We don't belong here. We're not German. We're Americans, not United Europeans or whatever the hell they want to call us. I want to see *my* skies, my clouds, my stars. I want to watch CNN and go to the movies. I want—"

Clyde took her in his arms and rubbed her back gently. "I know, Mama, I know. I do too. But we've had this conversation before. We can't go back. Whatever happened cannot be changed, at least as far as I can tell. This is Germany, 1635. We've been here three, four years now. So," he said, pulling away from her and giving her a big, warm smile, "let's not talk about it anymore. This is Pop's day. Let's talk about him." He motioned to the Purple Heart in her hand. "Tell me how he got that."

"I've told you before, haven't I?" she asked, wiping away tears with her small, frail hand.

"Yes, but I like how you tell it. Dad always left out the gory parts."

"Well, he lived it, and I suspect that that's much different than hearing about it secondhand like I did. It was painful for him to talk about." She sniffled and cleared her throat. "But he got this in 1944 during the Elsenborn Ridge battle. He said the Germans hit the ridgeline hard, but were thrown back in chaos. It was the only place along the entire line of attack in the Ardennes that held. He was very proud of that fact."

"And how did he get that?" Clyde said, pointing to a silver medallion resting inside the box.

Ella Lou's eyes lit up as she put the Purple Heart down and pulled out the medallion, running the red leather cord tied to it through her fingers. "Oh, this thing? You know exactly where he got this."

Indeed he did, but it was a game they played. All the children played it. Every year on the vigil, their father would put it around his neck and wear it proudly, and the Rice kids would all say, "Where'd you get that, Daddy?" And he would tell them, his face beaming with delight, his eyes wet with tears. It was a great story, a painful story, and John Thomas Rice made sure his children heard it every year.

"He got this during that very same battle," Ella Lou said. "It's an old family heirloom."

"How did he get it?"

Ella Lou leaned back on the couch and held it to her chest. She closed her eyes and told the story, as she remembered it, from her husband's own words. . . .

December 1944, near Wahlerscheid, Siegfried Line, Belgium-German Border

John Thomas Rice hated recon duty, especially in the frigid wind that now cut across his vision, blinding him in a bitterly cold white mist. Why he was out here was anyone's guess. Hadn't the 2nd Infantry Division cleared this area once already? But reports of heavy German movement near the Siegfried Line had spooked HQ, and Lieutenant Colonel McClernand Butler wanted a peek. The lieutenant colonel had reconstituted part of his own 395th Infantry Regiment, combined with elements from the 393rd, to form a new regimental combat team, and had loaned it out for special duty. *The Second shits and the 395 scoops,* was the saying among the men. Rice could not argue with that. He growled and spit into the rising snow.

"Spitting into the snow? Onto God's green earth? For shame!"

Rice recognized the high-pitched, impetuously youthful voice. He smiled. "Stow it, Davis. We ain't in Kansas anymore."

"You know I'm not from Kansas," Davis said in his best country-boy drawl, picking up a handful of snow and casting it toward Rice. It scattered in the wind. "I'm from the greatest place in the world. Wild, and *wonderful*, West Virginia."

Davis was no older than eighteen by Rice's estimation. Perhaps even younger; it didn't happen often, but once in a while a sixteen- or seventeen-year-old faked papers and got in. This West Virginia boy had the unmistakable exuberant immaturity of youth, coupled with a sense of faith that both impressed and annoyed Rice. He'd never been religious himself, and never intended to be. But it would be nice in times like this to give oneself up to some higher power, to not worry about what lay on the path tomorrow, or what lay beyond the tree line before them today.

What did lie beyond those trees? Rice did not know. The world was quiet, deathly so, and Rice would give anything in the world to be back in Höfen, bundled up in some foxhole, smoking a cigarette and drinking black, bitter coffee. The small German village was just a few miles behind them: not very far at all, but a world away in terms of safety. That's what Davis did not understand. None of the young men around them had that much combat experience; their regiment had just recently been put into the field. But Rice was twenty going on twenty-one, and Davis was...not. A big difference there as well.

They reached a narrow road that wound its way through the woods. They stopped, went prone and held their rifles forward, watching the sparse tree line, a line that had already experienced heavy fighting, tree bursts, downed foliage, and abandoned bunkers. "West Virginia, eh?" Rice said, keeping the mood light while he fumbled through his coat pocket for a smashed pack of Luckys. "Where from?"

Davis held his rifle forward, his hands bone-white from the cold but his face brilliantly lit with the thought of home. "Oh, a great little town. Best of the bunch. Grant—"

"Quiet!" Sergeant Greene said, waving his hand down. "No talking!"

Rice shook his head and chagrined. Greene was

a pain in the ass, but soon the wisdom of the order became clear.

The ground began to shake, lightly at first, like the impact trees might make in falling. Along the road, the snow danced and spread down the bank in tiny avalanches. Rice let the cigarette he had placed to his lips fall, unlit.

The quiet and cold air made the echo of German tanks ring loudly. Through the wood and down the winding path, diesel engines for sure, but how many wasn't clear. Rice tried to squint through the relentless snow, tried to pick out some motion, some flash of a barrel or the shaped hull of a Tiger or Panzer IV. It was a game the men played, trying to figure out the composition of the enemy armor by sound alone. He tried but could not make an accurate account.

"The Germans mustn't be too happy with the ass kicking they got from the 2nd," Davis whispered. "They're sending a few tanks our way." He said the last words as if here were disappointed, as if he wanted more. *Poor young fool.*

Rice nodded but wasn't so sure. This wasn't just a few tanks. This was many. More than he had ever heard before. And where there were tanks, there was infantry, Grenadiers, half-tracks, and artillery. He gripped his rifle tightly and tried to think of Ella Lou, his beautiful girlfriend.

The muffled *boom* of artillery filled the air, and Sergeant Greene screamed, "Back! Back! Take cover!"

The men were moving before the order was finished. Rice tucked his rifle close to his chest and rolled down the bank. He disappeared under the snow and felt the hard stomp of a boot on his shoulder as another man bolted for the tree line. He came out of the snow, shook his face clear and fell again, this time from the impact of young Davis against his back. Rice fell forward, further down the bank and under a pile of broken limbs. He paused. This might be a good place to hide, he considered. But no. The Germans were moving forward fast, too fast. Stay here and they'd be found and killed.

He pushed Davis away and got up. "Get off!"

"I'm sorry," was all Davis could say, his face bleached with fear.

Rice grabbed him by the collar and pulled forward. "Stay with me."

Through the artillery barrage, they ran. Trees burst apart as each strike pounded the space around them. It was foolish, really, to be running through the forest. It would be more sensible to stay in the open. Among the trees, an artillery barrage was far more deadly with nasty chunks of wood flying through the air. But surely somewhere nearby lay a vacant foxhole, an abandoned bunker in which to crawl. The Germans had held this line efficiently for a long time. Rice kept running and looking for cover.

Davis was about ten yards behind. Rice turned to tell him to get his ass on the move, but the boy stumbled on a root and planted his face square into the snowy mud and leaves. Despite the situation, Rice couldn't help but smile. *It's not a winter wonderland anymore, is it, boy? You're getting a real education now.*

"Get up, you country bump—"

A shell burst behind Davis and blew him apart, scattering his body into a dozen bloody pieces. Rice screamed and fell away from the impact. The sting of hot shrapnel pierced his right arm and chest, cutting through layers of clothing and striking his neck as well. A wince of pain cut across his cheek. A warm trickle of blood ran down his face.

He panicked. He had promised himself when he had disembarked at Le Havre, France, that he would not do so, that he would keep his cool no matter the circumstances. But this was a far cry from the comfort of a transport ship, and he had never been struck in battle before, had never felt so much pain.

He ran, and ran, and ran. Was he going in the right direction, toward Höfen? He could not say; he had changed course a couple times, trying to avoid the incessant shelling. He kept running and in time, the sound of the guns tapered off until they seemed leagues away. He stopped, his heart racing, his blood pounding in his ears.

He leaned against a tree. He panted heavily and looked left and right. Where were his men? Where was Sergeant Greene? Had they all died? Sweat filled his eyes and his neck felt wet and mushy. He reached in and drew his hand back. Blood, a lot of it. He squeezed his eyes shut and shook his head. *I'm going to die...alone*. He fought the urge to cry, stood upright and turned around the tree to run again.

And there they stood. Two of them: German soldiers dressed head to toe in winter camo—difficult to see even this close with the wind and snow and sweat in his eyes—forward observers, perhaps. Rice put up his rifle and pointed it at the closest, the one screaming, *"Runter! Runter!"* The man motioned down with his rifle, while the one behind trained a pistol at Rice's chest.

Rice couldn't understand the order, but the motion was clear. Slowly, he lowered his rifle and bent his knees as if he were going to sit down. Then he moved quickly, as he had been trained, bringing his rifle forward and pulling the trigger. The rifle kicked back against his shoulder, knocking him off balance, but the bullet hit the German square in the chest and put him down. One shot. One kill.

The other fired his pistol but missed, as Rice fell back into the snow. He put his hand down to keep from falling all the way. He pushed himself up and aimed his rifle again. This time, he spoke.

"Get down! Down, you fucking Kraut!"

He had never screamed so loudly in his life, had never felt such anger and fear. The German must have felt it too, for he dropped the pistol and fell to his knees, arms in the air. *"Bitte nicht schießen!"*

On weak legs, Rice moved forward until he was but a few feet from the man. No, not a man. A boy. He saw that now. A mere child, much younger than Davis. His small, red-chapped face peeking out from underneath a thick, padded helmet. His frail, tiny arms raised in the air, thin and girlish. On his knees he didn't even come up to Rice's waist. He was a boy.

But still a killer. And as Rice stood there, looking down at the boy, anger overtook his fear. He raised his rifle, aimed it carefully at the boy's chest, and fired.

September 1635, Grantville

Mary Jo Blackwell and Sandra Sue Prickett sat in Ella Lou Rice's living room, sipping tea and sharing pleasantries. Ella Lou didn't know these women very well, but they came highly recommended by the Grantville Library. "They know their stuff," the librarian told her. She would find out the truth of that soon enough.

"More tea?" she asked, holding up the teapot with mildly cold hands. A month after John's death and the air already had a chill of autumn in it. Her old bones could not take the changing weather anymore, but she had opened the window a crack to oblige the hot-blooded youngsters sitting before her.

"Please," Mary Jo said, holding up her cup.

Ella Lou poured then set the teapot down next to the heirloom. "Thank you both for coming." She cleared her throat. "As you know, my husband John Thomas recently died. He was a veteran and served with distinction, being promoted to sergeant during World War Two, and then to lieutenant afterwards." She picked up the silver heirloom and ran her thumb gently over the worn image on its front. "He got this during the war."

She handed it to Sandra Sue and both ladies studied it, turning it over and over to see the details. "It's pretty old," Sandra Sue said. "It looks like the image of the Virgin Mary, perhaps holding the baby Jesus."

"Yes," said Mary Jo, "and they're looking at something in the sky. Perhaps a cross or the face of God? It's hard to tell. Very religious, though. Catholic, maybe, or Lutheran. But we're not antiquities experts, Mrs. Rice, so don't take our word for the gospel. We're genealogists." Mary Jo laid it back down. "What exactly can we do for you?"

Ella Lou breathed deeply, then said, "Ladies, in case you hadn't noticed, I'm quite old, and not long for this world. I'm trapped in this century against my will. I've tried to adjust. I've tried making friends with down-timers. Some have even moved in nearby and are very friendly. But this is not my world, not my place. My husband has died. Five of our children were left up-time. All that remains is my son Clyde and his wife, my memories, and this." She picked up the heirloom and held it close. "Before I die, I want to honor the memory of my husband and the time that we had together. I want to make an *altruistic* gesture, as my son would say. I want to find the ancestors of the German soldier this heirloom belonged to . . . and give it back to them. Can you help me do that?"

There was a long pause as Mary Jo and Sandra Sue exchanged weary glances. Sandra Sue exhaled as if she had just finished off a good bowel movement. Mary Jo finished her tea in one gulp, crossed her legs, and said, "Well, Mrs. Rice. Ella? Can you tell us a little about this German soldier? What do you know about him and his family?"

Ella Lou placed the heirloom on the table and nodded. "I'll tell you what I know."

December 1944

Oh, dear God, I've killed a child.

The thought raced through Rice's muddled, confused mind. The shot echoed through the trees and put the German boy down. Yet, despite the ever-growing clangor of approaching armor and enemy soldiers, he could not run. He had to know for sure.

Rice fell to his knees and crawled through the snow to the boy. He pulled the boy close, tugged at his thick clothing and ripped the white coat open at the chest. The bullet had gone clean through the coat, leaving a moldering black hole of torn and scorched fibers. Rice's numb fingers clawed at the coat, tearing through it, seeking the place where the bullet hit.

He found it to the left of the heart, a neat wound, blood running down the boy's pale white skin. Rice pushed aside a medallion that hung from a chain around the boy's neck, whipped away the blood, and found the bullet lodged in a rib bone, just below the skin. He breathed relief. Not dead. Not yet, anyway. The boy moaned and tried moving. Rice held him still and cupped a hand over his mouth.

"Shut up! Don't move."

Gunfire erupted somewhere up ahead in the forest. Diesel engines, yelling, screaming, orders barked in German. Rice thought he could see a line of figures moving toward them. He turned and looked the other way. Perhaps if he ran, he could outrun the advance. Perhaps . . . if he were lucky. But life had never dealt John Thomas Rice a winning hand. There was nowhere to go.

He grabbed the boy's arm and dragged him toward a pile of brush and broken tree trunks. The boy winced in pain and yelled something indiscernible. Rice ignored him, fell back to his knees, and pushed his way underneath the debris.

Another push and they fell into the remains of an old foxhole, wet and muddy, stinking with shit. It stunk like death and dried blood too. Rice swallowed hard to hold down the nausea. He shook his head clear. There would be time later for getting sick, if he survived.

He pulled the boy in all the way and pressed his hand over his mouth. The boy's eyes were open, wide with fear and pain. Rice looked into those eyes. This wasn't a soldier, he thought. This was nothing more than a boy.

"Keep quiet."

For the next several minutes, all he could hear was breathing, heavy with exhaustion, heavy with doubt and terror. Rice found that he was just as anxious as the boy; perhaps more so, for above them, line after line of German soldiers passed by. One slip of his hand and the boy would cry out, and he'd be dead. Rice realized he was pushing down on the boy's mouth too tightly, pushing too hard against his nose. "Sorry," he whispered. He loosened his grip.

The boy gasped for air but kept quiet.

The German soldiers filed away and all that remained were echoes of firefights and far-off artillery fire. Rice removed his hand and lay back. If the boy screamed, it would hardly matter, and he couldn't very well keep his hand in place forever. Rice was behind enemy lines now; it was only a matter of time before he was found, killed, or died alone like whoever had died in this gross hole already.

"You speak English?" Rice asked.

"*Ja,*" the boy coughed. "A little."

"Good, because I'll be damned if I'm going to speak your language. I don't know it too good anyway, and every word sounds like shouting. You got a knife?"

The boy coughed again, nodded, and motioned weakly at his boot.

Rice reached into the boot and found a small blade, nicely crafted, slim and sharp. He held it in the faint light bleeding through the dead canopy of leaves and branches above them. He recognized the markings: a swastika on the grip; a Reichszeugmeisterei inscription on a blade with no blood groove. He'd seen a knife like this once before.

"*Hitlerjugend*?"

The boy nodded slowly.

"I thought your unit was smashed at Normandy."

"*Ja*, many dead. But not all."

Rice huffed and shook his head. "I should kill you now, you brainwashed little fool. But I've already lost one boy today; I'll be damned if I lose another, no matter what color your uniform is."

Rice leaned over the boy and opened his coat. The bleeding was not as bad as before, but it was still flowing. "I'm not good at this kind of business, but you learn a thing or two about gunshot wounds in the Pennsylvania hills. I've got to get that bullet out now or you're going to die. Do you understand?"

The boy nodded as his eyes closed. He was weak and getting weaker.

Rice reached into a pocket on the inside of his coat and pulled out a white handkerchief, nicely embroidered with tiny red and yellow flowers. He sighed. "I got this in France. I was going to give it to Ella Lou when I got back home, but I guess she won't mind me using it to save a life." He placed it near the wound and grabbed the boy's hand and pressed it against the soft, silk fabric. "Now, you push down as hard as you can, grit your teeth, and try to think about something pleasant. This is going to hurt."

As Rice began cutting an incision around the wound, he said, "I don't understand how this bullet got lodged like this. At the range I fired, it should have torn right through your chest like it did your partner." Rice shook his head. "I don't know...must have had a bad ammo load. That's happened to me before. You're one lucky little sot."

The boy gritted his teeth against the pain. "*Ja*, maybe." He reached feebly for his chest and grabbed the medallion that lay there. He held it forward with thumb and index finger. "But this helped."

Rice stopped cutting and took the medallion. It lay somewhere between the size of a silver dollar pancake and a silver dollar. An heirloom of some kind, maybe, tarnished and worn in many places. He squinted to try to make out the pattern on the front of it: some religious symbol with a cross and the faint outline of a face. He turned it over and saw what the boy was talking about.

The bullet had hit it near the bottom, chipping away a piece and leaving a gash that cut through some phrase that had been etched into it years ago. Rice tried to make out what was left of the words, but he could only discern *Ich*.

"I...what?" Rice asked. "What did the rest of it say?"

The boy did not answer. He had passed out.

The Black Dragons roared all night.

Rice heard the distinctive sound of the American 240mm heavy artillery, and it was music to his ears— that is, until some of the shells strayed into their area and rocked the ground below them. Rice did everything he could not to scream. Mighty flashes of heat and light broke through the latticework of tree limbs that covered their foxhole. Rice shook with fear, but held himself close to the boy, giving him as much warmth as possible. He had covered them both with a thin blanket he had pulled from his pack and had even piled up old, dried leaves over their legs for extra protection against the night freeze.

The boy lay at his side, moaning quietly, feverish and fitful, but alive. The bullet had come out easier than expected, and Ella Lou's handkerchief had stopped the blood, which he had placed tightly against the wound with the aid of a bandage from his med-kit. Nothing now but uninterrupted sleep could do the rest. Rice had checked the pockets of the boy's coat for anything else: matches, a flashlight, an extra blanket, a morphine syrette, food. Nothing. The boy didn't even have a satchel. His commander had put him in the field with nothing more than a coat, a gun, and a knife. Rice huffed. This war was over; the Germans just didn't know it yet.

The next morning the boy awoke and was hungry. Rice gave him some rations. He gave him a drink from his canteen too, then checked the wound. The area around the broken rib was red, raw, swollen, but for the most part clean. "I think you'll live," he said, laying back. He winced. The shrapnel bits in his neck were beginning to hurt badly. The blood had stopped, but the skin was tender and smelled awful.

"Would you like my blade?" The boy said, holding up his youth knife. "You have something in your neck. It looks infected."

Cautiously, Rice took the knife and wiped it against his pant leg. "What do you know about it?"

"My grandfather was a surgeon in the Great War."

"*Hm.* My grandfather was a pig farmer from Ohio." Rice pushed against one of the larger pieces lodged in his neck. He then placed the knife blade beneath it and yanked quickly. The piece burst through the skin and flew out. He pushed the collar of his coat against the blood and said, "What's your name, boy?"

"Oswin, sir. Oswin Bauer."

"John Thomas Rice. Don't call me sir. I'm a private like you, and not much older I guess. How old are you anyway?"

"Fourteen."

Jesus! "Well, Oswin, when you get back home, you can tell your family and friends that you bested an American, left him for dead in a foxhole. You can embellish the story if you like. I won't tell."

That got a smile from the boy. "Thank you, sir—I mean, John. But I don't have friends or family anymore. They are dead."

"What do you mean? Where are you from?"

"Darmstadt."

Rice shook his head. "Don't know it. Is it close?"

Oswin nodded. "It is not too far away, I suppose, but it is gone now. British bombers set a fire in it. A fire that would not stop. It destroyed almost everything. My mother, father, my little brother. All are dead."

Rice had heard of this kind of bombing. First, incendiaries were dropped around the city. Then, high explosives were released, which ignited the incendiaries and created a self-sustaining fireball that grew and grew as winds were sucked in to feed the flames. It was a terrible, brutal way to wage war, and rumor had it that more of these kinds of attacks were coming.

Oswin stopped talking and turned his head away.

From his coat pocket, Rice pulled a black-and-white wallet-sized picture of a girl. He smiled and ran his fingers across her bright face, trying to remember the color of the dress she had on. Red? Green? It hardly mattered. She looked good in anything.

"Is that your wife, sir?"

Rice ignored the "sir" and shook his head. "No, but I'd like her to be. I promised myself that when . . . if . . . I returned, I'd propose. But she's young. Not much older than you. Her father doesn't approve." He laughed. "He doesn't like me very much, and frankly, I'm not sure she likes me all that much either."

Oswin clutched the heirloom tightly. "My mother used to say that love is like the weather. There are many rainy days, and sometimes winds blow so strong that you can't stand it anymore. But you put your head forward and push through, and eventually, you will find the sunlight."

Rice picked another fragment from his neck. He gritted his teeth and hissed. That one stung. "She sounds like a smart lady. Did she give you that thing?" he asked, motioning to the heirloom.

"Ja. She got it from my grandfather. He used to wear it during his surgeries. He said it brought him good luck. He got it from his father, who got it from his mother. They say it's over three hundred years old."

Rice chuckled. "And you believe that?"

"Why shouldn't I?"

He picked another shard from his neck, wiped the wound clean and handed the knife back to Oswin. "Son, I hate to tell you this, but it's probably not that old. More likely than not your grandfather, or his father, got it from some shop secondhand. I'm not even sure it's real silver."

At those words, Oswin seemed to deflate. He dropped

the heirloom and laid back. Rice saw the hurt in the boy's face and immediately regretted the words. *Damn, my stupid mouth!* But it was *his* mother's fault that he was like this. She never filled his mind with romantic notions of love and perseverance. She never had any family trinkets passed down from his grandfather, no good luck charms given to him from his father, a man who drank too much and got himself killed in a card game. No, Mama Rice spent her idle time trying to figure out how to keep a family alive during a depression. She worried herself to death over it. Love was the furthest thing from her mind.

Rice rubbed his face, cleared his throat, and said, "Okay, then, tell me about this heirloom. Tell me about your family."

The boy sat up slowly, still in pain, but the hurt was gone from his face. He began to talk, and as he did so, Rice laid his head back. Oswin's voice soothed him and he thought of home, of Pennsylvania, of his mother and his sisters, and of Ella Lou in the soft green dress. Soft red dress. *I promise, sweet girl, when I return, I will ask. I promise.*

He closed his eyes and slept.

September 1635, Grantville

Ella Lou paused to let the ladies absorb what she had told them. They sat there, blank-faced, mouths opened slightly as if she had just sung them a dirty limerick. She smiled, proud of herself, proud of her good memory. John had told her everything, and more than once. Surely, with these details, they'd be able to help her. They must.

"Well, what do you think?"

They did not speak for a few moments, then Sandra Sue cleared her throat and said, "That's quite a story, Ella. I can't imagine being in such a terrible situation. Your husband is to be commended for his honorable service." She shot a glance at Mary Jo. "But, I have to be honest with you. Good genealogy requires good and obtainable records. Birth and death certificates, census data, marriage licenses, diaries, even criminal records. Do you have anything else from this German boy? Any further details?"

Ella felt her heart sink. "No, I'm afraid not."

"Then I'm sorry to say that it will be impossible to find this boy's ancestors."

"Why? Can't you people trace lineage through oral histories, stories?"

Mary Jo nodded. "Yes, and if we were still up-time, we'd probably be able to do it. But in this alternate timeline that we live in, Ella, we are missing the intervening centuries. They haven't happened yet. Your story took us back to about 1850, give or take, before your husband passed out, and apparently the heirloom was handed down from father to daughter, daughter to son, son to son, and so on. I didn't quite catch all of the surnames you mentioned, but there were many. Based upon what you told us, we can't be sure at all that it's as old as the boy claims. But even assuming that it is, there's been so much displacement from wars and famine and sickness—the wars going on right now, the time of Fredrick the Great, Napoleon—there is no research material, no body of evidence, that we can build upon. I'm . . . I'm sorry, Ella. It's not possible."

Ella crossed her arms and tried to look away. She was angry, but not at Mary or Sandra. It wasn't their fault. It was the fault of a foolish old bat who should have known better. How could they possibly help her with such slim details? She should have thought it through better, should have consulted Clyde first. She was making a rash decision based on emotion. She needed the cold practicality of her son, the calm calculations of her husband. Oftentimes, those qualities in her men were maddening, giving her no small amount of grief. But what she needed now was her children to help her through this. She needed her family.

She laid the heirloom down and stood slowly. "Well, thank you both for coming. I appreciate your time."

She walked them to the door. As she opened the door, Mary Jo said, "Ella, didn't you say that the boy was from Darmstadt?"

"Yes, that's what he said."

"Well, Darmstadt is just south of Frankfurt am Main. It's not that far from here. You could, I suppose, give the heirloom back to the town. You know, as an *altruistic* gesture, like your son says."

Was it possible? Would it be the same? Ella Lou wondered. No, it wouldn't be the same, but it would be something. Honoring the town, and its citizens, for the service of one of its own, even if that person did not exist yet. Oswin Bauer was a phantom in this timeline, a non-person, a figment of the wild imagination of some up-time witch. But the gesture didn't have to be a big, elaborate affair. It could be a small presentation, a few people, perhaps only the *burgermeister*, a council member or two, nothing fancy. Just the way John would have preferred.

Yes, I will give the heirloom to Darmstadt, she thought as she bid them goodbye and returned to her tea. *That would be a nice thing to do.*

October 1635, Grantville

Three weeks later, Ella Lou greeted her son at the door when he arrived on a Sunday afternoon for their weekly checkers match. "Good afternoon, Mother," he said as he bent down to hug her. She pulled away, angry and agitated.

"What is this?" she asked, holding up a piece of paper with a broken wax seal.

Clyde smiled. "Ah, you got it. I was hoping you wouldn't open it until I arrived." He reached for it. "Here, give it to me. I'll read it to you."

"Don't bother, Honcho. I had a neighbor translate it for me. What have you done?"

He shrugged and put up his hands in surprise. "Nothing. What are you talking about? I just did a little prep work before we leave for Darmstadt on Wednesday."

"Prep work? You've told the whole goddamned world about this."

Clyde shook his head. "No, I haven't. I just contacted Jason Waters in Frankfurt am Main and had him post a little announcement in the newspapers around there. And I had Rolf contact a few of his merchant buddies in Darmstadt. Word just got around a little. It's no big deal."

"No big deal? Clyde, I wanted a small affair. Maybe just the *burgermeister*, perhaps his wife if he has one. I just wanted to drop by his office, or wherever it is these people do their business, and give it to them."

"Mother!"

Ella Lou could hear the frustration growing in her son's voice, but she didn't care. He had disobeyed her instructions.

Clyde took a deep breath, then exhaled slowly. "You can't just waltz into town and say, 'Here I am, look at me, I have a present for you.' No, you have to plan for it, make appointments. Yes, we are exotic up-timers and these Germans will stop whatever it is they're doing to look at us, but as far as that goes, we're just commoners like most everyone else. We *had* to tell them we were coming."

"Okay, fair enough. But you've taken it too far, Clyde. Look here," she said, holding up the letter with clenched fists, "you have the entire town council attending, *and* the landgrave, this George II. The landgrave! And it's going to be a public presentation in their . . . *Schlossplatz*?"

"Yes, their market square. Rolf tells me it's a lovely place. Very spacious. It should be a great day, assuming it doesn't rain."

Ella Lou shook her head. "That's what this is all about, isn't it? A business venture. What are you going to do when we get there? Hand out business cards? How about T-shirts saying, 'I saw a wild West Virginian'? Or perhaps mugs with a picture of the heirloom saying, 'I survived Elsenborn Ridge'? Or—"

"Stop it, Mama! I don't appreciate the accusation. You're the one who wanted to do this. And he's my father, don't forget. I have a right to see that his memory is respected just as much as you."

"Yes, he was your father, but he was my husband. *My* husband!"

Crying, she turned her back to her son and stumbled into the living room. There, she fell into one of the chairs that she had set up for their game, and placed her hands on the table. She sniffled. "He was my husband, and I wanted to do this my way."

There was a long silence. Ella Lou could feel her son's eyes upon her back, angry eyes that had every right to be so, she knew. Clyde was right: it wasn't fair for her to sling accusations at him. She had asked him to look into the travel arrangements, had asked that he contact the government there in Darmstadt. She just didn't realize that he would go further than that. She should have known, though. Clyde was a business man: dot your i's and cross your t's. Leave no stone unturned. But . . . "I'm no good at public speaking," she said, rubbing her face. "I'll get nervous. I'll slur my words. I'm not smart like you, Clyde. I didn't even finish high school, and I don't know German at all. They'll laugh at me. They'll think I'm some old country bumpkin who—"

"Nonsense." Clyde put his hand upon her back and began to rub gently. "You're a wonderful speaker, mom. What about that time when you took to the picket line in Dad's union dispute? I remember you giving the company serious hell. And what about your work in the PTA when we were kids? There were many times when you got up and spoke your mind, and not from a prepared speech either."

Ella Lou shook her head. "Those days are long, long gone."

"The days are, Mother, but not the woman." Clyde took his seat and grabbed her hands. He held them firmly. "You can do this. I know you can. I'll prepare a speech for you—your words—not mine. And I'll be there if you stumble. We'll do this together. Okay?"

What could she say? She could refuse, cancel the whole thing. But if she didn't do it now, when? Winter was coming, and she wasn't about to go traipsing through the German countryside in a wagon and be stuck in the mud or snow in the deep freeze. So, if not now, they'd have to wait for next year. And would next year even come? Behind her son's hopeful remarks, Ella Lou could see concern. He'd just lost his father; would his mother be far behind? He wanted, he needed, closure on this matter just as much as she. It was not right of her to deprive him of the last good memories of his father.

"Okay, Clyde," she said, wiping off her face, "we'll do this your way. But I swear, if I mess up, I'm going to beat you around the head and neck until you scream."

Clyde nodded and smiled. "Good, but not before I get to beat you in checkers." He got up and went for the board. "And while I'm doing it, continue your story about dad."

As Clyde set up the board, she began. . . .

December 1944

The world exploded around them. A full-scale retreat was in progress. Rice could tell from the wave of German soldiers pounding the ground above them, running back in the direction they had come, their voices so close that he could make out some words. Whatever gains the initial assault had accomplished were now crushed, as he kept his head low and prayed that some stupid Kraut did not step right on top of them. Oswin had tried to cry out, but Rice held his hand strong against the boy's mouth. Oswin wanted to leave and he was certainly capable of doing so. His wound had improved considerably in the last two days. Not so Rice. He had dug out the shrapnel from his neck, but his right arm was swollen from the deep cuts there, and he was having trouble breathing. His rations were gone, his canteen was empty. It was all he could do just to keep the boy quiet.

Then the motion stopped above them, and the canopy moved a little. Rice could hear German voices, whispering. He heard a boot scrape against a thick tree limb. Loosened snow fell on top of them as branches were moved. Oswin struggled against Rice's hand. The boy was stronger than he looked. Rice tried to keep Oswin from moving, but before he could react, the boy's knife was at his throat. He tried to struggle against it, but his arm hurt too much, his heart raced too fast. He just didn't have the strength to fight.

The boy pressed his lips against Rice's ear and said, "Please . . . Herr Rice. Be quiet, and trust me. You saved my life. Let me save yours. *Ja?*"

Rice nodded.

Oswin raised his head toward the canopy and said, "*Heil Hitler!*"

The bolt action on a Mauser K98 locked in place. "*Wer da? Nennen Sie Ihren Namen!*"

Rice could understand little of their conversation. His head was stuffy and light, words blurred into words, and they spoke at such a pace that even if he wanted to, there was no way he could keep up. The German soldiers above the foxhole asked a couple questions; that much, Rice could infer by tone and inflection, and Oswin answered with his name, rank and unit. The Germans asked another question and Oswin replied, "*Nein! Nein!*" An order was barked, and the boy replied, "*Jawoll, Herr Hauptmann!*" And that was all.

Oswin returned the knife to his boot then grabbed the heirloom and pulled it from his neck, letting the chain snap and fall away. He placed it in Rice's hand and whispered, "I want you to have this, John. I have no family anymore, and I never will again. I have sworn to defend *mien Fuhrer*. When he dies, I die. You take it and give it to your Ella Lou when you get back home. Share it with *your* family. *Ja?*"

Rice tried to refuse, but before he could open his mouth, the boy was gone.

"Wait," Rice said, rubbing the place on the heirloom where the bullet had cut out the words. "What—what does it say?"

But no answer came. Only the sound of artillery, gunfire, and desperate, dying men filled his troubled mind throughout that long, dangerous night.

October 1635, Darmstadt

"A few hours later," Ella Lou said as they neared Darmstadt, "some GI's found him, all cuddled up in that thin blanket, half buried, half dead. They rushed him back to Höfen just in time. Another hour and he would have died. They tried taking the heirloom from him, he claims, but he wouldn't let it go. He clutched it so tight, his fingers bled." She laughed. "That sounds like your father...a dog with a bone."

They sat in the wagon while Clyde's business partner,

Rolf, drove. There was concern about their safety as they made their way across the USE. With the announcement that Clyde had put in the newspaper and his description of the artifact therein, what thief wouldn't want to get his hands on a trinket from the past, or rather, the future, especially one of pure silver? Rolf had brought his two sons along to ride horses in support, and Clyde had gotten out his father's old .45 and 10-gauge just in case. Clyde had also commissioned the USE for assistance, perhaps a gun or two as well to tag along, but with the recent events surrounding Henry Dreeson and the Huguenots, they politely declined. The government's time, resources, and attention were elsewhere these days. There was no official support from Piazza's office on this one.

"Did Dad ever try to find the boy," Clyde asked, "you know, after the war?"

Ella Lou nodded. "He thought about it a lot. The boy had told him that he would die if Hitler died, but you know how boys can talk, especially under brainwashing. He didn't believe that bull for a second. Yeah, he wanted to find him, and even once looked into travel to Germany, but life kept getting in the way. You kids starting coming and then we moved to Grantville shortly after you were born. Time slipped by."

"Why did we move to Grantville?" Clyde asked, gathering up his pistol and the small wooden box that contained the heirloom. They were approaching the entrance to the city. "I mean, we had no family there at the time."

"Well, after work dried up in Harrisburg, your father got this wild hair to move to West Virginia. That boy, Davis, the one he saw being ripped apart by German artillery, would go on and on about how wonderful it was, how beautiful and majestic. He was from Grantville, and so when the chance came, we moved. One of those altruistic gestures you talk about."

Clyde got up and moved to peek out the front of the wagon. Ella Lou did the same, holding onto her son's arm. Before them, Darmstadt lay. It was a beautiful place, she had to admit, similar to Frankfurt am Main, but even more pleasant in her eyes. Her heart leapt into her throat. She felt a little dizzy, her stomach queasy at the thought that soon, she would be facing people she did not know, people that did not know her. And how would they greet her? Would they be kind and gentle? Would they open their arms and accept this lady from the future? Would anyone come at all? Were they as upset at the arrival of these Americans, these West Virginians, as she was in coming through the Ring of Fire?

There was ample evidence that with the formation of the USE, the lives of Germans within its borders had improved—or, at least, stabilized a great deal. But would that last? Human nature being what it was, Ella Lou did not think so. And how would they take a story about their lovely city being ravaged by RAF bombers, even if it hadn't happened yet, and even if it never happened. Ella Lou had not finished high school, but she was smart enough to understand the concept of an alternate timeline. Just because such terrible things had happened in her time, in her world, did not mean that it would happen here. The Ring of Fire *had* changed everything. Everything, of course, but human nature. And would the kind citizens of Darmstadt greet her as a positive sign of things to come, or a reminder that in all things, life is chaotic and uncertain?

"Are you ready, Mother?"

Ella Lou breathed deeply and shook her head.

It turned out to be a pleasant experience, all things considered. The landgrave, George II, a seemingly bright young man in his early thirties, presented himself with much fanfare and celebrity, accompanied by his wife Sophia Eleonore of Saxony. They were also accompanied by their small children and various council members and important personages as could be imagined attending such an event. Though Ella Lou could not fully understand the speech that George II gave to introduce and welcome her and Clyde to Darmstadt, Rolf translated for them. The landgrave spoke eloquently about his appreciation for the USE and the Americans, and how they had helped stabilize the political situation. He also wished for continued prosperity between himself and the USE. He also took this opportunity to take a not so subtle jab at Hesse-Kassel. Apparently, no love was lost between these two states over some dispute with an inheritance line pertaining to Hesse-Marburg. Ella Lou shook her head. This was the kind of thing she wanted to avoid, and what Clyde, with all his savvy and intelligence, could not understand. All he saw were dollar signs; the bigger the event, the greater the circus, the better the profits and exposure. All she wanted to do was to honor the memory of the boy who had saved her husband's life and be done with it. Now, local politics had been attached to her gesture. And what would become of that in the days and months to follow?

Then she got up to speak to a handsome round of applause from those who chose to attend. The *Schlossplatz* was quite crowded, despite the cool day, and the hastily constructed podium in its center gave her weak eyes a good view of the crowd. The heirloom itself had been hung from a nail on the front of the podium, and all those who wished could come up and look at it as she spoke.

From a speech that Clyde and Rolf had prepared for her, she told them the story of her husband and how he had met Oswin Bauer, a distant son of Darmstadt, near the small town of Höfen. She told them about how this young boy, though misguided in his politics, had put aside his ideology and had given John his family's heirloom to hold and cherish and to share with *his* family. She told them too of their experiences during the Ring of Fire and how John had finally passed away, and how he had always wanted to give the heirloom back to the boy, but time and distance had kept them from meeting again. But now that the opportunity was afforded her, she, Ella Lou Rice, would give it back to the town that had given the world a boy, a man, who would one day meet her John Thomas and help him return home safely, and to one day, give her the best years of her life.

She told them all this and more, and when she was done, she thanked them by bowing low and blowing them a kiss. They treated her fondness in kind, applauding and cheering as she was escorted away from the podium by her son.

"You did good, Mama," Clyde said, helping her into a jacket. "Dad would have been proud."

She rubbed her cold arms. "I hope so. I did the best I could."

He kissed her forehead. "You were wonderful, just wonderful. Now, let's go find something to eat and—"

"Frau Rice?"

The voice was so small that Ella Lou hardly heard it over the bustle of people. The voice spoke again and she turned to see a thin girl standing there in a simple white and brown frock, holding the hand of a young boy, no older than nine or ten perhaps, his head a shock of curly brown hair.

"Yes?" Ella Lou said, looking to Rolf for help in translation.

The girl smiled, curtsied, and said, "Frau Rice, my name is Nina Weiss." She held up a piece of paper. "I read your announcement in the newspaper. The description of the medallion was so vivid, so specific, that I had to come and see."

"See what?" Clyde asked.

The girl motioned to the boy. "This is Stefan, my son. I named him after his father who died in Wallenstein's army near Dessau. Before he left, though, he gave me a promise. Go ahead, Stefan, show the lady."

Stefan nodded and opened his shirt. He reached in and pulled out a perfectly round medallion, hanging from a piece of rope and shining in the bright sun.

Ella Lou fell to her knees and took the medallion in her shaking hand. "Clyde," she said, with quivering lip. "Go get the other one, please."

Clyde returned with the other and handed it to her. He knelt down beside her and they looked at the medallions side by side. Ella Lou's hands shook as she ran her fingers over the old, worn etching of the one John had given her, but it was clear that the lines matched the one in her other hand. Mary the Blessed Virgin, holding her son Jesus, looking into the sky at a bright, glowing cross. *This is it*, she thought, her eyes filling with tears. *This is the one.* But was it truly? What was on the other side? What did it say? She was afraid to turn them over, for if the words, the phrase, that the bullet had rubbed out was not on the other one, then it would be another disappointment, another failure. She closed her eyes and prayed.

She flipped them over.

"Stefan had etched a promise on the back of it," Nina Weiss said. "I told my son that if those same words were on your medallion, it would mean that his father had kept that promise, at least in some small way. Is that promise on your medallion, Frau Rice?"

Ella Lou opened her eyes. At the bottom of the heirloom, where the bullet had struck, the word *Ich* lay. On the other one, in the same place, was the full promise.

Ella Lou held it up to her son. "What does it say, Clyde?"

"*Ich werde zurückkehren*," he said. "I will return."

Ella Lou could not contain her tears anymore. She let them flow, and as she placed both medallions around little Stefan's neck, she smiled through those tears, took the boy in her arms, and hugged him tightly. "Yes," she said, "it does. Your father has kept his promise, Stefan. He has come home . . . and so have I."

Sole Heir

Terry Howard

Grantville, early spring 1636

"I got a letter today from Wolmirstedt. They wanted me to know that Otto Schmidt died. His shop is sitting empty. They are asking if we're coming back. And, they want to know what we're going to do about Anna," Arnulf Meier announced to his family, and everyone else at the dinner table.

The dining room table seated all ten members, eleven counting the baby, of the three families who shared the house when they were all there at once, which they usually were at supper time. Everyone except Madde and the baby had jobs. Not that Madde didn't work. She had a baby to take care of, plus she kept the common areas of the house and cooked most of the meals for all three families.

All four of the boys worked full-time, or part-time before and after school, in the old mine they, along with Officer Lyndon Johnson of the Grantville Police Department, leased from the government. They still had not gotten around to mentioning to their parents just how much money they had in the bank from selling the large stash of aged moonshine they had originally found in the mine where they now grew mushrooms, aged cheese, and processed copper for wire. Nor had they ever mentioned what they were doing with that money in the way of investments and business start-ups.

Herr Meier looked at his eldest son Paulus. "You remember Anna. When you were apprenticed to Herr Schmidt we assumed you would one day marry her. She was his only living child so you would eventually take over the shop. You couldn't take over the shop now even if you wanted. You aren't a shoemaker, and you have no interest in being one. And even if you were and even if you did, you aren't old enough.

"But that still leaves Anna. On the one hand, there never was a formal betrothal agreement. So we have no legal obligation to see the two of you married. And, her dowry is a shoemaker's shop which doesn't have enough business to make a living and isn't going to, the way things are. This means, she doesn't really have any other prospects.

"On the other hand—" Arnulf looked at his oldest son, "—the letter made it clear that some people there are still assuming you will marry Anna. The letter also made it clear that some people there feel we have some obligation to take care of the girl. Which, I suppose we do. As much as there was a shoemaker's guild in Wolmirstedt, we are what is left of it.

"So, Paulus, what are you going to do about Anna?"

Paulus looked back at his father. The blank look on the boy's face caused Arnulf to suppress a smile. He knew he had caught his son in an unguarded moment. He was sure his son's face completely and exactly reflected the boy's state of mind. It looked like the thought of marrying Anna, or anyone else at this time, for that matter, was, to his son, a completely unparsed sentence. Arnulf felt certain that, regardless of what things were like here in Grantville, the boy was still used to the idea of men getting married around thirty to women around twenty.

Shortly Paulus spoke, "Father, that is not for me to say!"

Arnulf worked hard at keeping a smirk off of his face. "Son, you can't have it both ways. When I suggested you help me out in the shop and finish learning the trade, you told me you were over eighteen and therefore an adult. You told me you've got a good job working in Officer Johnson's mine with the mushrooms and the cheese. You said that as long as you're paying your share of the rent and expenses, which I have to admit is true for both you and your brother, I don't have anything to say about how you spend your time or your money. I am still trying to figure out how Ebert managed to apply the same logic to stay out of the shop. He isn't eighteen yet. But, now you want to turn around and tell me you are too young to take on an adult's responsibility when it comes to dealing with the hard questions of life. Well, make up your mind. Are you an adult or aren't you?"

Arnulf continued with a solid demeanor and a straight face. "You're legally an adult only because we are in Grantville. Anywhere else in the civilized world, you would be right. It would not be for you to say. But, here in Grantville, up-timers see nothing wrong with a boy getting married as soon as he's out of high school as long as he can make a living. You're out of high school. You've got a good job in Officer Johnson's cheese mine. You can afford to support a wife and kids."

Herr Meier lost the fight at keeping a straight countenance. His face glowed with a smirk like a pig with a secret stash of apples. The three men at the table had figured out, at least in general, what their sons were up to, even if they had no idea just how much money the boys were worth or just how many different businesses they were shareholders in or how much property they owned (besides the house they all lived in), or even where exactly the money had come from in the first place. The boys were paying a reasonable amount of money every week to the support of the families and the three families were enjoying what they all considered to be a very comfortable standard of living. So Herr Meier and the other two fathers had agreed amongst themselves to sit back and wait for the boys to bring it up. But, since he could put his son in an uncomfortable spot without breaking the secret, it amused Herr Meier to do so.

"So there it is." Arnulf recapped the pertinent facts, "Anna is probably assuming you are going to marry her someday. Wolmirstedt is assuming we will take responsibility for the girl, even if there never was a formal betrothal. So! What are you going to do about Anna?"

Paulus blinked. As he thought about it he realized, somewhere, not far from where his id hid from his ego, he still assumed he would one day marry Anna Schmidt. This was perhaps part of the reason why dating was not something he had taken an interest in, no matter how many girls threw themselves at him. He was a plain-looking fellow, and no one had been particularly interested in him before he went into business. Now he assumed it was his money they were interested in. This was a perfectly reasonable reason for them to be interested in him, when one looked at it logically. But, now that he dragged his unexamined thoughts into the light of day, he found that his logic had been corrupted by up-time romantic thought. On the one hand, if they didn't want anything to do with him before, he didn't want anything to do with them now. On the other hand, in another unlit crack or cranny, one that had not been corrupted by Grantville's improbable and improper ways, dating was courting, and he was ten years away from being old enough to have a family of his own and therefore he had no reason to be courting anyone, not to mention the expense of doing so. These were the first assumptions he looked at. His second thoughts were of Anna herself. He hadn't seen her in over five years. His father had collected him from Herr Schmidt's shop on his way out of town. Herr Schmidt had decided to stay and hide and thought his apprentice should stay with him. Paulus tried to conjure an idea of what she might look like now. He couldn't get past the picture of a scrawny redheaded lass standing under her mother's hand, while his father and her father yelled at each other.

Still, the idea that she would one day be his wife was, upon reflection, just as comfortable in the light of day as it was lurking in the dark shadows. His father was absolutely right. He was more than capable of supporting a wife and family. His father had no idea just how true that was. When they had found the stash of aged moonshine they did not tell their parents because they feared their parents would take the money and use it to leave Grantville. Instead they invested it. Now, after all this time, telling them would be difficult.

Paulus blinked again. "If we are going to play this by Grantville rules, and apparently we are or you would be telling me what to do instead of asking, then Anna will have something to say about it. I suppose I ought to go find out."

His father nodded. "I suppose you should."

"But, even by Grantville rules, we'd have to wait. She's not sixteen yet," Paulus said.

"She can get married at fifteen, with parental consent," his brother Ebert pointed out.

Paulus turned to Ebert. "Well, we can't burn that bridge until we get there. If she says yes, we can find her a place to stay here in town and she can work in the mushrooms if she can't find something else, while we work out the details. If she doesn't say yes, then we will see if a stay in Grantville might not change her mind."

Ebert smirked, "What's the point of asking her if you're not going to accept her ans—"

The words, "Shut up, Ebert," were accompanied by an elbow in the ribs.

Magdeburg, early spring 1636

Some days Anna could turn her mind off and think of nothing but cutting shoe parts out of the hide in front of her. It made the twelve-hour workday go faster. And some days she couldn't. This was one of those days.

The millwright and the mechanic were assembling a stamping press for cutting uppers like the one already in use for cutting the soles. They might not get as many units out of a hide as they did when they cut them by hand, since they'd be cutting several hides at once, but the savings on labor would make up for the loss on the materials. Besides, they were getting a good price, a very good price, on scrap leather. Once they'd chopped it into tiny bits, the gunsmiths were using it for bluing barrels and they could sell all they had. The cutters and the kids tracing the patterns for the cutters to cut had been told not to worry. "No one is going to lose their job. We'll still be cutting the odd sizes by hand and some of you will move up to other jobs because output will go up."

Her mind went back to the days in Wolmirstedt, when she was a little girl and she had a mother and a father and knew she would one day marry her father's apprentice and keep the house while he kept the shop. Then came Tilly's men. Paulus' father took him and fled. Momma got sick and died that first winter when there was so very little to eat. Her father caught a fever and died just a few months ago.

There was no one to take over the shoemaker's shop. Where there had once been two shoemakers in town before Tilly's men, now the town was about one-fourth of the size it had been before and there wasn't enough business in Wolmirstedt to keep even a single shoemaker busy. It didn't help that the people could buy shoes out of the Wish Book cheaper than her father could make them. With no one to run the shop, Anna moved to Magdeburg and got a job in one of the shoe mills. It was either that or starve. The town council told her they couldn't support another charity case.

Anna's thoughts went from worrying about the future to dreaming the impossible dream, Adolf's dream. Before she met Adolf, she dreamed Paulus' family would return to Wolmirstedt, that they would take her in and she would, in due time, marry him and he would run the shop in Wolmirstedt. Now it was a different dream.

Adolf, his sister, and his mother lived in the same two-room apartment she did, along with sixteen other people. He had almost been a journeyman before Tilly's men came through. He was sure he could make a living in Wolmirstedt if he could get one of the heavy machines for sewing the uppers onto the soles like he was running now, and one of the light machines for sewing uppers. He had in mind a style of shoe not found in the Wish Book. He'd seen it in a used clothing store. It was from Grantville and it was a baker's shoe, called a loafer. It was suitable for a townsman who didn't want to wear the heavy work boot like the ones the mill was making for the army, and sure didn't want to wear a wooden shoe like a peasant. He'd have to cart them to market in Magdeburg or somewhere else not run by the guilds. And if anyone ever opened a mill making them, he might be out of business. Still, Adolf had a dream and she and her father's shop were now part of it. When she couldn't turn her mind off, the dream was often the only thing she had to keep her going.

Anna heard voices. One was the plant manager.

He was escorting someone through the mill. This meant some bigwig, usually a shoe buyer, sometimes a shareholder. But the bigwig was too young to be a shoe buyer. He was little more than a lad of a boy; he was very plainly dressed to be someone important like a shareholder and yet his voice was oddly, distantly, familiar.

"You can see we are nearly done assembling the new stamping press for cutting uppers. We are expecting a fifteen percent increase in production once the new press is on line. And over here is the old cutting area."

Anna took a second look at the bigwig. Her mouth fell open. "Paulus?" Her hand flew to her mouth. But it was already too late. The name was out. The plant manager turned to look at her with a frown on his face. The idea of someone on the floor addressing one of his guests greatly annoyed him. His people should be concentrating on their work. They shouldn't even notice he was there.

Paulus stopped and stared. No one would call the girl beautiful. But no one would call her ugly either. Mostly she was clearly Anna and that was comfortable.

"Anna?" Paulus answered. "I was just in Wolmirstedt looking for you. They said you'd gone to Magdeburg."

"How did you ever know to look here?"

"I didn't and I didn't think I'd ever find you. So I wasn't even looking. But since I was passing through town I thought I'd see how things were going in the shoe plants." He couldn't help doing a little bragging. "Having stockholders dropping in for a look around from time to time is supposed to be good for keeping the management on their toes."

"You're a stockholder?" Anna could see that the shop manager was starting to fidget on top of turning red in the face. "I've need to get back to work."

"No you don't." Paulus said. "You need to quit."

"*Quit?* I can't do that! I need this job!"

The plant manager spoke up, "Herr Meier, I would hate to see her quit. She is a good worker. She is on the list for trainees for the new press."

Paulus ignored the plant manager and said to Anna, "No you don't."

"Yes I do! How will I pay my room and board?"

"Anna, you're fourteen. You're too young to be working full-time in a shoe mill."

"Paulus, there are lots of people younger than me working here."

"Yes, but they're not wards of the Wolmirstedt Shoemaker's Guild."

"There isn't such a thing as a Wolmirstedt Shoemaker's Guild."

"Well, there was. It was your father and my father and your father was the guild master. So I guess my father is now. It really doesn't matter. When my father finds out you're working in a shoe mill, he'll put a stop to it. You can't work here if you're going to school in Grantville where my parents can keep an eye on you. So you can quit now and come to Grantville with me. Or you can wait and make my father come and get you. You don't want to make him do that! He won't ask you to quit. He'll tell you to. Then if you don't he'll have them fire you."

Several thoughts and emotions flashed through Anna's mind pretty much at the same time. First was the old dream. The Meier family would not be returning to Wolmirstedt; but, they would take her in and take her to Grantville. They would take care of her, even send her to school, and in due time, she would marry Paulus. This caused her to smile in relief. Secondly she did not want to make Herr Meier angry. This thought linked into the unhappy memories of her own father in a drunken rage as he was so often toward the end. This caused her to wince in remembered pain and grief. Then came the new dream, Adolf's dream. Now the dream would not happen. This thought brought sadness and with the sadness came guilt. For Adolf's dream to work, they needed the shop in Wolmirstedt plus what she could add to the family's savings. How could she turn her back on her new family? She now shared one of the big beds in the apartment with Adolf, his mother and his sister. It was cheaper than renting a cot. When the nightmares came, Adolf's mother would snuggle her and whisper comforting words and prayers in her ear.

When Anna's mind and face settled down what remained was resolve tinged with sadness. "Paulus, I can't. I'm going back home to Wolmirstedt just as soon as we save up enough money."

Shock fought with puzzlement for dominance in Paulus' mind. He'd never really considered the possibility that Anna would say anything but yes. "Anna, we need to talk about this.

"Herr Wiesel," Paulus asked the plant manager, "would you be kind enough to give her the rest of the day off?"

"Paulus, they'll dock me."

"I'd object if they didn't!" he said. "Don't worry, I'll cover it. Go get your coat and meet me in the office. We'll go to an early lunch."

"But, who will do her job?" The manager objected. "We're barely keeping up as it is. I'll end up sending some people home early when we run out of uppers and we'll miss our production goal for the day." He knew he had a winning argument because Paulus had been asking rather critically about missed production goals.

Anna turned back to cutting uppers with a vengeance and was steadfastly ignoring him.

Recognizing defeat Paulus said, "Anna, I'll be here at the end of the day."

Back in the office, Herr Wiesel asked, "If you don't mind my asking, what is your interest in our Anna?"

"I was her father's apprentice. I'm going to marry her."

"Oh? I thought she had an understanding with Adolf."

"What? Who?"

Now her reaction started to make sense. The startlement transformed into anger. *Anna had other plans. But, Anna is mine! How dare she?* But the anger gave way to reason. *Well? Why not? We never were formally betrothed. I wasn't there when she needed me.* The reason which replaced the anger slid into acceptance. The acceptance became relief. *I don't have to look after her. She is going to marry someone else.* The relief became sadness. The death of a lifelong expectation was still a death and while it was not a devastating loss it still needed to be grieved. In his grief he thought of three girls in Grantville, each prettier than Anna, who had flirted or at least tried to flirt with him. Still, Anna was his. *Am I just going to let this fellow Adolf steal her?*

The manager answered Paulus' question, "Adolf Braun, he's one of our machine operators. He's been trying to raise a loan to buy a sewing machine to go into business. They won't sell him the sewing machines on installments because he isn't a master, so they don't consider him qualified. If he can manage to get a loan, the rent would be cheaper out of town. So he's been talking to Anna about her father's empty shop and his family has been saving their money."

"But, he can't compete with a mill," Paulus said.

"He doesn't want to. He wants to make a town shoe instead of a work boot. He wants to buy cut soles and whole hides and his other supplies from us and then he wants to sell his shoes out of our retail store here in town. You remember, we originally opened it to have someplace to sell the seconds we can't send to the army. We're selling out of seconds and we're getting a good rate for firsts going out the door too."

"Would the scheme work?"

"When we get the new press for uppers up and running, we're going to have to cut more soles than we can cut in a twelve-hour shift. So we're planning on opening up a partial night shift just for running the sole press. If we do that, then we could run enough extra soles to let some go off site. The more soles we cut, the more scrap we can cut up into tiny little bits and from what we're getting for them we could quite possibly turn a small profit from cutting up whole hides. As for the rest of the supplies, the more we buy the better. Even after we charge him a handling fee, we can still sell to him at a better price than he can get anywhere else and it all helps our bottom line. But that would be a matter of policy and I'd have to kick it over to the board."

Paulus smiled. "I don't think it will be a problem as long as you're sure it will be profitable."

"If he pays cash for the supplies and we take his shoes on consignment I don't know why it wouldn't be."

"Well, my father is making a lady's high-heeled dress shoe that is selling well in a dress shop in Grantville. Do you think your retail store would be interested in taking some on consignment?" If they were and his father decided to do it, then, he would have to take on an apprentice or hire help. He might try insisting that Ebert do it and that could cause all kind of problems. Maybe he shouldn't even bring it up. It would mean more money but sometimes there are other things, like domestic tranquility, that need to be considered.

The manager smiled. "Considering who's asking..."

"Yes, I see your point," Paulus said. "Just one more thing, well, two actually. First, would this Adolf be good for her? And by that I mean good to her."

"Yes. Adolf is a fine young man. He takes good care of his mother and his sister."

"Well, I guess the real question in my mind is whether or not this Adolf is up to it."

"If I had the money I'd loan it to him. He's a hard worker, he's level-headed, I have absolutely no doubt he'd make it work."

But still, Anna was his! The relief shifted back into anger and the anger became resolve. He found his answer in a favorite phrase he'd picked up off a Grantviller who bought so many of their fresh mushrooms, *The answer isn't no, it's hell no!* Dammit, Anna was his!

By quitting time Paulus had calmed down and was prepared to admit that he had no claim on Anna and that he would let her go her own way if that was what she wanted. Still, he was waiting for Anna outside the employee door at quitting time. She was nearly the last to leave. When she came out she was with three other people. The girl, about his own age, was pretty, and was clearly the younger model of the older woman. The male was presumably Adolf. The four of them stood together in a way that somehow said "family." Even in the light of his resolve to let things alone, Paulus found this, for some reason, to be disconcertingly annoying and sighed.

"Anna? Over here." Paulus called. The four of them stopped and spoke briefly. The mother gave Anna a peck on the cheek before sending her off. It was obvious to Paulus that she was concerned. Adolf started to follow Anna. But he stopped when his mother laid a hand on his arm.

"Where would you like to eat?" Paulus asked Anna.

"I've heard a lot about Grantville Ribs with french-fried potatoes and coleslaw," Anna said.

"You've never tried them?"

"We get our meals with the rent. Sometimes it's not very good. More than once dinner has been a big tub of apple peels she'd bought out the back door of some eatery that was making apple pies or something. She just sets the tub down in the middle of the table and everybody digs in. We eat a lot of dumplings, but the meals come with the rent so we don't eat out."

"Well, let's go find ourselves some ribs then." Paulus led her into the office.

"Hey, Herr Wiesel, who has the best ribs in town?" Paulus asked.

"Carry out or eat in?" Wiesel asked.

"Eat in I think. It's a little too cold for a picnic."

"Cheap or fancy?" Wiesel asked.

This left Paulus in a bit of a dilemma. He wanted to say "the cheapest," but he didn't want to look chintzy in front of Anna. He settled on saying, "The best ribs. I'll happily eat at some place cheaper if the food is better."

Herr Wiesel gave him directions and they headed out into the cold.

Anna didn't say anything until they were seated and Paulus had placed the order. They had been shown to a table back by the kitchen and Anna was very conscious of her shabby clothes. Paulus' coat was new, but he had the only coat she could see in the restaurant that had plain leather buttons.

Finally she asked, "Paulus, do you really own part of the shoe mill?"

"Well, I own a quarter of the McAdams Mining Company. And it owns twenty percent of the mill you worked in, along with twenty percent of several other things."

"How did you end up owning part of a mining company?"

"It took a lot of hard work, and then we had some very good luck that landed us with a nest egg. After that it took a lot of common sense, and even more hard work and yes, it is true, even more good luck."

A very anxious Anna didn't press him for a better

answer. Instead she asked, "You said the mill I worked in? Are you really going to have me fired?"

"No, but, unless you tell me to take a hike, you really are going to have to quit. I think you should go to Grantville and enroll in school where my parents can keep an eye on you, and then we will get married if you want to when you're old enough. So you'll have some time to make up your mind. I don't think you should stay in Magdeburg alone."

"I'm not alone. And besides, I don't want to stay in Magdeburg and I don't want to go to Grantville. I want to go back to Wolmirstedt," Anna said almost in tears.

He knew for certain what her answer would be but he was, somehow, still, hoping he was wrong so he said, "But there's no one to run the shop and the shop can't make a living."

"Adolf can."

"Adolf Braun?" Paulus asked.

"Yes. Adolf thinks he can make it work if he can get a loan for the sewing machines. He's a journeyman, almost one, anyway. If he can't get a loan, we're saving up to buy one," Anna whispered.

"We?" Paulus asked.

"His family and I. They've been good to me since I got to Magdeburg. Adolf's mother looks after me.

"Momma died four years ago and Poppa took to drinking when things got bad and that made it worse of course. At first when he got drunk he'd beat me. Later, when he was drunk almost all the time he—" Anna had tears running down her face and didn't finish saying what it was her father did when he was drunk.

"So you feel like you're part of a family and you

want to take them back to Wolmirstedt and try running the shop."

"Yes, but Adolf can't get a loan. The Wolmirstedt town council won't or can't help. It would be easier if Adolf had his master's papers but he doesn't. If he had them, the machine sellers would sell to us on installments since we have a shop. But their guildlines require the buyer to be a master, if you want to buy on time."

"Okay, Anna." Paulus found himself, once again angry. At Wolmirstedt for not taking care of her, at Anna's mother for dying and her father for being a jerk, at Adolf and his family for stealing Anna's affections which he thought should be his, at Tilly for turning the world upside down and at the world for letting it happen. He found himself wanting to tell her that what she wanted did not matter, she was coming to Grantville. But it was plain that wouldn't work. "If you want to go back to Wolmirstedt, then I guess it's time we talked to Adolf and see about making it happen."

"Do you think you can?"

"Probably, but I need to talk to Adolf.

"The ribs are here. You rip them off the rack and gnaw them off the bone. The only thing you need the fork for is the coleslaw."

A bit later Paulus asked, "How are the ribs?"

"Good," Anna answered.

"Do you remember the time when—" Paulus wandered off into happier times and kept up the chatter all the way through supper, including a rather fancy desert.

As he helped her on with her coat he said, "Let's get you home and I'll talk to Adolf."

"Can you get him a loan?"

"Probably not. But the mining company should be willing to go into a partnership with you and front the start-up cost. I'll have to go back to Grantville and talk to my brother and our partners, but I don't think there will be a problem. It's just another start-up company and it has a good business plan with what should be a better-than-average return as long as Adolf is willing to work it."

"Oh, Adolf is a good worker. He figures with the sewing machines he can keep ahead of his sister and me cutting out the uppers. Then his mother can take care of the house. Eventually we'll get married, I'll take over running the house from his mother and maybe he can get an apprentice or two."

They never got to the apartment. Adolf was waiting for them in the street outside the restaurant. Despite his mother's wishes, he'd followed them there and waited for them through the meal.

"Anna, is everything all right?" Adolf demanded as soon as he saw her.

Paulus read the hostility and worry written plainly on the man's face. But mostly he took note of the club the man had managed to come up with somewhere along the way. It was in the fellow's hand, hanging against his leg, half-concealed.

"Adolf, this is Paulus. I told you he used to be my father's apprentice and he owns part of the mill. He's going to help us get set up in business."

"Why?" Adolf barked belligerently, locking eyes with Paulus.

"Because Anna is an old friend. Because my father feels our family has an obligation toward her and I agree." He didn't say, *Because it is the first step in a plan to get Anna away from you.*

"Paulus can get us the sewing machines," Anna said.

"You can?" a conflicted Adolf replied.

"Yes," Paulus said, "but understand. We're not talking about a loan. We're going to want fifty-one percent of the business. You will run it, we'll help with set up and marketing. You can pay yourself, your sister and Anna the same wages you're making now but we're going to take half the profits."

"Is that fair?" Anna asked.

"I think it is." Paulus nodded. "You're living on wages now, aren't you? This way, you get your living and a nice incentive program, half of the profits. If you don't make it work you can come to Grantville and he can go back to the mill and we can sell the machines."

A surprised Adolf spoke up, "Half of a business is better than none, Anna. At the rate we're going it could take us years to save up the money. If your friend will help us get the loan then I guess we will do it on his terms."

"Adolf? What's that?" She meant the club. "What are you going to do with it?"

"Nothing! Not anymore. But with his telling you that you had to quit and if you didn't he'd get you fired, well, I wanted to talk some sense into him and I thought I might need it to help get him to see things our way."

The next day Paulus returned to the office of the shoe mill. "Herr Wiesel? You said you would loan Adolf Braun the money if you had it. Will you stand by that?"

"What do you mean?"

"If you can get the money, will you loan it to him?"

"Where would I get that kind of money?"

"Borrow it and lend it to him at a higher rate of interest, or buy a percentage of the business. If you're sure he can make it work it should be safe enough."

"Who would loan me that kind of money?"

"I think it could be arranged."

Back in Grantville, Paulus and Peter had a chat with the other two partners at lunch time at the high school.

"Look," Paulus said. "Yes, it's too far away for us to keep an eye on it. And I still agree that normally we shouldn't invest more than five percent in anything we can't keep an eye on. But, this is different and it's got a better-than-average business plan. Yes, we're buying a twenty-six percent share instead of the usual twenty percent share or fifty-one percent share, and we're making a loan to the shop manager in Magdeburg so he can buy a twenty-five percent share, but he's putting his money where his mouth is and is willing to sign for an unsecured loan. Which, really, it isn't. With his job, he's good for it if the business fails. The main expense will be the sewing machines and they're durable goods with a good resale value. The mill is getting new machines and the shop is buying used ones. So the risk isn't that high and it's spread three ways."

"So this is just business?" Ebert asked. "Nothing personal?"

"We do owe her something, Ebert. At least, Papa thinks we do. This way she's not just a dead expense to our family."

"And that's all?" Ebert asked.

"What else would it be?" Paulus asked.

Ebert smirked.

"Shut up, Ebert," Paulus responded.

"Sounds good to me." Peter said.

Ludwig nodded. "It's not that much money and it's not that big of a gamble and Paulus really wants it, so I figure if we go along with it he owes us one, especially if it goes bust."

At this last thought Paulus' countenance darkened.

"It's settled," Peter said. "Let's go get the ball rolling."

"I didn't say I agreed," Paulus said.

"Well?" Peter asked.

"Are you sure this is just business?" Ebert asked his brother.

Paulus just glared at him.

"Actually, it is a good business plan," Ebert said. "I can see us doing a lot of these partnerships between the mill and struggling shops. I've only got one thing to say."

"What?" Ludwig asked.

Ebert got a shit-eating grin on his face and in a sing-song voice associated with a grade-school playground he said, "Paulus has a girlfriend. Paulus has a girlfr—"

"Shut up Ebert!" a flushing Paulus demanded rather more adamantly than usual.

That night over dinner, Paulus' father asked, "Where's Anna? Did you leave her in Wolmirstedt?"

"No. She wasn't there. But she found me in Magdeburg. She is working in one of the shoe factories."

"And you left her there?"

"I offered to bring her to Grantville but she'd rather go home. She's found a journeyman who thinks he can make the shop in Wolmirstedt work if he can get a couple of sewing machines. The plant manager thought he could too."

"And you think he can get someone to give a loan to a journeyman?"

Paulus, not wanting to admit that he and his partners had the money to make it happen, lied by telling a half-truth. "The plant manager is going to arrange things. They will get the machines and their supplies through the mill and sell their finished product in the mill's outlet store."

Herr Meier wanted to know, "Is she going to marry this journeyman?"

"Maybe, in time. She's still too young to get married. But, he's taking his mother and his sister to Wolmirstedt with him to help make the shop work, so it's all right. And I promised that if they sent Anna to enroll in the accounting program at the high school here in Grantville next fall so she can learn how to run the business, we'd look after her and find her a part-time job and a place to stay she could afford."

"Yeah, right," Ebert said. "She's coming to Grantville to learn to run the business."

Paulus blushed a very deep red and pushed an elbow, rather harder than usual, into his brother's ribs.

"Ouch! Hey, that hurt," Ebert objected.

"Shut up, Ebert!"

Aerial Donkeys

Herbert Sakalaucks

Saalfeld Railroad Station, April 1635

"Where is the local?"

Karl looked at the station agent, who shrugged. "I don't know, Herr Alpendorf. Reinhardt telegraphed when the train left Kamsdorf, but then closed down the station and went home. He didn't say if they were having any trouble. But if the local's delayed another thirty minutes, I'll have to hold you for the southbound from Grantville. The traffic's gotten so heavy, I can't delay a train that's running. They may only be talking about war coming, but if this is just talk, I'd hate to see what our traffic will be like when war breaks out! The steel mill is working overtime and shipments are way up. We're using every engine we have. It's your decision if you want to wait. If something broke down on the local, it might not arrive at all and your wait would be pointless."

The decision was clearly Karl's, along with the consequences. As the head conductor, Karl was responsible for seeing that his train arrived on time. Management was less and less accepting of conductors whose trains were late. He needed to get his train moving as soon as possible.

Karl jogged to the engine and swung up into the cab. Nobody there seemed to share his concern about the missing local. The fireman raked the fire to spread the coals. He tossed another shovelful of coal in and then closed the firebox door. He sat down on his seat, pulled his cap down over his eyes and started to snore. The engineer didn't even turn when Karl entered the cab. He just rapped the water level to make sure it was true and then turned a valve to slowly add some water to the boiler. Karl reached over and tapped him on his shoulder to get his attention. "Gunther, I want you ready to roll just as soon as I give you the highball. The local's over twenty minutes late and we have to make up time." Gunther just nodded and went back to checking the gauges. Karl couldn't remember Gunther ever saying more than five words at a time, but his trains were never late because of mechanical problems.

Karl realized waiting in the cab wouldn't get the local in any faster, and it might make the crew upset. So he swung down, out of the cab, and paced back down the platform. He had to do something. He pulled out his watch and checked the time again. It was only four minutes later than the last time he checked. He stopped and took a deep, long breath to relax. The decision was his. He had been on this run for three months now and was third in seniority on the railroad. For someone twenty-two years old, that was exceptional. He snapped the watchcase closed. He was very proud of that watch. He'd been presented the watch by Mr. Lowe himself when he made head conductor. They were very expensive, but kept very accurate time. The railroad considered them a safety investment, and only had enough for their head conductors. He slid the watch back into his vest pocket. He'd give the local another ten minutes, then they were leaving. As soon as he had made up his mind, in the distance he heard a familiar "*Aahooogah.*" It was a Goose's horn. The local had finally arrived.

By the time Karl reached the platform on the last car, the Goose had emerged from the trees across the river. It was struggling to pull two freight cars. The extra load explained the lateness. As the Goose pulled on to the side track, the station agent signaled for it to stop alongside the last passenger car of the train. As it rolled by, Karl checked for riders. The passenger compartment was full! With a squeal of brakes and sparks, the Goose came to a stop. The station agent quickly placed a step at the rear door to help the passengers down. Immediately, all the passengers tried to get off at once and jammed up at the door. The station agent called out, "One at a time! One at a time! The train won't leave without you."

When the first passenger reached the ground, Karl called out, "All aboard for northbound passengers. We depart in two minutes." Passengers scrambled to retrieve their luggage from the Goose's baggage compartment. Karl helped them board while the harried agent passed out their bags. Karl calmly announced, "Please show me you have a ticket. Anyone for Grantville or Rudolstadt, I'll punch your tickets now. Everyone else, I'll punch them later. Grantville and Rudolstadt passengers remain in the last coach, through passengers go to the first coach." He did a double take as he helped a pretty, red-haired young lady to board. He had seen her before, but hadn't had the nerve to talk to her. He made a silent vow this trip would be different. He was determined to get to know her better. All he knew now was that she traveled from Kamsdorf and, from her clothes, she was probably an up-timer. He turned back to the line as the next passengers stepped up. Two workmen showed him their new employee passes and asked, "*Ludwigsstadt bahn?*" From their dress, they were heading to the end of track to start working. Karl quickly replied, "*Nein, dreissig minuten, Sie gehen nach Süden,*" and pointed south. They nodded and stepped back to wait for the southbound train. Karl helped a last family of four to board and then picked up his signal lantern from the platform. Swinging it side to side so Gunther could see, he called out, "All aboard. Let 'er roll!"

Gunther gave a short pull on the whistle as a warning. Then a cloud of steam poured from the cylinders, as the wheels spun, briefly, for traction. As the train slowly started to roll, Karl grabbed a handrail and let the momentum pull him up. He waved to the station agent and then entered the coach. He made his way through the Grantville crowd and went to the first coach. He punched the tickets for the through passengers and hung them on the hooks above the seats to show they had paid and remind him when they needed to get off. By the time he was done, they were almost to the Ring Wall. He hurried to the car's mail room and unlocked the door. He had only a short time to sort the Grantville and Rudolstadt mail that had just arrived. With a practiced ease, he tossed the letters into the waiting sacks. The remainder of the trip to Grantville passed quickly. A whistle sounded in the distance.

The southbound train was waiting at the switch for them to clear. As soon as their last car passed, the yardman threw the switch and the southbound train whistled for departure. As the northbound rolled into the Grantville depot, Karl leaned out the door and tossed the Grantville mailbag at the feet of the waiting mail clerk, who was also the station agent's oldest son. Karl then hurried back to the last car. He opened the door and called out, "All out for Grantville!" The station agent and his youngest son already had the steps positioned to assist the passengers down by the time Karl reached the back platform.

The odor of fresh-cut lumber, mixed with the usual steam, coal smoke and oil scents, was heavy in the spring air. Karl looked up. The new passenger platform was almost completed. Soon the passengers wouldn't have to worry about getting wet when going to or from the station. The railroad was trying to accommodate the rapid growth in the number of travelers. Along with the new structures, new rails were a priority and tracks were already being relaid to shorten grades and distances and replace strap rail. Right now, the platform work was stopped. The workers were taking a break, waiting for the train to depart before resuming work overhead. The straw boss seemed perturbed by the interruption, but the workers took the opportunity to admire the young ladies that detrained. Through the crowd, the agent hurried over to Karl. "You arrived twenty-five minutes late! The northbound freight will have to wait an hour for you at Jena."

Karl took out his watch. "You're right, twenty-five

minutes. We've got fifteen minutes in the schedule to load and be off. If I keep standing here chatting, we won't be able to make any of it up. If you can get the mail and packages loaded, while I board the passengers, that will save at least ten minutes." He gave Joseph a pat on the back and turned to the group of waiting passengers. "All aboard for Magdeburg and points in between!" Four minutes later, the train pulled out.

A quick glance into the mail room revealed only a lone mailbag and some luggage had been loaded at Grantville. Sorting would go quickly. Hopefully, they wouldn't have to stop at Rudolstadt. No one was ticketed for there.

As they approached Rudolstadt, Karl could see the signal arm was down. More passengers to load! They wouldn't make up any time here. He repeated the routine from Grantville and managed to make up a whole minute. With no local passengers, the last coach was temporarily empty. He headed back to the first coach to see to the needs of his passengers. The next stretch was the longest on the route. Maybe he could finally get a few free minutes to meet the young lady and chat with her. He entered the mail compartment and quickly sorted the Grantville bag. The day promised to be sunny, so he extinguished the fire in the small stove and quickly rehearsed the introduction he planned to use with the young lady. Straightening his coat and hat, he opened the door and stepped out into the passenger compartment. The object of his attention was seated alone, three seats away. Just as he reached her, the elderly grandmother across the aisle tugged at his coat sleeve. "How long until Jena?"

"Three hours, Grandmother." The reply was automatic. He turned back to the redhead but the interruption caused him to completely forget his prepared speech. Instead, all he could come up with was, "Do you travel this way often?" As soon as he said it, he wished he had just kept walking down the aisle. It sounded so trite. The smile on her face as soon as she realized he had spoken to her drove the embarrassment away immediately.

"No, this is only my second train trip. I'm on my way to Imperial Tech." She glanced around the car. "It looks like we're the only young folks on this trip. I was hoping we might have a chance to talk. I remember you from last time. You were so busy; you never said a word to me." She tried to pout, but almost giggled.

Karl's heart nearly skipped a beat. She remembered him! He stood there, lost in his thoughts for a second, before he remembered to answer. "I remember. That was my first week as head conductor for this train. I was so nervous about not making a mistake on the new job, I couldn't think of a word to say." And I'm still having trouble! Karl took a deep breath to relax and then continued. "It's been three months since I started this run and now I think I know every bump and sway in the track." Just then, the train passed a rough track section and the car gave a sharp thump. He held up a finger for emphasis. "And there should be another just . . . about . . . now!" Just like a musical conductor signaling a drummer, the car gave another thump as it reached the end of the rail section. They both laughed at the timing.

She gave him a thoughtful look and then asked, "Aren't you a little young to be a head conductor? I always thought they were old men."

Karl nodded. "Normally you would be right, but I started as a trainman before the railroad opened for business. My father was the foreman who helped build this section of the railroad and I worked on his crew. When they posted the job announcement for trainmen, I already knew the route and the engineers. Mr. Lowe decided to take a chance on a younger man and now here I am!"

"Is your father Fritz Alpendorf?" she asked with an amazed look on her face.

Karl was speechless for a moment. How did she know his father? "Why yes. How do you know his name?"

"I've met him a number of times when he came to my father's steel plant to check on the new rail production. I must say, you do bear a strong resemblance to him."

Karl started to get a tight spot in his chest. She was way above his station in life. The short hair and open attitude had left him with the impression she might be a shop clerk. The daughter of a steel mill owner? Never! Nevertheless, he had to ask, "Who exactly do I have the pleasure of addressing?"

"Oh! I'm sorry. I should have introduced myself. Father says my manners are atrocious at times. I'm Lynn Pierce. I'm on my way to Imperial Tech to study mechanical engineering." She stuck out her hand. "And you are?"

Karl bowed, took her hand and kissed it, as he imagined a nobleman would. "I am Karl Alpendorf, head conductor on this train. Very pleased to meet you." They both laughed at his performance. A chuckle from across the aisle caught their attention. The old grandmother there was smiling.

"Such a nice young man. And so polite," they heard her whisper. "I wish I was still young."

Turning back to Lynn, Karl asked, "Are you really planning to study engineering? Why would you want to study in such a boring field?" Lynn's eyes went wide. Karl realized that had not been the right way to ask the question. Before he could recover, Lynn launched into an explanation that evidently had been used numerous times before.

"It's not a boring field! I've worked the past few years for my parents as a draftsman and engineer on all sorts of projects at the mill. And done a good job too! If I'm going to be able to do the more complicated work that the mill will need in the future, Father says I have to have the training that will be needed. He agreed that after two years at Tech I could take on larger projects. I helped with the design of the machines that rolled the rail we're riding on!"

The conversation was interrupted by a small boy walking up to Karl and tugging politely on his coat sleeve. Karl turned and asked, "Can I help you?" The boy, who seemed to be bouncing more than the car motion would explain, motioned for Karl to bend over so he could whisper in his ear. Karl nodded and then stood up. "We'll be right back." He escorted the child to the restroom at the end of the car. Opening the door, he said, "Here you go. Just pull the latch back when you get ready to come out." He walked back to Lynn. "Just part of my job, running the train."

Lynn looked puzzled. "I thought the engineer ran the train?"

"Oh no, he only drives the engine. The conductor runs the train. He's responsible for arriving on time, making sure everything is run safely and that the passengers are taken care of properly. A very important job!" He straightened his coat and, unconsciously, struck a pose. The youngster chose that moment to leave the restroom and announce to his mother in a loud voice, "They even have running water!" as he raced back to his seat.

Lynn's rejoinder, "But you're still pretty young!" brought Karl back to earth.

They talked for almost twenty minutes about Karl's work, Lynn's plans for school, and her ideas on new products for the mill. Karl held his own in the technical discussions, describing the engineering problems his father had encountered with construction at various points on the line. Lynn described what the mill was doing for rolling the new steel rail. As they passed over a short trestle, Karl described the headaches they had encountered with the pilings. "The land in this area is very soft and marshy. It took them almost two weeks to get the pilings down far enough to hit solid ground. They had a lot of problems with supplies and equipment sinking into the ground. We've had to keep real close watch on the track to make sure it doesn't buckle or slide. They were eventually able to find a solid ridge up ahead that rises above the soft ground. It's close to a stream and follows its course for about a mile." The train started to slow down as it reached the foot of the uphill grade.

Karl noticed the door on the stove had come open. "Excuse me. I need to attend to the stove." He walked over and checked the coals. They were dull, with lots of ash. He shook the grate and cleared the ash. Not much was left of the fire so he reached for the water pail, which hung nearby, to douse the remnants. As he tossed the water in, he felt a vibration that was unfamiliar. Suddenly, he felt more than heard a loud series of crunches through the frame of the car. A loud screech of steel on steel came from the direction of the engine. Without thinking, Karl dropped the pail, slammed the door of the stove closed and locked it. At the same time, he yelled out, "Everyone grab something and hold on!" He looked up and saw Gunther and the fireman fly past the window, heading for the soft ground alongside the track. The car reared up in the air. Lynn was thrown from her seat and a small trunk flew off the luggage rack and struck a glancing blow to her head. A wrenching crash, then the car stopped abruptly. Karl grabbed hold of the overhead rack to keep from being thrown onto the stove. When Lynn's limp body was thrown, he grabbed her with his free arm and hung on. A sharp, grating pain in his arm meant something had broken, but his grip on the luggage rack held.

A loud, metallic snap sounded from the car behind them. Karl frantically looked toward the rear. The second car tilted almost ninety degrees in the opposite direction his car was leaning. The crash posts had held and they were safe from that direction. The cars gave one last groan, settled and stopped moving. Amazingly, he and Lynn were the only ones who had been thrown forward. Everyone else had heard his warning and held on. He called out, "Anyone else hurt? Check those around you."

A voice from the far end of the car called out, "I think I broke an ankle."

Still holding Lynn, Karl called out, "Can someone help him?"

Surprisingly, the grandmother from across the aisle got up and went back to help. She managed to walk on the sides of the seat legs with little difficulty. Karl checked Lynn's pulse. It was strong, but a nasty gash on her head was bleeding freely and already starting to purple. She moaned a little, but didn't waken. He set her down, then took out his handkerchief and pressed it firmly to the cut.

The stove was still secured to the floor by its stay bolts and the door was shut. Fire, the other major concern in train wrecks, wouldn't happen here, but Karl could smell a faint smoke odor. It must be the stove on the other car. Fighting back nausea and pain from his broken arm, Karl gathered up three fire grenades that were fastened above the stove and made his way back to the second car. Luckily, the doors were unlatched, but he still had trouble stepping across, clutching the grenades to his chest. When he finally entered, the stove was still attached, but the door had come off its hinges and coals were spread on the floor. He quickly threw all three grenades. Their glass shells broke and spread the chemical on the coals. Holding his breath, Karl grabbed two more grenades from above the stove and added them to the effort. The flames sputtered out, Karl ducked out of the door, closed it and sucked in a lungful of clean air. While the grenades were very effective in killing the flames, he had also been warned that they were equally effective in killing anyone who breathed in too much of their fumes.

Karl gingerly descended to the ground and looked around. His arm was beginning to throb. He cradled it with his right hand. He thought he knew every foot

of the line, but he didn't remember a pond on this
section. The passenger cars had come to rest leaning
in opposite directions, but still on their wheels. They
were headed downhill, with their wheels resting on
opposite sides of a small ravine. The first car had
struck a pile of coal, which accounted for the sudden stop. The coal had no business being piled there.
Karl stepped around the pile and the reason for its
existence became evident. The tender had struck a
large stump and flipped over, dumping the coal in
its flight. The tender was twisted around a large tree,
upside down, about fifty feet farther down the ravine.
By some fluke, the engine had missed the stump and
the large trees on both sides of the ravine and simply
continued down the ravine, to settle in a large pond.
It was wreathed in a cloud of steam. Karl started to
head toward the engine to check on the crew but
then remembered seeing them bail out. They were
lucky! Bailing out had kept them from being scalded
to death. Karl started to turn, still wondering where
they were, when a voice behind him caused him to
jump. The arm reminded him forcefully that it needed
attention soon.

"Do you know what happened?" Gunther yelled.
"The rails gave way! When we started riding on the
ties, Hans and I jumped." Suddenly, the cloud of steam
seemed to register with him. His eyes went wide and
he started to stammer, "O-otherwise we'd have been
cooked alive!" Gunther pointed toward the engine.
"My poor Annalise. What has happened to you?"

It took Karl a moment to understand who Gunther was talking about. Gunther had a name for his
engine! Even more astonishing was that the shock

of the accident had finally loosened his tongue and he had said more than five words at the same time! Karl grabbed Gunther with his good hand and pulled him back toward the ravine to help check further on the passengers. "Come on. They'll get her out all right. She's just in some water. Help me get this arm splinted and then we can see about getting a message out to get help." Gunther kept looking back over his shoulder as they climbed onto the nearest platform.

Karl looked around again to try and get his bearings. "Do you recognize where we are? I don't remember any pond on this section. I thought we were about ten miles from Jena."

Gunther nodded. "We are ten miles out. This pond is new."

Karl fumbled for the key to the mail room. He finally stuck out his hip for Gunther to reach into his left coat pocket for the key. "Help me get the telegraph rod and key rigged up so I can send a message for help." Gunther found the key and opened the door. He got the emergency telegraph key and the long rod to tap into the wire. Once Gunther hooked the pole end over the telegraph wire and attached the key, Karl sent the message calling for help and gave their approximate position. Both Grantville and Jena acknowledged and said help was on the way.

"Oh . . ." Karl was seeing spots before his eyes. Then nothing.

"Karl? Karl?" A soft patting on his cheek.

"Wh . . ." Karl opened his eyes.

Gunther stopped patting his cheek. "You're awake. Good." Then he began to give Karl a report. "Besides your broken arm, there are two broken ankles and numerous cuts and bruises."

Karl looked around. Someone had removed a pair of seat bottoms and Lynn was resting on them, with a makeshift bandage around the cut on her head. The grandmother was sitting beside her. Karl struggled to his feet, then walked over. "Do you need anything?"

Lynn looked up, but the grandmother remarked, "Young man, I do believe your estimate on our arrival time may be a little off!" Laughing at her attempt at humor she then pointed toward Lynn. "She should be fine."

Lynn's eyes opened and immediately fixed on him. *A good sign, according to what doctors said.* She looked over his injury and then asked, "Is it true you broke your arm saving me from landing on the hot stove?"

The question was totally unexpected. Karl was still a little woozy and had to pause and reconstruct what had happened. It had all happened so fast. He hadn't been thinking, just reacting. When he realized what might have happened if he hadn't caught Lynn, he almost fainted again. He managed to mumble, "I suppose so. I was just doing my duty." He quickly realized how unfeeling that sounded. "I mean, I'm glad you're safe. Everything happened so fast, I couldn't let someone as nice as you get hurt if there was any way I could help it." He started to blush and quickly left before Lynn could see it. He missed the smile that lit up her face.

With a sense of duty pushing him, Karl walked around the wreck assessing the damage in detail. His arm was throbbing with every step but he pushed on. Both cars appeared to be in remarkably good condition. The coupler was missing on the first car, but there was no damage to either car's frame. With a little work, they should be running again soon. The same could not be said for the rest of the train. The tender was smashed and twisted and only the wheels looked like they could be salvaged. The engine, what could still be seen, appeared to be undamaged. The problem was that it was slowly sinking into the pond. With the soft ground in the area, that was going to be a nightmare trying to raise. The large, old-growth trees might cause a problem with access to the site.

Gunther and Hans approached with worried looks on their faces. "Come with us, we need to show you something."

They started back down the track, past the wreck. When they reached the start of the damage, Gunther pointed to the ties. "Do you see it?"

Karl stared but didn't understand what Gunther was pointing at. "I don't see a thing!"

"Exactly!" Gunther pointed to a long stretch of ties with wheel marks gouged in them. "There are only a few spikes on the outside edge where the rail was. They weren't pulled out by the rail; they're just gone! Someone's taken the spikes! The track crew wouldn't notice because they don't see the outside of the rail as easily on the curve when they're riding the hand car."

Hans held up a spike bar that he had found nearby. "It looks like someone used our own tools for the job!"

Karl realized that he was in over his head and needed help. Just then, a familiar *Aahooogah* sounded from the direction of Grantville. Help had arrived.

Hugh Lowe sat in his office, rereading for the fifth time a copy of the terse telegram that had notified the railroad of the wreck. No doubt by now, word was spreading like wildfire, since the telegraph message had been sent in both directions in the clear. A commotion in the outer office broke in on his thoughts. His secretary discreetly knocked on the door and then entered. "Mr. Lowe, a messenger just arrived from the radio station. He says that a government official from Magdeburg is trying to reach you and they say it's extremely urgent he speaks with you."

"Tell him I'll be right over." He looked once more at the message, still trying to decide whether it was a harbinger of more sinister problems. With a sigh, he folded it and shoved it in his pocket, and then headed for the radio station.

Brendan Murphy, from the Secretary of Transportation's office, was still holding for him when Hugh arrived. The operator showed him how to work the equipment and then stepped out to give him some privacy. Sterling immediately asked, "Was it a raid, Hugh? As soon as word of the wreck reached us, our first thoughts were another raiding party, what with all the war rumors flying about."

Hugh stuck his hand in his pocket, but left the message there. "All we know, there was a wreck. The conductor said nothing about a raid in his message. It may have been sabotage and it might not. I would greatly appreciate any help you could lend in that area. By the way, who's going to be responsible for the investigation? I sure hope it's not your office. No disrespect intended, but you guys never struck me as the CSI types."

"I was afraid you might ask that, Hugh. Right now, no one is. I've recommended that TacRail handle this and I'm waiting for the army to give its approval. They could also help with the cleanup and repair. I've spoken to Colonel Pitre and she says they should be able to get there within a few hours. I'll get back to you within the hour. Magdeburg out."

Hugh took off the headset, muttering, "It sure sounds like someone's lit a fire under him! I hope he can follow through on that promise. I've got too many shipments that are going to be delayed if the main line is tied up waiting for someone in Magdeburg to make a decision about investigating." He summoned the operator back.

Less than ten minutes later, a follow-up contact came in. "Please tell Mr. Lowe that TacRail will be arriving in the morning to investigate the wreck and assist in repairing the track. Magdeburg out."

"Of all the damn places to have a wreck! Miserable terrain and soft ground, a winning combination!" Colonel Pitre's sarcasm was drowned out by the bellowing of the oxen hitched to a passenger car as they pulled it back onto a temporary shoo-fly track. One car was already back on the rails and workers from Vulcan Werks were checking the brakes so it could be hauled back to their shops for repairs. During a pause in the salvage work, Beth pulled Sergeant Cooper aside. "I want you to conduct an investigation. It's obvious someone removed the spikes on the track, causing the accident, since the spikes are gone." She pointed toward an obvious break in the undergrowth. "There's a trail that leads off into the woods from the tracks. It appears to be quite recent and shows signs that someone has traveled back and forth with a heavy load." Jim Cooper gathered a squad to follow the trail and see where it led. He'd been gone almost two hours and Beth was beginning to get worried.

A bellow from the oxen brought her attention back to the salvage work. The car had reached the rail and the straining oxen had managed to pull the first set of wheels onto the track. The drover had pulled them up short because some of the timbers had moved. A short pause was needed while the timbers that were guiding the rear wheels were repositioned for the final pull. For the umpteenth time in the past hour, the lack of an adequate-sized crane to work on rough ground came back to the top of Beth's Christmas wish list. As she finished checking the timber placement, she heard a commotion from the group trying to decide how to proceed with the locomotive. She stood up and walked back around the car. Coming out of the woods was the squad, with Sergeant Cooper leading the way. Two civilians were being escorted, with their hands tied behind their backs.

Dragging his captives with him, Sergeant Cooper pulled up in front of Beth and saluted. "Mission accomplished, Colonel."

Thuringen Gardens, Grantville, late April 1635

A quick glance at his watch showed Vince that he was ten minutes early. Even so, he increased his pace. Dark clouds were threatening rain any minute and he detested wet clothes. As he approached the entrance to the Gardens, the doorman held the door open for him and motioned for his attention. "Herr Masaniello, your party is expecting you. Herr Lowe has the private room in back reserved for you."

Vince was surprised. This was so unlike Hugh. He never went out for lunch, and the added cost of a private room had probably unleashed a swarm of moths from his wallet when he paid for it. This had to be something important, and most likely involved last week's train wreck. If he was going to make another plea for faster delivery on the locomotives they were assembling, it was a waste of time and money. The current schedule was already overambitious and the delay in the wheel castings was out of his control. He chuckled to himself. He'd wait until after the meal to tell him that. A free lunch from Hugh was too good to pass up!

As Vince entered the private room, Hugh Lowe rose and shook his hand. A quick glance at the table showed it was set for three. "Somebody else coming, Hugh?" He motioned toward the settings.

"A little later. I wanted to have a chance to eat with you in peace before getting down to business. This is my first chance to relax since that business last week." Outside, a rumble of thunder and patter on the roof announced that the rain had arrived.

A discreet knock on the door announced the arrival of the third member of the meeting. Colonel Elizabeth Pitre opened the door. "Am I on time?"

Hugh waved her over to the extra place setting. "Beth, we're just starting dessert. Tell the waiter to send in an extra serving if you're hungry."

"If that's today's special, you don't have to twist my arm. I'll definitely join you." Beth took her seat facing Hugh. "Good to see you again, Vince. Any new toys for us to play with at TacRail?"

"Maybe. If you're really interested, I'll send some-one over to your office later this week to brief you. We've finally solved the bottleneck on the boiler tubes shortage. Would you believe, we're recruiting gunmak-ers? The steel barrels they use for muskets only need some minor changes to be used as boiler tube stock. We should start seeing a steady supply of boilers for larger industrial uses."

Hugh visibly perked up at the news. "Does that mean I'll see my new locomotives sooner?"

Vince winced. This was what he had expected! "I'm sorry, Hugh, but the casting delays on the drivers and cylinders are what are delaying the construction. We already had the locomotive tubes built. It's still going to be July before the next order of engines could even remotely be ready." *And more likely October,* was the unspoken thought.

"Well, that's why I invited the two of you here." Beth and Vince looked at each other, hoping the other would explain. "Colonel Pitre, has your investigation come up with any answers?"

"I do have answers to both of your questions. First, we have discovered the reason for the accident."

"Excellent." Hugh clapped in appreciation. "I knew bringing TacRail in was the right approach. I told Brendan he wasn't equipped to handle this type of investigation. So who sabotaged us?"

"I'm sorry if you think I was implying sabotage," Beth said. "It was nothing as dramatic as that. It seems one of the local landowners was building a dam to power a new mill and needed something to hold the structure together. Somehow, the spikes were 'liber-ated' and used to beef up the cross braces on the dam. We're holding the landowner and his foreman in custody until we can sort out who was responsible for giving the orders and removing the spikes. I suspect both were equally involved and I suspect the railroad may be the proud owner of a new mill when this is all settled."

Hugh was stunned. He shook his head. "What were they thinking? Just pull up the spikes and no one would notice?"

Beth nodded. "They didn't think the outside spikes were that important and figured the track crews wouldn't notice them missing since they were on the outside of a curve. We found a trail leading straight from the accident site to the dam. When my sergeant questioned them, they each implicated the other."

"That was fast work. I'll have my lawyer get with you to start the court proceedings. Now, you said you had an answer to both questions. What were you able to do about getting us back in operation?"

"There's good news and bad news. The good news is that between your track crew and my unit, the track is repaired and back in operation as of late yesterday morning. The two cars were hauled back to Grantville and are already over at Vulcan Werks for repairs. Martin said they should be finished in a week. The tender, as we suspected, is a write off. I was able to retrieve the wheels and they went back with the coaches to Vulcan."

Vince nodded agreement.

Beth continued, "The bad news is the locomotive. The ground there is now part of the pond that the dam was built to deepen. The surrounding ground is either too steep or too soft to try and set up any equipment to lift the engine out. Even if the pond is drained, the ground would still be too soft. The loco has sunk so far in that it's impossible to drag it out either. Believe me, we tried! We could squeeze six oxen, yoked to a cable, into the ravine. All we managed to do was drive the engine in deeper. As far as I can see, the only hope is that it doesn't sink too far by the time it starts to freeze. We *might* be able to dig it out next winter."

Vince sat there, taking in the report and wondering why Hugh had asked him here. When Beth emphasized digging, a light began to flicker. Hugh interrupted his thoughts with a question for Beth.

"So what you're saying is that I'm short an additional locomotive until the winter freeze?"

"Basically, yes. Unless Vince can come up with some way to lift the engine out without losing his equipment to the bog, you'll have to wait."

"I suspected as much from the description Karl, the conductor, gave me of the accident site. But as short as we are for engines, I had to hope. Vince, if there ever was a time you could pull a rabbit out of a hat, this is it." Hugh looked like a drowning man searching for a rope.

"I don't know about rabbits, and without seeing the site, I can't say for certain, but we do have some new toys that may be of use." The prototype boiler he'd had Arlen working on was ready and had the power needed. Adapting it would be the problem. "Colonel, could you stop by the Werks with me when we finish and describe to my chief engineer what you're facing? I think with a little brainstorming we might come up with some possibilities."

Vince's optimism brought a smile to Hugh's face. "I'd like to send Karl with you, Colonel, as my liaison. He's laid up right now with a broken arm, but has had some exposure to railroad engineering. He knows everyone on the line and should be of some help."

Beth just nodded, her attention fastened on the kitchen doorway. The waiter had just arrived with the additional strudel. It was smothered in fresh whipped cream and perched on a huge scoop of ice cream. Beth checked her belt, to make sure proper attention could be given to the dessert.

Two sets of legs stuck out from under a damaged passenger car. Recognizing both, Mimi Goss walked over and gave the longer pair of them a kick. "Arlen Goss, are you going to let Martin have a lunch break, or are you both planning on starving me to death?" The aroma of cheese and oregano brought both men out from under the car. Mimi stood there with a fresh pizza and two bottles of beer. "Junior is kicking, telling me it's way past time to eat! Now go clean up and get back here before I finish this whole pizza. The doctor says I need to watch my weight and you're definitely *not* helping."

After a quick, apologetic kiss to his wife, Arlen grabbed Martin and headed to the nearby wash sink. As they cleaned up, Arlen surveyed the crowded shop. A crew was unloading car part castings from some flatcars. "You know, Martin, we may need to expand again. Those ore cars are taking up a lot of space, especially broken down like they are for shipping. The work keeps coming in faster than we can finish it."

Martin gave Arlen a poke in the ribs and pointed

to Mimi with a bar of soap. "Work here's not the only thing expanding. When is she due?"

Arlen smiled at the jest. "Not for a couple of months yet. The doctor isn't sure, but it may be twins. She goes back to see him next week. We should know then." The object of the discussion picked up her second piece of pizza and scooped the cheese string into her mouth. "We better hurry or there won't be anything left!" Arlen tossed a hand rag back on the sink and headed toward his wife. When he got to the table he was rewarded with a cheese-flavored kiss.

Just about the time the last of the pizza disappeared, Vince Masaniello came through the open shop doors with Colonel Pitre and two others. Mimi turned to Arlen. "Looks like my cue to leave. Your boss is here with visitors."

Arlen motioned for her to remain seated. "Stick around. He mentioned he might be stopping by with visitors and needed to discuss a large project. I'll want your thoughts if it involves travel. With a baby coming, I don't want to get stuck too far from home. Your being here may remind him of that fact. Vince can be a little too focused at times."

Vince pointed out the cars that were in for repairs to the visitors and then brought them over to the table. "Arlen, these are the visitors I mentioned. I believe you know Colonel Pitre."

Arlen nodded a greeting. He had worked with the TacRail commander on a number of projects. Her presence at least reduced the likelihood of a long trip. "Good to see you again, Colonel. Were those parts I sent last week what you needed?"

"Yes. We didn't even need to do any extra machining."

Arlen turned to the other two visitors. The female was familiar, but he couldn't place her name. The man with the arm in a sling was a total stranger. Vince continued, "This is Karl Alpendorf, a conductor on the railroad and his companion is Lynn Pierce, a mechanical engineering student. They'll be involved on this project."

Arlen snapped his fingers and pointed at Lynn. "Now I remember! You work at your father's steel works. I thought I remembered seeing you somewhere. You were there when I was meeting with him on that large parts order for the ore cars." He pointed to the arriving castings. "You made the design suggestion that reduced the weight on the wheels."

Lynn smiled. "I'm flattered you remembered."

A swift kick under the table reminded Arlen of his manners. He turned to his table companions. "Let me introduce the head of our car construction, Martin Erlanger, and my wife, Mimi." Both nodded acknowledgement.

Vince pulled up some nearby chairs. When Martin and Mimi started to rise, he told them to stay. "This is just a preliminary brainstorming session. Outside ideas would be welcomed."

Arlen asked, just a little puzzled, "And just what, exactly, are we brainstorming? If it's about the wreck, the cars are here and should be relatively simple to repair."

Vince shook his head. "The problem is the locomotive. The railroad needs engines, badly, and the wreck has left one mired in a bog. The colonel has spent the past few days trying to lift, pull, or push it out. All that's happened is that it's stuck even deeper now in the muck. You know as well as I do that USE Steel is making parts as fast as they can, but we can only build locomotives if the parts are here. If we can get this engine raised, it should be a simple repair job. You were at the site to get the cars here for repair and know what the situation looks like. Is there any way we could use the new prototype steam engine to get that locomotive out?"

Arlen said, "That site is heavily wooded along the ravine and around the pond the loco is submerged in. There's no way to pull the engine out until the ground freezes. I assume we can't wait for winter?"

Vince sighed. "Nope. Hugh needs it now!"

"Just asking." Arlen looked over at the prototype. It was supposed to generate over two hundred horse-power. It could be mounted vertically on a sledge for transport to the site and outriggers added for stability. The problem was finding a way to lift the weight of the loco without toppling the equipment. Somehow, the lift point had to be right over the loco. He started to get an idea. He doodled on a napkin, laying out the site as he remembered it. When he finished he pushed it across the table to Beth. "Is this about how you remember the site's layout?"

Beth studied the drawing for a minute. "That's very close. You've got extremely good powers of observation. Now, what's your idea?"

"I remember a story about a railroad that faced a similar problem. They solved it by rigging cable between a number of large trees and running some type of pulley mechanism out for the lift. I was stuck for a minute on what the mechanism looked like, but remembered an old model train crane I had on my layout. There would be a set of pulleys connected to the steam donkey for lifting and lowering and other sets on the end of the mechanism and trees that went back to the donkey engine to run it out and back." He paused, gathering his thoughts. Abruptly he asked, "Colonel, how much pull do you have with the navy?"

"I know Admiral Simpson from meetings we've both attended, but all we've ever discussed professionally was how much more rail he needed for his ironclads. What do you need?" Beth asked.

Arlen started to sketch in lines on the site map, connecting back to a point on solid ground. "We'll need some anchor cable to handle the main lines. Two-inch might work, but three-inch would be better. Probably around ten sections of hundred-foot lengths. We'll return it when we're done, but it will be stretched." He turned to Lynn. "I'll also need some custom casting work to make the pulleys and blocks to handle cable that size. Can USE Steel handle something like that with their current workload?"

Lynn studied the rough sketch and then got a far-away look. After a minute she replied, "I'll have to check with Dad, but I think they could do it if Mr. Lowe asked and explained why." She looked over at Karl. "No offense, but your boss has been pushing real hard for loco parts and rail. He'll have to decide how important this work is."

Arlen walked around the flatcar, double-checking the rigging holding down the donkey engine for shipping to the accident site. Six weeks of very intensive labor was sitting on the car and he didn't want anything to happen to it. The engine's "accessories" had taken up all of his time. The gearing system for the two cable drums was simple in theory, but Vince's extra requirements had complicated the final design. The trade-off had been that the company could use the design on a wide range of other steam-powered equipment. Vince was already in contact with the navy on one of his pet projects concerning the new boilers.

The aerial lifting dolly sat next to the engine, strapped to the deck. At just over six feet long and eight hundred pounds, it would need special handling to simply get it into the proper position once they arrived at the site. It had been ready a week ahead of schedule, thanks to Lynn's efforts at USE Steel in overseeing the finishing machining. Word had arrived two weeks ago that the cable had been delivered by train, along with four navy riggers to help the TacRail detachment install it. It would be ready when he arrived. Hopefully, it should only take a day or two to finish the project once he got the engine set up. The prospect of camping in the woods, even with an army tent and cot, wasn't too inviting. Besides, the doctor said Mimi was inside a month for her delivery. He planned on being there for the birth of their twins.

Arlen finished his inspection. Only one strap had needed some tightening. The shop crew had done a good job loading the equipment. He signaled for the waiting Goose to back up and couple on. Since there was only one car and they couldn't leave the car blocking the main line once they unloaded, the railroad was sending a Goose to pull the car out and return with the empty. As the Goose bumped into the flatcar, Arlen connected the air lines and signaled it was coupled. He grabbed his duffel bag and swung up on the Goose's rear steps as it pulled out. He looked around for Mimi, but she was nowhere to be seen. Arlen shrugged. *She probably went inside for one of those increasingly frequent pit stops the pregnancy is causing.* He settled down on the bench seat for the short trip to the accident site.

An hour later, when the freight special arrived at the accident site, Arlen was amazed at the work that had already been accomplished. The forest canopy had been limbed out and cables ran like a spider's web between the trees. A dirt ramp with a wooden deck was waiting to assist in unloading the engine. The pond where the engine had landed had been drained and a caisson of timbers erected to help in removing enough mud so that cables could be slung underneath the engine's frame.

Beth Pitre met him as he climbed down from the Goose. "We're ready as soon as you can get your engine set up." Beth guided him around the site and kept up a running commentary. "I've had my detachment build rollers to ease the hauling. The site is leveled and the lifting cables are already rigged around the bottom of the locomotive."

They were interrupted as a crew of local workers swarmed over the donkey engine, loosening the tie downs and attaching ropes to manhandle the load off the flatcar. Beth continued, "They should have it off and in position before dinner. They're being paid a bonus if we have the work done in the next three days. The army needs all the logistics transport it can round up to support the forces in the east." With a wave of her arm she added, "Can you see where we might have missed something?"

Arlen was amazed by the coordinated mayhem around him. TacRail was taking this assignment seriously. He looked around and then asked, "Did you get the softeners made? I don't think Admiral Simpson would appreciate us cutting his cables, much less Mr. Lowe having his locomotive dropped back in this mud hole."

Beth smiled. "Two old truck tires cut up and positioned as recommended! I have to confess. One of my squad worked for a crane company right after high school." Pointing to the tent area, Beth went on, "Why don't I get you settled in your tent? You can unpack and then have lunch while we get the donkey engine in position and rig up the aerial gear. We might even have time to finish the rigging before dark."

"Sounds fine," Arlen said. "The sooner we get done, the sooner I can get back to town. The doctor says Mimi could give birth any time now."

After lunch, Arlen watched as the ship riggers moved the aerial lift dolly into position. The riggers took their time. While the process looked easy to the uninitiated, one wrong move could sever a hand or finger in the blink of an eye. When the dolly reached its destination, four cables were waiting and were strung through the pulleys on each end. The entire dolly was slowly hauled by teams with ropes, into position over the locomotive. Arlen was surprised to see Karl in a group gathered around the engine, helping to transfer water to the boiler and overseeing the laying of the coal in the firebox. "Aren't you a conductor?" he asked.

"I am, but when my father started with the railroad, I was his assistant and got to learn a lot of jobs. Mr.

Lowe says I'm a fast learner and he's kept me here to get an education in what he calls the 'hands-on part of project management.' He said he may even send me back to school if I do well."

Arlen reached over to give him a congratulatory pat on the back, but managed to stop at the last second when he recalled Karl's recent injury. They both laughed at the near miss. Arlen noticed that the sun was starting to cast shadows, making for less than ideal visibility. Colonel Pitre stood nearby surveying the work too. When the TacRail squad finished securing the cables to the drums on the donkey engine, Sergeant Cooper looked to Beth, who considered the scene one more time and then nodded. A shrill blast from the sergeant's whistle brought the work to a halt. "Pack it in for the night, everyone! We'll get the donkey engine steamed up overnight and start the lift in the morning!" All around the site, men started to tie down their lines and insure the gear was safe.

Arlen approached Colonel Pitre. "I'm not sure why you need me here, Colonel. It looks like your people have everything under control!"

"It's not the prep work we need you for. Your time comes tomorrow when your engine shows us what you can make it do. There are a lot of people following this effort. Vince has a number of other projects riding on how well your baby performs." She nodded a good night and headed off for her tent. Arlen checked Karl's efforts on the boiler, left some instructions to be called if something unexpected should happen and then headed for his tent, too. His dreams that night were a confusion of small babies flying through the air.

☆   ☆   ☆

A whistle roused Arlen from his sleep. From where he was lying on his cot, it could be argued that there might be a hint of light just breaking out in the east. Sergeant Cooper was turning out his squad to a chorus of groans and complaints. Arlen's joints agreed and refused to budge. The cot wasn't the worst place he'd ever slept, only the worst in recent memory. He finally rolled out and stretched to get the worst kinks out. A nearby washtub provided cold water to clean up. The smell of ham and eggs cooking erased most of his ill thoughts about the army. An hour later, after a delicious breakfast and two of Dr. Gribbleflotz's blue pills, he went to check on the donkey engine. Karl was already there, adding a small shovelful of coal to the bed of coals in the firebox. The heat from the fire was a welcome relief to the damp morning air. A quick check showed that the steam pressure was up.

The sun was casting visible shadows when Colonel Pitre approached. "Is everything ready? It looks like we might have a hot day today, so we might as well start now."

Arlen did one last safety check, to make sure everything was tightened properly. "It's ready! Warn everyone we're starting!" Arlen winced when Sergeant Cooper blew his whistle from directly behind him.

"Stand by to start the lift! Everyone man your assigned ropes!"

Arlen slowly advanced the throttle to start the engine. The gears engaged and the slack on the lifting cable slowly came in. Overhead, the lifting dolly started to descend as the cables to the locomotive took up the strain. After a moment, Arlen backed off on the steam and disengaged the gears, letting the slack run back out. He turned to Beth. "Just like backing a car out of a ditch, I'll have to rock it to break the mud's suction!" She just nodded in agreement. On the third try, the engine straightened and started to lift. Arlen slowed it down, calling out to the ground crews, "Keep your lines tight! We do not want it to twist!"

As the locomotive rose above the pond, the entire clearing reverberated with cheers. Arlen stood, sweating from the heat of the boiler and the tension. He muttered under his breath, "Don't cheer until it's on the flatcar. A lot could still go wrong." He locked the gear for the lift and shifted to the moving drums. Just then, a gust of wind hit the locomotive and started to twist it. One man was pulled off his feet and deposited into the nearby mud, but the locomotive was stopped before it could jump the upper carrying cable. In their anxiety to stop the twist, the ground crews over-corrected and started the loco in the other direction. Luckily, the wind now helped and they were able to get it straightened out. When everyone was back in place, Arlen called out, "Starting the move!"

Slowly, the cables paid out to the far side and wound in on the near side, pulling the engine over to the waiting flatcar. Another hour and the locomotive was safely lowered to the flatcar and tied down.

Colonel Pitre came over to congratulate Arlen. She had a message in her hand. "Well done! I'll make sure the proper people are informed how well your equipment worked. By the way, this message came in shortly after you started the lift. I didn't want to break your concentration, so I exercised command prerogative and waited." She was smiling from ear to ear.

The message read:

Congratulations! You are the proud father of a six pound four ounce baby girl and a seven pound two ounce baby boy as of 5:15 this morning. Mother and babies doing fine. Mimi says she'll give you and Vince a one hour head start when she gets out of the hospital!

Deidre

Arlen stood there stunned. Finally he managed to blurt out, "I'm a father!" The nearby soldiers heard the comment and started another round of cheers. Karl came over and spoke in his ear, "I've got a handcar standing by that will get you to Grantville inside the hour. Just grab your bag and go. We'll finish up here." He pointed to the nearby handcar and crew. Still in a daze, Arlen trotted over to his tent, stuffed everything into his duffel bag and raced over to his transportation.

An hour later, he was shown into Mimi's room. Deidre Hardy, Mimi's best friend, was there, along with both sets of grandparents. The twins were wrapped up, one on each side of mom. Mimi fixed Arlen with a stare. "Took your time didn't you?" Arlen stood rooted to the floor, unsure what to do or say. Finally, Mimi and Deidre couldn't hold back any longer and broke into peals of laughter. "Just don't make this a habit!" Mimi quipped. "We heard how the lift went. My labor started just as you were leaving with the engine, but the doctor thought the delivery would take longer. I told them to wait and let you finish the job. Too many people were counting on you to try and rush you back without an emergency. I'm still not sure, though, if I'll give Vince the same benefit of the doubt!"

As if on cue, a knock on the door announced Arlen's boss, Vince Masaniello. "How's the new mother doing?" he asked cheerily.

Mimi scrunched up a pillow and let fly. "Just you wait, Vince Masaniello! When I get out of here, you have a one-hour head start and then I'm going to get you."

Vince feigned a hurt look. "How would that look? Killed by the wife of my new vice president?" He turned to Arlen and shook his hand. "Congratulations, Arlen. Colonel Pitre reported that everything went as planned. I'm starting a new division for marine and heavy equipment and I want you to head it up. We'll expand at the current site so you won't need to move." He looked toward Mimi. "And, in the future, you can send someone else out on the projects."

Mimi looked torn between throwing another pillow and hugging Vince. She finally relented and gave Vince a hug. Then, she fixed Arlen with another stare. "You're still forgetting something!"

Arlen quickly realized he still hadn't kissed her and quickly remedied that oversight. When they both finally came up for air she asked, "And?"

Arlen was totally clueless, until Deidre poked him in the ribs and whispered, "Their names!"

"Oh, right. Their names?"

"Since you weren't here, I decided on Ariel Marie and Donald Kevin. That's how they are entered in the hospital's records." Mimi and Deidre picked up the twins and handed both to Arlen. "This is your daddy, kids."

Arlen was flustered. "How do I hold two at once?"

Mimi smiled wickedly, "You'll learn quickly!"

☆   ☆   ☆

A week later, two letters went out from Vulcan Locomotive Werks, addressed to the Hudson's Bay Company in Copenhagen and to Admiral Simpson in Magdeburg. The first read:

Dear Sirs,

I am writing to inform you that your order for ore cars left by rail this day and should arrive in time for your scheduled sailing date. The pumping and mining equipment you had requested we develop have been designed, the power supply has been tested and they should be ready for the requested spring delivery.

Vincent Masaniello

The second letter was much more informal:

John, the engine works! It's producing well over two hundred horsepower under load. Colonel Pitre said she's sending you her evaluation by separate letter. I've got the walking beam assembly in production and should be able to ship the first power plant before winter sets in.

Vince

Buddy

David W. Dove

A home near Pittsburgh, Pennsylvania
Spring 1987

Louis Garrison set the cardboard box he carried down just inside the front door. "I'm home!"

From around the corner, his two kids came running: Christy, ten, and Mike, six. He gathered them up in a hug.

It only took Christy a second to notice the box. "What's that, Dad?"

"I brought home a surprise."

"What is it, Dad?" asked Mike.

"I can't tell you until your mom gets here."

His wife, Tina, came around the corner just then, drying her hands on a towel. "I'm here, Hon," she said sweetly.

Louis stepped over to gather her up in a hug. "Hello, love of my life," he said and then kissed her.

"The box, Dad?" Christy reminded them impatiently.

"You'd better tell them before they explode," Tina told him, with a knowing wink.

"Okay, okay," he said and leaned down to lift the top off the box.

A young, golden-haired Labrador retriever lifted its head out of the box.

"A puppy!" the kids cried out in unison.

Louis reached down and picked up the dog. "Your mom and I decided that you were old enough to have a dog now, but you have to help us take care of him."

"We will!"

He laughed and put the puppy on the floor. "His name is Buddy."

Late summer 1999

Louis looked up from his book and noticed Buddy watching out the window. For years the dog had waited by the window to watch for the school bus. He smiled and shook his head. "He's not coming home tonight, Buddy." Mike had just left for college at Penn State that morning.

Buddy looked over upon hearing his name and whined.

Louis patted his leg. "He's gone to college, Buddy, just like Christy did." His oldest had started college four years before.

Buddy trotted over and sat next to him.

Louis reached down and rubbed the dog's head. "There's nothing we can do about it, old fellow; kids grow up. It's just us and the wife now."

Buddy looked toward the window and whined again.

"I miss them too, Buddy."

Sunny Sunday Morning, spring 2000

Louis Garrison leaned over to give his wife a final kiss after she climbed into the driver's seat of her car. "Have fun shopping with your mother."

"Are you sure you don't want to come with us?" she teased.

He rolled his eyes back. "Wouldn't that be an adventure, with me sitting on a bench somewhere while I wait for you two ladies to come out of a store with your latest acquisitions? No, thanks. While you two are out trying to throw away all our money, I'm going to drive down to the franchise in Grantville and check out the store. I understand the owner is having a difficult time and I thought I'd have lunch there and observe his operations. Maybe I can help him. I'm going to take Buddy with me; you know how much he likes to ride along."

"The two boys out on an adventure, huh? Are you sure he's up to it?"

"He's an old dog and doesn't get around that well anymore, but he always enjoyed the car rides. I don't think he has that many rides left; it's the least I can do for him."

She nodded sadly. "Are you going to be gone all day?"

"No, it's a short drive down there and back. I'll be back in plenty of time for dinner."

"Well, you boys have fun."

"We will. You too." He closed the door to her car and watched her back out of the driveway. As she started down the street, she waved, so he waved back.

He walked back inside the house and called out. "Come on, Buddy; let's take a trip."

Mere seconds later, Buddy walked into the room, carrying his leash in his mouth.

Louis took the leash and snapped it to the dog's collar. "Ready to go, aren't you? Well, then, let's go to West Virginia."

That afternoon in Grantville, West Virginia

Louis leaned over with the plastic bag over his hand to pick up the dog droppings. "My God, Buddy, what have you been eating?"

The dog's face was completely innocent as he waved his tail happily.

Both Louis and Buddy jumped at the sudden flash of light and loud thunderclap.

"What in the hell was that?" Louis wondered aloud.

Three days later

Louis sat in shocked silence as he thought about what they had said at the town meeting. Four centuries? They had traveled back almost four hundred years to Germany? How could this have happened? How could a town suddenly find itself four centuries in the past with no way to return?

He pulled out his wallet and fished out the picture of the one person who meant more to him than anything else. His wife's sparkling blue eyes seemed to be looking straight at him. Her perfect smile was as dazzling as ever. The one lock of her blonde hair that always managed to escape curled along her left cheek.

"Four hundred years!" he choked out as the tears

ran down his cheeks. Everything he knew was gone, his entire life.

He felt the cold nose nudge his hand and looked down to see Buddy resting his head on his leg.

Louis smiled and scratched the dog's ear. "Yeah, you're still here aren't you Buddy? I guess it's just the two us now."

Summer 1631

Louis sat down on the hillside and waited for Buddy. The dog was having trouble making it up the hill, but soon joined him.

He scratched Buddy behind the ear as he looked out over the landscape. Just down the slope was the smooth wall of dirt where the West Virginia hills didn't quite line up with the German countryside.

Reaching into the bag he carried, he pulled out the small strip of spiced jerky. He tore off a piece and gave it to Buddy, then took a bite for himself. The spices in the jerky weren't really good for Buddy, but the dog liked it.

Louis laughed to himself. The spices didn't always agree with his system either.

They had just come from the vet and the news wasn't good, but then it wasn't anything he hadn't heard before. Buddy was old and his joints were getting stiff, probably arthritis or something similar. And there wasn't really anything that could be done; even back home all they could do was give the dog drugs to lessen the pain. Here, they were just waiting for it to get too bad for the dog to endure. After that, well, he didn't want to think about that yet.

Spring 1632

Louis shivered as the wind cut through him. He reached up to flip his collar higher on his neck and then shoved his gloved hands back into his pockets. He knew that the world was in the middle of the Little Ice Age, but damn it, it wasn't supposed to be this cold at the end of April.

He and Buddy were on their evening walk through the streets of Grantville. Buddy seemed to have a definite destination in mind as he pulled strongly on the leash.

Louis laughed. "Easy there, boy. I'm not getting any younger and neither are you."

Buddy pulled him along and then suddenly stopped as they rounded a corner.

Louis looked up at the black-and-white building in front of him. This was the restaurant he had come to visit that fateful day when the Ring of Fire had ripped them away from their home.

Because the store's owner, Nino Sanabria, Jr., had been out of town doing business that day, he had been left up-time, separated from his family just like Louis. The store had been closed shortly after the Ring of Fire. With no owner to run it and no supplies due to the rationing of the previous winter, no one had bothered to open it again. All the former employees had gone on to either the military or other jobs, with the exception of one poor woman who now lived at the Manning Assisted Living Center because her medicine no longer existed.

With Nino gone, ownership of the shop had reverted to his wife, Michelle, and because the financing was with an out-of-town bank, she now owned the store free and clear. But Michelle knew very little about running a restaurant and had sold or used the supplies within.

Louis stood staring at the building for several long minutes and an idea began to grow in his mind. In the last year, Grantville had grown by leaps and bounds as both refugees and the curious poured into the area. More people meant a need for more services, especially when many of those people were travelers and other temporary residents. And those people would need a place to eat, a place like the empty building standing in front of him.

He looked down to where Buddy stood beside him and the dog looked at him with questioning eyes. "What do you think, Buddy? Should we see if we can make this place work?"

Buddy wagged his tail and barked happily.

Summer 1632

Andreas Muller took a few moments to calm down and build up his nerve. He was getting desperate and there were few options left. The last thing he wanted was to go back to being a soldier. Unfortunately, many people were reluctant to hire a soldier. They had too many bad memories of what soldiers had done, if not to them, then to family or friends.

Now he stood before the building of the business he was about to enter. Like so many of the up-timer buildings, this one had a lot of glass, letting anyone see what was inside. He could see the gleaming counters and tables. He didn't hold out much hope, but he had heard that the owner needed help.

Andreas took another deep breath and pulled open the clear glass door. He heard the small bell tied to the inside handle tinkle as the door closed. His eyes took in the gleaming black-and-white tiles on the walls and floor and the shiny metal of the counters and table legs. The tables were not filled with people, but then it was the middle of the afternoon, not really mealtime. Several people were seated at the tables and two young women were moving among them, taking orders and serving food.

Near the door, a golden-haired dog was resting on a mat. The dog raised its head and looked at Andreas.

Andreas gently reached down and patted the dog's head. The dog accepted the attention and laid his head back down.

A tall man sitting at the counter was motioning to get his attention, so Andreas walked over to him. As Andreas took a seat on the stool next to him, the big man extended his hand in greeting. "Hi, my name's Louis. I haven't seen you in here before, have I?"

The man's accent was definitely that of an American. It was hard to tell his age, since all Americans seemed to be younger in appearance, but Andreas guessed he was probably in his forties. Andreas took the man's hand. "Hello, Louis. My name is Andreas Muller. No, I have not been here before. I was told that the owner has need of help."

The man's face widened in a broad smile. "Well, welcome to the Amideutsch Lunch Counter. I think you'll like it here; I'm in here all the time. The manager will probably introduce himself shortly. Are you new in town?"

"Yes. I am looking for work."

Louis nodded in understanding. "I wish you luck with that. What did you do before you came to Grantville? Are you one of the refugees?"

Andreas paused as he considered his answer to the question. Would telling the truth keep him from getting the job? But would telling a lie not be bad as well? He exhaled deeply. "I was a mercenary, but I am tired of fighting."

He could see Louis considering what he had said. But then the big man nodded. "Well, this seems to be a great place to work. You should try some of the food."

Andreas was hesitant in his reply. "I do not have much money."

Louis laughed a bit and patted him on the shoulder. "Don't you worry about that, Andreas; this one is on me."

Louis motioned to the elderly woman working behind the counter. When she approached, he spoke to her. "Magda, please bring my new friend here a cheeseburger and one for me too."

"Thank you, Louis," Andreas said as the woman left to fill the order.

Louis waved his hand dismissively. "Don't mention it. If you don't mind my asking, why are you interested in working here?"

Andreas took a moment to collect his thoughts. "As I said, I am tired of being a soldier. But before I was a soldier, I worked in a tavern. When the wars started and people were struggling to survive, they did not have the time or money to spend in a tavern. My wife had died of disease and my children had grown and married, so I took work as a soldier. But I do not like being a soldier, so I need to find other work. I was told this place needed help."

Louis nodded. "Yes, it could use an extra hand or two. With the way people keep coming to Grantville, I think it's going to be pretty busy."

Andreas looked around. "This is not like any tavern I have ever been in."

"That's because it's not a tavern," Louis answered. "This place is sort of like what we called a diner up-time, but of course the menu will have to be changed to foods that can be found in the area."

Andreas thought about what Louis was telling him. "I must admit, Louis, I have eaten some of your American foods, but I do not know how to make them. I may not be of any use to the owner."

Louis again waved his hand to dismiss Andreas' doubts. "You don't need to worry. You won't be expected to know that, at least not at first. It sounds like you know something about running a restaurant. That's what's important."

Magda brought two plates and sat one down in front of each man.

"Magda," Louis said, "This is Andreas Muller. He's considering a job here. Andreas, this is Magdalena Bacherin. She does most of the cooking for the place."

Magda gave Andreas a cold, appraising look and nodded in greeting. "Herr Muller."

"Frau Bacherin," Andreas responded.

As Magda walked away, Louis chuckled. "Don't mind her. She seems cold at first, but she's really a nice person." He gestured to the plate. "There you go, Andreas, one cheeseburger. Dig in."

Andreas picked up the sandwich and took a bite. As he chewed it, he had to admit that it had a lot of flavor, but he still didn't understand the obsession Americans had with hamburgers. He looked around nervously. "Louis, I enjoy talking with you, but when is the owner coming back? If I cannot get this job, I must look elsewhere."

Louis chuckled. "You're right, Andreas, and let me apologize. I haven't been completely open with you." The big man stood and extended his hand again. "Andreas Muller, my name is Louis Garrison and I'm the manager here. You've got the job."

"Thank you, Louis, uh, Herr Garrison."

"Please, it's been Louis up to now; let's keep it that way. I think you're going to do well here, Andreas. You passed the most important test as soon as you came in the door."

Andreas was confused. "What test, Louis?"

The big man pointed to the dog by the door. "Buddy seems to like you."

The dog heard his name and looked toward the two men, his tail wagging happily.

Fall 1632

Veronika Heyder put the last touches on her sketch as Buddy lay on his sleeping mat in the store. The dog made an excellent model; he barely moved.

"Veronika!" Magda called out. "You have a customer."

Veronika finished the last bit of shading and then put down the sketch pad. She walked over to the table where the man had been seated. "What will you have, Mein Herr?"

The man leered at her. "Bring me some beer and something to eat, girl."

Just the man's gaze made Veronika feel dirty, but she had a job to do. "We have several items to eat, Mein Herr. If you would look at the menu, you can see our selection."

"Don't talk back to me, girl. Just bring me some food!"

"Yes, Mein Herr," she answered and quickly walked away from the table. She could almost feel the man's eyes on her.

"A basic sandwich and a beer," she said to Magda when she reached the counter.

Magda began to assemble the sandwich. "Do you need any help with that one?"

"No, I think I can handle him. I just want to give him his food and get him out of here."

Magda placed the finished sandwich on a wooden tray and then quickly poured a beer. She placed it on the tray next to the sandwich. "Be careful."

Veronika picked up the tray and carried it back to the table. "Here you are, Mein Herr. Can I get you anything else?"

She let out a short scream as the man grabbed her, pulling her onto his lap.

Louis heard Buddy's barking and immediately rushed to the front of the store. In the dining area he quickly spotted the problem. Buddy was barking furiously at a dirty-looking man he had backed up against a wall. Magda and Veronika were behind the dog with angry looks on their faces.

"What's the problem here?" he asked.

The man quickly answered, "That dog is mad; he attacked me!"

Veronika countered angrily, "He touched me, Herr Garrison!"

"She asked me if I wanted anything else," the man protested.

"I didn't mean that!" Veronika spat at him.

"I'll handle this," Louis said calmly. "Magda, take

Ronnie back to the office." He waited until the two ladies had left and turned back to the man. "You scum, who do you think you are? I don't know how you're used to doing things, but that's not the way we do things around here. Now get out of my shop."

Buddy growled to back up Louis' statement.

The man looked at Louis, then the dog, and apparently decided not to argue. He quickly gathered his things and walked to the door.

As the man opened the door and stepped out, Louis released the breath he had been holding. "And don't come back. You're not welcome here."

Magda left Veronika in the office and went out to the dining area. She saw Louis starting to clean off the table where the man had been seated.

"Herr Garrison, I will take care of that," she said to him.

"Are you sure Magda? It's no problem."

"Yes, you have more important things to do." She waved him away from the table.

She quickly gathered up the untouched food and put it back on the tray. Just as she started for the kitchen, she changed her mind.

She walked over to where Buddy had returned to his mat and knelt down by the dog. Buddy raised his head in response. She could tell that the confrontation had taken a lot out of him.

"I know we do not want you to beg for food from the customers, but you have earned this one," she said and placed the uneaten sandwich down in front of the dog.

As Buddy began to eat the unexpected treat, Magda gently patted his head. "You are a good dog."

Spring 1633

Louis was startled when Johannes came bursting into the store, breathless from running.

The teenager panted heavily as he spoke. "Herr Garrison, come quick! Something is wrong with Buddy."

"What is it, Johannes?"

"I was walking Buddy at the park and he lay down by a tree. He won't get up, Herr Garrison!"

Louis flashed a worried look at Andreas.

"Go!" his partner ordered.

Louis grabbed Johannes by the shoulder. "Show me!"

The boy nodded and the two of them ran from the store to the park as quickly as they could.

"Over there!" Johannes panted.

Louis looked where the boy pointed and saw Buddy lying by the tree. He quickly rushed over and knelt by the dog. "Buddy, what is it?"

The dog carefully raised its head with a painful expression, but didn't get up.

"Oh God, Buddy!" He carefully scooped up the dog and began to run. The veterinarian was several blocks away, but Louis carried Buddy at a full run the entire distance.

Louis gently stroked Buddy as the dog lay silently on the examination table. The veterinarian had just told him that nothing more could be done for Buddy and that it was only a matter of time before the dog died. Buddy was in a lot of pain and it wouldn't get any better.

Louis knew that it was time for Buddy to go. "We've been through a lot together, haven't we, Buddy? You helped me raise my kids and get them off to college, took trips with me."

He chuckled sadly. "Who would have thought that the two of us would take the most amazing trip of all together, a trip through time?

"We had to start a new life together, a new home, a new job; and you were right there with me every step of the way. I don't know what I would have done if you hadn't been here.

"But it's time for you to go, isn't it, old friend?"

He looked up at the veterinarian and nodded that he was ready.

The vet brought the syringe over to the table and gently injected its contents into Buddy. As the injection took effect, Buddy's breathing slowed and finally stopped. The dog's eyes closed, never to open again.

"Goodbye, Buddy," Louis choked out quietly.

Andreas walked into the veterinarian's office and found Johannes sitting there.

"Herr Garrison is in there," Johannes quickly told him, pointing to the door.

"Thank you, Johannes. Have you been here all this time?"

"Yes, Herr Muller. I did not want to leave them."

"Go home, Johannes, you have studying to do."

"But Buddy and Herr Garrison!" Johannes protested.

"I will look after Herr Garrison. Stop by the restaurant on your way home; Magda has some sandwiches prepared for you."

"Yes, Herr Muller," the boy said and hurried out the door.

Andreas walked through the door that Johannes had

shown him. Inside he found Louis tightly clenching Buddy on the table, his face buried in the dog's side. He hated to interrupt. "Louis?"

Louis looked up at Andreas; his eyes were red and his cheeks were wet with tears. He looked sadly at the dog's body on the table. "I had to let him go, Andreas."

"He was old and in pain; it was a kindness to let him go."

"He was the last I had."

"The last what, Louis?"

"My last link to my old life!" Louis choked out and buried his face in his hands. "I'm completely alone now."

Andreas quickly pulled up a chair and sat beside Louis. He put his arm around his friend's shoulders. "I know you were close to him, Louis. Our animal friends can come to feel like one of the family. But you are wrong, my friend. You are not alone."

"But they're all gone now, all of them. Tina, the kids, and now Buddy. Everything I knew and loved is gone."

"And I say again, Louis, you are not alone. Buddy saw to that."

Louis looked up, confusion on his face. "What do you mean?"

"Buddy was how old, fifteen?" When Louis nodded, he continued. "That is a long life for a dog, Louis. He has had sore joints and could not walk well for the last two years. Even the veterinarian didn't know why he held on for so long, but I think I know."

"What are you talking about?"

"Buddy was looking after you. He couldn't leave

until he knew you would be okay. He had to wait until you had a new family."

"But my family is all gone. Buddy was the last I had."

"Your old family is gone, Louis, and I will help you mourn them. But you have a new family now: Magda, Veronika, Johannes, all of them. And you have me, Louis. I heard one of you up-timers say that friends are family that you choose. Louis, I am your friend and your brother. Buddy's final act was to make sure you had a new family so that you weren't alone."

Louis looked up at Buddy again. For several long moments he stared at the dog before speaking again. "Will you help me bury him, Andreas?"

"It would be my honor to help you lay your friend to rest, Louis."

Louis looked up when he heard the knock on his office door.

Veronika stood there, looking unsure. "Herr Garrison, I am so sorry about Buddy. We all loved him; he was one of us and will be missed."

"Thank you, Veronika."

She pulled something into view. "I made this for you."

Louis took the large square object from her and looked at it. It was a framed sketch, one that Veronika had drawn of Buddy sleeping by the window. On one side a verse was written. He could feel the tears forming in his eyes. "Thank you."

"A friend from school gave me the verse when I told her about Buddy. She said it brought her comfort when she lost her pet."

Louis glanced at the words. "I'm familiar with it, Veronika. Please, thank your friend for me."

Veronika nodded and started to turn away. She quickly turned back and wrapped her arms around Louis in a hug. "I'm going to miss him."

Louis held her tight and let his tears fall. "We all are, Ronnie."

Veronika released her hug and quickly left the office. Louis could see she was wiping away tears. He looked down at the picture and read the passage silently.

The Rainbow Bridge

Just this side of heaven is a place called Rainbow Bridge.

When an animal dies that has been especially close to someone here, that pet goes to Rainbow Bridge. There are meadows and hills for all of our special friends so they can run and play together. . . .

Andreas watched as Louis hung the picture on the wall next to where Buddy's sleeping mat had been.

Louis stepped back and looked at the picture. "Do you think it could be true, Andreas?"

Andreas looked over the words of the poem. "I don't know, Louis. I am not a theologian, but I cannot believe that God would forever separate us from those who bring us so much happiness and love."

Louis nodded toward the window. "It looks like the storm is over."

Andreas looked outside. The thunderstorm had passed and the last of the rain was dripping down the window. The cloud front was passing to the east and the afternoon sun was coming out. In the eastern sky a bright rainbow was forming.

This story is dedicated to all those who have friends waiting for them by the Rainbow Bridge and was written in memory of the friends who wait.

Transit

James Copley

"Making Ideas into Reality Since 1975"
—An old soldier

Hambühren, 5 miles west of Celle

Hans stopped just outside the door. The sun had barely cleared the horizon, and the sky was a great golden canvas with wispy streaks of pink clouds strewn across it like bits of cotton candy. It was a cool, crisp morning with the promise of a sweltering summer afternoon in store. The horses were standing in the courtyard of the small inn, indifferent to the hour.

This could not be said of their riders. With bleary eyes, and pillow creases still marking their faces, his two assistants, barely awake, moved to load the survey equipment onto the packhorses, while the inn's stable master finished preparing the saddles on the visitors' geldings.

The horses seemed to be watching a small dog scamper back and forth barking first at the kitchen window, then at the kitchen door. Its frantic efforts to be noticed were finally rewarded when the door opened and a well-used ham bone was tossed in its direction. The dog demonstrated remarkable agility by catching the bone and proudly bore its trophy into a corner of the stable to enjoy the largess.

This was all lost on the assistants, as they strapped down the last saddle bag. The precious transit was not trusted to the pack horses, but was mounted in a special harness behind the saddle on the master's gelding. Finished, they plopped down on the hard bench alongside the stable.

Hans watched and listened. He had always been fascinated by their interplay, and wondered how it could have possibly developed between the two demonstrably opposite personalities.

"So, Chaim," Andrew asked. "What, perchance, is going to happen today to ruin this beautiful morning. I'm sure you have spent all night determining the different ways we shall meet our end." Andrew restarted the years-old game between the two friends.

Chaim cracked his eyes open against the morning glare and glanced over at Andrew. "Just for you, you little guttersnipe, I will apply my boundless wit to the endless cosmos to produce for you...a prophecy." Andrew's eyes rolled as he prepared to receive his friend's sarcastic response.

"First, my friend, we will never smell the homey stench of our favorite London slums ever again. We shall lose our jobs within a fortnight. Our trust in this upstart German student will end in disaster after he is discovered hanging from the trellis outside some woman's window. Second, the duchess our little Hans has been cultivating will decide we are all guilty of malfeasance, and order our unjust imprisonment. Third, a giant horse will step on my foot crushing it completely flat, and the owner of said horse will blame me for the horse losing a shoe, at which point my nose will fall off and my hair will turn bright blue." His deadpan voice rose to a crescendo as he finished with the description of his hair. "And finally, after all is said and done, a pretty girl will come looking for you, just for the opportunity to wipe that silly grin off your face!" He raised his arms in the air as he declaimed, *We're doomed!*

The horses skittered away from the loud outburst, losing any interest they may have had in a small four-legged animal. The two-legged variety were proving more dangerous. Hans overheard the stable master as he glanced at the two foreigners and shook his head, muttering to himself; *"Dummkopfs,* there is no need to frighten the horses."

Andrew eyed his friend, "You have had entirely too much time on your hands lately, my friend. Which movie was that one from?"

"Mine!" Chaim's face crinkled with myriad laugh lines as he grinned back at his companion. "The one I will someday write about our adventures together."

Hans turned away at the sound of the loud guffaws coming from his assistants. "Well, at least someone's having fun this morning," he muttered.

At this point, his presence was discovered by the laughing japesters. "And there is the star of my future comedy!" Chaim said.

Hans could hardly disagree. The hair on the back and one side of his head had been shaved partially away giving him a mop of ridiculous looking, misshapen mange, poorly covered by the hat sitting gingerly to the other side. A new bandage had been applied to the place where he had been bashed and bloodied.

He was sure his assistant thought he looked rather like Bozo the Clown on one of the Grantville TV screens that Chaim found so fascinating.

"At least I managed to shave this morning, and my clothes and boots are clean. I've saved that much of my dignity even if I do look like a Grantville TV buffoon." He rolled his eyes at his own sorrowful attempt at levity.

He had a massive headache left over from being thumped on the head. When he paid the innkeeper, he discovered he was liable for the bar tab his former bodyguards had run up. This news, while not surprising, was decidedly galling, and hadn't helped his mood. The mercenary escort hired to protect him had instead gotten drunk and turned the local tavern into a shooting gallery. While it earned the idiots a quick trip to the gaol, Hans was not entirely satisfied with the outcome. On the other hand, astonishingly, an agent for Duchess Anna Eleanor had already arranged for the damages to be covered, and while it certainly made a difference in the dent the entire episode made in his purse, he wondered at the motivation. Why would a duchess worry about a surveyor's expenses?

"Good morning, sir!" "How's the head?" His assistants asked as they moved to greet their employer. "Are we ready to go, sir?" "Where we going, Boss?"

"One at a time! And quieter, please!" Hans grimaced a bit at the mild pain their volume had produced. "We're going nowhere until our guards arrive, and then we will still have to wait for the representative from the manor." The new guards, having replaced the mercenaries at the order of the duchess after the mercenaries in question had been arrested, were in the direct service of the duke. One of them had family living in the village, which prompted them to choose to stay there instead of at the inn.

At that moment, a pair of horses rounded the corner. Thinking that it was the arrival of new guards, Hans turned to berate them on their tardiness. "Wh—"

Oops...

Dorotee and her father's retainer, Hermann, appeared from behind the adjacent building, with a third horse and rider following behind. Dorotee wore the same riding jacket he had seen before, but today she wore a divided riding skirt and billowing underskirts. She had a blue and gold ribbon wound artfully through and around her braids, keeping most of her hair up and away from her neck. Secured with another ribbon, a light blue sunhat hung from her neck, swinging along her back as her mount swayed to a stop. Wisps of hair floated like a halo around her head, sparkling in the morning light.

He was stunned... This time, even though taken by surprise by her sudden appearance, he took the time to truly study her. Her flaxen hair was a perfect match to the blue and gold that made up her dress and ribbons. The colors flowed across the glossy black coat of the mare, their silken sheen giving the illusion of liquid metal. Her eyes were a dusky hazel which seemed to change with every fleeting thought. And her skin was lightly tanned from time spent on her beloved horse. To say he thought her beautiful was an understatement.

His paralyzed mind retreated to his concept of the divine for a suitable reference. He whispered, "*Ave Maria, gratia plena, Dominus tecum. Benedicta tu . . .*"

His assistants glanced back at Hans. "Oh, yeah," Andrew said, "the boy is definitely smitten. Send for a priest, he needs the extreme unction! The man is taken away with love and shall surely die ere the sun comes up tomorrow."

"That or Lust has taken him already," Chaim whispered.

"*Ooof!*" Andrew landed a solid elbow in his friend's ribs and he gasped for air. Chaim nearly collapsed from the ensuing laughter.

As she pulled on the reins, halting her mount at the entrance, Dorotee stared at the laughing assistant. Recognizing him as the one who had retreated at her father's approach on the day of "the incident," she dismissed him as irrelevant and refocused her attention upon the master surveyor. His face seemed frozen in the same manner as in their first encounter, although this time it gave her a flutter of something she had never felt before. Sadly, it also reminded her that she was here as a representative of the family and that there was business to conduct. Hermann and Marie, her mother's designated chaperones for today's activities, were an additional reminder of her duties as they pulled even with her.

Her mother had designated Hermann as the primary representative, but admonished her daughter that even knowing the devout loyalty of their retainer, care should be taken to ensure that all the terms of the duchess's negotiation be carried out. While Dorotee had no concerns about Hermann's abilities on that score, she understood her mother's intended message. If you fail to watch out for your own interests, don't be surprised when your interests are compromised by those around you. Even Hermann could make mistakes, in other words. She intended to monitor the proceedings carefully.

Marie's presence, on the other hand, was a bit more of a mystery to Dorotee. While she suspected that most of the reasons for her mother's insistence upon Marie's going along was simply that of a trusted female companion for propriety's sake, she couldn't help the nagging feeling that there was more than one agenda being advanced by her being there.

The master surveyor finally seemed to break out of his trance, noticing the laughter coming from his assistant. Uttering a quick admonishment that managed to stifle the laughter to mere chuckles, he approached her horse, sweeping off his hat and doing a surprisingly good approximation of a courtly bow.

"Good morning, *gnaedige Frau*! We are nearly finished with our preparations, and await your command!" His performance was marred, however, for when he made his sweeping gesture, the unholy mess that was his hair became fully visible to everyone.

Chaim again went into paroxysms of laughter and even Dorotee could not hold back a giggle at the ridiculous state of Hans' hair. He straightened abruptly and jammed his hat back on his head, wincing as his bandage shifted. His face blazed bright red in embarrassment.

Dorotee took pity on him. Fixing his assistants with a piercing glare, she dismounted and moved toward him, striding with a purpose born of experience. Hermann, realizing what was coming, quickly followed suit, grabbing the reins of Dorotee's abandoned horse and handing both sets to the stable master, who moved quickly to take them.

"Turn around, please." For a moment Hans froze in place. "Come, come, I'm not going to hurt you. Now turn around so I can look at it." He turned reluctantly, glancing at his assistants in trepidation. She pulled off his hat, handing it off to Hermann, and proceeded to remove his bandages, being careful to minimize his discomfort. She cringed in sympathy but was undeterred at the sight of the ugly gash along the back of his head. The disgusted look she gave her retainer bounced off him with no effect.

Dorotee closely examined the wound for infection, sighing with relief at finding none. She motioned to Marie, waving her forward with one hand while she reached toward Hermann, retrieving the hat.

"Well, this is a right mess you have here. I'm certain that is no bandage I put there." She turned to Marie, who had dismounted, and rattled off her instructions. "Go inside and have water boiled, and have the innkeeper find some clean cloth, you know the type we need, and scissors."

Hermann interrupted. "Lady Dorotee, I'm sure that Master Blum is well able to take care of himself."

"Considering you are the one who put that crease in his head, I believe you have absolutely no room to talk at this point!"

Hans kept silent, for which Dorotee was grateful, as she didn't need to have any distractions when dealing with Hermann's obstinacy. While her father commanded his instant obedience, with her, he was quite a bit harder to order around.

"He is going to get a new bandage put on, and that is that." She shoved a bemused-looking Hans toward the entrance of the inn, forcing Hermann to follow if he wanted to continue arguing. The surveyor's assistants moved to follow, but were held by a glare from the retainer. Dorotee maneuvered her new patient into the common room of the inn, and plunked him down on one of the benches.

"I do not want to watch our surveyor keel over just because no one thought to properly care for his wounds."

To this, Hermann voiced no reply. He simply applied his baleful stare at the object of the conversation, triggering yet another round of chuckles from the assistants, who by now had moved to observe the action from one of the open windows.

While waiting on bandages to be prepared, she decided it would be an ideal time to brief the surveyor on his new tasks.

"You are aware of your obligations, I am told?" She stood above him busying her hands by brushing his remaining hair away from the wound.

"Ah... Yes." Hans began to recite the tasks that had been conveyed to him via the duke's sealed message. "I am to survey and prepare the plans for a resupply way station, with the location for such to be chosen by your family, with the additional caveat that it is to be in a stable area, easily built upon, with immediate access to both Hambühren and the new road.

"Speaking of which, have you considered yet where your first choice might be?"

By now, Marie had arrived with the bandages that had been requested. With a sideways glance toward Hermann, she began to lay out the materials for Dorotee. Hans tried glancing at the array only to have his head jerked back around by a quick flip of Dorotee's hand.

"Hold still, or this will hurt." Dorotee reached down with the precut lengths of cloth, dipping it briefly into the near boiling water. After letting it cool for a few moments, she quickly applied it to the gash on Hans' head, drawing a flinch. "Hold still!"

She heard him hiss as she finished placing the sterilized pieces of cloth onto his scalp. As they began to dry from the heat, she wrapped the wound in the rest of the cloth, making sure to cover the open sides of the dressing with the tails as she had been taught by the up-time trained nurse who had helped during the aftermath of the French raid on the oil fields. She tied off the ends with a loose square knot and tucked the remnants into the sides.

Examining her handiwork, she looked to Hermann, motioning for him to inspect her work, as he had done in times past. Though still glaring at her patient, he acquiesced, passing judgment upon her first aid skills, producing a satisfied grunt.

Hermann turned back to her, this time with considerably more insistence. "Are we quite finished? It is past time that we should be on the road."

"Of course, I'm finished," she replied with a hint of a self-satisfied smile.

Hans rose from his seat, and began placing his hat back upon his head, only to have it snatched away from him by Dorotee.

"I'll not have you destroying my work in mere minutes! You will have to do without this for at least today!"

"I thank you for your care." He began to stare at her again, only to give a slight shake of his head, like a horse shaking off a fly, and returned his attention to Hermann. "I agree, sir, it is definitely time we should be going."

As they exited the inn, Hans' two assistants could be heard arguing over something, but with Hans' quick command they mounted their horses, leaving off whatever they had been discussing. Hermann and Marie soon followed suit.

Dorotee sent a grateful look toward Marie before mounting her own steed and they headed south out of the village.

Just south of Hambühren, 5 miles west of Celle

Chaim rode close beside his partner's horse, leaning over to whisper "What's your bet, now?"

Andrew glanced back at Hans with a calculating look. "Three months. It'll take that long just for him to gather the courage to ask her father. And that presupposes that he can get past Stone Face back there."

Chaim gave his own appraisal. "I say no more than two months. In less time than that he'll be hanging from her trellis." His eyes traveled from Hans to the girl. "Or she'll be hanging from his! Did you see the looks she gave him at the inn? I thought he was going to burn up on the spot, with the heat from her eyes. That was no act of a spurned woman! Like as not, soon she'll be stringing the bait. I wonder if he realizes she fancies him. He's dense enough sometimes to put a brick wall to shame."

"Aye, he is that!" Andrew chuckled. "If only he were as smart with women as he is with mathematics. It's too bad she's not an equation. He'd be able to make her sit upside down and dance in circles!"

Chaim gave his friend a knowing look. He had observed their master's lack of experience with women several times over the last few months.

Andrew returned the look. They both burst into laughter recalling the last disastrous encounter Hans had endured, involving a serving wench in Celle who had unaccountably taken a liking to the shy surveyor. To say that he was unsuccessful in maintaining her interest was an understatement. His comparison of her to the Pythagorean theorem simply put the icing on the cake, as the up-timers put it.

As the survey stakes hove into view, the party began to loosen into its constituent parts. The assistants rode toward the road survey stakes and dismounted, beginning to unload their equipment. Hans oversaw this activity while giving the surrounding area a quick once over. Hermann had indicated a long but narrow area adjacent to the road, but had not given any particular preference to exactly where to start.

Hans watched him confer with Dorotee as she established herself under a nearby oak set in a small clearing in the center of the proposed way station. With her hair gently blowing in the wind, she seemed a picture of tranquility. Hans was drawn to the fact that she had pulled out a book to pass the time. It was too far for him to determine what kind of book, but in his mind, any book was better than no book. Books were the window to the world.

He began his survey work, quickly deciding that the first thing to be surveyed was a central stable and livestock area, offset from the main road along a bypass, which he imagined would have attached blacksmith and farrier's shop, with a pair of inns at either end of the way station. His mind began to build the station in his imagination. It was a satisfying but time-consuming task, taking up most of the day. Several times, he conferred with Hermann, ensuring that the plans he was making were within the bounds of the agreement. Hans was surprised to learn that Hermann was a former *Jägermeister*, and that he heartily approved of Hans' decision to work around the trees in the area as much as possible. Nearing the completion of his task, he prepared to give his presentation to Hermann. Hans returned to the meadow where Dorotee had arranged herself, then he paused, gazing about, taking in the myriad details surrounding him in an all-encompassing gestalt.

He turned in place, allowing his eyes to match up his inner vision with the untouched reality. The picture before him stopped him in his tracks. A sudden spark of inspiration snapped across his synapses.

The image of Dorotee, sitting under the oak tree and reading a book jumped from the back of his eyes to the front of his thoughts. He sat down right where he was and drew a sketch of her leaning against the tree. In his mind he added a circular bench around the trunk, with flowers and a gravel path leading up to and surrounding the tree. It was one of his better sketches. In the drawing, escaped wisps of her braided hair were shown blowing gently in the breeze. Her dress was playfully twitched to and fro by the wind's gentle fingers and the branches seemed to embrace her in a loving, tender fashion, playing along the edges of her shoulders like a lover's arms.

Then a clearly frustrated Dorotee slammed her book closed and dumped it back into the saddlebag. Wondering what the book might contain that would cause such rancor, Hans began walking toward her, signaling to his assistants to begin packing their equipment.

Her eyes seemed to lock onto him as he approached, although with her current mood he wondered at his courage in approaching her. Her hazel eyes had shaded to gray, seeming to match her dire expression. Coming within comfortable speaking distance, he slowed, suddenly unsure of himself as her mood seemed to sour from bad to worse.

"Yes?" she queried sharply. "What is it?"

"A thousand pardons, *gnaedige Frau*. I simply wondered what might be troubling you. I noticed that you were reading earlier, but seemed upset at what you had seen."

"It's my mother. She wants me to learn this idiotic new math that is being taught to children in Grantville. I don't understand it! How can you solve something that already has been solved, and why would you mix letters and numbers in math? I don't see how to solve for x when it has no numerical value."

Hans brightened up considerably at the mention of his favorite subject. "Ah . . . if I may explain . . . x is not a letter when it is used in math, it is simply a placeholder in an equation, used to represent a number. When you are solving for x, you are simply determining what x should be for the equation to work."

Dorotee raised her eyebrows at this revelation, but quickly deflated again. "How do you make the equation 'work'? It has an answer on the other side of the equal sign already! I don't understand!"

Hans smiled at her, pulling his drafting notes out of his knapsack, flipping to a blank section. He quickly scribbled on the sheet and showed her the page.

$$456 - 342 =$$

"This is the kind of question you are used to seeing, correct?" Dorotee nodded. "Okay, now look again." He made an additional notation and held it out again.

$$456 - 342 = x$$

"This is called an equation because the idea is the values are equal on both sides of the sign. When you are doing normal arithmetic, you are really doing this."

Dorotee's eyebrows furrowed in thought. Hans pointed at the x on the paper. "For this one, in order to solve for x we simply subtract three hundred forty-two from four hundred fifty-six."

"Well, that's simply one hundred and fourteen." Dorotee focused on this new perspective with a sharpened gaze. "What about when there's numbers and letters on both sides?" Hans scribbled franticly on the paper, excited to be showing someone algebra for the first time. He showed her the new set of notation.

$$4x - 10 = x + 5$$

"Now to solve for x, we must think about this 'equation' in terms of equality. We want to isolate the *x* on one side so we must eliminate the numbers accompanying it. But! Whatever we do on one side, we must also do on the other."

Hans finally sat, relaxing from his uncomfortable perch. He plumped down onto a convenient tree root next to her. He continued to write, but this time showing her as he drew in the next step.

"Easiest thing to do would be to remove the five, so we will then 'add' a minus five to both sides of the equal sign."

Dorotee interrupted with a start. "But why not simply subtract it?" Hans shook his head.

"It doesn't matter now, but in higher math, there is no such thing as subtraction, only adding together positive and negative numbers..."

Hans continued his instructions for several minutes, walking her through the basic process of the solution, answering questions, and pointing out common errors. Proceeding from basic algebra and the Pythagorean theorem to polynomials and quadratics, he continued in his ad-hoc instruction. She leaned closer, her eyes wide with wonder. Dorotee seemed fascinated by the information, as if a whole new existence was opening before her eyes.

Hans was so engrossed in his teaching, he failed to notice the time. The sun began to set over the horizon and reading the book became harder and harder.

Suddenly, he was interrupted in midsentence by a long shadow crossing in front of the faded light. He glanced up in startlement to find Dorotee's mother, Margarete, standing there watching them. He sprang from his seat next to Dorotee, almost knocking her over in his haste to create some distance between them.

"My apologies! I did not mean to presume." Surprise tinged with fear in his voice as he hurriedly gave greeting to Margarete. Finally noticing the time, he began to apologize once more, only to be interrupted by Dorotee.

"Mother, you would not believe the things this book holds on its pages!" She cried. "It's like it's from another world, but it all makes sense!"

Seeing the significance of her mother's raised eyebrow, she quickly came to Hans' defense. "He was helping me to understand the 'equations,' that's all," she stated primly. Butter would, apparently, not melt in her mouth.

Her mother gave her a look that said "We'll talk later" and turned back to address Hans. "I trust you have some progress to show us at dinner tonight?"

Hans was dumbstruck. He had expected to be fired instantly. Instead, by implication, he was being invited to sup at their table! What strange world had he fallen into? Were the angels of heaven going to blow their trumpets?

Again, Dorotee came to his rescue. "He has been working diligently, Mother. I requested his assistance after it became apparent that he would be able to explain this new math to me. He has been a great help! I could not imagine understanding these new 'equations' without his patient instruction."

"Very well. I had expected to see you at sunset, Master Surveyor, but it seems that we all will be a tad late to dinner tonight. I'm sure you have a few things to tidy up first. We shall expect you in about two hours. Is this acceptable?"

The direct question finally broke him from his

trance, which seemed to be becoming a regular state of mind for him since meeting this family.

"Oh, of course!" He jittered around in place for a moment before realizing that his sketchbook was in Dorotee's hands. Hesitantly, he moved toward her, hoping that she could read his mind so he could speak as little as possible. Talking to women had gotten him in more trouble in recent months than anything else, so he almost feared to say anything. Fortunately she figured out what he needed and he was spared having to speak again.

At the Harenberg Manor House

The meal was proceeding smoothly enough, considering the circumstances. Herr Harenberg was silent for most of the meal, only responding in grunts to the questions and comments of his wife. Hans, he completely ignored. On the other hand, Margarete had plenty to say, both about his drawings of the plans and the new math he had spent the afternoon teaching Dorotee.

Dorotee as well had many things to say. Her ideas and commentary about the possible uses of algebra were astounding to him, considering she had only learned of their existence earlier that day. He watched in amazement as she reached a conclusion about one of the applications of the Pythagorean theorem, discovering completely on her own that it could be used to determine distance. She didn't quite know how it would be done, but knowing that $a^2 + b^2 = c^2$ gave her the clue that led to a quick discussion of geometry and trigonometry. Before he realized, he was hired on the spot as a temporary tutor, earning him a steady glare from her father.

However, after a sharp glance from his wife, Otto turned back to his meal, again ignoring the dinner guest. Clearly there had been some words said, and Hans was certain that he had been the subject of the discussion. Needing more than ever to be on his best behavior, he managed to hold his tongue better than usual, speaking for the most part only when spoken to.

His meekness seemed to satisfy Herr Harenberg that he was harmless enough. His wife, on the other hand, appeared to want something different.

After dinner, they retired to the sitting room where the servants had laid out a bottle of port wine, hot tea and some small deserts. Dorotee and her mother sat together in a low couch and began to lay out his drawings onto the table in front of them. They commented back and forth about the different facilities, occasionally asking Hans for clarification. Otto remained silent and foreboding, as if daring Hans to step out of line.

"Why is it that you have two separate inns? I would think that one would be satisfactory for here, and putting just one in the center seems like a better use of space than having one on either end."

"Yes, ma'am. However, there is one thing I have learned about inns from my travels. If one enters the town to find the inn, by the time you get to there, you are already halfway through the town. Moreover, Celle is only a few miles further down the road. Better then to tempt one to stay at the inn as soon as they reach the way station, when they are tired from the journey and just looking for a place to stay as opposed to being halfway through town and realizing how short the rest of their journey truly is. Also, giving the illusion of longer travels beyond helps nudge them in our direction. There is of course an ulterior motive to all of this, which was my true reason for locating them there. The stables and livestock yard are located off the center of the way station, and they are going to smell. I prefer to smell flowers and a healthy breeze in the morning instead of manure. The rest of the reasons I figured out later, justifying my choice to myself." Hans gave a self-deprecating laugh.

The discussion between mother and daughter grew heated for a time, but there seemed to be no true consensus yet. Suddenly both of them stopped, staring at the sketchbook. Hans looked over, trying to see what they were both looking at, hoping that he hadn't left any of his scribbled notes from the road survey in his sketchbook.

"My word! How beautiful!" Margarete exclaimed.

Dorotee looked up from the sheet of paper they were examining, eyes wide, staring at him as if seeing him for the first time. Silently she passed him the sketchbook, still open to the page in question.

It showed the sketch he had drawn of Dorotee while she was sitting under the oak tree. Its flowing curves and gentle shading contrasted jarringly against the stark straight lines of the surveyor's notes. Seen now in the gentle light of the lanterns and fireplace, it seemed to come alive, the flickering flames giving the illusion of movement to the delicate design of pencil on paper. One could almost see the wind playing gently with Dorotee's hair. The look of absorption on her face gave her a peaceful demeanor. Fluttering around her, oak leaves were painstakingly and exquisitely depicted.

Her eyes brimming with moisture, Dorotee turned to her mother. "*Mutti...*" She shook her head in disbelief. "That can't be me!" She fled the room; her footsteps echoed hurriedly up the stairs, and a final thump marked the end of her retreat as the door to her chambers swung closed.

Hans was mortified. Somehow his drawing had upset her horribly. Everything was going wrong again! That damned demon Murphy had struck again, and he silently cursed the day he decided to become a surveyor.

"I...I...I'm so, so sorry! I will go now..." he stammered, scrabbling for his notes. He was stopped by a large hand placed on top of his own. He froze, looking up in terror as the glowering bulk of Otto von Harenberg loomed over him.

"Hold, boy..." His voice was deep and gravelly, forceful, but not aggressive. "Let me see that." He reached out and plucked the sketchbook from Hans' unresisting fingers. He turned the pages, slowly and deliberately examining each diagram and picture, reading the notes given with them, until he reached the sketch. Holding it to the light, he stared into the picture as if memorizing every line. Hans quailed in fear as, for a seemingly endless moment, a frown came upon his face. It was replaced finally by something Hans had never before seen on Otto von Harenberg...

A smile. Not a very big one, and in truth, it could very well have been his imagination. Almost certainly was a figment of his hyperactive hindbrain, which the people in Grantville stated was the home of terror, the fight or flight reflex. It was only a small raising of the edges of his lips. Hardly anything at all.

Hans could only look on anxiously as Herr Harenberg turned to his wife. "He does good work. And I find no fault with his ethics." He handed her the sketchbook, nodding to her as he gathered up his wineglass and made for the door. "You were right, Margarete. You were right..." With this final cryptic statement, he opened the door and stepped down the hallway and up the stairs, moving slowly. His tread was heavy, as if a great weight had settled onto his shoulders during the few strides to the stairway.

Hans stared after the departing noble for nearly a minute before a polite cough reminded him that he was still not alone. No longer terrified, but immensely confused, he turned back to Margarete, several questions burning in his mind.

"I truly am sorry I made her cry. I'm not sure what I did, though."

A gentle smile washed away some of his apprehension. "It's not every day one is handed a masterpiece where one's self is the subject matter." Margarete rose from her chair, motioning him toward the foyer.

"But it was just a sketch! Not a work of art! Seeing her there is what gave me the idea of a park instead of a town square!" He got up quickly, gathering the rest of his notes, and stuffed them into his portfolio.

"In that case, dear boy, you are truly underestimating your own worth." She opened the front door and he stepped through, glancing back at the stairs as she spoke. She followed his eyes as they tracked upwards.

"Good night, Master Surveyor. We shall meet again in the morning."

With that she closed the door. Hans wandered back to Hambühren's inn, his feet hardly touching the ground. He was halfway back to the inn when he stopped in his tracks...

They still have my sketchbook!

A few weeks later, Dorotee stared out the window, drinking in the night sky with its flickering stars and gentle gusts of wind. Behind her, framed in expensive glass, the sketch hung in splendor amid paintings and childhood fancies leftover from her youth. The candle, flickering in the breeze from the open window, gave off a sepulchral light, barely illuminating the room beyond its immediate environs. The starlit sky shone upon the low brush and meadows outside like a blanket of shimmering dust, not quite visible to the eyes. The moon was a mere sliver of its normal self, hazing over occasionally as ghostly wisps of clouds occluded its meager glow.

In some ways, the sky matched her mood. Hans had been to dinner again, as he had every week since the first, this time with construction plans and suggestions on how to attract renters and merchants. His time was being increasingly monopolized by her father. While this came to her as something of a relief, considering the rocky beginnings of their relationship, it also meant that he had less time to spend teaching her and talking with her. He also brought with him a letter from the Duchess Anna Eleanor, which according to her mother, included a promise of investment and patronage. This seemed to Dorotee a giant boost for the potential success of her father's way station, which, in turn, would cause her father to spend even more of Hans' time on the project.

Though she realized that the idea had originated with her mother, her father had certainly opened his mind to the concept, especially now that he had the free services of a highly trained surveyor at his disposal. She had overheard him stating that it was almost like having the Royal Architect doing all the design work for them. Hans, of course, stinted at nothing in providing the absolute best work he could, going far beyond the limits of the original negotiation.

In all honesty, it was not the way station that held her attention when Hans came to visit. He was always unfailingly polite and courteous, sometimes to extremes, but there was another side to him that she was beginning to catch glimpses of.

When he was tutoring her in mathematics, he seemed to be an entirely different person, no longer shy and unassuming, but confident. Always gentle in his corrections, nonetheless he drilled her relentlessly, ensuring that a certain method was solidly ingrained in her memory before moving on to the next. That confidence showed through in his work as well, demonstrating to her that there was much more to Hans than a simple servant or merchant. Here was genius, floating just beneath the surface, supporting the passion and joy he held for his chosen fields. It was contagious, infecting her with the same passion, the same drive, and the same desires. Oh, if only she had the same opportunities!

Her world had undergone a paradigm shift. No longer were her thoughts solely concerned with her next outing, her next lesson, or her next meal. Suddenly her mind was filled with an image so profound it overwhelmed her. She imagined herself, sitting, reading a book as she had done countless times with her mother. This time, however, her mother was not her companion, and the location was not her mother's solar.

The memory surged upward from the depths of her mind, flooding away nearly every other thought. She saw herself, sitting at the base of an oak tree. Beside her, writing in his sketchbook, was Hans, a look of concentration and determination locked on his face as he produced wonders on paper. Never before had such images occurred to her. Their power was almost overwhelming, nearly turning her normally analytical mind to something resembling porridge.

A knock sounded on the door to her room, and after composing herself for a moment, she was surprised to find her father on the other side of the doorway. His eyes were solemn, seeming to carry a great weight. He strode ponderously inside, taking a seat on the room's only chair, leaving Dorotee to sit on the edge of her bed.

"Your mother showed the young man to the door. I trust that your reaction the first time we had him here was not because you hated him..." His eyebrow quirked upward in a query as he spoke, to which she quickly responded with a shake of her head. "I thought not."

A long pause followed as he seemed to gather his thoughts. Dorotee waited patiently for him to begin, realizing that whatever he had to say meant a great deal to him. His eyes wandered the room, as if taking into memory everything he was seeing.

"Your mother has taken a liking to this young man." He glanced up at her for a moment before continuing. "As have you, I suspect."

Dorotee was astounded to hear her father discussing Hans so openly. Normally, whenever any young man was mentioned, he glowered and growled, saying nothing but meaning everything.

He took a deep breath and focused back on her, his eyes drilling into her, as if he could see into her soul.

"Your mother has discussed it with me, and apparently also discussed it with the duchess. They are in agreement, and while I am a little reluctant to place so much trust in this young man's abilities, his work ethic is good, and he has good deportment. He has much better sense and tact than your half-brother in fact, which is, admittedly, not hard to do these days. His employment with the duchess will see him in good stead in the future, and I am ashamed to admit, I was wrong about him. He is not nearly the uncultured ruffian I first took him to be."

Dorotee's head swam with much confusion and a hint of exultation. She had to be sure! "Discussed what, father?"

"Eh?"

"What did my mother and the duchess discuss?" Dorotee was near bursting with anticipation..

"Your marriage, of course! What did you think we were discussing?"

Dorotee leaped from her seat and ran to her father, enveloping him in a fearless embrace.. Hesitantly, his arms wrapped around her as well.

"If he asks for your hand, I will not tell him no, though it pains me to think that my youngest daughter might one day marry and leave this place, her home and mine."

"Thank you, *Vati*! I love you."

Otto's eyes widened at that bare statement of affection. So rarely do parents receive such unbidden messages from their teenaged daughters that for a moment he was paralyzed with indecision. As the paralysis faded, his arms tightened on his daughter's shoulders, returning her affection a thousandfold.

"I love you too, dear. I love you very, very much. And I have always wanted the best for you, in all things." He drew back from her embrace, regaining some of his composure. "Though if he is as hesitant in other things as he is in conversation, I dare say the deed will never be done!"

Dorotee chuckled. "Leave that to me, *Vati*! He'll never know what hit him!"

Otto's laughter chased her through the hall as she raced for the stairs to talk to her mother.

The Ducal Palace, Celle

Hans fidgeted with his waistcoat as Chaim opened the door, then waggled his eyebrows. Andrew was helping arrange the last of his formal evening-wear.

"There's a huge crowd out there! The duchess is holding court right now, but I'm sure that will not last for long. Are you ready, Hans?"

Hans gave his assistant/new business partner as withering a look as he could manage, although it looked more like a grimace with the green color that was beginning to appear around his eyes. A whimper was all the response he could muster to his employee's gentle teasing.

Showing a bit of mercy, Chaim relented. "Don't worry, Hans! You'll do fine. Just remember your lines, don't lock your knees, and try not to faint like you did that one time in the foyer!"

Finally, at Andrew's signal, Hans gathered himself and stepped bravely into the next room. As he left, he overheard Chaim accosting Andrew.

"I told you he'd make it! Two months, nearly to the day, now pay up!"

The monsignor watched as the duchess finally joined her husband at the front of the groom's procession in front of the *gasthaus*. While he normally disapproved of the kind of matchmaking the duchess was becoming famous for, he considered this time to be one of the rare exceptions to his rule that love should find its own way. The couple whose wedding he was witnessing seemed to him a near perfect match, both in mind and in manner. The boy's intellect was at times astounding, but erratic and needed a steadying hand, while the entirely too pragmatic girl on the other side of the coin was finally beginning to discover the wonder and joy that little bouts of impracticality can bring.

In all honesty, he had been astounded at the request for him to witness this marriage, coming as it had from the cardinal-protector of the USE. It had been nearly fifty years since a Catholic clergyman had been truly welcomed in this staunchly Lutheran area. After having met Cardinal Mazzare in Rome, he had developed a deep respect for the man's intellect and compassion. He had even come so far as to consider the cardinal one of his friends. The monsignor had spent many a night acting as attendant to discussions held in His Holiness, Pope Urban's sitting room, listening to the constant challenging and debating of the merits and demerits of Cardinal Mazzare's books among those who comprised His Holiness's inner circle.

Although the monsignor could not truly be considered a member of that most rarefied of groups, he had been welcome to observe and, occasionally, be brought into the conversation by the ever-engaging priest from the future, who was invariably at the center of those lofty discussions. It ultimately proved both educational and daunting. The core foundations of his belief, already eroded by the constant political upheaval inherent in Vatican life, took what seemed a terminal blow from the revelations of the future that Cardinal Mazzare brought into the mix.

Considering the war's effect on this area of Germany, he was frankly astounded that the Catholic church could have made such inroads in the face of steadfast Lutheran resistance, even under the inspired leadership of Cardinal Mazzare. He had initially balked upon receiving the Cardinal's missive. On the other hand, when one receives a request from a cardinal, one is obliged to accommodate said request if at all possible. And amazingly, it had been no onerous task. The townspeople, while guarded and less than entirely welcoming, were far from hostile. It had not hurt the situation that the young Catholic man who needed his counsel was a likeable sort and well connected to the local nobility.

In fact, the boy showed much promise. The streets on either side of the church door were crowded it seemed, with nearly everyone the young man had met in the last few years. Besides the duke and duchess, several of his fellow students and even a smattering of his teachers from the Imperial College were present.

This also included the dean of Grantville's technical college, the head of the school where he had studied modern surveying, and with whose recommendation he had obtained employment from the duke and duchess of Kalenberg. His brother and sister-in-law held pride of place near the front. According to the tales overheard from their corner of the gathering, his older brother had always teased him, saying that he wouldn't dare miss this day, as it would be the vindication of all the times that his brother had saved him from bullies, proving that he was destined for greatness. The monsignor chuckled to himself as he considered the happy rivalry he had with his own brother, remembering similar phrases being touted about after his investiture ceremony as a monsignor within the Sistine Chapel.

The bride's procession represented a substantial crowd as well. With several dozen of her family members in town for her sister's long-awaited wedding only two weeks prior, it seemed to most that the sensible course was to simply stay for the second one as well. Considering how long the dowry negotiations had taken for the first, few could believe how quickly the bride's father had capitulated for the second.

But most agreed; it was a love match. There would be no stopping the tide, no matter what his desires on the matter, especially knowing the girl in question. Better to surrender with dignity than go down with bitterness.

Coming from the right side of the church, Hans moved toward the center of the stairs leading to the church entrance, Chaim and Andrew following behind, both of them in matching finery on loan from some friends they had made in town. As they passed the monsignor, Hans paused, again thanking the Catholic clergyman for his attendance in what normally would be a very hostile environment for one of his faith. The monsignor looked back bemusedly, his prayer book, a precious up-time printed volume given him by Cardinal Mazzare himself, held lovingly in his hands, a smile on his face. He gave greetings to the obviously nervous young groom, reassuring him that things would work out just fine.

The bride's arrival was heralded by a small girl-child carefully placing flower petals onto the path with all the exquisite care her three years could manage. The monsignor heard a murmur of awe arise from the congregation as the vision of an angel came into view.

The bride wore a simple but immaculately designed, fashionable new dress, beautifully hand-embroidered with pearls and a wealth of lace. A wreath of roses, along with various grains and other symbolic items, adorned her hair. Carried gently in her hands was a prayer book.

The father of the bride stepped slowly to his daughter's side. With quiet dignity, and a bit of reluctance common to all fathers, he escorted his offspring to her future partner. Onlookers stared unabashedly at the blushing bride as she passed.

The bride and groom met in front of the church, turning together toward the church, gingerly alighting upon the steps.

As they approached their destination, the monsignor suddenly recognized the roses as belonging to the same vines that had been presented as a gift to the duchess several months ago by Lady Margarete. He had known that the duchess had received the prized roses, but had not realized that they had grown so much.

No doubt, he mused, as people began to comprehend how much the duchess had involved herself in this young woman's wedding, speculation would rise as to the reason. Assuredly, the bride's future social calendar would be full to bursting within weeks, but hopefully, not before the honeymoon was over.

The monsignor watched the groom gaze at his intended with a dumbstruck expression. A whisper of sound escaped Hans' lips, traveling softly to the clergyman's ears.

"Unglaublich, einfach unglaublich!"

Simply unbelievable, indeed! He smiled at the thought. The duchess had outdone herself this time. He would have to congratulate her on a masterful endeavor.

Finally, the bride arrived before her family's minister, a man, it was said, of impeccable morality and tact, and transferred to the arm of her prospective mate. Her father kissed her forehead and turned to shake Hans' hand. It seemed that a certain mutual respect had grown between them, which was all to the good.

What a joy to be seeing this! His hands moved of their own accord in following the Lutheran minister's benediction in the ancient blessing of the ages.

"In nomine Patris et fillii et Spiritus Sancti..." he whispered, as he listened to the Lutheran minister's exhortation to the couple about their duties to each other and to the community. He glanced down at his prayer book one last time before focusing his attention

upon the wedding before him. Looking down, he saw the dedication handwritten on the blank folio of the book.

"Go with God, my friend —Fr. Larry Mazzare"

So be it ... If His Holiness was of a mind to follow in the footsteps of a future church as represented by such a man, it might be that such evils as once threatened this world's future might never come to pass. The monsignor's eyes misted in joy as he reached an epiphany, at long last understanding the absolute faith and hope represented by a future guided to peace by one man's conviction that all faiths were valid. In so doing, one validated one's own faith as being true to the Word of God.

The monsignor crossed himself, offering a silent prayer of thanks to a God he now knew was real, despite years of living in the intensely politically charged world of High Church politics. Decades of self-doubt and recrimination washed away in a surging wave of peace.

"We are gathered here to witness the wedding vows of Hans and Dorotee..."

M. Klein Fashion Dolls

Caroline Palmer

Ronneburg, Saxe-Altenburg, 1636

Margarethe Klein looked at the half-carved wooden figure on her workbench and tried not to break out in tears. Even though she had been carving dolls since she was a little girl at her parents' knees, she could not seem to create anything that resembled the up-timers' famous Barbie dolls. In fact, her latest effort resembled something like a monster instead of a graceful lady of fashion.

The image she had acquired after months of searching and most of her savings was of little help. The head had been the easiest part, not dissimilar from the heads Margarethe was used to creating for her regular dolls, the *poupée des modes* she made to order, but the body was beyond her. Because the doll in the picture wore a full-length gown, Margarethe had no way of knowing the doll's true proportions, how the joints moved, or her true size.

Gazing at the shiny paper she had taken from the magazine Julius Wolf had sold her, Margarethe fervently wished she had access to the market the merchant had told her of, the one called eBay. It sounded like the miracle from the Lord she needed right now. It was almost, almost enough to make one turn Catholic.

If only she could see, touch, hold a real Barbie or one of those others she had heard called Dollar Store Knockoffs. Once Margarethe had a model, she could do so much! Perhaps she could even create Barbie replicas designed to look like famous people as the magazine had advertised!

Just the thought of presenting someone like Gretchen Richter or Rebecca Abrabanel with a miniature doll that looked like one of them, with Margarethe's mark on the back, made her heart ache with frustration. And her hands itched to see what techniques doll-makers in the future had come up with.

Margarethe thought of the Princess Kristina doll that sat on a stool just behind her. The size of an up-timer doll called an AG (which was even more expensive than a Barbie according to the magazine), it was probably the most ambitious doll Margarethe had created, a slightly idealized version of Princess Kristina. It had cost Margarethe much of her savings to get a color portrait of Princess Kristina and even more time to make the molds and get beeswax to create the princess's face, lower arms, and legs. The expensive angora wool for the hair, not to mention the fabrics a *true* princess required was beyond her means at the moment and for some time to come.

"If only . . . If only!"

☆   ☆   ☆

"So did you get them or not?" Agathe Wolf put her hands on her hips and regarded her husband impatiently. Julius was a good man, and a successful merchant, but sometimes (more often since the Ring of Fire) Agathe felt like taking over the business and leaving the housework to her husband.

Julius smiled at her calmly. "Of course I got them! I said I would, even if I had to search to the ends of the earth, did I not? And I was lucky, I happened to meet the famous Frau Higgins herself at the market and her husband gave me an excellent price on them. Discounted on account of Emma's wedding. And they refused to let me buy them a drink in the tavern. Insisted they do all the business in back and wouldn't go in."

Agathe sniffed, not believing a word her husband said. Always, always soft. Julius could charm an inquisitor of the Holy Office into buying a copy of Martin Luther's *Small Catechism* and a Lutheran into buying saint's relics, but when it came to collecting money he would accept a blessing from the Lutheran and a prayer from the Catholic and never see he'd been cheated.

"How much Julius? Don't forget there's still the matter of the wedding feast and Emma's clothes and dowry. We cannot let the Brummes think us stingy or poor."

"Don't worry my love, everything will work out, just as it always does."

Everything works out Julius my love, she thought, *because you married* me. "How much? And if you got these dolls where are they?"

"Be easy Agathe, my love, be easy," Julius said, putting a box on the table. "Here they are."

With a heavy sigh, Agathe tore open the wrapping.

"Julius! What in the name of all...How could you have possibly!"

There were definitely two dolls in the box, one a female with breasts so large her tiny waist couldn't possibly have supported them if she had been a human being. The other was a male, thankfully not anatomically complete.

But the woman's leg and one of her hands had been chewed. Her hair had been cut, or styled, to the point where it was a mere stubble. The male doll was in slightly better condition, but had been marked on with several different colors...

"Julius...What..."

"This was all there was, Agathe. I tried, I really did. It took me ages, and all the money I had to buy these. I know they have no garments, but I thought... I mean you're so good with a needle..."

"For mending and embroidery, but fitting clothes? For a figure so misshapen? Honestly I cannot imagine a corset even with the up-timer's materials that would create such a silhouette! I have never seen an up-timer woman, Julius. Do they look like that? They must have to break their ribs! And how could they work like that?"

"I don't know, Agathe. None of the up-timer women I saw had figures like that, nor did I see any of the men who...well...they did *seem* to be normal in every way if you know what I mean. I did hear of men and women whose job it was to display the latest fashions to merchants. Perhaps this is how they looked."

"I cannot imagine why anyone would do such a thing. It must have been incredibly painful to have your ribs destroyed like that."

"Yes indeed. I must say, my dear, that you are the loveliest woman in the village, especially since all your ribs are intact. I am sure that you will be able to solve this problem and get these dolls suitably garbed for the wedding."

Patting her cheek fondly, Julius took himself off to his business.

Agathe sighed. She knew of course, and so did Julius, that Margarethe Klein, the town dressmaker was the only person suited, but that wasn't the problem. How were they to *pay* to dress the dolls?

"These are very fine, Master Wolf," said Margarethe as she leafed through the sheets. "You're a gifted artist."

Christoph blushed. "Thank you. Papa and Master Brumme think I should stick with learning business but I've always hoped to be an artist. At least with the new roller printers I can combine the two."

Margarethe smiled. "And you've found something no one else is doing. Every printer in the Germanies is busy printing how-to's and political tracts, but who thinks of fashion? Papa and I had to scrimp and pinch to save for a Higgins sewing machine in order to stay in demand with our noble customers, but how are people to know what they want to wear? And who can afford to go to Magdeburg or Paris for clothes? These days I do more business in dolls to display the clothes than the clothes themselves. Any seamstress worth her salt can rescale a pattern, but it's exchanging patterns in the first place! Your papa has been very kind in helping with the shipping, but...there is so much more I could do! I wish I could create a Barbie doll of my own, a 'doll for the masses' as it were."

She waved her hands in the air in exasperation and longing.

Christoph grinned. "Speaking of Barbies, Mama sent you these." He placed the box on the table in front of them. "Papa bought these in Bamberg from Frau Higgins, but they came unclothed. Mama wants to know...well we *are* spending a great deal on Emma's wedding and the dowry..."

Margarethe opened the box and stared, blushing a little at the unclothed forms. "You say your papa bought these in Bamberg? From *Frau Higgins*? Of the Higgins Sewing Machine Company?"

"That's what he said. Well, not from Frau Delia Higgins herself, but from her husband."

"Oh, Christoph, Christoph! Don't you know that Frau Delia of the Dolls lives in *Grantville,* not Bamberg? And according to my information she is a widow and not married at all! Her daughter is the one who's married!"

Christoph shook his head in disbelief. "I cannot... I didn't...What if they're stolen? Mama would have a fit! Then these are not the right kind of dolls?"

"Of a sort." Taking the woman doll out of the box, Margarethe pulled one of the legs out showing him the plastic ball joint. "You see? From my research the *true* Barbie dolls are made of better plastic and don't come apart as easily. Then there's the 'Made in China' label on the back of the neck. Barbies were made by a company called Mattel. I cannot imagine a manufacturer or artist not labeling their work. I always mark my dolls with an MK even if I'm not selling them. I would say that these are the cheaper kind of doll. Whoever sold your father these at least gave him the 'bang for his buck' as the up-timers say, even if they weren't who they said they were."

"But you could make clothes for them? And perhaps other accessories? And... well... as I said... umm...*cheaply*."

"I tell you what, Christoph, let's make a deal. If I could *borrow* these to make patterns to create other dolls like these, then I will make clothes for these, a whole trousseau if Emma would like."

"Is that even possible? I mean... I know you said you wanted to make figures like a Barbie, but we don't know how to make plastic."

Margarethe laughed. "Plastic? Who needs plastic to make dolls? Artisans have been making dolls and other figurines for centuries!"

"Out of what? Clay?"

"Clay, certainly. Clay isn't as fragile as you would think but it's hard to keep painted. Artists use wax mostly, for big projects with a rich patron like a king's burial effigy or a saint for a cathedral. Wood is also good for making dolls, a lot of my *poupée des modes* are carved wood, jointed if I've got the patronage. Cloth is very good for dolls as well. I do a fair business in cotton or muslin dolls, especially muslin. You cannot imagine the amount of muslin and linen scraps I collect as a dressmaker to use in my dolls.... Sometimes I wish I could focus on making dolls instead of sewing clothes for people. Dolls at least don't complain if you poke them with pins."

Christoph smiled. Margarethe's eyes had lit up and it seemed as if her whole face had taken on a glow as well. She was more attractive than he'd realized before, with her straight medium brown hair and blue-grey eyes. It must be hard on her, being all alone in her parents' shop, and he knew she'd been lucky that the area needed a seamstress so she hadn't had to move after her parents had died two years ago.

"Then there's a market for such things?"

"If I didn't have a market I wouldn't sell any. Not every noble can afford to have a *toile*, or mock-up of a dress sent from Paris like the books say Elizabeth of England did. A doll is easier to ship, easier to make samples for, and easier for the client to see how they would look in the dress. Come let me show you."

Taking him to the back of her shop, she showed him the dolls she had lined up in various stages of completion. She held the Princess Kristina doll out for him to inspect.

"You see? Wax head, arms, and legs, sawdust-stuffed body. Wax or tallow is easier to tint like skin. You can paint clay once it's dry or bake it in before you fire it, but either way you have to seal it."

"You're like a painter."

"Very much so, and like a masterpiece my art is hard to play with sometimes. But if I was able to create a small fashion doll that is easily jointed and has a similar *shape* to a Barbie doll, then the possibilities are endless." She waved her hands in the air again.

Christoph frowned, turning the Princess Kristina doll in his hands. "I've watched Mama and Emma making candles and soaps, and I see your molds. Wax, as you say is more fragile than wood, and wood is cheaper.... You could reproduce your molds and mass-produce your wax parts, but wood is hard to mass-produce with a lot of carving. I know, my sister's betrothed is a printer and a printer's son,

and I helped with the new printing device. Bert and
Master Brumme spent hours, sometimes days, carving type. Now, with the wringer printer, it takes as
long as Bert, Gunther, and I can draw them. What
you need, is something that can shape wood quickly.
And for that we need a smith."

"We? Since when did this become a twosome?"

Christoph grinned wider. "Since my father used
my sister's entire dowry to purchase abused knockoffs
from a pair of frauds. Besides, you'll need someone
to help with the marketing once you start producing,
and then there are clothes patterns that need to be
reproduced for sale..."

Margarethe laughed and took Princess Kristina from
his hands. "Then I had better get started designing
dolls and leave the rest to...what do they call it?
Marketing and production?"

"More like marketing and distribution, if I have
the up-time words right."

"Mass-produce wood parts? Perhaps if they were
larger...like that..." Johan nodded to the Princess
Kristina doll that Christoph and Margarethe had
brought, carefully wrapped in fabric, next to the
plastic dolls.

Margarethe shook her head. "I need wood pieces
the size of the smaller dolls, not damaged, like this,"
she unfolded her picture. "The heads don't need to
be so detailed, at least at first. But if we're going to
make a Barbie-like doll that a lot of people can afford
it needs to be out of a sturdy material like wood and
we need to mass-produce it."

Johan tugged his smock and picked up the small

woman with a wink. "Not much in the way of clothes, eh?"

"Yes, yes we know. I'm working on it," Margarethe said testily. "But you need to see how she looks."

Johan flexed a leg gently. "Don't bend, like yours, Margarethe. The little lady you made for my girl has better joints."

"Those are ball joints, like buttons. I carve those too."

"Need to mass-produce those, too. Could make buttons cheap." Johan nodded. "You can't make feet like that with a lathe like I have, have to be carving. Carving for the details like the face and hands too."

"But you can mass-produce the pieces to be carved?"

"Not now. I've got too much other work to do, and you'd have to wait for after the harvest to get much from the farmers."

"So we are stalled until after the harvest and then during planting. Time, we are wasting. Money, we are losing."

Margarethe patted Agathe's hand. "People have to eat, Agathe. We may be able to survive without more than a kitchen garden but some people don't have a kitchen garden. My prototypes, as the up-timers call them, are finished, both the boy and girl. Now I can work on some patterns for clothes to sell."

Gerta Brumme shook her head. "Even if the farmers are available to work, they don't work for free. We need something to pay them for their work even if these dolls don't sell. What about your big dolls?"

"My *grande pandores?* The heads are wax or tallow depending on what I can get. I have tubes I fit into the molds so they can go on the bodies easily. I don't make a lot of them, because making the bodies is expensive and so is the wax, which is why I mostly use tallow. I inherited a few from my father and they don't travel well. Too big, unless we ship them in pieces."

"Could we make the heads to sell?"

"We could, but I doubt it would work. Most seamstresses and tailors like to use *pandores* that resemble the local nobility."

"You have the mold you made for the Princess Kristina doll, couldn't you reproduce it for a . . . what did you call it?"

"A *pandore*? I would have to change the scale on the head, which would mean I'd have to carve a new model. The same if we wanted to make any new heads I don't have. Molds have problems though, after so many uses the mold deforms and you have to make new ones."

"So what do we do?"

Agathe cleared her throat and raised her hand. "I think we start with Christoph's fashion books while we send someone to Grantville. *After* Emma's wedding."

"Emma's wedding was amazing, wasn't it, Mama?"

"Hmmph. The Wolfs and Brummes spent a lot of money on the wedding feast. All those individual cakes . . ."

"Emma said the up-timers call them cupcakes."

"Whatever. Then there were those place cards. Who does Gerta think her daughter's marrying, a nobleman? I can't imagine how they stayed up."

"They were birch. I saw the workers peeling and steaming them," said another woman. "What I wonder is how they got those dolls."

There was a collective sigh of envy.

"The Wolfs must have spent Emma's entire dowry on those. I heard Julius bought them damaged, but I couldn't tell. I bet Julius bought them stolen and had Gunther paint the eyes to hide them from the true owners."

"I thought it was a good touch that Margarethe made them costumes to match Emma and Bert's wedding clothes."

"What *I* find outrageous, Mama," said one of the young ladies. "Is that Christoph spent the entire feast dancing with no one but Margarethe and Mistress Wolf allowed it. How many other girls like me had to sit out or dance with another girl because of him! It was incredibly rude. And what if he marries her? She's just a seamstress, and an orphan. Margarethe should have sold her father's business and gone to live with relatives like any *respectable* girl would."

"Well I wonder what exactly young Christoph is doing at Margarethe's at all hours of the day," Master Lukas Gench said. "I believe he visits her *very* frequently, and without a chaperone. Just like several other of her 'clients.'"

Several of the listeners looked thoughtful.

Lottie's mother patted her daughter's arm reassuringly. "You needn't worry about Christoph marrying that girl, Lottie my dear. Your father intends to make an offer for you soon enough, and with your dowry, the Wolfs won't be able to resist."

"You know what I heard? Emma and Albert left for Grantville the day after the wedding. It must be costing a fortune!"

"Those Wolfs and Brummes are getting above themselves," Master Gench said. "The Americans are giving young people too many unsuitable ideas. What *are* the Germanies coming to?"

"You want to do *what*?"

"Make limbs, bodies, like for people."

The up-time researcher blinked and nudged the boy next to her. After whispering in his ear, he shook his head.

"I...Uh...That's...I don't think you can do that. Maybe like Dolly...You know the sheep-clone? Except in sci-fi..."

Emma stared in confusion and shook her head. "Dolly? Is she related to Brillo?"

"No, no, never mind. Look, maybe we're working at cross purposes, not understanding each other. Why don't you start at the beginning?"

Emma nodded and sat down across from the up-timer. "My parents, they got me and my husband those plastic model dolls, like Barbie, very expensive..."

The girl snorted. "Tell me about it. The girls from the Consortium cleaned up, um, made a lot of money from even the cheap ones. I wish I'd been able to join, but my mom gave all my dolls to my cousin before the Ring."

"My friend, Margarethe, is a seamstress and she makes dolls to help her business. She wishes to make dolls like Barbie, only of wood, but it takes time. What we need is a fashion doll like Barbie that we can produce quickly."

The researcher nodded. "Well...I see. I tell you what, let's look in the craft section."

The craft section of the library was not very large.

"Susanna Oroyan's *Designing the Doll* has a lot of

neat ideas. Your friend might be familiar with a lot of them if she does a lot of doll-making, but it might be worth it to copy the text."

Emma nodded enthusiastically as she flipped through the pages. "Margarethe does do a lot of doll-making in her spare time, especially since her father died. I wish there was some way to copy the pictures..."

"Here, Dawn Herlocher's *Two Hundred Years of Dolls* might provide you with some ideas about what was done up-time, and so might Douet's *Identifying Dolls*. But you know, if you wanted to do something really quick, you could do paper dolls or maybe coloring books. I hear the grade schools are crying for them."

"Paper dolls? Why would anyone buy paper dolls? Those are easy to make. Mothers make them with their children for games during the winter. Or you can buy them from a printshop."

"You can buy paper dolls?"

"Oh yes. My father-in-law says they were the second thing Master Gutenberg printed after he finished the Bible. They're expensive though. You have to color them after printing or buy watercolors or something to color them with after you buy them."

"Like a coloring book?"

Bert, who had joined Emma, scratched his head. "What's a coloring book?"

The researcher led them to the kid's section and pulled out a thin book. "See? It's a basic outline drawing that kids color in. My teachers used it to teach us to draw inside the lines."

"But how do they color them?"

"Crayons...Oh, right. I forgot we don't have them

yet down-time. Let me at least see what I can find out about how to make them."

"The fashion books are doing well," Christoph reported at a business meeting. "But not the coloring books."

"We need something to make them stand out," Julius grumbled. "The printers I sell them to place them on their shelves with the American's how-to guides and the Brillo pamphlets so they get lost. Who wants to buy something they could make at home just as easily?"

"I told you they should have the coloring sticks with them," said Emma.

Julius shook his head. "It would take time and another investment to make them work."

Bert grunted. "Researcher said tallow would work. A bit greasy but with the cheap paper we're using it would be fine."

Margarethe smiled and bounced slightly, noticing Christoph's jealous look at his brother-in-law. "I love this!" she said, just to make Christoph jealous.

Why did Bert have to choose this of all times to make a speech? grumbled Christoph silently.

"Ah, thank you my dear. That was just what I needed after a long trip."

Margarethe smiled. "It is good to see you, Master Gench. You were so kind after Papa died."

"Hardly a trial, Margarethe, child. Your papa was a good man and an upstanding member of the guild. My wife and I shall be proud to take over Calvin's business and welcome you into the family."

She stared. "Take over Papa's business? Welcome me into the family? I . . . I don't understand."

"Of course you do, child. Surely you've heard your neighbors' complaints? You are a young unmarried woman living alone. Even in this new world the Americans brought, it is unacceptable. Completely unacceptable!"

"I don't . . ."

Master Gench waved her to silence. "Here is what we shall do. My boy is almost past his apprenticeship. We will post the banns now and you can marry once Rolf has finished his apprenticeship. You will, of course, live with us until the wedding."

"No. I will not marry your son. My papa left his business to me and I will keep it and I will *not* hand it over to you or your son! Not *ever*."

"Margarethe, child, I just have your best interest at heart. If you were a seamstress to a noble family, few would question your unmarried state. But the guild cannot allow an unmarried orphan female of your age to continue to operate on her own in a town, and it will not. Either you will marry my son or you will end in a charity institution. Those are your only options."

Agathe cradled Margarethe as she cried.

"And he can do it! He can take everything! Everything my mama and papa, everything my grandparents built . . ."

"How?" Emma asked. "The guild doesn't have control over who people buy their clothing from. We've always bought clothes and fabric from your family and so have the Brummes."

"They can find other ways. Convince my suppliers to stop selling to me or increase their prices. Vandalize the shop. Convince the city authorities to arrest me on some crime or make me leave town. Undercut my prices until all my customers leave, then bring their prices back up once I'm in the poorhouse."

"Isn't there any relation you could stay with while you work?" Agathe asked. Gesturing to Emma to bring Margarethe a cup of tea while she mopped Margarethe's face with her handkerchief as though she were a child.

Margarethe shook her head. "Papa was an only child. Mama had some family in Altenburg, but it's been years since I heard from any of them."

Emma came back carrying a mug. "Well I don't see why a woman can't run a business on her own if she's good enough at it. Or why a woman *has* to marry. I'm happy to have Bert, don't get me wrong, but I'll always wonder what *I* could have done on my own. Papa, what about that woman in Bamberg? The Ram printer? She defied the guild."

"She had a powerful political movement behind her by the time it came to that. Unfortunately, Margarethe doesn't. What do you think, Gus?"

Gus rubbed his head. "As I see it there are three choices. First Margarethe marries Rolf Gench as soon as his apprenticeship is over."

Christoph stiffened. "I know Rolf. He's a fool and a bully. There's a reason why his parents haven't been able to arrange a marriage for him yet."

Gus waved Christoph's comments away. "Second, Margarethe continues to run her seamstress business until the guild shuts her down. Hopefully by then the doll business will have taken off and it won't matter. The third option, if you want to find a better husband than Rolf Gench, and that wouldn't be hard..."

Christoph sat up in his chair, smoothed his hose and pulled his doublet down. Emma and Agathe noticed and exchanged smiles.

"...is to stop sewing clothes and concentrate on the dolls. The tailor's guild doesn't have jurisdiction over them, in fact as far as I know no guild regulates doll-making."

"But what happens if the dolls don't take off? And how do I live in the meantime? If I refuse Rolf Gench, his father may go to the town council and find a way to make me leave town. And I can't accept him and then call off if the doll business does well..."

Tears formed again in Margarethe's eyes and Agathe motioned for a clean handkerchief.

"I have an idea."

Everyone looked at Bert, surprised since he rarely spoke.

"Emma and I could rent Margarethe's house and she could live with us or with my parents. It will buy us time to find a good lawyer."

Gus put his hands on his hips. "And just where do you plan to get the money to rent a house? And what happens to the three of you if this business doesn't succeed?"

Bert set his mouth in a tight line. "We'll cross that bridge when we come to it, Papa. But I'm not going to abandon a friend."

Lukas Gench didn't expect the hearing to take long. He *was* the head of the Tailor's Guild and member of the town council, a man of influence in the duchy. And if that wasn't enough, he'd made sure to send an exquisite bolt of his finest cloth and a silver cup to the magistrate. Once he had Margarethe's inheritance and her share in the fledgling doll business it would be easy to repay the Jew money lenders, not only for the money to bribe the magistrate, but for his other debts.

"Master Gench, please present your case."

Lukas bowed and swaggered forward. "Mein Herr, Margarethe Klein is an unmarried orphan, currently residing in this town and holding herself out as a member of the Tailor's Guild. It is my duty as a friend of her late honored father and the head of the guild to see this situation righted. I insist that Mistress Klein be placed under my guardianship so that a proper marriage may be made for her so that she is no longer styling herself as a tailor."

The magistrate nodded and Lukas permitted himself a triumphant smile at Margarethe who sat with Masters Wolf and Brumme and their families on the opposite side of the aisle.

Then the town's Swiss-born lawyer, Walter Boose stood. "Mein Herr, if I may?"

The magistrate nodded again and Boose approached him with a sheaf of documents.

"As you can see, in the Year of Our Lord, Sixteen Hundred and Thirty-Four, Calvin Klein, master of the Tailor's Guild, applied for and was granted, legal emancipation for his only daughter, Margarethe. As you know, Mein Herr, this law grants a woman the legal rights of a man..."

"Yes, I know. Hmmm. These documents do seem to

be in order... Master Gench, do you have any proof that these documents are false?"

"I do not, Mein Herr. I had no idea such documents existed!" It was a lie of course, but since Lukas figured he was on the side of the angels putting that girl in her proper place, it wouldn't matter. Why didn't the magistrate just rule in his favor as he was supposed to?

The magistrate sighed and continued flipping through the documents. Finally he looked up.

"Well...these could be forgeries..."

Lukas glanced at his opponents, not quite able to suppress a smile of triumph. Victory, vindication! Perhaps he ought to have that engraved on a plaque for the wedding...

"Mein Herr! As you can see, the seals of the notary..."

The magistrate nodded. "Still it is highly improper for a young woman to live alone..."

"Mistress Klein is not residing alone." With a flourish, the lawyer presented the magistrate with another wad of paper. "As you can see, Mistress Klein is currently renting a portion of her home to Master Albert Brumme and his wife, an upstanding young couple. Also, there is an affidavit from Mistress Klein's pastor stating that she is a regular attendee at church and..."

Lukas felt his elation disappear. Why hadn't he thought of bribing the pastor as well? It would have meant more money he'd had to borrow against the girl's inheritance...

"Hmmm...well..." The magistrate looked over the pile of evidence that had accumulated on the table. "I need time to review all this evidence in detail.

Yes. Great detail. And consult a few people. Master Gench deserves time to review the evidence himself, and perhaps see counsel. Yes, yes. Time. One month."

Lukas smirked at Margarethe, assessing her as Emma Wolf guided her out of the room. So she'd thought to win easily had she? *Well, well. A stalemate is better than a failure, at least for me.* He'd been right that this hearing wouldn't take long...

"Monstrous! Simply monstrous! That man ought to be ashamed of himself!"

"He smells profit, Agathe, profit he and his family can collect without effort on their part. Those *pandores* have made us a modest profit and we've started getting orders from the catalogs we sold with them. The little ones Emma calls 'farthing' dolls are beginning to pick up too. And once the farmers start producing a wood Barbie replica, we stand to make a fortune if all goes well. And let's not forget Calvin's house and equipment. She may not be a catch for a noble family, but for us she's quite an heiress."

"Then why have you prevented Christoph from making an offer? I told you when Master Gench started this whole thing what we should have done. If Bert and Emma hadn't moved in with her, those Genches would have swallowed the poor girl and her fortune up by now."

"And I told you, Agathe, I want to be sure this doll-making venture didn't ruin us. It still could. And then what would we do with an extra mouth to feed?"

Agathe put her hands on her hips, anger making her face red. "We would have a hard-working daughter-in-law with enough skills to help keep us afloat. I want you to announce that you have taken care of the matter by arranging her marriage to Christoph. And if you don't, Julius Wolf, I swear I will!"

Margarethe was crying as Christoph led her into the workroom. Silently, he sat beside her and offered his handkerchief, which she took with a sniff.

"They haven't made a judgment yet, and even if they rule for Master Gench, Papa and Master Brumme can appeal to the duke."

Margarethe mopped her eyes and shook her head. "The duke will never listen. I suppose I could sign everything over to your papa and run away, but Master Gench would find me and force me to marry his son."

Christoph reached out and brushed a strand of hair away from her face. "Margarethe, I have a present for you."

"Oh? For me?"

"Two presents actually, one from Papa and the other from me."

Gently, he opened a cloth bag and pulled out a large hank of angora wool, dyed a soft blonde. "I know you ordered this from the crayon profits, but Mama told Papa she'd never forgive him if he charged . . . well . . . family. The salesman called the color 'Kristina Blond' so he was sure it was the right color."

Margarethe stroked the soft wool in amazement, her tears slowing. "Ohhh! Christoph! It's perfect! Softer than I could ever imagine! But you said *you* had a present for me?"

Smiling he handed her a box. Opening it, Margarethe stared. Lying in the box were two wooden dolls, one boy and one girl.

"I . . . I made them special. With the knob joints in the arms and legs like Emma's . . . I painted them too . . . I know the hair is only paint . . ."

"Oh . . . Christoph! They're exquisite! I don't know what to say!"

"Say you'll marry me, and not just to avoid Rolf Gench. Though it would be a massive blow to me if you preferred him. I want a room full of dolls and little girls of our very own to play with them."

Margarethe smiled. "And what if we have boys?"

"We could always expand the business into toy soldiers. But first we have to do a little promotion."

Magdeburg Palace security, plagued by crackpot religious fanatics, spies, and an ever-widening circle of foreign and native enemies, were pleasantly surprised to find that the package contained not a bomb, but an eighteen-inch doll of Princess Kristina holding a miniature Brillo doll and a note:

TO HER ROYAL HIGHNESS
FROM M. KLEIN & COMPANY, FASHION DOLLS

Epilogue

"Hurry up! Get that wagon loaded and going!"

"Lukas, calm down!" Hilda Gench placed her arm on her husband's, trying to calm him, but he shook it off.

"Hilda, be silent and get that useless son of yours out here! We need to get out of town as soon as possible!"

"But there's no reason . . ."

"Of course there's reason, fool woman! Were you

deaf when you heard the pastor read the banns for the Wolf boy and the Klein girl? Well, if you did, then you also remember the loans I took to try and get that girl for our boy! Money to bribe the other guild masters, money for the magistrate, not to mention our other debts! If we don't get out of town *right now*, we're done for!"

Hilda whimpered as Lukas raised a meaty hand toward her. "But Lukas..."

"*Go!*"

"Men coming," Rolf called from where he slouched in the doorway.

Toward the end of the street, Lukas saw men dressed in the uniforms of the town guard riding toward the house. Ignoring his wife and son, he clambered onto the wagon and grabbed the reins. "I'll write from Prague!"

Orlando Delivers

Sarah Hays and Terry Howard

On the road to Augsburg, late May 1636

"Stare all'erta!" the caravan lookout cried, as bandits boiled out of ravines on either side of the trail. "We are attacked! Robbers! Bandits!"

Orlando Rosalez glanced first one way then the other. Neither direction offered escape; ahead of him lay just over half the caravan, behind him the rest. The bandits would arrive before he could get away. From the left he counted four; from the right half a dozen, but those had twice as far to run before they reached him. He concentrated on the nearer group, hearing his father's voice in his memory.

"When the bandits come, run. When you cannot run, fight." As a pair of the caravanner's hired guards stepped up to block the oncoming foursome, Orlando listened to his father's remembered voice: *"Fight just long enough to get away, son."*

The caravan guards' advance delayed the four

brigands. Orlando's wheel-lock pistol, steadied over the back of his donkey, went off in a blast of choking smoke; he never knew whether he hit the man he'd aimed at or not. He pocketed the empty pistol, out of habit, on the saddle and drew his rapier.

The thickest smoke didn't so much clear as split open, showing him an oncoming giant bearing a club raised overhead in both hands. If it connected, Orlando had no doubt he'd be driven into the ground.

"Hell," said Adolfo Rosalez de Circassia in his son's memory, *"needs fuel, son. That's why Adonai made so many Gentiles. When all you can do is die, an angel will guide you home. Take as many of the sons of dogs with you as you can, eh?"*

Adolfo, three years ago, had taken four with him.

"I guess it's my turn to see what an angel looks like, Papa," the young Jew murmured, stepping quickly forward inside the blow and turning sideways to meet his foe.

The club came whistling down, but by the time it landed Orlando's head had moved. The blow glanced off its moving target, striking instead the top of his shoulder, driving him to his knees. Orlando thrust the blade of his rapier before him as he fell. It went through his opponent's belly.

With a cry he fell, his heavy body covering Orlando from view. His club hit Orlando's thigh with all his weight behind it. But Orlando didn't feel the pain; he wouldn't know about that injury, or the slice above his ear, or his dislocated shoulder, until he could be wakened. First the caravan guards had to drive off the rest of the brigands, then they had to find Orlando. Then they had to figure out he hadn't been killed, and get the body of the bandit off him.

Then they had to wait for him to wake up.

"Tell Jano he's coming around."

Orlando opened his eyes. Above him stood the owner of the caravan he had joined to cross the Alps. Hostility and anger boiled off a man usually noted as tranquil and uncommonly reasonable. "What did you have on your ass," he demanded, "that got three of my men killed?"

"What?" Orlando asked, puzzled.

"Three of my men are dead. Once the bandits made off with your ass they fled," Jano snarled. "What were you carrying? Gold? Gems? Had you mentioned valuables I would have charged you for extra guards. Now your treasure is gone, three of my men are dead and seven more wounded, and it's all your fault! What did you have?"

"A book."

"A book? Was it covered in gold and studded with gemstones?"

Orlando started to shake his head. Pain stopped him. He started to shrug. Pain stopped him. He settled for speaking softly: "A rich man, an American up-timer in Augsburg, just bought this book from a dealer in Venice. I'm delivering it."

"You're hand-carrying a *book* to Augsburg, from Italy?" Jano began to yell. "You do not hand-deliver *just a book*!"

Orlando protested, "It *is* just a book. In the up-timers' world something happened to make this book special. Now, here, it is just a book—a beautiful book, and one of a kind, but nothing more."

The caravan master's jaw worked. "So much trouble for just a book?"

"Well," Orlando conceded, "Some people screamed bloody murder because the dealer sold it to a Gentile." He didn't add many others had screamed the book should be destroyed, nor how the doge of Venice had what he believed to be the original safely deposited in his library. Orlando doubted the notion of abomination and blasphemy as surely as he knew the doge possessed only a copy. "At least two or three cardinals want it. A dozen more people would want it if they knew about it."

"So you brought this *book* on my caravan?" Then he glanced at the man treating Orlando's wounds. "How is it?"

The man laughed. "He's not cut. Just one whopper of a bruise."

"Can he walk?" the caravan master asked.

"Sure, he can walk. It's going to be very sore and he might limp, but not much."

Glancing back to Orlando, the caravan master said, "I've got all the injured I can carry. Walk, or stay here."

Before the caravan master could stalk off, the guards' captain came up on a horse. Jano shifted his gaze to this target. "Yes?"

"You're right," the man said flatly. "Alfredo's band attacked us. But you knew to watch for them, when you didn't find his man waiting in the usual place to be paid off. The party with the ass went one way, the rest of the band another. I got a good look at them going over the ridgeline, Alfredo bringing up the rear."

"I hoped he'd retired." Jano sighed. "Move out. We've got lost time to make up for."

The guard looking at Orlando's thigh helped pull him up. "Here," the fellow said, handing Orlando the club, "you'll need a walking stick. If I was you I'd keep the thing as a good luck charm."

Somewhere in an Apennine pass, a few days later

Orlando sighed, sliding from his saddle. He slipped his mule's bit to let the beast drink, and stepped upstream to dip a pan into the water for himself. Orlando hadn't stayed with Jano's caravan. He wanted to follow the thieves' trail in its freshest hours. He bought a pair of horses from the guards, and took off on an overpriced horse in his travel-worn boots. When his horses wore out, he'd traded for a mule and the other supplies he'd need to travel light. He'd no idea where this trail might lead; a mule did much better over rough ground than a horse.

Orlando glanced at the sky and saw three stars, marking the official start of the Sabbath. He whispered a promise to say a prayer later and spoke to the mule.

"At least you can rest awhile." He hobbled it to graze while he made himself a meal. Not bothering with a large open fire, he struck a spark from flint and steel and teased the frayed edge of charred rag wick in the little brass lamp he had purchased at the caravansary to flame.

While he waited for the water to boil he murmured a prayer. Once the water boiled he divided it, leaving a little in the pan to keep warm against the needs of washing-up.

Orlando finished his meal then cleaned and packed away his gear, and glanced at the moon. Perhaps an hour had elapsed since he'd set the mule to graze. He wanted to give the sentry, if his quarry had set such a precaution, about that much longer to grow inattentive. He opened his saddlebag and drew out his cloak, turned its darker lining to the outside, and wrapped it around himself. He slipped off his boots to rest his stocking feet among rocks still warm from the cooking lamp.

Some time later he woke, feet now cold. A glance at the moon showed he'd slept longer than he'd meant to; but the night's clear sky provided enough visibility to find the mule. He undid the hobbles, replaced his saddle, and convinced the mule to accept the bit so he could lead his mount as he approached his target.

So, they'd posted a sentry. But Orlando's patience paid off: the man leaned against a tree, head on his chest, softly snoring. Orlando looped the mule's rein over a branch. He crept quietly round where the four travelers' horses had been tied up for the night, and carefully slipped the long rope looped through all their headstalls from its moorings. He'd hoped to find his ass on this picket line, to no avail. Orlando led the picket string down to the creek, pulled off all their tack, and left them to graze or roam as they pleased. Within a quarter hour he'd deprived the horses' riders of their use and come back to the camp where the sentry still sat, fast asleep.

Orlando studied the fire-lit circle. The sentry's blanket lay empty on the fire's far side; beside it he could see another, snugly wrapped over a slim shape. No packages there; the sleeper nearest him had similarly taken full advantage of his meager bedding. The fourth form sprawled, half-on, half-under, a cloak instead of a blanket. He turned to the saddles; the first boasted no bags at all, but a pouch looped over the horn, too small for the prize Orlando sought. The second lacked even so little room for cargo. The third bore a bundle.

Slipping quietly around the camp, Orlando reached the saddle and cut the thin leather string holding the bundle, slipped the covering off, and grinned. A moment later he'd secured it across his back; another moment sufficed to ensure he left nothing valuable on the last saddle.

Orlando slipped away, worked his way quietly back to the mule, and departed in the moonlight, thoroughly pleased. He walked a hundred paces before he swung into the saddle.

Not wanting to attempt the passage over the mountains alone, Orlando continued south. Picking up another caravan or even returning to Venice seemed like a good idea. He did not wish to make another mistake; his last had nearly ended up killing him. He'd stolen back his book from people who'd already shown themselves ready to risk life, limb or prison.

The moon set; beneath his saddle the mule slowed, not out of a normal reluctance to work but genuine weariness. Orlando took stock of his surroundings. Half a mile behind him the trail he rode clung to the edge of the mountain like a burr to a homespun stocking; before him, it narrowed.

On his right the slope spun down steeply into blackness. To his left a fold in the face of the stones led upward. Orlando slid out of his saddle and cinched the strings of his prize more tightly, then led the mule into the defile. A couple of mule-lengths from the trail, he looped the rein over a stubby branch, turning back to check for tracks. With a wisp of brush he erased the marks of his passage away from the well-traveled route. Presently the mule began to reach toward nearby graze.

"It's too soon. Come on," Orlando said, and led the mule upward again. When he could see over the peak, at least partially, he drew a breath. No one, canny soldiers of fortune or otherwise, waited there. A boulder twice his height marked the shoulder of the slope; he circled it, silently, one careful step at a time. No one waited on the far side. The view he had from here, of the valley below and the trail across it, would take a man's breath away in daylight, Orlando thought. By starlight, he could tell only that so far, at least, he and the mule had the place to themselves... except for the wildlife.

The boulder sheltered a hollow a little wider than Orlando's outstretched arms, perhaps twice as tall as a man on muleback; from the hillside wall ran a fast trickle of water, collecting where it had worn away the stone. Overhead a sleepy-sounding bird complained as Orlando led the mule into the space, but finding them harmless, subsided. Past the crevice between boulder and mountainside, a little hollow opened toward the stars; it might reach twenty feet long and half again as wide, its walls barely less than straight-up cliffs. Knee-deep grass covered its floor.

Orlando hobbled the mule, parked himself in the narrowest part of the entryway, unrolled his cloak and murmured a lengthy and apologetic prayer.

☆   ☆   ☆

Twelve days and nights of similar travel, daring difficult passages to avoid roads where ambushes could be set, ensued. Orlando came to think of the mule with some affection; it proved a faithful beast of burden, if not a companionable one. Seeing the valley below, Orlando understood why the longer, steeper, less-traveled route existed.

"Well," he told the mule. "A few hours more, and you'll have a stall, with water and grain and somebody to brush you. A bit of luck and you might even get to stay there three or four nights, eh?" The mule, after the manner of its kind, did not answer. Fallow fields, vacant towns and weathered bones, presumably left by plague, explained the empty trail. Orlando rode onward. "Might be I've mistaken our chances," he told the mule. "We could have to do without a stall or bed again tonight."

Crossing two more ridges, he left the devastated valley behind before coming to a run-down inn.

"A Jew's money spends as well as a Gentile's," the gray, work-worn host said flatly. "I'd as lief take yours as not. Custom's not easy come by, lad. My business has been slow since the last full moon."

Curiously, Orlando said, "What makes you think I'm a Jew?"

"Cut of your clothes, boy," the man lied. The tale of the Jew with golden book full of treasure maps, worth a fortune to any prince of the true church, had made its way even here. "Either you're a Jew or you stole them from a Jew. You don't have the manner of a thief."

Orlando left his mule with the lass in the stable, then trod cautiously inward. A group of young men carried on over bowls of stew and mugs of...something...passing hunks of dark bread to one another and carving thick slices from a slab of cheese in a platter on the bar.

"Buy an ale, stranger," advised the slightest of the customers. "Bread and cheese come with."

"All right."

The crowd studied him a little more carefully after he let a small coin fall on the bar with a chiming sound. A woman who might've been the innkeeper's wife—or sister—picked up the coin. "Help yourself," she said, handing him a bowl. "Stew's on the hearth. I'll bring your ale to your table."

He nodded, and then used his dagger on the cheese. He cut a triangular slice, broke it in half and tucked it into his bowl. The stew had onions, garlic, and bits of something green in the gravy with the long-cooked, soft white beans. Orlando tore half his fist-sized hunk of bread into bits and stirred them in.

The woman brought him a wooden mug. Cautiously, he sipped; the taste ran like fire down his throat. He ate, sipping as he went, rationing his bread to match the drink and stew, until bowl and mug held no more. Then he set his dishes down.

"Thanks," he murmured to the stable-girl, now waiting on his table. She dimpled at him, a child of ten or maybe twelve.

"Welcome," she said. "The mule's fed and brushed and watered, like you asked."

"Thanks. Where will I find my night's lodging?"

"Upstairs," she said. "I'm to show you when you're ready. Mika'll see to the others."

"I'm ready now," Orlando said quietly.

The girl led him up a narrow, winding stair to a sturdy planked door, pulled a string and shoved her hip against the edge. One long wall sported three short shelves, ranging up from waist-height; a basin and jug stood on the lowest. The next one up lay bare; the third, not much more than a handsbreadth wide, sported an oil lamp. The girl offered him a candle.

"Haven't had oil for the lamps for a spell, but the chandler down the way sells these cheap," she said. Gravely, Orlando thanked her. "The latch works on a string. You'll need to loop it over this hook if you don't want anyone disturbing you." He nodded, watching her demonstrate. "Now if there's nothing else you need... Oh, under the bed's a necessary," she said. "See you downstairs in the morning, then."

With a sketch of a curtsey, she fled. Orlando tied his latchstring tightly.

What he wanted most in all the world amounted to a long hot bath and a good night's sleep, but he doubted he'd have either until he'd delivered the book to his cousin's buyer in Augsburg. He finished his prayers, hung his saddlebags from the wall-hook, and considered the bed. It actually didn't have visible bugs writhing in the wrinkles of the blankets; indeed, he couldn't smell anything vile on the bedclothes. He moved the candle for a better examination, ignoring a knock at his door.

"Faith," he murmured to the night. "No bugs at all?" He studied the rest of the room's furnishings: four hooks in the wall by the door, the (for a wonder, empty) necessary vessel under the bed, a curtain he could drop over the window by undoing a string, and what looked for all the world like a washcloth and towel, rolled up neatly on the shelf behind the basin and pitcher. And the pitcher, when he checked, actually held warm water! "Well, well, well," he said tiredly. "I believe I'll have a night's rest, anyhow. A bit of a wash-up won't hurt, either."

Another knock came at the door. Orlando sighed. "What is it?"

"Did you want anything else tonight, mister?" The voice didn't sound like the stable-maid's, nor the woman who'd brought ale to his table.

"More water, in a bit," he said. "I'll set the pitcher out."

"All right," the voice answered. Orlando grinned. She sounded disappointed.

One of the little pouches in his saddlebags provided him a lump of soap the size and shape of an egg, his razor, and a comb. He lathered the soap, then tackled his ablutions, a hint of a reckless grin on his face as he worked, glad he'd first seen the too-young stable-girl and the too-old crone of a common-room hostess. Otherwise he'd have hoped for a little easy company, perhaps.

Twice Orlando emptied soapy water from the ewer and wrung out the cloth before he felt he'd done his best to clean himself. Wiping out the basin with the rag last, Orlando wound the towel around his waist, knotting it at a catty-cornered fold. It flapped against his thighs, eight inches above his knees. He rinsed the basin, put away his tools, and poured the last of the clean water into his own mug. Then he untied the string to set the pitcher on the landing.

Out of the shadows stepped a girl, her eyes as big as saucers. She wore a shift so thin he could nearly see through it. Not the stable-lass, this girl might have been her sister. Now she asked, "Can I do anything for you?"

"I want more water," Orlando said. "Is there a laundress here?"

"Mika does our washing. Tomorrow is the regular day," the girl said. "Do you want clothes cleaned? I can take them down to her for you."

He bundled his slops and hose into his shirt. "These, then, if you please," he said. "Once they're dry I'll be on my way."

She reached out, running one hand along the muscle of his arm as she took the bundle with the other. "I wish you could stay longer with us."

He laughed gently. "I am a man working for another. My time is not my own, but if it were I might stay... with you."

She pulled the clothes against her chest. "I might like that."

He watched her bend to lift the pitcher, the outlines of her body barely hidden by the shift... and nearly didn't see the club whistling toward his head. For the next little while things moved very fast. In the room's half-shadows, Orlando didn't recognize the face of the man pushing in, but he couldn't miss the glint of a blade. The thug's rush bore him back beyond the bed, where he could not reach his own sword.

He slammed his own head into the face of the man who'd tried to stab him. With a cry the fellow fell back and dropped the dagger. Orlando did not dare look for it, for the assassin grabbed Orlando's own sword and swung it blindly like a club. It hit nothing but one stone wall of the tiny room; its wielder cursed as the blow reverberated into his hands and arms.

Desperately, Orlando yanked the curtain down from the arrow-slit, swinging the slender pole like a mace on the end of the ragged material; far more by luck than design, the stick struck his attacker in the eye. The man fell toward Orlando, who shifted his grip from the rag to the branch, his motion from a swing to a stab, and drove the end of the curtain rod into the man's eye. A strangled scream followed; Orlando twisted his grip, breaking the stick. The man kept screaming, unable to do more.

Fueled by desperation, Orlando grabbed his fallen sword and turned to face the new flickering light in the doorway. He found himself staring straight at the innkeeper. The startled man held a light, expecting to greet the triumphant young tough from his dining room. He'd depended on his lamp for light to finish Orlando's murder. Now the innkeeper's eyes went wide.

"Please," the man got out, ashen-faced and white-lipped, "please, good sir, I heard a noise and came to see. That's all. I had nothing to do with this. You must believe me."

"Sure. Help me get this—" Orlando kicked the writhing blinded body at his feet "—out the door to close it. Set the lamp down. You'll need both hands."

The landlord stooped to set down the light. Orlando brought the pommel of his rapier down on the back of the man's head. Still filled with rage and adrenaline, he turned to the girl who'd played the bait. The girl had curled up in a tight ball on the landing, whimpering softly around her thumb.

He jerked a handful of her hair hard; her whimpering ended, replaced with a scream of fear as high-pitched and primal as anything Neanderthals once heard in the caves across the valley. Still she continued to hug her shins tightly with both arms, trying to hang onto the comfort of a fetal ball even though he more than half lifted her from the floor.

She'd played the bait, a knowing accomplice. Had the night's events gone her way she'd have helped murder him. Yet the fear on her face, the total lack of comprehension in her blank blue eyes, her insistence on retreating into a world he could not see, hit him like a torrent off a mountain glacier.

The girl's desirability vanished. He dropped her head. She tucked it against her knees, once again found her thumb, and went back to whimpering.

Orlando dressed, collected his things and headed to the stable. He saw not a soul anywhere. He saddled his mule while apologizing and promising it a good long rest as soon as a safe place could be found.

"Wait," said a voice at his back.

Orlando spun, drawing his rapier. At its point stood the lass who'd tended his mule—and by the look of the beast she hadn't done a half-bad job.

"Whatever for?" he asked with some of the viciousness he had directed toward the older girl.

"If you leave now the men who left earlier will ambush you," she said. "That's what they did to my father and brother. Mika is my mother's uncle's widow—when he died she hired my father to run the inn. When we came here to work for her, these men . . . killed my father and my brother. I watched them beat my mother to death outside the kitchen when she tried to stop them raping Luna."

He looked at her. "Luna?"

"My sister," the stable-girl said. "They made her pretend she wants to sleep with you. They planned to kill you while she had you distracted."

"The one who came to my room tonight won't do such things anymore," Orlando said calmly. "I'm sorry about your family."

The girl lifted her chin. "Call me Salome. You're Orlando, the Circassian. Right?"

"How do you know my name?"

"I heard them talking about you. Orlando the Circassian and his golden book full of treasure maps."

"Great. That story's probably been told in every caravansary in the Alps by now." Orlando let out a deep sigh. "I won't be able to show my face anywhere."

"If we meet anyone," she said, "best we have some story to tell, that sounds the same no matter which of us they ask. Luna's sick; I'm taking care of her and you're helping us get to my uncle in Innsbruck."

"The truth, as far as it goes. All right, then. My name is Orlando—Orlando Rosalez, from Circassia. Son of Jaime Adolfo Rosalez, the caravan master, at your service," he said, with a slight, mocking bow. "I still don't know why I should trust you."

"Luna cries in her sleep and talks of Father as if he will return any day now. She only gets up when they beat her. She . . . they hurt her," Salome said, "badly. She's weak and like a baby sometimes. You're the first traveler who's stopped here and lived out the night since my father died. I thought I could get help from the first large group to stop, but there hasn't been any. The word seems to have spread. Doesn't anybody care?"

Orlando listened.

"You can get out over the mountain and down to the caravan route by the back way. But I want to go with you."

"How would you know about the mountain trails?" Orlando asked.

"I don't. Otto does."

"Otto?" Orlando asked.

"Here," a voice came from the hay loft. Orlando glanced up and a boy about the same age as Salome climbed down. "My grandmother is the cook here."

Salome said, "Before those men killed his parents, Otto's papa ran the stables here. I found Otto in the hayloft—I hid there too, the night they beat Mama to death. I stole food for him, and for me, until Mika caught me."

Orlando sheathed the rapier.

"I didn't tell her he's here. We talked about running away, but he doesn't want to leave me behind and I won't leave Luna here."

"Why didn't you go alone?" Orlando asked the boy.

"I don't think I can make it," Otto said. "I don't know how to fight."

"How do you know the trails?"

"Papa took me hunting," Otto answered, "a lot of times. After the plague, business got bad. If we wanted meat to eat we had to hunt."

Orlando nodded. "So what's different, now?"

"You can fight. If those men come after us, you'll stop them." The boy's complete confidence in him flattered Orlando. Charmed, he found himself not wanting to disappoint the lad.

He said, "I'm leaving now. If you're ready you can come with me. If you're not you can stay here—"

Salome interrupted, "I'm ready now, but Luna is still upstairs. It'll take me a few minutes to get her down."

"I won't wait. She helped them try to murder me tonight. You're lucky—I left her alive. I'm not taking any chances on her."

"We can't just leave her," the girl said.

Orlando said, "She's . . . not quite right. How will she handle the journey?"

"She's not dead yet," Salome said, pleading. "But she will be, as soon as those two men get back with their friends. They'll kill us both if you don't take us with you now."

"Go get her dressed, then," Orlando said, disgusted with himself for being softhearted. "Let's go."

Otto chose trails barely visible, when they could be seen at all.

Orlando quickly dismissed all thought of riding his mule. More than once Otto led where even a mountain goat would not have gone. Salome, burdened by Luna, scarcely seemed aware of where she trod. When Luna stumbled, missed her footing and fell, Orlando lifted her into the saddle. Salome crawled up behind her to hold her in place.

Several times Orlando, despite having a guide, felt sure he would fall off the face of the mountain. Without a guide he would never have found his way even in the daylight; even with one, after the moon set, he feared every step along the precipitous route.

"Are you sure you know these hills?"

"We hunted all over them," Otto said. "There's a place ahead where shepherds stop when they move the herds. The trail widens. There's trees and grass there."

"We'll stop," Orlando said firmly. "The mule's tired."

No knots of livestock dotted the slope when they arrived. Even Otto had trouble staying on his feet by the time they reached the shelter the few dozen thin-trunked evergreens offered. The mule snorted, shoving its muzzle into the pool of water in the middle of the grove. Orlando let the beast drink its fill; Salome sank down in the thick cover of needles with Luna below the nearest tree, dull-eyed and silent.

When daylight woke him, Orlando studied their surroundings. The three children lay huddled together like puppies trying to keep warm. His mule, a few yards away, cropped grass with more energy than the beast had shown for days along the trail.

The youngsters gave no sign of waking. Orlando built a tiny fire, then toasted some of the bread. The smell finally seemed to rouse his companions. Salome took bread out of a bag on her shoulder, then showed him a bota. He shook his head; she shrugged and dripped ale into Luna's mouth, waking her.

The mule drank and ate again; Orlando cleaned his gear and packed it away. As they started back out, the trail climbed, narrowing.

They stopped to rest often through that day and night at any place wide enough and flat enough, especially if it had a bit of grass. They walked over trails a horse could not navigate. When they stumbled, exhausted, onto the main trail, Orlando turned south.

"No," Salome said. "We must go north. You're known to be traveling south and they will look for you there. Besides, I have an uncle in Innsbruck."

"Innsbruck is out of my way."

She snorted. "Staying alive is never out of the way."

"All right. But we stop as soon as we find a suitable spot—my mule is nearly as tired as you. Let's find somewhere out of sight. We'll rest until moonrise. Do you have anything to eat?"

"The last of Mika's bread, from the inn," answered Salome. "Ale, too."

They found a small, mostly hidden clearing. By then Orlando himself wanted to rest and eat. They stayed put through the rest of the morning and into the late afternoon. Near dusk Luna woke from a nap, screaming, frightened of the unfamiliar surroundings, alerting Orlando. The younger sister calmed the elder.

"Shut her up!" Orlando said. "And we might as well go on, after all that noise she made!"

But before they could return to the trail, a handful of men went by in a rush. Salome clapped a hand over Luna's mouth as her sister's eyes went wide in recognition.

"That's them," Otto said, running back from a hiding place near the trail. "They're looking for us."

In the next village, the inn sounded rowdy.

Luna recognized the voices of her tormentors, forcing Salome to muffle her sister's mouth again. When Orlando approached the kitchen door to buy bread and cheese, the innkeeper hesitated, glancing back over his shoulder at the noisy crowd within.

He looked likely to refuse until he spied Otto with the girls. "Otto?"

"Yes, Herr Hess?"

"How are your parents, lad?"

"Killed, sir," the boy returned. "By the men in your common room."

At these words the innkeeper hissed to his wife. "A cheese and four loaves of bread. Hurry!"

"Can we buy a horse?" Orlando asked.

"Otto, at the far end of the stable . . . my oldest nag and an older saddle. Quick, now—saddle up and begone." Again he glanced at the noise in the common room as if he could see through the kitchen wall.

"I can hold Luna on the horse in front of me. You and Salome ride the mule," Orlando said. "We need to be elsewhere, and we're in a hurry."

They went on, traveling mostly by night, resting from daybreak until sunset. Orlando bought provisions along the way, sparingly. Luna burdened the horse a little less every day, just as the pack on the mule grew lighter.

Innsbruck, August 1636

As twilight gathered, Salome led the horse through the streets to her uncle's place. Once there, she handed the reins to Orlando, who had been leading the mule, and went inside. Otto stayed on the horse to hold a half-conscious Luna in the saddle.

The kitchen door burst open and a small crowd poured out.

"Damnation," a large stout fellow bellowed at Orlando.

"Wait, Uncle Paul!" Salome practically hung off her uncle's upraised hand as Orlando turned to look at them, dropping a hand to his rapier.

"I came out to cuss you soundly for treating my nieces so foully," the burly man said. "But I've seen men three days dead who looked better than you."

Orlando blinked.

"Even on a horse, she looks more dead than alive," Paul went on. "Hermina, help me get Luna down," he turned to his wife, "and you get her to bed." His wife, a woman the same age but not so broken-down as Mika by far, obeyed with quick hands and a look of pity at her niece. "Someone get these poor mistreated animals into the barn and looked after! Sarah, take the young man's gear to the good room upstairs." Turning back to Orlando, Paul clapped him on the shoulder. "And you, sir, need a meal. You're as dead on your feet as Salome. We'll find you a bath and a bed."

Through bowls of thick stew and stout bread, Salome's family left Orlando in peace. When he finished bathing, someone else's clothes awaited him, his own having been whisked away for washing, although the laundress allowed that some of them really ought to just be burned. Dressed enough for indoor public spaces, he let a maid lead him to his room; there he fell on the bed, and did not stir until sometime after noon. Upon waking he found the chamber pot, then the kitchen.

While he ate, Luna's uncle came in.

"So you're back from the dead, are you? You'll be happy to hear Luna's awake. She's resting. She even remembers her last visit here." Paul's voice grew quiet. "Though she talks like it happened yesterday. She sounds as if she's still that little girl I remember, as if what happened never took place."

He paused. "Salome told us everything, including how she thinks you came to be at that inn alone. My family owes you a debt."

Orlando shook his head. "I'd have never gotten

out of that place without Salome's help. Give Otto a place, send Mika help, and we'll call it even."

"I hate to rush you on your way, but I need to tell the duke's men about the murders. If you're still here, they could hold you up. They might take an interest in that book everyone in the carrying trade is talking about."

Orlando grinned. "I see the rumors are still swifter than I am."

"Could I see it? Is it really covered in gold?" Paul sounded wistful. "Is it true it's written in a language only the Americans from the future can read, and that's why no one else found the treasure maps?"

Orlando snorted. "It's written in ordinary Hebrew. Doesn't have any maps in it at all, never mind treasure maps. Of course it's one of a kind and it's very beautiful; but if this up-timer hadn't wanted it, the previous owner could never have sold it for a tithe the price."

"Why did the up-timer want it, then?"

"My boss says he took a notion for it because, in the world he came from, something happened to make this book very famous, and worth a lot of money. That's not going to happen now, but the up-timer still wants the book. There, he could never have owned it, even as rich as he is, because of how famous it became, and what a price it could fetch. Here, he can have it for a fraction of that cost."

Orlando stretched. "I'll show it to you. Can you find me a good horse and a decent saddle to take the place of the nag that carried Luna here? I'll pay for the horse, if it isn't too much; I'm afraid my traveling money is about gone."

Paul shushed him. "What you've done for my brother's children is pay enough, if you want to leave the nag and the mule."

"Hang onto the mule for me. I'll pick it up on my way back to Venice. I've grown oddly fond of the beast."

The innkeeper nodded. "You can leave in the morning. Otto will guide the duke's men back to the inn to see after the old woman there."

Augsburg, a week later

"Were there problems on the trip?" Avram Ben Rubi, head of the Augsburg firm who handled local business matters for the Abrabanels, knew Orlando's journey had been anything but smooth. Every caravansary from one side of the Alps to the other buzzed with one tale or another. A good tale travels faster than any other freight. Many tales had taken wing along Orlando's route.

"Nothing I couldn't handle," a very confident courier answered proudly, refusing to admit that he'd almost lost the package at least three times and nearly got killed twice in the bargain.

"Well, it's good you're not early. Word arrived from Venice three days ago. They want you to bring it back to Venice," Avram said, in a firm, serious, senior-partner voice.

"Back to Venice!" Orlando didn't, quite, shout. "I've been clubbed, stabbed, shot at, and beaten for this book, and now you want me to take it back to Venice? I've gone without sleep for more nights than I can remember, starved and freezing! I've been robbed and nearly killed in order to protect this priceless relic, this precious, one-of-a-kind book!"

"But it's a forgery," Avram said. "We promised the genuine article!"

"Tell the customer it's a fake, or not," Orlando cut him off. "I don't care. He won't ever see the difference by looking at it."

Avram stared at his young associate.

Orlando, one hand on his hip and the other on the pommel of his sword, stared right back. His voice dropped to a snarl. "I'd never have left Venice with this book if anyone could tell it's a fake! You don't know for certain, either. So I'll deliver this book into your buyer's hands, but I'm not taking it anywhere else."

Avram tried to soothe him. "I cannot take a forgery to our client—it's a matter of trust and honor!"

"It's killed at least seven men, Avram, and maimed more than I can count," Orlando exaggerated. Avram Ben Rubi stepped back. Orlando's voice rose and kept rising. "I've been ambushed, beaten, fallen down a cliff and dragged a girl halfway over the Alps, all to deliver this book to H.A. Burston—your client. Now, you want me to take it back! Are you completely insane?"

Avram's mouth fell open. Such passionate defiance struck him as completely out of the norm. Orlando looked at Avram's face. Then he laughed—a laugh half a cry, a laugh he couldn't choke off until it brought tears to his eyes. When his laughter ran out Orlando gasped, overcoming hiccups, endeavoring a calmer demeanor.

"After I hand the customer the package, you can explain that it is not what he ordered. Then, if he says to take it back, I will. Not until then."

Eliyahu, Avram's partner, came into the room at the sound of raised voices. "One of us will go with you to see him, then. Rest, and refresh yourself. Tomorrow is the Sabbath. We go the next day."

Orlando nodded. "Where will I find a mikvah? I've time for a bath before sunset, if the mikvah is not too busy. Is there a synagogue? If not, where do you meet for evening prayers? Do you know someone who can make room for a guest for Shabbat dinner?"

Eliyahu scribbled a note. "Take this five doors down, on the left. Ask if they'll find you proper clothes. You look like a Gentile, 'Lando."

"You should see me fight," he answered, a reckless gleam in his eye.

"No," Avram put in quietly, "I'm pretty sure I shouldn't see that, 'Lando. Do you honor your father in this?"

Memory filled the youngster's eyes with sadness, rage, and then defiance. "I honor his memory every day I don't let his only son be murdered, Avram. Every day."

"Forgive an old man," Eliyahu suggested. Like Avram, he could be no more than thirty-five. "Forgive both of us, Orlando."

Orlando shrugged. "Wasn't you who murdered Jaime Rosalez, stole his goods and livestock, killed his employees and left his son to die in the desert, was it, Avram? You've no more to be forgiven for than Eliyahu, here—or your client, for that matter. A man doesn't always remember the awful things that happen, if they don't happen to him."

Ben Rubi bit his lip; Eliyahu bowed his head. They said nothing.

Orlando folded the note. "Will you keep the book here, until we're ready to deliver it to your customer, Avram? I would rest to honor the Sabbath, and I cannot do that if I'm keeping this book safe."

"I'll keep it," Eliyahu said. He took the leather bag Orlando had worn around his waist for so long, and shook his head. "So small a thing, to cause such trouble."

Relieved of his burden, Orlando de Circassia smiled. "To think, if one man hadn't wanted an old book, all this trouble never would have happened."

He left their office to seek the mikvah.

Later Orlando spent the evening and the Sabbath day in prayer and study in borrowed clothes, while his own lay waiting for cleaning and mending, once the Sabbath passed. Avram offered him a bed in a loft both nights, and Orlando gratefully accepted.

H.A. Burston's home, Augsburg, the morning after the Sabbath

Eliyahu, Avram and a younger man arrived at Horatio Alger Burston's door.

Horatio Alger Burston's name, bestowed upon him by the unthinking cruelty of his father who considered it heroic, and the inability of his mother to tell the man no, had marked Al Burston for life. As a child he answered to Al; now he signed his name H.A. Burston. His business associates addressed him thusly, or he did no further business with them.

His visitors arrived as he prepared to go to church. While Horatio never dishonored the Sabbath, his business associates knew quite well they wouldn't disturb him by appearing on a Sunday. Orlando Rosalez de

Circassia stepped forward at Eliyahu's introduction, with a beautifully illuminated Haggadah in hand.

"At last," H.A. said. "Not before time!" After repeated delays and excuses, the book he had coveted for more than a year had appeared. H.A. looked at it and remembered the words of Keats, "A thing of beauty is a joy forever."

He said as much aloud.

"Yes, it is beautiful." Avram hesitated. "But, Herr, ah that is, Mister Burston, it is not the book you ordered. This is, alas, but a forgery. As of our last correspondence, the original has been recovered, but remains on its way here."

"Why," H.A. Burston asked in the quiet voice a man uses when he's trying to hold on to his temper until he can straighten out a confusing and outrageous situation, "did you bring me this one now, then?"

Avram paled. H.A. Burston didn't have to be the noble, angry Gentile who could order a Jew's head separated from his body or send him with all his family into the streets with nothing but the clothes on their backs to invoke his almost inborn dread. Indeed, both Avram and Eliyahu knew this man would not behave so. H.A. Burston didn't know how to act like that. Yet Avram's ingrained reaction to the situation would not bow to mere knowledge.

"As a sign of good faith," Avram answered, "and because the courier insisted."

H.A. lifted an eyebrow.

"Yes, he had quite a time getting here."

"Oh?" H.A. said. "Join me for breakfast and tell me about it."

Avram glanced at his associates.

"Eliyahu and Orlando can stay. I must get back to the office," he said. As an Ashkenazi, Avram kept *kashrut* far more closely than either Sephardic Eliyahu, a cosmopolite at ease when eating with Gentiles, or caravan-bred Orlando, who would eat anything with anyone. Avram considered the former highly improper and the latter only dubiously Jewish. Had Orlando not often prayed fervently in his hearing, he'd entertain no doubts at all.

Augsburg, May 1637

Orlando came back to Augsburg via the first spring caravan, with the original manuscript H.A. Burston referred to as the Sarajevo Haggadah. Avram and Eliyahu studied the illuminated manuscript with care, comparing it to the photographs in the magazine article H.A. Burston had provided. Neither could find any discrepancy between the article Orlando carried and the book pictured.

H.A. Burston's wife Catharina had finally fallen asleep. H.A. nestled Catharina's fourth child, their first daughter—his second child and the newest apple of his eye—in the crook of his arm a few feet away from the crib beside his wife's bed. Once the child, too, began to snore, he raised an eyebrow at Maire, the nanny. She crossed the room on quiet feet and lifted the baby into her own arms.

"Thanks," he murmured, watching her settle the child next its mother. Standing up, he stretched until his spine crackled, then left as quietly as he could walk to his office; the sun hung half over the horizon. It had been a long night and a difficult labor, nearly nineteen hours of shrieking pain. His daughter presented as a breech birth, with all the complications and dangers such events entailed.

A chambermaid appeared. "Herr Burston, a Jew and an up-timer are asking to see you at the door."

"Don't you mean in the parlor, Inge?"

"I will see them to the parlor, Herr Burston."

"In the future, do that first," he said firmly. "Then come find me. But in this case offer our guests breakfast. I'll be down to meet them in the dining room shortly."

"Yes, Herr Burston."

H.A. went to the bathroom he'd had retrofitted into the house. A rich man did not live without running water and flush plumbing. After the night he'd witnessed, he needed a shower. But for courtesy's sake, he did not dawdle.

At the dining room table, Horatio recognized the "up-timer," Orlando Rosalez de Circassia, whose dress had inspired the chambermaid's confusion. The young man worked his way through a massive breakfast as Eliyahu sat and watched.

"Good morning, Eliyahu. Please forgive me for keeping you waiting; we had an eventful night. Catharina just gave birth to a beautiful baby girl."

"*Mazel tov*, Herr Burs...ah...H.A. Do I have the pleasure of being the first to offer my congratulations?" When Horatio nodded, Eliyahu continued, "You remember Orlando de Circassia. He arrived last evening, from Venice. At last we can deliver the book you ordered."

Orlando stopped eating long enough to set a carefully wrapped package on the table. As he gave his attention back to what was left of the six light, fluffy, scrambled eggs with just a hint of dill and chives,

H.A. stared at the wooden box. Silently, he stood letting that stare linger. Finally Eliyahu said, "So if we could make the exchange, Herr Burston, we will be on our way."

"No," H.A. said. "I mean to keep both copies. With the delays in delivery, I expect a good price on the forgery. I bought the original as an anniversary gift for my wife. That occasion has long since passed; but it arrives perfectly for giving to her as a birthing-day present."

Eliyahu nodded. Orlando smiled.

"I want the copy for my daughter. I will tell her it is hers when she is old enough to understand that she owns a book she cannot touch."

Eliyahu named a price. H.A. named a much lower one.

They finished haggling just as Orlando finished his eggs, grits, biscuits, gravy and links of the smoked turkey sausage Horatio preferred. Orlando made eye contact with his host. "What your cook does with eggs..." He shook his head. "These are incredible."

"They had better be," H.A. said. "He's a French chef. His cooking should be the best in the Germanies, even if I did have to send him to Grantville to study with someone who does Cordon Bleu for fun." He helped himself to some eggs and sausages, took a bite, and nodded. "How was your trip? Less exciting than last time, I hope?"

The young man who'd affected the *lefferto* style of dress since his previous appearance here produced a genuine smile. "The only troubles were the late snow and the cold of the high passes."

☆ ☆ ☆

A few days later Catharina looked at the two books side by side. "Tio Al, these are exactly the same."

"No, Mrs. Burston, on that point you are quite mistaken," Horatio told her, thumping one of the two volumes. "This is a copy, but still worth a tidy sum. Even now the original there is a very old book, unlike any other, written in Spain two hundred years ago."

H.A. glanced from the newly delivered, beautifully illuminated manuscript past the copy to his wife. She cradled their daughter. His joy of ownership paled a bit, despite the obvious care in the copy's craftsmanship and the historical significance of the original. When he weighed the book against having a healthy wife and child—a treasure Horatio had feared losing more than once during Catharina's unbearably prolonged labor—the thrill of owning the Sarajevo Haggadah faded away like a forgotten tear.

He looked at the two-hundred-year-old book. He knew he would forever after think of it, not as some national treasure Horatio Alger Burston never could have dreamed of owning in his own place and time, but instead as the book Orlando had delivered on his daughter's birthday.

"One is yours," he told his wife as he gathered her in his arms. "The other is our daughter's. Both are, therefore, priceless."

Stockholm Syndrome

A.P. Davidson

June 1634, Stockholm

"It's a dump," Sandra whispered as she looked around the city her lunatic husband had dragged her to. It was only remarkable in its appearance of bland unattractiveness. She could tell its inhabitants were energetically improving it from all the construction going on, but compared to Grantville and Magdeburg, it seemed like a sleepy village. She sighed as she turned to watch her husband dragging a trunk down the dock. *Rob, what have you gotten us into?*

Robert Aronian, head of the Grantville Credit Union, had been hired as a consultant for the new Swedish Riksbank, with the support of the king no less. The king, along with merchants from Sweden and elsewhere, had drawn investments together and taken out huge loans to hire a slew of foreigners knowledgeable in banking in hopes of benefiting from better financing. Now that the war with the League of Ostend was mostly over, the plans were developing rapidly. Robert was the latest hire.

Paid an obscenely large fee and even shares, Robert had uprooted his family from their friends, their community and even their plumbing.

"Don't worry, honey. I'm sure whatever it is, it'll only take a couple months, three tops," he reassured her.

"Herr Aronian!" They turned to see a young man pacing toward them, waving his arms. "We didn't expect you for another few days."

"Hans, it's good to see you. Yeah, the winds were pretty favorable or something, so we're early." Hans Hering had worked at the credit union from early on, then had moved to the new Federal Reserve. A brilliant and charming man, the new Swedish bank had hired him months ago.

"That's good; you can be one of the first to see it." Taking Robert by the arm, he pulled him toward another ship that was docked beside a large crane. It was lowering a crate into a waiting wagon. With a few feet left, the cable jerked and the crate fell with a loud crack. Hans quickly ran over and inspected the damage.

He leaned in and whispered, "If that thing is broken, you'll be next to hang from the crane."

The crane operator turned ghostly pale. "I'm sorry, sir. I'm sorry. It won't happen again."

When he returned, Hans smiled. "It's fine, there's no damage, I think."

"What is 'it'?"

"Our printing press, newest model, the Johnny-four."

"Wait, they usually use those for money," Robert blurted. "You're printing money?"

Hans turned to him with an incredulous face. "No, Herr Aronian. You are."

☆   ☆   ☆

They had rented a house in the middle of Stadsholmen, the main island of Stockholm, and Hans had been gracious enough to let them use his wagons.

"Printing paper money was the emperor's idea, though I definitely thought it was a good one. I'm sorry that you didn't know about it beforehand. Herr Kock will visit soon; he's the boss so he can fill you in." He reined in the horses, got down from the wagon and grabbed one of their trunks. "Here's your place. I have to deliver the goods, so I'll see you another time."

They unpacked their things quickly and Sandra attempted to get a fire going to heat some water, but couldn't figure out how. She sighed. Being a housewife had never been her goal in life and it was evident in her lack of skills around the house. She could barely handle a stove, much less a seventeenth-century open hearth. "We should get a maid," she told Robert while digging into a box for a lighter.

"I'll look into that."

Their conversations of late had been terse and stiff. Sandra was still feeling angry at him for unilaterally deciding they would all go to Stockholm. There was also a bit of guilt, she admitted. As she built up the fire, she heard Robert shuffle off to another room. For reasons she never understood, he always preferred praying alone.

The Ring of Fire had hurt all the Americans, separating them from their family and friends. But few felt the separation that Robert had experienced. He was the last of the Baha'i, a religion that didn't even exist yet. For the past few years, he had spent quite a bit of their savings trying to find a small place for Baha'i to flourish. He had met with limited success and now had a handful of members.

That small start had filled Robert with huge ambition and he had decided to open a small Baha'i center outside Grantville. The expense would be high and most of their savings had already been invested in other areas. So Robert needed a new source of income. That was why they were sitting in a house in the middle of Stockholm.

When someone knocked on the door, Sandra opened it and saw an older man dressed in clothes that instantly said "filthy rich."

"Hello. I am Marcus Kock, chairman of the board at the Swedish Riksbank," he said. "May I come in?"

"Of course. We can wait in the living room. Robert will be down in a moment."

After they arranged themselves at the table, Robert entered. He immediately got to work and asked, "What's this I hear about you guys printing paper money?"

"We are not printing yet, but we intend to. Or rather, the king intends to. He has seen how the USE dollars are working in Germany and wants something similar for Sweden. Most of the board members feel the same." Marcus' face was stony and Sandra wondered which side of "most" he had been on.

"Anyway, since we don't really know much about how paper money works, we decided to hire an up-timer who does. You were one of the people who helped create the USE dollars and establish the Federal Reserve. A natural choice."

"Well, that seems straightforward."

"You are also expected to aid our distribution of the money and integrate it into the new services the bank is offering."

Sandra interrupted. "Wait. That sounds like it will take a lot more than a couple months."

"I'm not sure where you got that idea, Mrs. Aronian. We're paying a large sum for your husband's expertise and we expect him to be worth it." Kock leaned back in his chair and crossed his arms, exuding an aura that simply said "I'm the boss."

"Sorry, Sandra, but he does speak some sense. They want to milk me for all I'm worth. But don't worry, I'll get it done fast and we'll be back in time for your mom's Thanksgiving feast."

Sandra got up, went to the kitchen, and set out some cups as the water had started to boil. Then she picked up the coffee container, wondering how much it would cost here. She liked tea, but Robert practically had coffee for blood.

She came back to Robert and Marcus having a heated discussion about something and left the cups on the table. Quietly, she slipped away to the bedroom, physically and mentally exhausted. *I wonder how I'm supposed to keep myself from snapping.*

Marcus Kock was nearing fifty and felt more than his share of aches and pains. He hadn't wanted this job, but because he was from Liège and had done much business with the Wisselbank, the people organizing this new bank had felt he was the best man for it. This new bank hadn't even opened yet and he was already lost. He was not a banker, and felt like things were getting increasingly out of his control. He now left most of the problems in the hands of his capable bank manager, Hans.

And now this. Kock wasn't sure what to make of

the up-timer, but he was certain it would mean more work. On the other hand, he was hopeful it would mean more profits. *Well, it's not like he could make it worse.*

The money situation in Sweden was in a grim state. True, nothing compared to the times of Gustav's father, but still bad. Officially, it was somewhat simple, the main currency being the riksdaler with smaller coins of varying value: the mark, öre, örtug and penning. However, the reality was that these coins had been severely debased and were a fraction of their official value.

Then in 1624, Gustav Adolf had created the notorious copper money, complicating an already fragile system. Every coin now had both a copper and silver equivalent. It had been, in their view at least, a necessity since Sweden had been short on silver. By now, the Swedes simply did not trust the government with their money.

After a few days of settling in, Robert left for his first day at the bank bright and early. Sandra had about a dozen things happening at once and didn't get a chance to say goodbye.

"Bobby, get down from there! Dangit, where's Fruit Loops when you need them? Bobby! Don't get close to the fire. Now where was that good towel I had? Jesus!" She turned and stared face to face with a young woman. "Who are you? How'd you get in here?"

"I-I-I'm sorry, milady. The door w-was unlocked. I'm Margaret Kilpatrick, and I'd like to be your h-housekeeper," she murmured at the floor. Then she held up a scrap of newspaper with an advertisement on it.

She was probably not even eighteen, very pretty, but so tense you could pluck her like a guitar string, Sandra thought. The thought, however, was overcome instantly. *I'm saved*. She gave Margaret a crushing hug. "Thank God! Can you cook? How about clean? And you speak English! I can't believe I found an English speaker. I'm terrible at languages; my German accent is still laughed at. Yes, I'm hiring you right away. Please help me with breakfast. Can I call you Marge?"

Each exuberant phrase from Sandra only seemed to intimidate Margaret more. "Um, y-yes milady, I can do all of that. I think. I'm from Scotland, ma'am. If it p-pleases you, you can call me whatever you like."

"A Scot? Really? Are there more of you here? I should go check it out, maybe I have family here."

Margaret explained that there were quite a few Scottish immigrants in Stockholm, mostly families of the mercenaries in Gustav Adolf's service but there were plenty of merchants and peddlers as well. Sandra felt her mood brighten.

Across the island, Robert was in a considerably less joyous mood. He sat at a table in the main hall of the bank. They were waiting for Hans.

"I just got here and you're already piling more jobs on me. Now I'm a tutor?"

Marcus smirked. "We are wandering into the unknown. None of us on the board know about your American banking. You need to teach us, oh wise-and-all-knowing up-timer."

Robert just glared.

"I'll help you as much as I can." That was Lars

Claesson, Robert's new assistant. He was a slightly-more-than-half-trained bank teller, but seemed competent enough.

Robert sighed yet again. "Fine, I'll dig up my old books and we'll meet up when we can. Maybe I'll print out a booklet for you guys...heck, maybe for everyone. Lars, I'll need you to get me a few people to help design the money and find suppliers for ink and paper."

Lars grabbed a pen and began writing down a list of supplies they needed to print their new money.

Robert heard a chuckle behind him.

"You seem like you have a handle on things, Herr Aronian." Hans smiled. "Come on, I'll give you the grand tour." He walked off with Robert and the others trailing after him.

The bank was certainly a substantial edifice. It stood on a corner of the Stortorget, the Great Square, a few blocks from the palace. Slightly bigger than the Grantville bank, it had been converted from an old warehouse. The main floor was dominated by rows of tables for the bank tellers. They were being drilled mercilessly by a couple of Germans. They needed to learn quickly, before the bank opened up. Soon, the bank would be getting deposits, servicing loans, savings accounts and exchanging the silver and copper dalers for new paper dalers.

They walked down to the basement and Robert stared. "That is some bank vault you got there."

Two guards stood in front of an open metal door, beyond which was a small room. *It actually glows.* The credit union rarely held silver, even now. The stacks of silver bars, the bags of silver coin were foreign. Robert shivered.

"About twenty-five thousand riksdalers worth of pure silver, that's...almost three million dollars," Hans whispered. His eyes reflected the bright precious metals. Substantial loans from the USE and selling shares of the bank had given the bank its initial assets.

Lars smiled proudly. "That's why we have this fancy safe, several inches of concrete, the six-inch-thick iron door and you need that fancy new key to open it." He pointed at the brass key on a chain around Marcus' neck.

The upper floors contained the various offices and meeting rooms. Hans opened a door to a small room. "And this is your office. I took the liberty of making it as close to your old office in Grantville as possible. I hope that I remembered everything? Your religion is important to you, naturally, so I want to help you maintain your, ah, worship." He stared intently at Robert.

The desk and drawers were plain and ordinary and only served to highlight the other items in the room. A small but beautiful prayer rug lay on the floor. A table sat beside it with a water basin on top. Finally, on the shelf were several important Baha'i texts.

Robert experienced both surprise and fear at once. Surprise at Hans having remembered and gone to the trouble of arranging his office like this and fear of...he risked a glance at the other two men who had become eerily quiet.

The agent who had hired Robert had suggested that he keep quiet about his religion. "Swedes are already suspicious of Catholics and Calvinists and they restrict public worship. The king holds the worst of them back, but if they see your...practices, I can't be certain what will happen."

Marcus cleared his throat and commented, "You can decorate your office all you want, but it's still smaller than a closet."

Then Lars chimed in hastily, "Shall we finish the tour? I very much want to inspect the new presses."

They walked down the hall, with Robert following after a few seconds, never noticing the way Hans just stood there, staring at their backs.

After the tour they arrived at a largish, very well-appointed room with hardwood table and chairs, wall hangings and down-time-made Coleman lanterns set in nooks along the walls to provide lighting. Robert would finally meet the board members.

They took their seats and Marcus Kock started the ball rolling. "So, Robert, how do we get people to accept paper money? We are having enough trouble with copper money and at least copper is worth something."

Robert had heard about the copper coins but had never seen one. "Perhaps you could explain about the copper coins a bit. I understand they are larger than the silver coins of the same value?"

There was a moment of profound silence, as though Robert had said something along the lines of "I understand that oceans have water in them," and everyone was wondering whether he was joking or just an idiot.

"Ah . . . yes," Hans said, and it looked like he was trying to hide a smile. "Perhaps we should show Mr. Aronian a few of the copper coins. Lars, would you mind?"

They waited while Lars went out and came back pushing a cart. From the cart he pulled a huge plate of copper. It was roughly rectangular, apparently hand hammered into that shape. It had been stamped in the four corners with crowns and in the center with EIGHT DALER. The thing—Robert couldn't think of it as money—must weigh thirty-five or forty pounds.

"This," Lars said, "is a copper eight-daler coin."

"That's not money," Robert said. "It's a commodity." *Or a serving platter! Jeez.*

"Money is a commodity, is it not?" Marcus asked.

"No. Money is a medium of exchange." A couple of members responded with slow, awkward nods. *I guess I really do need to teach them.*

"Is that how you get people to take pieces of paper?" asked a member of the board whose name Robert couldn't remember for the life of him.

"I guess... in a way. Mostly they take our money because of what they can buy with it and partly because they have faith in its value."

"Then we should be able to do the same thing and reserve the silver for foreign trade and certain preferred customers just like we did with the copper." The man was smiling and Robert had a sudden urge to check and see if his wallet was where it was supposed to be. At the same time, Robert wasn't in a position to tell a member of the board not to be a crook.

"I honestly don't think that will work. One of the reasons for the huge loans that have been made to the bank was to provide it with enough silver to restore Swedish currency."

"But I thought the reason we brought you in was to convince the common folk that the paper money was good," said Marcus.

In other words, Robert thought, *to front for the*

bank. "As I understood it, sir, I was hired for my experience in banking and finance. Since I have arrived, it has been pointed out that you intend to use paper currency. I was not completely convinced that that was a good idea till I saw *that*." Robert pointed at the copper plate on the table. "Paper is certainly better than that."

Marcus grumbled, "When the idea of the Riksbank was first suggested, I wanted to get rid of the copper and go back to silver, but the majority wanted to use paper money. So I guess we should just start printing it."

"You can't use fiat money," Robert said quickly.

"Fiat money?"

"Money that is money because the government says it is," Robert explained. "Like we use in Grantville."

"Why can't we use fiat money?" asked the guy who made Robert want to check his wallet, proving that he wasn't stupid even if he was greedy as hell.

"Because it won't keep its value," Robert said. "Money is all about confidence, the confidence that your customers have in the bank, and especially in the money itself." Robert stopped and thought for a moment. "How many copper dalers are there to the silver daler?"

Clearing his throat, Marcus murmured, "Legally, it's worth the same."

"A copper daler is worth about two-thirds of a silver daler," Lars said.

"The market value." Marcus sighed. "I admit copper isn't worth much compared to silver and they are inconvenient to use."

Robert nodded, and then braced his arms on the table. "Then I propose that the Riksbank take the copper dalers and all the other copper coins at face value. One copper daler can be exchanged for a paper daler or for a silver daler, and vice versa. Same goes for the marks and öre and all of the others. All will be exchanged at a legal and fixed value."

Robert just sat there as the room exploded. Words like "idiotic" and "treasonous" were launched like so many verbal grenades at the heresy of giving people good silver for over-priced copper—just because they said they would years ago.

"That's insane! They'll exchange the copper for paper, then immediately turn around and exchange that for silver," Hans declared.

"This is a matter of honor," Robert said. "It is a matter of the king's word to his people. Will you make the king of Sweden a liar?"

"But the cost!" howled the smart crook.

"Temporary, I assure you, gentlemen. If handled right, this one act will go a long way toward restoring Sweden's credit. We have to do this if Sweden is to have the sort of booming economy that is found in the USE. If you're just patient, the rewards you receive will be many times the cost."

They argued about it for the rest of the day. And off and on for some time afterward. Eventually, Robert had to write Gustav Adolf and Coleman Walker, who apparently also wrote Gustav Adolf. Gustav had to personally intervene, but it was finally settled. The Riksbank would take copper coinage at face value, for now.

Sandra walked excitedly down the street pushing Tommy in his stroller. She had been invited to a private worship meeting by a Scots Presbyter. "So you haven't been to worship in a long time."

"Well, I would have liked to, ma'am, but see, I had to take care of my mother." Marge shifted Bobby in her arms. "First the drinking, then the illness. I never had time for such matters."

By now, Sandra had gotten to know Margaret very well. Her father had been an officer for the Swedish army, one of the many Scots. He had died in a battle and was buried somewhere in Pomerania. Her mother had become alcoholic and died soon after, leaving Margaret with no family in an unfamiliar city.

"Don't worry, Marge." Sandra patted her on the arm. "I'll take care of you." She knocked on the door of a large house.

They were greeted by a beaming woman in fancy clothes. "Welcome! You must be the up-timer! It's so good to see you, come in. I'm afraid it'll be a bit cramped."

There were indeed many people in the room. A few of them were Dutch, but most were Scots; young children scrambled between the legs of the adults. "I'm Anna Fife. My husband's off in Antwerp somewhere, my boy Will is somewhere around here." She craned her neck to look over the crowd. "Please, make yourselves at home."

"It's nice to meet you, Mrs. Fife. I'm Sandra Aronian." Sandra paused, then asked, "I'm sorry if this is rude, but shouldn't these kids be in school or something?"

"Sandra, dear, are you mad? Send our boys to the Lutheran schools?" Anna left to chase after a group of young boys, leaving Sandra with her own thoughts.

☆ ☆ ☆

Months of long, exhausting hours had come to fruition. They had begun exchanging the old silver and copper dalers for the new paper dalers. Robert pulled out a one-daler bill from his pocket and examined it with pride.

It was slightly bigger than the USE dollar and instead of green, it used blue ink. The standard odd shapes and unnecessarily large amounts of the word ONE and the numeral 1 scattered on it surrounded a portrait of Gustav Adolf's head in its regal splendor.

The line of customers stretched quite a bit. While the Stockholmers were still a bit skeptical, they wouldn't miss an opportunity to rid themselves of the copper dalers.

An old man sat down at a table as two employees lifted the heavy copper coins onto the scale. He eyed the sign in the middle of the room nervously. It listed the fixed prices for the money exchange.

The teller didn't even glance at Robert anymore. Not at all the same as it had been the first day when—in spite of his reassurances—both tellers and customers were constantly turning to Robert to see if he really meant it, the tellers afraid and customers prepared to be belligerent if he backed down at the last minute. Today she smiled at the man and said, "Well, you have nine dalers in copper, would you like to exchange or deposit?"

Robert was confident in his plan. The Stockholmers would certainly make a run on the bank, grabbing as much silver as they could, but in the end it would only help gain their trust. Only when they saw every transaction being treated fairly and honorably would they gain faith in the bank. They would start using the paper money once it had shown its value. As for the silver, they would hoard it, at least some would for a while, but that wouldn't hurt anything, not too badly, anyway.

The old man stroked his beard and then pulled his bankbook out of his coat. "I will add four dalers to my account and take the rest, in paper dalers and marks, please." And that was another change, one that was just starting to happen. The first few days it was copper in and silver out, almost exclusively. But now some of the customers were leaving money in the bank and accepting paper dalers. Partly, that was because they had to have an account before they could even apply for a loan. But Robert knew it was more than that. People knew how the Grantville bank and credit union worked; they knew how the new banks in Magdeburg worked . . . and they were starting to trust the Riksbank.

The teller took the bankbook and flipped her ledger to the correct page. After scribbling some numbers, she stamped the bankbook and returned it to the man and opened a drawer. "You now have seven and a half dalers deposited here." Then she counted out three paper daler bills and sixteen-mark bills and handed them over. "Thank you and have a good day." No doubt tomorrow the man would return to exchange some paper for silver.

There had been a minor cost to Robert's dealings. He had wanted them to use a decimal system using cents. Unfortunately, he was fighting tradition here and had to compromise. However, they were able to establish a system of eighths where one riksdaler was eight marks, sixty-four öre and so on. The simple and precise structure was more proof that the bank was here to bring stability and confidence. The dalers and marks would be paper, while smaller denominations were copper coins.

Robert had been surprised at the speed in which the new bills and coins were being made. Later, he had found that the mint that was creating the coins just so happened to be owned by the Kock family ... with a slice of the profits going back to Marcus. *That swindler doesn't do anything without taking a cut for himself.*

A few hours later, Sandra knocked on Robert's office door. "Looks like you guys are doing well down there." She had come to visit. She was holding Bobby, while Margaret trailed with Tommy in her arms.

Robert smiled. Sandra's mood had eased considerably as she became friends with Margaret and other ladies in the city. Robert was grateful for the small community of Scots and Germans she could speak to (literally, her Swedish was still terrible) and befriend.

"Hello Tommy," he said as he picked his son up. "Yeah, it's a madhouse down there. People are coming in every day for paper or silver or other business. I feel sorry for the poor tellers. I have to go with Marcus later to check out the new scale we got from Grantville. You headed out again?"

"Mm-hmm. Marge and I are headed over to Anna Fife's. We're going out for a day at the spa and some shopping." Of course, by spa, she meant going to one of the fancier public baths and shopping was going to a seamstress, but you made do.

Tommy started gnawing on a key that hung around Robert's neck. Sandra cried out, "Tommy, no!"

Robert handed him back to her.

Sandra accepted her son back, then asked, "Of all the people here, why do you have the key to the vault?"

"They probably think I like people kissing my butt." Everyone now saw that Robert had the full support of the king and were hurrying to get on his good side. Except Marcus, of course. He had offered to take the key off of Robert's hands. When Robert told him that he thought it was a bad idea, he replied in his snarky way, "I thought you wanted to increase the money supply? I can surely help with that."

"Well, I have to get back to work. Have fun, Sandra." He gave her a kiss.

"Goodbye, dear. Don't overwork yourself. Come on, Marge, or we're going to be late." Margaret jumped up and fumbled a goodbye to Hans, whom she had been talking to.

The bath had been quite refreshing, but the seamstress was dreadfully dull. Being fitted for clothes was nothing like going to the mall.

"I think Margaret actually smiled," Anna Fife said as Margaret was being fitted for a dress.

Sandra nodded. "I accomplished that a week ago. I'm trying to get her to say my first name now." They had made it a quiet mission to get Margaret to open up and each day was a small victory. "I can't believe, of all things, she wants something like that for her birthday." Her voice lowered. "It looks like a curtain and a puff ball had a baby."

"Well, that's fashion for you," Anna said as she examined the skirt she was wearing.

"She needs a cocktail dress or something. I mean

I've never been one for too much skin showing, but I don't know how you can get a man wearing this. You got to go a bit sexier and..." Sandra stopped as she noticed Margaret's intense focus.

Anna laughed. "Something you can't say to the young one?"

"Who knows? Depends on how your sex-ed is here." That gave way to a lengthy discussion about what sex education was.

"Mistress Aronian, c-can I ask you something?" Margaret sat down, having finally finished.

"Of course."

"What is your Grantville high school like?"

"Hmm, I guess I'd have to say...an opportunity. And a fun place. A lot of kids make great memories there. And as a counselor, I always enjoyed watching them graduate and go out into the world."

"The future sounds like a fascinating place," said Anna. "My husband doesn't want our boy in the school here. Says he doesn't want him turning Lutheran on us. So we home school him."

"That's unfortunate. The high school is secular; it has to be to get public funding. All the religious schools are now...I mean, will be...or would be, dammit, all private."

"What is private?"

"It just means not paid by the government. The parents usually pay for their kids to go to a place the parents like more."

Anna looked at her keenly. "So, since the government doesn't pay for it, they cannot get involved."

Sandra knew that tone. The gears in Anna's head were turning. Living in Stockholm, Sandra had been pleasantly surprised that women were not the quiet, homemaker-type she'd expected. That resulted from so many of their husbands and fathers being off to war. Inheritance and legal powers were still a problem, but they could be worked around. Having a woman as the head of a household and controlling a business was not that strange here. Anna took that to a new level. "Huddle up, I have an idea."

November 1634

"No, Marcus. N. O. We are not lowering the reserve rate."

Robert and Marcus' arguments were commonplace now. The other board members were intimidated by both of them and, knowing that they were out of their depths, wisely remained silent.

Robert was frustrated. The bank's stock of silver had taken a major hit in the first weeks of operation. Then gradually people had started putting the new minted and milled silver coins back in the bank and accepting paper money or even leaving their money in the bank till they needed it. The bank had steadily improved its standing and popularity. Desiring more profits, Marcus had just demanded—again—that they be allowed to print and loan out more money. As a rule, they did all their business with paper money, but kept a large reserve of silver to exchange.

"We set it at forty percent for a reason. Everything is still unstable and we need a good supply of silver on hand. I won't support this."

This effectively ended the debate. The board almost always sided with Robert. The last letter of support from King Gustav had had subtle threats to those who sought to undermine the bank's efforts.

"Now if you'll excuse me, I have a bank to run."

Back in the main hall, he met up with Lars as he was closing up. "Well, that's the end of that. We've managed to survive another week without something blowing up in our face."

Lars chuckled. "You shouldn't be so hard-hearted, Mr. Aronian. Everyone's working overtime and we're all a bit stressed. Even Mr. Kock is trying his best."

"Oh, that is definitely true. Marcus always tries his best when there's money to be made." Robert walked down to the vault and, with the help of a guard, heaved the heavy door closed. Quickly locking the vault, he met up with Lars at the front door. There, he noticed Hans and several large men lifting copper onto a wagon.

Robert ambled over. "So how are you, Hans?"

Hans looked up. "Terrible, I'm utterly exhausted. I'll be glad when this is all over."

"I don't know why you volunteered for this."

"If I'm not here to watch, the idiots would screw it all up."

The money exchanges had resulted in huge amounts of copper just sitting in the bank. So now the bank was in the business of selling copper. Somehow, Marcus had gotten a contract written and approved, making him the dealer for the bank. It was only a coincidence that he also owned extensive copper and brass works.

Hans climbed into the driver's seat. "So you've been here nearly six months. How long do you plan on staying?"

"Once things settle down for the bank; probably no

more than a month or two. They don't really need me when they have guys like you managing things."

"Ah, good timing then. Past December, they say there's some chance of the harbors freezing over. Then, you'll really be stuck here, and you wouldn't want that would you?"

Lars came up and patted Robert's shoulder. "Come, Mr. Aronian. You promised me that drink did you not?"

Robert nodded and they headed off down the dimly lit street.

As Hans was preparing to leave, he heard a voice.

"Hans! Hans! I need to talk to you." It was Marcus, who looked like he was in a foul mood.

"What is it sir?" Hans put up his most appealing smile.

"I received a letter from my copper works manager. He says he isn't getting the amount of copper that's reported. There's some missing."

Hans frowned. "You think someone's pinching some copper?" He turned to the laborers, who quickly averted their gaze. "Are you accusing my workers?"

"I accused no one, but they are the ones in the best position to steal."

Laughing, Hans pointed. "Herr Kock, there's a room full of silver right there. Who would want to take some cheap copper? But don't worry; I'll keep an eye out." He shook the reins and the cart began a sedate roll away from the bank, leaving Marcus behind.

Gritting his teeth, Hans muttered, "Old bastard."

As he and Lars sat down in a nearby tavern, Robert asked, "Come to think of it, I've barely seen Hans lately. What's he up to? He seems to go in and out quite a bit."

Shrugging, Lars replied, "He says some side project. To be honest, I think he's growing weary of all of this. He doesn't like you much. In fact, I daresay he hates you."

"What? He hates me? Why?"

"It's not too hard to see. You've essentially become our new bank manager. We used to go to him to solve problems, but now we go to you. Not to mention, you get paid a lot more than he does. When you're not looking, he glares at you sometimes." Lars paused, taking a big gulp of beer. "You don't think he fixed up your office out of the kindness of his heart, do you? He was trying to embarrass you. He's jealous of your position." Lars nodded his head toward Robert's chest.

"Well that's just preposterous. I . . ." Robert felt the weight of the key around his neck. *It ought to properly be his. Is he really jealous?* "Are you sure?"

"Maybe. I have six brothers and sisters, so I know about jealousy and hate."

Silence hung between them as Robert stewed in his thoughts.

Lars tipped the rest of his drink and waved the barmaid for another. "So, Mr. Aronian . . . you are still planning to leave?"

"Of course I am. Why wouldn't I?"

"Mr. Aronian, you don't have to lie to me or yourself. I know you're enjoying it here."

"What?" *Is Sandra giving him psychology tips?* "I am enjoying it, I guess. In Grantville, the credit union is small and the bank of Grantville gets all the attention. But here, it's like we're pioneers. You can just feel the energy coming from the customers. We're making a difference, Lars, helping ordinary citizens."

"I like your attitude, sir. It's much better than Hans', for sure. Here's to prosperity...for everyone." Lars lifted his mug in a mock toast and his beer quickly disappeared.

Later that night, Robert and Sandra were sitting and watching while Margaret played with Bobby. He decided to broach the subject.

"Honey, do you...like it here?"

"Yes? Why?"

"How would you feel about living here...permanently?"

Her eyebrows rose slightly. "What are you talking about? Your contract ends pretty soon. What are you going to do for a job?"

"I don't know. I might just open up my own bank or even a credit union out in the other islands around Stadsholmen. I just feel like I can do a lot more here than I ever did in—" He stopped when Sandra started laughing. "What's so funny?"

Clearing her throat, she replied, "That's actually what I wanted to talk to you about. I kind of want to stay as well."

Now it was Robert's eyebrows that shot up.

"I've been talking with some families here and we want to open up a private school."

"A school?"

"It'll be for all the kids who don't fit into the regular Lutheran schools. Anyone can join with any religious affiliation." She sidled up close to Robert.

"And with my hubby so friendly with the king, I'm sure he could be persuaded to approve it."

"I . . . see. So, I guess we both want to stay?"

"Stockholm isn't that bad a place once you get used to it," she said, leaning on his shoulder.

"Yeah, it really does grow on you."

Suddenly, Margaret leapt up. "Excuse m-me, milady. I feel a bit ill right now. If it is p-possible, I would like to leave early."

"Um, sure that's fine. Go rest up, Marge." And Margaret hastily left the house.

"I think she has a boyfriend."

"And how would you know that?"

"Women's intuition."

Two nights later, Robert stumbled back home, shaking the rain off his coat.

"Herr A-Aronian, w-w-welcome h-home," Margaret said.

"Thanks, Marge." He handed his coat to her. *Is it just me, or is Marge even more jittery than usual?*

A few hours later, Sandra and he were lounging by the new Franklin stove they had installed in the living room. After a big dinner and a warm bath, life was good.

Sandra looked over and decided now was a good time to ask. She smiled. "So, did you talk to them about a loan for the school?"

"Yes, and they approved! I have the paperwork in here, so you can sign." Robert opened his briefcase and ruffled around inside. "Hmm, where is it? Ah dang, I must have left it in my office. We were really busy today and I must have forgotten. You know, I'll just run back and grab it."

"You sure? It's already dark out and the weather is awful. I can just get it tomorrow."

"No, it's fine. The weather service said it will get even worse tomorrow. I don't want you to walk in that mess. Besides, tomorrow's the twelfth, I'm not working then." He lit a lantern and walked out into the stormy darkness. "It's only a short walk, I'll be back soon."

When Robert arrived in the square, he passed by several large wagons. *Ah, there's a shipment of copper going out tonight. It's pouring, though.* He entered the open doors into the darkened hallway and heard voices and glints of light from the basement. *That's odd; we don't have any copper down there.* Edging closer, he peered down the stairs. The vault was open. In shock, Robert dropped the lantern with a loud clatter.

Three faces turned toward him. Two were unfamiliar, but they were faces that didn't seem to invoke friendship.

The last face was Hans. He smiled. "How unfortunate, Herr Aronian. I had hoped this would go quietly."

Slowly Robert's eyes adjusted to the scene and another shock hit him.

There were bags of coins at their feet. *The silver!* "Hans, what the hell are you doing?"

Hans shrugged, his smile never wavering.

And I used to think that was a happy smile.

"Let's just say it's a bit of vengeance." Here, his smile positively gleamed. "Also, I like money." He jerked his head and his goons (there was really no other way to describe them) began climbing the stairs.

Robert turned to run and saw two other unpleasantly large men behind him. *Well, I think they call this a less-than-stellar situation.* His eyes darted around for anything to use.

One of them lunged, but Robert grabbed the dropped lamp and swung it at his face. With a loud grunt, the man fell and Robert tossed the lamp at the other man. With the distraction, Robert bolted up the stairs and headed for the door. He yanked it open and ran outside, the pounding rain matching his heartbeat.

Behind him, one man pulled out a matchlock and fired. Robert cried out as he felt a stinging heat on his shoulder and tripped, landing painfully on the cobblestones.

"Damn you! Do you want to wake up half the city?" Hans' voice echoed.

Pure adrenaline shook Robert and he leapt up. *Damn, it's dark.* His panic disoriented him, but all he wanted was to get as far away as possible. Then he was tackled from behind. He fell to the ground hard. The last things he heard were thundering shouts and the deafening rainfall.

"He was lucky the night patrol heard the gunshot. They chased those bastards away before they could..." Sandra let out a deep breath. It had been an exhausting night. Robert was still unconscious, but the doctor had done as good a job as could be hoped.

Lars nodded grimly. *Indeed, he is lucky the tavern nearby is frequented by many watchmen.* The thieves had made off with nearly all of the silver; almost two tons worth. Troops were searching high and low throughout the city for any sign, but they had vanished.

With a knock, Marcus came in followed by Anna. She came and sat at Sandra's side while Marcus cleared his throat. "Hans was missing today."

"What? You think he did it?"

"I went to his home and he wasn't there, either. I have to say that it doesn't surprise me too much."

Sandra interrupted, "So are they searching for him? Door-to-door? Where are the police? Where's the cavalry?" Her eyes burned bright and for a minute the others did not want to speak.

"The robbery:...it's a secret, Mrs. Aronian. We have to tell as few as possible, though I'm sure there are plenty of rumors already," said Lars.

Marcus nodded. "Think about it, Mrs. Aronian. If it gets out that all of the town's money has been stolen, there will be pandemonium. Everything we have worked for would be ruined. We have a few squads searching ships and patrolling the roads, but that's all. I've instructed the staff to keep quiet, and we still have a bit of silver left. That's all we can do until we find him or the money."

Sandra's ire had swelled with each word, but by the end a strange calmness had settled her. "Okay." She stood and went to a drawer near her and pulled out a small up-timer pistol. "We'll just find him ourselves."

Seeing the shock on all of their faces lifted her mood considerably. "Come on, guys. We're smart people. We can do this if we work together." Then quietly, "Please. For Robert's sake."

Anna stood up. "I'm with you, Sandra."

Lars' grin was predatory. "The game's afoot."

Marcus wondered where that strange idiom had come from, then noticed their stares. "Fine. But I want it noted that I am very reluctant. So what is the plan?"

A long pause followed.

"We go to the scene of the crime!" piped Lars.

A short time later, they were at the bank, leaving Margaret at home to watch the kids.

She wouldn't be much help with stuff like this, Sandra thought. "Well, shit, you idiots tampered with the evidence." They watched as the last muddy footprints were being mopped away.

Anna ran her hands over the vault door. "My, how did they break this thing open? It looks impenetrable."

"They didn't." With a start, Lars darted forward. "The key is here. Hans had the key, but how?"

Marcus shrugged, "He must have stolen it." He pulled the key out from the keyhole and examined it.

"Well, none of this helps us. We already suspected Hans. What we need is to find out where he's hiding." Sandra was getting frustrated already.

Walking down the hall, they discussed what options they had. Anna's husband could bribe some of the stevedores to search vessels. They could quietly have the bank guards walk through the neighborhoods.

"Wait."

They all turned to Marcus, but he had his eyes on the large stack of copper plates in a corner. "I just remembered. There was supposed to be a delivery of old copper dalers today. I knew those men seemed suspicious. They must have used the wagons for the silver."

Tapping two guards, Lars rushed out, followed by Marcus.

"Do you know where they're going?" Anna inquired.

"Not a clue and I'm not going to wander around in that downpour." The storm's ferocity had only increased as the day passed. Sandra pushed down a desire to go home and see Robert. *The doctor is there and Margaret too.* She rubbed her stomach then stifled a giggle. *Five years ago, I was helping kids go to college, now I'm chasing a fugitive in a hurricane.*

After an hour, Marcus, Lars and one of the guards returned, drenched from the rain and looking quite dejected. They came and sat beside Sandra and Anna.

"No good. The teamsters have disappeared too. They were probably working for Hans. We have people out looking for the wagons." Lars shrugged and plopped his head down on the table, exhausted.

Marcus sighed, massaging his neck. "I'm getting too old for this. We can't let this go on much longer with the little money we have. If they ask for silver and we can't give it, there goes any trust we had."

"Don't worry, sirs. We're certain they're still in the city. This storm is keeping the ships from leaving. Any fool who slips out of harbor will be seen right away. All the roads are being watched as well," said the guard, obviously some naïve young fool.

"Mrs. Aronian! Mrs. Aronian!" an older man ran in, shouting.

"Doctor? Is everything okay?" Sandra leapt out of her chair.

"Yes, your husband is awake. He seems fine and..."

But Sandra had already run off.

☆   ☆   ☆

Robert found himself smothered by his sobbing wife, who apparently had gone swimming, the way she was drenched. Amid wet kisses, she murmured, "I was so worried, Robby."

When the others came in, they found a much more composed Sandra sitting by Robert's bed.

"We are glad to see you awake, Mr. Aronian."

"Thanks, but that's not important. Have you caught Hans and the silver?"

"No, not yet, but we are doing everything we can..."

As the conversation wore on, Anna noticed Sandra had been ignoring them. No, rather she was staring at a table by the door.

"Sandra? Are you all right?"

"The key, it's right there." She had whispered, but shock coursed the whole room.

"I understand it now," Sandra said, and she explained.

Hans had needed the key to open the safe, but couldn't steal it outright. He had made a copy. Only one person could have taken it; only one person who was in their home when they were asleep and could slip the key out for a while.

"Margaret!"

"Yes, milady!" the girl said as she rushed in.

Everyone could see she was visibly shaking, sweat coming down her face.

Looking into Margaret's eyes, seeing her guilt, Sandra found her own eyes tearing up. "Oh God, why did you do it?"

That broke Margaret immediately and her story came out in a rush. She had been a naïve and lonely girl. A month ago, Hans began courting her. Against his wit, charm and handsome features, she hadn't had a chance. He had taken advantage of her, in more ways than one. He seemed fascinated by her life as a maid and took every chance he could to get to know her. But when she revealed that the Aronians wanted to stay in Stockholm, he had snapped. He had persuaded her, by sweet words and subtle threats, to take a mold of the key one night.

"I-I'm sorry, m-m-milady, I w-was a fool. I never exp-pected him to-to steal from you." Quivering and sobbing on the ground, she made a pitiful sight.

Lars knelt down and firmly said, "This may be difficult, but we must know where Hans is."

"I don't k-know. I've only ever been to his home." At that last statement, her cries became much louder.

"Have you ever seen him write odd plans or speak with anyone strange, anything?"

"I saw him t-talking to a sea captain once. He k-kept making rude comments at m-me. I think his name was Pills or something like that."

"Captain Piltz?" Anna said. "Ah, that would make sense. The man has a creaky old boat, hauls pretty much anything for anyone. My husband dealt with him once. He leered at me like some old lecher and my husband got so mad he threw him out the door. A man fit to deal with criminals."

"Then let us go pay him a visit at his ship. And bring some friends with us."

Everyone stood up except Robert, who was still not in a condition to run around. As they turned to leave, Margaret tugged on Sandra's shirt. "He never loved me, did he?"

Sandra embraced her. "No. He didn't."

☆　　☆　　☆

The decrepit-looking ship was not hard to find. Lars and Marcus had brought a dozen or so guards with them. A dirty-looking sailor looked over the railings at them, staring with wide eyes.

Lars stood at the foot of the boarding ramp, looking quite dashing with a gun at his hip. "Halt! Come out with your hands up or we will use force. Surrender or face the consequences, fiends."

The guard captain rolled his eyes then pulled out his sword. "Let's go." Seizing the ship and crew was anticlimactic. The guards were former soldiers and did their business quickly and efficiently. The seven men found on board surrendered; they weren't stupid.

The guard captain flipped a chest open. "Tear the ship apart. Leave nothing unturned. We must find that silver."

Lars came out as the captives were being tied up. "Nothing so far. Not many places on board to hide that much silver."

"Where is it, Hans?" asked Marcus, but the man just lay there kneeling on the ground, brooding. "The courts may have some mercy on you if you tell us." Silence. *He is a spiteful man; simple as that, I suppose.* If he could not spend the money, he would derive satisfaction from knowing its absence would hurt Stockholm.

"Enough!" Sandra ran up to Hans and kicked him in the stomach. He fell to the ground groaning. She yanked him to his knees. "Listen up, you son of a bitch, you hurt my husband. If you don't start spilling all of your guts right now I will make you hurt *a lot more*." She pointed her pistol at him and Marcus' legs gave a small lurch when he saw the anatomical part it was pointed at.

Anna came up and gave the most devious smile Marcus had ever seen. "Nonsense, Sandra, that small thing won't work. My husband bought some cannon for his ship recently. I'm sure he will let me test them out."

A dark stain slowly spread from Hans' pants and he whimpered, "I'll talk, I'll talk."

Early next morning, Marcus gulped down his coffee as he watched the line on the crane lower. "Was he really that clever if we figured it all out in a day? By the way, remind me never to get you mad." The diver had surfaced and said something to the crew on the dock.

Sandra smiled. "We were just cleverer than him."

Lars yawned. "He panicked, maybe. The town watch had raised the alarm and with the storm, he couldn't escape that night. So he dumped it in the water, hoping to get at it when things cooled down. He probably didn't think about how cold the water is, even when it's only twenty or so feet. A man could freeze before he gets the silver up." He went down to the dock as the net brought up the accumulated wealth of Stockholm.

Sandra looked at the up-timer thermos and fresh coffee in Marcus' hand. "Where did you get those things?"

He wisely remained silent.

A week later

Everything seems different, yet the same, thought Robert. They had now made their move permanent. Robert and Sandra had decided to donate their old home in Grantville as a new Baha'i community center and his people were probably beginning the remodel. Little Tommy was having his birthday party and it seemed every burgher and person of note in the area had come. In the case of Hans Hering and his ilk, the trial was to commence soon. Robert wasn't sure what punishment was like here, but he was certain it wouldn't be pleasant.

As for Margaret . . .

Robert glanced at the corner where she was hiding. The ones who knew the truth had decided that they would keep the secret. She had been coerced, seduced by a cunning wolf, and they all agreed that she deserved a second chance.

Marcus came up and greeted him with that annoying smirk of his. They stood in friendly silence for a bit.

"There's not enough room in Stockholm for a second bank. Not yet."

Robert decided to match smirk for smirk. "Scared that I'll beat you?"

Marcus' smirk became a full smile now. "Why beat them when you can join them?"

"So you're offering me a job? The one Hans . . . left."

"No, I'm giving Lars that job. I'm offering you mine."

"What?" Robert choked out.

"Mr. Aronian, I may not like you, but I respect you enough to admit you are better at banking than I am. So, please, make this bank something to be proud of."

Robert sat in a nearby chair, silent for a minute. Then he said, "I hear that you're trying to open up an investment bank division. With a small cut for yourself."

Marcus nodded silently.

"I also hear you deposited a thousand silver riksdalers in the bank immediately after the theft."

He nodded again, letting himself be examined by Robert.

"I'll give you my answer tomorrow."

The big smile was back. Marcus got up and began walking away. Then, turning for a parting shot, he stated, "Excellent. I'll move your personal effects to the new office."

Soon, Sandra came and sat next to him. "I want you to meet a few people later. They're backers for our new school. Though it seems you already met one."

That took a bit to figure out. "Marcus Kock?"

"Yep, he wants his own kids there, too." She lifted his arm and put it around her shoulder. "By the way, you said yes to his job offer, right?"

"How did you know I had a job offer?" Robert felt his brain was getting slower and slower. "He asked you first?"

She laughed. "I think he's scared of me. I said I'd help persuade you to say yes if he helped grease the wheels to get the school accepted. But, of course, I knew you'd say yes anyway."

"You must know Machiavelli or something."

"Nonsense, he's dead and I'm Scottish-American, not Italian."

"Any other devious secrets you want to tell me?" He poked her lightly in the back.

"A few. I got Lars to dance with Margaret. Wait, you never answered. Are you going to accept?"

"Yes."

She laid her head on his shoulder and placed her hands over her belly. "Well, the baby and I are proud of you."

"What?" Robert choked.

"Robert, I'm pregnant." She smiled radiantly.

Robert beamed back, and then promptly fainted.

Boom Toys

Kim Mackey

"Come on, Nick. What's bothering you? You've been like a—what's the American expression?—like a bear with a sore tooth. All day, I might add, even at work. You can tell us; we're your housemates. And best friends. If you can't trust us with your secrets, who can you trust?"

Nicki Jo Prickett sighed. Tobias Ridley was a shrewd judge of character. It had been a mistake to let him be the odd man out in the three-handed game of gleek that Katherine Boyle, Solomon des Caux and she were playing. It gave him way too much time to ponder.

Katherine smiled. "Better tell them, Nick. They'll find out soon enough, as it is on Monday."

Nicki Jo nodded. "I suppose you're right Katy." Then she looked at Tobias Ridley and Solomon des Caux. "But don't talk to anyone until Monday, do I have your promise on that?"

Both young men nodded solemnly and Nicki Jo shook her head.

Almost three years since the Ring of Fire. How

421

could she have suspected how much her life would change in those three years? Right after the Ring of Fire she had been nearly all alone in a hostile Grantville where she had effectively burned all her bridges by "coming out," exposing to the world her lesbianism by bringing her Fairmont lover to the senior prom. It hadn't seemed that important at the time. She'd gotten a full ride at WVU in Morgantown because of her grades in science, especially chemistry. She'd never expected to return to Grantville except for rare—*very* rare—trips home to see her dad and sister. Her dad hadn't been that concerned that one of his daughters was a lesbian, but her mom . . . her mom had stopped talking to her for good.

When her sister had called her the Friday before the Ring of Fire and told her that Mom would be out of town visiting relatives, she had seized the opportunity to get in a last trip home to pick up her few remaining belongings. Amy Kubiak, her best friend throughout her years in Grantville, despite being a class behind, had come home with her from Morgantown that weekend. And been caught like she was. Fifteen minutes. Fifteen minutes was all that had separated them from being on the other side of the Ring of Fire.

At first Nicki Jo had blamed Amy and her bitterness and depression had lasted months before she finally made up with her friend.

But when she finally did, it had been Amy who had saved her, just as she had saved her in high school, by introducing her to Colette Modi who had hired Nicki Jo to help develop the Essen Chemical Company.

For months after the Ring of Fire Nicki Jo buried

herself in her work for the biogas plant and in studying chemistry. At WVU Nicki had been taking both
organic and physical chemistry her sophomore year,
giving her as good an academic background in chemistry as almost anyone else caught by the Ring of Fire.
But she needed more, especially practical experience,
if she was to achieve her goal of getting a patron
outside Grantville. She had been relieved to discover
that seventeenth-century Europe was not as hostile
to lesbians and homosexual men as she had thought.
True, there were cases of women and men being tried
for sodomy in Europe, but the cases were rare and
usually involved women and men who were already
on the margins of society.

It was odd, really. Right after the Ring of Fire
Nicki Jo had cursed her luck thinking that she had
wound up in a universe where Grantville, filled with
her enemies, was the most tolerant town in the world
instead of just a hick little village. Only gradually had
she learned that homosexuality in the seventeenth
century was tolerated, even ignored, except in certain
rare cases. Of course, you didn't want to actually go
out and flaunt your sexuality, but that was as true of
heterosexuals in many ways as it was of homosexuals.
So long as you kept things discreet and didn't go out
and parade around for gay rights, people were willing
to look the other way. It helped, of course, if you
were rich and powerful, or had friends who were
rich and powerful.

But even that wouldn't help if you weren't discreet.

The case of Mervyn Tuchet, Earl of Castlehaven
in England, had been a cautionary tale in the value
of discretion.

In 1631 the earl and two of his retainers had been beheaded for sodomy. But the case would never have come before the courts if the earl's family life hadn't been highly dysfunctional. Besides being a sodomizer, the earl had also allowed—even encouraged—his retainers to rape both his wife and his new daughter-in-law. That alone would still not have been enough to draw the attention of the courts if he hadn't also threatened his son with disinheritance. In the end, it had been his son who had brought the case before the courts. Other noblemen, disgusted at the earl's inability to control the chaos of his manor—a chaos that they loathed even more than the earl's sexual barbarities—had applied pressure in the right places to ensure his conviction.

With that tale in mind, Nicki Jo and Katherine Boyle had invited Tobias Ridley and Solomon des Caux to share a house with them in Essen. Gossips would assume that they were living in sin, but the more normal and recognized sin of a heterosexual relationship between unmarried couples.

Only the couples themselves, and Colette and Josh Modi, knew that the relationships were homosexual ones.

"Okay," Nicki said, "This is the situation." Nicki thought for a few seconds and then continued. "We've been making toluene so we can methylate morphine to produce codeine efficiently, right?"

Both men nodded.

"Well, after we provided some codeine to the Essen Intelligence Service, the director must have mentioned it to someone, because the ordnance team for Essen Steel is now breathing down our necks to make trinitrotoluene, TNT. Colette and I have been putting them off for a month, but they finally went to the governor-general and he's starting to put the pressure on. So we've got to produce some explosives to get them off our backs."

Nicki Jo wrinkled her nose in exasperation. "Not that I want to. I want to save lives, damn it, not make boom toys."

Tobias laughed. "Boom toys are fun, Nick. Besides, the Republic can't afford a very large army, so we need to keep a tech edge."

"I know, Toby," Nicki Jo said, "but our feedstock situation isn't that great. Until we can get a steady supply of nitrates from Peru or Asia, we're limited in how much nitric acid we can produce. We can't produce it with electricity like Grantville can. At least, not profitably. And every ton we use for explosives will cut into our profit on stuff we can get higher margins on."

Tobias looked at Solomon. "Let me and Solomon work on it. We're good at nitration, aren't we you old catamite?"

Solomon gave Tobias a mock scowl. "Catamite am I? Who was on top of who last night, you sodomite?"

"Sodomite? Sodomite am I? Buggerer!"

The two men looked at each other and grinned. Nicki Jo laughed. "Please, guys, I don't want to hear about it. Male sexual bonding is not my thing." She smiled at Katherine, who smiled back.

She knew she shouldn't do it, of course. Tobias and Solomon just weren't quite ready to be on their own yet. Oh, they were good chemists, but they still didn't understand, deep down, how dangerous some of the processes were that they were dealing with. But it would get De Geer and the ordnance team off her back.

"Okay, I'll let you guys have building number one. But you've got to be careful. That was our original pilot plant and it just doesn't have the safety features we've built in to the major production facility. Remember . . ."

Tobias and Solomon laughed, then chorused together, ". . . it's hard to make miracle drugs when you've blown up the chem lab." Nicki Jo had had that sign posted in three different languages at all entrances to the Essen Chemical Company's facilities and laboratories. It seemed to have worked because they'd had no major accidents except for some minor burns, spills, and inevitable glass cuts. But there was always a first time.

Nicki Jo shook her head and wagged her finger at them. "I'm serious, guys. Watch your damn purity. Distill, distill and then distill again. If you even suspect you have too many impurities, destroy it. And for God's sake, make small batches. Just telling the ordnance team we're starting to work on it will keep them satisfied for a few months. Understood?"

Both men nodded solemnly again. Nicki Jo sighed. Now she knew what it felt like to send children off into the world where you couldn't watch them every step of the way. It wasn't a pleasant feeling. She resolved to drop in as often as she could to check up on them.

"Okay, Toby, your turn to play gleek. You still owe me two guilders from last week."

Three weeks later, Nicki Jo was deep in conversation with her head chemist, the Hungarian Banfi Hunyades, when Katherine Boyle came hurrying through the door of the Essen Chemical Company's main research lab. The lab was an impressive assemblage of glassware, earthenware and stoneware. Alembics, retorts and ovens were everywhere and the building had been designed to take into account the needs of a down-time chemistry lab that had to depend on seventeenth-century materials and apparati. The majority of the glassware, thermometers and other instrumentation was manufactured by the Essen Instrument Company, a separate subsidiary started up by Colette Modi, Nicki Jo and Katherine, with financial backing from Essen Steel investors. Stoneware came from the Raeren workshops south of Aachen. Ovens, alembics and other metal apparati were built to spec by metalworkers in the Steele area who worked for or contracted with the Essen Steel Company. To the eyes of a twentieth-century chemist, the lab would have seemed a dangerous Rube Goldberg mishmash filled with safety hazards. In the down-time universe it represented the best state of the art chemical research lab in Europe, outside of Grantville.

When Nicki Jo saw Katherine's face, her guts began to twist inside her. Normally there was nothing that could get Katherine Boyle upset. So the worried frown on her face was not a good sign.

"What is it, Katy?"

"I really don't know if it's that much of a problem," Katherine said, "but Tobias and Solomon have kept it a secret for a week, so I thought I better tell you as soon as I could."

"What?"

"According to Franz Dubois, Tobias and Solomon decided they weren't getting enough toluene out to work with, so they decided they'd try distilling out phenol and nitrating that for an explosive instead."

Nicki Jo's face turned white. "Oh shit."

Banfi Hunyades shook his head. "Young fools. Don't they remember the lectures? Or do they simply think they are immortal?"

Of all the alchemists and chemists hired by Essen Chemical Company from the members of the Acontian Society, Banfi Hunyades had the most experience. A man in his late fifties, Hunyades not only came from a long line of Hungarian alchemists, he had also instructed students in chemistry and chemical medicine at Gresham College in London. His experience and intelligence had enabled him to easily pick up on the principles of up-time chemistry and help adapt up-time laboratory techniques and methods to seventeenth-century materials.

"What?" Katherine said. "Is it that much more dangerous than working with toluene?"

Hunyades nodded. "Trinitrophenol is also known as picric acid. Many of the metal salts of picric acid are highly unstable, even more so in some ways than mercury fulminate. And you know what kind of precautions we take in *its* manufacture."

"So what are we going to do?" Katherine asked.

"Tear those boys a new asshole, for one," Nicki growled. She looked at Hunyades. "Will you back me up on this one, Banfi? Sometimes I think Tobias and Solomon are still stuck in male dominance mode. If you help ream them out, it might make more of an impression."

Hunyades nodded. "Whatever you wish, Miss Prickett. Do you want to go now? The experiment still has an hour to run."

"Yeah," Nicki Jo said, "let's shut it down. We may

not be back in time and I don't want to leave this up for someone else to stumble across." It took them five minutes to break down the apparati and arrange for a clean-up crew.

Building one, two hundred yards away from the main research lab, had been the first coal tar pilot plant built by the Essen Chemical Company in the spring of 1633. It had been mainly a proof-of-principle plant, designed to establish the needs for a more sophisticated coal tar distilling facility.

Banfi Hunyades, Nicki Jo and Katherine Boyle were thirty yards from the plant when it blew up.

It all could have been much worse, of course. Banfi and Katherine were hit by non-lethal splinters from the door while Nicki Jo was knocked unconscious when a bigger chunk dug a groove along the left side of her head. The plant itself had been designed with a weak west wall in case of a hydrogen explosion and that fact helped save the lives of the ordnance team and Solomon des Caux who had also been protected by heavy equipment between them and the blast. The only serious injury was Franz Dubois, who lost an eye to a splinter.

But the three men closest to the blast, including Tobias Ridley, died.

It was the fourth day after Tobias' funeral when Nicki Jo's subconscious baggage forced itself into her forebrain. She was in the dark, alone, in her bedroom.

You piece of shit, Prickett. You knew they weren't ready. You knew it was dangerous. And you wanted to absolve your conscience. So much easier to tell yourself you were busy, to let the oversight slide, wasn't it?

Her self-loathing, buried for years, made her choke. Carefully, quickly, she cut her wrist with the small dagger she always carried. Not a dangerous cut, just a nice shallow cut. For the pain. *Take that, you bitch.* Again, another shallow cut. It had been years since she'd even thought of cutting herself, let alone done it.

It all started in sixth grade. Stephanie Baxter, the Queen Bee. Pretty, petite, popular. She'd hunted around for someone she and her friends could pick on, someone they could all hate with a passion. Her sights had fallen on big, awkward Nicki Jo Prickett. It helped, of course, that Nicki Jo was smarter than any of them.

But that still wouldn't have been enough for Nicki Jo to turn to self-injury without her mother. Karen Prickett had had a difficult time with her first daughter, Angela. She had been bound and determined to do it right with Nicki Jo. The pressure to be perfect had been intense. Nothing Nicki did was good enough. When Nicki Jo protested, tried to rebel, her mother, a hefty woman herself, beat her, often after half-a-dozen whiskey sours. When her dad or sister tried to intervene, they were screamed at and beaten, too. She loved her dad, but he'd been too weak to deal with her mother. So he went passive-aggressive and retreated. Angela did what she could, but by the time Nicki Jo was in sixth grade, Angela had left the house to live with relatives.

So Stephanie had been the tipping point. It hadn't helped that Nicki Jo's burgeoning homosexuality had made her feel attracted to Stephanie. That only increased her self-loathing. By the time Amy Kubiak was in middle school and able to really help, the cutting addiction was already in place for Nicki Jo Prickett.

It was her sophomore year in high school when she finally cut a little too deep, nicking a vein and spraying blood around the girl's bathroom at Grantville High School. It had been a big scene, with paramedics, administrators cordoning off the hallway, everything. Only then, with Amy Kubiak's urging and the insistence of the school counselors, had she gotten the therapy she needed.

But there was no Amy Kubiak in Essen to help her now.

Nicki Jo watched the blood drip from the shallow cuts, feeling the pain, wanting it. She hadn't cried at Tobias' funeral. She never cried. Hadn't cried since she was five years old. She was getting ready for a good, deep cut when the bedroom door opened.

"Leave me alone," Nicki said.

"No," Katherine said, "I won't. I won't let you do this to yourself."

Katherine came over and took the dagger from Nicki Jo's hand. Nicki resisted at first but Katherine's grip was steady and unrelenting. Finally, Nicki Jo let go.

"It's my fault. I should never have let them do it."

Katherine shook her head. "God gives us free will, Nicki. Tobias knew what he was doing, knew it was risky. And Solomon bears as much guilt as you. He could have said something, stopped it early enough. He didn't."

"My fault, mine! I knew they weren't ready, I *knew* it! But I let my pride, my anger at being pushed into a corner take over. Don't you see?"

"What I see," Katherine said, "is my friend, my lover, letting guilt destroy her. I noticed when I was in Grantville that Americans seem to love guilt. But they don't love what should come from guilt."

Nicki Jo looked at Katherine, a puzzled expression on her face. "What should come from guilt? What do you mean?"

"Certainly not this," Katherine said, holding up the dagger and throwing it contemptuously across the room. "That is just indulging in self-pity. Penance, Nicki. You know that there will be pressure to keep making some kind of explosives. You know that if you don't get involved more of our friends may die. As difficult as it may be for you to accept, you have to get involved. Consider it your penance. It won't bring back Tobias, but at least you can say you did your best to keep others from making the same mistake."

"What if it's not good enough?" Nicki said. "What if other people still die?"

Katherine smiled sadly. "Then that is God's will. But at least you will have done your best to prevent it."

Katherine looked down at the cuts on Nicki Jo's arm. "I think we need to get a bandage on these. Not any worse than some of the glass cuts you've had, but we'll need to put some antiseptic on them."

Penance, Nicki thought, penance. With sudden resolve she went over to her bookshelf filled with chemistry books. Somewhere there had to be an explosive that would help the Republic and yet be easier and safer to make than TNT or picric acid.

"Go ahead and get the bandages, Katy. I've got work to do."

"Gelignite?" General De Vries said. "What is gelignite?"

The ordnance team for the Essen Steel Company, minus Franz Dubois, who was still in the hospital, was meeting with the Army of Essen's command group. Nicki Jo had temporarily taken over Franz's scientific advisory role.

"It's like dynamite, General, but safer. It doesn't sweat like dynamite does," Nicki Jo said. "A big percentage of it is potassium nitrate, so that will ease the feedstock burden for it. It requires some soluble gun cotton, but only a very small percentage. The main ingredient will be nitroglycerin. Up-time, Nobel patented gelignite in about 1875."

"Nitroglycerin? I thought that was highly unstable?" De Vries said.

"That's why we'll turn it directly into gelignite, General. Now, you won't be able to use gelignite in artillery shells, but you can use it for satchel charges for your engineers, and for these." Nicki Jo pulled a short piece of wood with a metal cylinder on the top from beneath the table. "Even with the reduction in active ingredients for gelignite, the army can only afford about a ton a month. So the ordnance team and I came up with this."

De Vries took the club-like weapon from Nicki and waved it in the air. It was light, less than three or four pounds.

"What is it?"

"Well," Nicki said, "Up-time it was called a 'potato masher.' But I think down-time it needs a more martial-sounding name, so I've suggested we call them 'warhammers.' It's a grenade, General. With half a pound of gelignite in the warhead, it should be a useful addition for the infantry for both defensive and offensive battles. Once the army has enough of these in inventory, along with whatever satchel charges it wants, we can use the gelignite in construction projects. For Essen Chemical Company's bottom line, making nitroglycerin will also be beneficial since we have to get a nice pure glycerin, which, up-time, had literally thousands of uses."

After the meeting, Katherine Boyle, Colette Modi and Nicki Jo Prickett walked back to the Essen Chemical Company laboratory.

"Well," Colette said, "General De Vries certainly seemed enthusiastic about your warhammers. And he even didn't think to bring up TNT again."

Nicki Jo laughed. "I know. But we give them some boom toys, and we get paid to develop a method for purifying glycerin, which will make us a pile of money, none of it related to explosives. Much better than that stupid old TNT."

Mitzi the Kid

Kevin H. and Karen C. Evans

Southeastern Poland
Summer 1634

The sun rose toward high noon. A buzzard circled slowly over his head as the gunfighter stepped from the saloon. Red dust puffed up from each step, and the sneer on his face was even more twisted than before.

Mitzi the Kid stood up from the chair in front of the marshal's office. "Black Bart, what are you doing in town? Didn't I throw you out yesterday?"

Black Bart spit into the street. "You're nothing but a sniveling little mouse, and I never listen to mice."

Mitzi stepped into the middle of the street. Women grabbed their children and hid inside shops. Black Bart's eyes were like flat river rocks. "Draw, you lily-livered coward." Mitzi stood and watched him for a movement.

There, Black Bart's finger twitched. Mitzi's gun cleared leather and started firing before Black Bart could get his gun out. The man in black fell to the ground, and there was silence...

Broken by whistling.

Mitzi sat up, suddenly aware that he had fallen asleep with his precious book on his face. He definitely didn't want to be caught with the book again, not when he should be picking rocks. He hid the book under a couple of rocks on the sledge, and hurried over to the first furrow from last fall. He would have to get the rocks out before they could plow and plant this spring. He found a rock, and tossed it to the pile at the edge of the field before the whistler could top the hill behind him.

Mitzi bent over, grabbed another chunk of rock, and with a quick twist of his shoulders threw the rock to the pile. At least he was still close enough to the edge of the field that he didn't have to use the sledge. Dragging a sledge full of rocks was one of Mitzi's least favorite activities. He bent, threw another rock, bent, threw rock, then more of the same.

He kept working as the whistling stopped. Then he heard a familiar voice. "Mstislav, I see you're picking rocks."

Mitzi looked over, and it was Aleksy! "I'm Mitzi. I'm fourteen, great-grandfather was Mstislav. And shouldn't you be at your duties? Were you dismissed? Are you back for good?"

Aleksy laughed as he gave his little brother a hug, and pounded him on the back. "No. The count declared a break. I think it is a new mistress. And while most of my workmates could only talk about having parties and entertainment, I'm here to see what you've been neglecting."

Mitzi grinned as well. "And you walked the whole eighty miles?"

Aleksy shook his head. "No, I was able to ride part of the way. Otherwise, I'd still be on the road."

Mitzi and Aleksy sat down on the sledge and pulled grass stems to chew on. Mitzi leaned back on his elbows. "I was sad to see you go. How long will you be home? Now that you're gone, it's been my job to pick the rocks before the first plowing. I was hoping you were back for good."

Aleksy laughed and leaned on his elbows as well. "Wishful thinking, brother. Even if I were back for good, I'd get a different job than picking rocks. That's yours!"

"I've been reading that book you brought. I've read it through twice already. Who is this man, the author? He sounds like some Frenchman, with a name like L'Amour."

Aleksy tousled Mitzi's hair. "From what I could find out, he was an American, but he doesn't live here in Europe. He was from before the miracle." Aleksy pulled a little booklet from his shirt. "But I learned about something even better than L'Amour. I brought it home to show the village elders. They probably will want to have a meeting tonight, so I don't think anyone else will have time to come out here and catch you sleeping again."

Mitzi blushed, but his discomfiture was quickly forgotten. "What is it? Is it a story as well?"

"No, it's in good German. It's just a couple of pamphlets. They're about something called the grange."

Mitzi arrived at the village meeting early, so he could get a good seat. He was perched on a barrel very close to the front. As always, the gathering was in the open area between all the houses.

With only seven extended families, and nine houses, this wasn't the largest village in the district. There wasn't a shop of any kind, so nobody sold spices. That meant that they were not a town. They had their own small scriptorium, but it wasn't really large enough for the meeting, so they met in the courtyard.

In the old days, when Uncle Olek was a young man, the village had been the direct support of the manor. But when the manor house had burned down twenty years ago, the Olbermann family moved off to the town and left the village elders in charge of making sure that the fields were planted and rents were paid. Even the manor was twenty minutes' walk from the village. And so the village became sleepier and less exciting week by week and month by month.

He smiled as he saw Frau Walczak, bustling around in the cobblestoned space between the houses. She always called it a courtyard, saying that even castles did not have so fine a space for their activities. It was not quite like a plaza or courtyard in a town. It really was just a wide space, with houses on all sides.

Herr Piotroski supervised the setting of planks on top of barrels to make the head table. The preparations were finished, and Old Uncle Olek came out of his house, and sat down at his seat. That was the signal, and the rest of the village council, all the heads of households, gathered around the table.

The meeting started. Mitzi let his mind wander as Herr Piotroski gave the same old announcements. Finally it was Aleksy's turn. Aleksy took out the pamphlets and put them on the council table. "Here are the basics for organizing our village into a grange. The grange will protect our farms and families by making us part of a larger coalition. More, it will get us access to *The Grange Proceedings*, which are newssheets about the advances in agriculture, and broadsheets on how to make improved tools that will work for us."

After he sat down, there was a moment of silence, then the talk began. In the tradition of the village, all the adults seemed to be talking at the same time, and as loudly as possible. Everyone, at one time or another, pointed at the pamphlets laying on the table and waved their hands in the air to emphasize some point or other. As it grew darker, lanterns and torches lit up the area, food and drink were brought out from the houses, but the discussion never stopped.

Uncle Olek waved his cane at Herr Piotroski. "But it's not new! This sounds just exactly like what we've been doing all along."

Herr Piotroski ducked, and nodded. "Yes, I agree. But if we form an organization, one that is bigger than just our village, we can get better prices and what money we do get will go farther."

Mitzi's father, Hans, picked up the pamphlet, and looked at it as the others shouted. Then he stood up, and raised his hand for silence. "It says here, if we set up this organization, we can have a voice in politics. And I like what it says about cutting out the middleman. It means that we could get more money, and even the people we sell to would get more."

As the night wore on, formidable quantities of both beer and bread were consumed. To Mitzi, it seemed that all the wrangling was really more about making sure everyone knew that everybody else had heard them, and that they had heard everybody else. The real selling point had been that everyone had heard about villages in Germany which organized and were having great success.

The last holdout was Herr Grabowski. He stood up and shouted, "You all sound as if we will have to pave the courtyard with gold bricks just to use up all the money we will make. You all act like enthusiasm will solve all your problems. You need to know, that if you're not willing to work this idea won't work for you."

Herr Piotroski banged his cane on the table when the whole village tried to shout down Herr Grabowski. When it was a little calmer, Herr Piotroski said, "So you're saying you don't think we should try this?"

All eyes went to Herr Grabowski. He frowned under his heavy black brows. "No, I'm not. I'm saying that if everyone is willing to make this work, I'll try it too."

The Duroski manor had fallen to hard times. It lay on the side of a valley closer to holdings of the Polish nobles. The family was almost nonexistent now. The only living heir when the old man died was his son, Jarusz. He was a bully and a wastrel, but the old man had no other choice. There were not even nephews he could leave it to. So the manor fell into disuse as Jarusz Duroski spent his inheritance on anything and everything except proper maintenance.

Now Jarusz was home and out of money. He and his band of lowlifes were camped at his old manor. The house itself was still standing but most of the outbuildings were collapsed and decaying. There were no servants, just he and his men.

Jarusz and his men were drinking in the old dining room. The table had been hastily repaired with a mismatched leg, and it was not strong enough to lean on, but it was able to hold the leather jack full of beer, and the map spread out in the middle. He leaned over and examined it for a moment, then placed his finger on an area next to his land. "And who owns this land here?"

Boris, his second in command, replied, "That land belongs to the Olbermann family. It is part of an inheritance that went to a German cousin about ninety years ago. They moved to town when their manor house burned. It has been almost twenty years since they have been in residence on that property, but I don't think that the land belongs to anybody else."

Jarusz stroked his beard. "So the family has not been there? That just may be the answer to our supply problems. There's nothing else here we can forage. Perhaps if we occupy the ruins of the manor, we can claim that we were just protecting the property from the bandits and thieves."

That brought a laugh from the men in the room. Jarusz laughed as well. They would really be "protecting" the land from themselves. He pulled his knife from the scabbard and started picking his teeth. "With a little effort perhaps we could convince the Olbermann factor that it should really be ours, and not belong to someone who abandoned it more than a decade ago."

Boris stood up, his eyes alight. "And even if we can't get the land for our own, we can claim payment for protecting it."

Jarusz nodded. "Very well, gather up the men. We'll go camp in the ruins of the Olbermann manor. It looks like a very nice little valley, and it would fit nicely into my holdings."

Boris nodded. "Yes, Your Excellency. Everything will be ready at first light."

Jarusz yawned. "No need to leave that early. We'll go when I'm ready in the morning."

With a crunch, the last rock landed on the pile at the edge of the field. Mitzi stood and stretched his back. *At least this field is now done.* Mitzi got his switch, and started the ox moving. He needed to get these rocks down to where they were building a new shed.

It had been a week since Aleksy returned to his posting. And the organization of the grange was complete. Mitzi himself had been appointed as clerk because he could write well in German. Even though he was still picking rocks out of the fields, he felt more important.

He came out onto the road, then noticed sounds of an argument drifting up the hill from the village. Mitzi shaded his eyes, to see who was waving their hands now.

Down at the edge of the village, there was a group of armed men that Mitzi didn't recognize. He'd never seen anyone like that in this area. Opposite them, a group of villagers stood shaking their fists in the air. He wanted to hear this, but he couldn't leave the ox up here untended.

He tried to hurry, but oxen are slow, and by the time Mitzi had the ox put away, and the sledge behind the barn, the group of strangers was gone. He ran over to his father. "What was all that?"

Hans was still angry. "Those Cossacks claim that they are protecting us from bandits. They have moved into the ruins at the manor, and they want us to provide them with food. I think they're the wastrels that have all but destroyed the Duroski holdings. But they definitely don't work for the Olbermann family, and we owe them nothing."

That evening was the regular meeting for the grange, so the tables in the courtyard had been set up again. Mitzi took his seat to the side of the head table, and had paper and his ink pot ready to take notes. He was interested to see what the leadership would decide to do about the Cossacks.

Herr Piotroski stood up and banged his cane for order. When it was relatively quiet, he began. "This opens the monthly grange meeting for New Olbermann. And while we settled on an agenda last meeting, let's talk instead about what everybody has on their minds anyway. What do we do about Duroski and his Cossacks?"

Mitzi's father, Hans, stood. "Yes, agree."

Herr Piotroski nodded. "Fine, we will open the discussion of Duroski and his men, and save the discussion of the cost of seed for next meeting. I'll go first."

There was some murmuring, but no disagreement. Mitzi got busy writing the record of the meeting.

Herr Piotroski laid out all of the particulars of what they said, and what we said, and then opened the floor for general discussion. There were a couple of moments of silence, as everybody waited to see who would go first. Then the shouting and hand-waving started. Tonight, the participants were grim and everybody showed expressions of concern.

Hans stood to speak. "But what can we do? These men are armed like soldiers. They claim they have feudal right over us."

Herr Piotroski stood. "Our leases, our grants, and

our loyalties have always gone to the Olbermann family. These men follow that blockhead Duroski. They have been camped at his old family manor for several months now, and have probably either destroyed or completely stripped anything there. I think they are hungry, and clamoring for new ground. I know for a fact that the son, Jarusz, has coveted this valley for as long as he can remember. Our village will never owe that parasite anything."

There were rumbles of agreement all through the meeting, but nobody stood to speak. Finally, Mitzi stood up. "I know I'm young, but I don't think we need to stand for this. It's just like in my book that Aleksy gave me. The people in town are being threatened by a rowdy gang, and they came up with a plan. That's what we need, a plan."

When he sat down, the meeting moved into the typical calm and reasoned discussion of the village. That is, everybody waved their hands in the air, and shouted their opinion at the top of their lungs. Groups began to form. People with the same general opinion tended to stand in the same area.

Finally, it began to look like there were only two groups. One was for the appeal to the law, and the younger group was for a more violent solution.

That was when Herr Piotroski stood and banged his cane for silence. "We haven't heard from Uncle Olek yet. Uncle Olek, which action do you think we should pursue?"

Everybody turned to the old man at the other end of the table from Mitzi. He had not allowed them to make him president, but he was still respected and expected to sit on the council.

Uncle Olek stood slowly, and looked at the entire village. His eyes were burning under his bushy white brows. "I think that we have a responsibility to the Olbermann family. So it is the right thing for us to send a representative to town and let them know what is happening."

That brought a huge reaction from the crowd. It sounded to Mitzi kind of like a roar. People started shouting at Uncle Olek, and then shouting at each other.

Uncle Olek was still standing up, waving his hands for quiet. Finally Herr Piotroski banged on the table and shouted until it was quiet. "There you go, Uncle Olek. What else do you have to say?"

Uncle Olek took a deep breath, and steadied himself with his cane. "I was saying, before I was interrupted, that we also have a responsibility to the Olbermann family to protect their land. So I think we also need a plan to protect the village. And it is here at the grange that we look for plans to protect our homes and families."

The shouting began again, and the discussion went on for a while. Finally, Herr Piotroski stood and banged with his cane. Mitzi decided that everybody was getting a little tired because it didn't take as long to quiet as it had before.

Herr Piotroski said, "As president of this grange, I've decided. Tonight we will send someone into town with a letter. Mitzi will write the letter for us, and we will send Wictor to town with it. Wictor, make sure you give it to the Olbermann family, and wait for their reply. The law should deal with this."

Wictor was Mitzi's cousin, just a year younger. He could also read and write a little, but not as much as Mitzi. The agreement between the village families and the Olbermann family was handed to Mitzi. He was to make a copy that would be presented to the intruders when they came back in the morning. And another paper detailing all the decisions of the grange would be prepared and sent with Wictor when he left in the morning. Mitzi realized that he would be up very late tonight getting all the paperwork ready for the confrontation.

Mitzi meticulously finished the minutes of the meeting, then started on the other articles. But he couldn't help but think about the trip to town. Wictor would be walking all day, and reach the inn after dark. It would take at least a day to negotiate with the factor for the Olbermann family, and then a whole day back to the village. Mitzi really wondered if there really was time to wait for the Olbermanns to respond.

Early the next morning, Herr Piotroski and Uncle Olek stood at the entrance to the courtyard. They watched as Wictor ran down the road and over the hill. There was no way Wictor could return for at least three days, and perhaps longer, if it took time for him to locate the factor, or convince him of the seriousness of their petition. He carried a sack with food and a blanket. Evidence of apprehension and discomfort were visible on the elders' faces. But they were resolved. The law said thus and such, and the law would be obeyed.

Now it was time for the Cossacks to return. Herr Piotroski and Uncle Olek stood by the road with the other adults. Mitzi stood with the other young men in the courtyard, near the doors of the homes, and the mothers had insisted that all the children stay with them inside the houses.

Herr Piotroski had been adamant that they should not arm themselves with axes and hoes because they didn't want to provoke violence, and would only resort to it as a final choice. So the boys stood as grim and threatening as possible with their hands at their sides.

Then on the road opposite of where Wictor had disappeared, Mitzi heard a clatter. A man on horseback, followed by twenty swaggering men on foot came down the road toward them. Mitzi nudged his cousin Karl. "Come on, I want to see this." He and the rest of the boys ran to Uncle Olek's house because it was the tallest. They hurried inside, and ran up to the garret, then squeezed out the window and sat on the roof on the courtyard side. From here, they could see the entire village.

Everyone in the village watched the splashy color and glitter of steel as Duroski and his men approached the village elders. The two groups finally met, and Herr Piotroski waved the paper in the air.

Jarusz Duroski stepped down from his horse. Mitzi was not close enough to hear everything said, but the captain waved his fist in the air, and then struck Herr Piotroski's paper to the ground.

The brigands laughed, and moved closer around Duroski as he pulled himself back up on his horse. He laughed with his men, then pointed at the hay barn just outside of the village. Then he shouted in a voice loud enough for Mitzi to hear. "Burn it to the ground!"

Several of the Cossacks were armed with swords or clubs. Some of them marched over to the hay barn just outside the village, and began lighting fires. When the grange elders ran over and tried to defend their barn, they were struck to the ground. Mitzi jumped up, and crawled through the window, followed closely by the other young men.

They hurried down the stairs, but before they reached the front door, they encountered Aunt Marie. She was Uncle Olek's spinster daughter, older than Mitzi's mother. She lived with Uncle Olek, and took care of him. Now she was planted firmly in front of the door, with her hands on her hips.

"Where do you all think you're going?" Aunt Marie's voice was stern, and the young men skittered to a stop in front of her. All of them were more afraid of Aunt Marie than they were of the intruders outside.

Mitzi felt a hand push him forward, and he cleared his throat. "Aunt Marie, we're going out to help. We can't just stay in here and let them burn down the village. They are threatening the village elders. We've got to go and help."

"No, you don't. You are to stay in here. We can't afford to lose you, and the brigands have already left. You just wait right here until I get word from my father."

By the time the boys were able to leave the house, the barn was fully engulfed. The brigands were outside the village on a hill. They stood and watched the blaze.

Mitzi's father and the other elders of the grange were frantically filling buckets to keep sparks from the barn under control, but there was no saving the barn. Herr Piotroski signaled the boys to come help with the buckets.

Duroski could be heard laughing as he and his men left for their camp next to the burned-out manor house.

☆   ☆   ☆

That evening, as Mitzi sat at his little table to take notes, he felt waves of anger and determination wash across the meeting. After the intruders had left that day, the village spent a long time dealing with hot spots in the barn. The only thing that kept it from burning other buildings were the old stone walls, and the fact that there was almost no hay left after the winter.

The leaders of the grange were seated at the front table. Everyone was streaked with soot, and exhausted. Herr Piotroski stood and announced that the brigands had demanded that the supplies be set out on the morrow. And further, if the supplies were not put out, two houses in the village would be set afire.

At this statement, the mood of the villagers became, if anything, more determined. Snatches of conversation drifted across the courtyard. Mitzi's mother could be heard. "But what if they have firearms? What can we do for that?"

There was more hand waving and shouting. It was very difficult for Mitzi to write down what was happening, because he had trouble telling what the consensus was.

Uncle Olek said, "We have six light crossbows in the village. And a couple of the boys are very good. But they would never stand against a concerted attack. There are still more of them than there are of us."

Finally the grim defeated mood shifted. More and more, the hand waving was to support a plan of attack. Ideas came faster, and eyes lit with hope and defiance. Herr Piotroski stood. "If this plan has any chance of success, everyone must do their part. If not we will have a disaster."

☆   ☆   ☆

Mitzi was at his post on top of Uncle Olek's house. His part of the plan was to watch the watcher. The Cossacks had a man at the edge of the clearing near the road. He had been there since first light.

Mitzi knew this because he had been out on the roof, lying on his stomach and watching the road all night. As jobs went, it wasn't too hard. The worst part was the almost overwhelming smell of bacon grease, and it was making Mitzi hungry.

One of the main sources of income in New Olbermann was rendered pig fat. They collected it in barrels and sent it in to town to sell in the fall after the slaughter, and again in the spring when they thinned the hogs.

Today the barrels of pig fat were being used for something else. In the center of the village, he could see the tables set up again. It seemed that nothing could happen in the village without tables being set up in the courtyard. But this time, instead of setting the table up at one end of the courtyard, the tables were right in the center. Food, barrels of beer, and other consumables were stacked in the open area on the tables.

After some time, the activity around the table stopped, and the villagers withdrew to their houses. Everyone waited for ten minutes, then Mitzi noticed the watcher nod his head in satisfaction. Then he strolled down into the grove, and ambled toward his camp.

"That's it! He's gone to his camp," called Mitzi. The tension in the village ratcheted even higher. Final preparations were made, and the smell of frying bacon lay over the village like a blanket.

From this point on, his job was to tell everybody in the village where the intruders were. It was just a faint clatter that attracted Mitzi's attention. Turning, he saw the brigands. They were all trooping over the hill, dressed in flashy tabards and shirts. "Uncle Olek, here they come. I think it's all of them, all right. They must all be really hungry."

Uncle Olek was inside the window, at the top of the stairs. "Mitzi, can you tell if they're carrying any guns?"

Mitzi shaded his eyes and looked carefully. "No, Uncle Olek, I don't see any guns. I don't see any crossbows, either. Almost all of them have a club or a sword, but that's all I see. I don't think they expect us to resist."

The Cossacks marched right up into the courtyard of the village. Everybody was safely inside. Mitzi crouched down on his rooftop so they wouldn't notice him, but none of them looked up.

Jarusz dismounted and walked over to the tables. "Very nice spread." He turned to the men. "You there, Pavel. You get the first taste."

Pavel was a young man, but Mitzi didn't like the looks of him. The wastrel had close-set eyes and greasy, unkempt hair. He stepped up to the table. "Smell that? Fresh food!" He picked up a piece of bread and tore into it hungrily.

The captain watched him for a moment and then grinned. He slapped Pavel on the shoulder. "I guess it's not poisoned. Have at it, men."

Pavel looked startled, but then grinned and picked up a hunk of cheese. The rest of the men surged forward. "That sure makes me hungry," said Pavel.

With a rush, the outsiders flooded into the court-yard, crowding around the table and grabbing samples for themselves. The mood among them turned almost festive as they congratulated themselves over their easy conquest of this village of sheep.

Mitzi watched closely. When the last man was inside the village, Mitzi called in a clear piercing voice, "Now!"

With a crash, barricades were thrown up across the entrances to the center of the village. At the same time, second story windows overlooking the intruders were thrown open, and cauldrons of boiling grease were poured on the men below. The resulting howls of rage turned to fear when flaming bundles of straw were cast down on the men. The grease caught fire.

The Cossacks ran from side to side, trying to dis-lodge the barricades, but these were the bolsters used at harvest time when the hogs were driven into town from the surrounding woods. They were very sturdy and pig proof.

The fire spread following trails of the hot grease, and the food on the table was now aflame. Many of the brigands were on fire as well. Some of them were trying to climb over the barricades, and others were pounding on the village doors, trying to escape the building conflagration. The houses had all been built in a day and age that called for fortification from time to time, so the doors were very thick and reinforced, and there were no windows on the first floor, only small arrow slits.

Now, any time a man came within range of one of the arrow slits, a rain of crossbow bolts drove him back to the center of the courtyard. Upstairs, now

that the grease was all spent, pots of boiling water
were dumped on the men in the center. And from
the rooftops, Mitzi and his cousins sent an avalanche
of field stones onto the heads of the men below.

A group of five or six men picked up anything they
could use as shields, and together they forced their
way through the barrier on one side of the courtyard.
But they were the only ones that escaped. Smoke
and steam obscured the sights below, and finally the
screams stopped.

For a moment, the village was silent. Mitzi felt
an odd feeling of horror. It had been much worse
attacking these men than it ever was dealing with
slaughtering the hogs. The picture of a man covered
in flame, trying to climb over the barrier kept repeating in his mind's eye.

Then his father, Hans, stuck his head out of the
garret window. "Mitzi? Are you all right? Come in here,
boy." As he scrabbled down off the roof, he started
thinking about exactly what they had accomplished.
They had won! The Cossacks were dead! He climbed
back into Uncle Olek's house.

When he walked out onto the square, he really
was a mixture of emotion. He was relieved that it
was over, he was still excited by the battle, and he
was sickened by the carnage.

The flames had only scorched the stone fronts of
the old houses, but he couldn't bring himself to look
at the bodies yet. He felt his stomach clench. A wave
a nausea flooded his mouth, and he had to run out of
the courtyard and empty his gut over and over. And
still the vision of the flaming man was before his eyes.

☆   ☆   ☆

The gunman lay crumpled face down in the red dust of the street. A wisp of smoke curled away from Mitzi's six-shooters. Mitzi looked around. In that window protruded a rifle barrel. From the door of the hardware store, Uncle Olek with his big old horse pistol looked out. And there was Mitzi's mother, gathering up the family pistols from his brothers and sisters. He might never know exactly who shot Black Bart, but he or his family, it was the same.

Mitzi bent over and grabbed another chunk of rock. With a quick twist of his shoulders, he threw the rock to the pile at the edge of the field. It just wasn't fair. After everything that happened, here he was picking rocks again. The more things change, the more they stay the same.

Then he heard a familiar whistle over the hill. Aleksy was home! He hurried out of the field just as Aleksy came to the wall. "Aleksy, you're back!"

"Yes, when the news of your difficulties came to the ear of the count, he insisted that I hurry home to help. But from what I heard in town, I'm too late. You have already saved the day all on your own."

Mitzi grinned, and then his face fell. "Yes, I guess we did. But Aleksy, you didn't see it. It wasn't like the book, not the same at all."

Aleksy nodded, and the two of them walked toward the village together, not speaking. When they came into the village, Mitzi shouted, "Aleksy is home!"

That brought everyone out of the houses. Herr Piotroski slapped Aleksy on the back. "It is definitely time for a party tonight."

☆   ☆   ☆

That night, the table was set up in the courtyard. Everything had been repaired after their encounter with the thieves, but the town still felt uncomfortable with the awful truth.

So the first thing they did that night was hold a torchlight procession out to the hill near the manor. There they placed a sign on the mass grave dug in the hill. And it said:

Here are the graves of twenty-seven men.
They came to steal our food and burn our houses.
They never left.

NEW OLBERMANN GRANGE

The Arrow

Gorg Huff and Paula Goodlett

Willem Krause watched the *Las Vegas Belle* fly over and the left side of his mouth lifted in his patented half-grin. He was a charming fellow. Which was something he both knew and worked at. Krause worked at everything. Very little had come easy to him. His title was real enough, but mostly meaningless. He made his living as a mercenary soldier. He watched and as he watched, he formed a new goal. *The goal of my life*, he thought. He would gain an airplane—buy one, or build, or steal one, to take him where he wanted to go and turn him into a whole scout company all by himself. With an airplane, he could sell his services anywhere. Anywhere at all. To Krause it was obvious just from seeing the airplane fly, that aircraft would be of immense value in war even if they could never fire a shot. He watched the plane for another moment, then turned away. He had things to do. And he needed to be in Saxony to get the money to do them with.

☆ ☆ ☆

"It's true, Elector," Willem Krause said. "I saw the airplane fly with my own eyes."

John George of Saxony asked for another beer—as was his custom, by dumping what was left of his present beer on the head of his servant. It was a boring old joke a hundred years before the Ring of Fire. But Willem smiled as though it was the freshest of wit. "They," he said, referring to airplanes, "will be world-changing, Elector. But I don't think the up-timers know it."

"Why not?" John George asked.

"Because of the resources—or rather the lack of resources—they are dedicating to them even now." Willem shook his head in only half-pretended disgust. Telling John George anything bad about the up-timers on his western border was always a good tactic, but in this case Willem was somewhat amazed at how little resources the up-timers were spending on aircraft.

The conversation continued, a mix of complaints about the up-timers and their destabilizing effects, upsetting the natural order of things. And the advantages of air power which, if invested in by farsighted members of the better classes, could stave off—at least for a time—the democratizing effects of the up-timers.

It took two more weeks and quite a bit of groveling, but Willem got the money and headed back to Grantville. During the groveling, they discussed whether it was better to simply buy an airplane or have one built. Krause managed to convince the elector of Saxony that having one built, and having the elector's loyal Willem Krause involved in the building, would mean that they were not dependent on the up-timer knowledge nearly as much as they would be if they simply bought whatever some up-timer sold them.

Back in Grantville, with a bank account filled with Saxony silver, Willem Krause started looking into the possibilities for airplanes. There were many people building many types of airplanes. The Kellys, an up-timer couple, were building three different aircraft at once. A pair of idiots, one up-timer, one down-timer, were trying to get people interested in building multi-engine bi-wing airplanes.

Money, Darius thought. Back up-time, big stars and rich people ran around in faded jeans and torn T-shirts. Not down-time. Down-time, real money was needed to have a wardrobe and having a wardrobe meant having real money. And at first glance this guy looked like he had real money. All those fancy clothes, and this dude was pretty well-padded, too. Not fat, but definitely nowhere close to starvation.

"How can I help you, sir?" Darius asked.

The guy looked at Darius and gave him this sort of conspiratorial grin, as if he had a secret but was willing enough to share it with Darius because he trusted him. "Aircraft. I'm interested in aircraft."

"Yes, sir!" Darius said in Amideutsch, half-unconsciously returning the grin, "Aircraft design and history have been two of our most popular research areas ever since the National Library was established. And they've gotten even more popular since the *Las Vegas Belle* first flew. We have a standard booklet you could buy. It has some basic research from the library and it contains the basic theory and the main formulas involved. It costs twenty-five dollars, but it's just an overview. There is a much more detailed and complete book that was put together by three researchers and examined by Herr Smith. He said it has enough information in it to get you killed."

The guy looked kind of surprised and a bit bemused by that comment. But it was exactly what Hal Smith had said about the book. And Darius told him why. "An airplane that never left the ground was unlikely to kill the pilot, but even the best airplane ever built is a death trap if badly-flown or poorly-maintained. The more expensive book *Aeronautics 101* has enough information in it to get you off the ground."

Darius continued with his sales pitch. "If you're actually going to try to build an airplane of your own, you want to read the second book. It's two hundred dollars, but it has a lot of information. After you've read it, you want to consult with Herr Smith and get his thoughts on any design you come up with. That's expensive too, but Herr Smith is a real aeronautical engineer and the only one in the world. There are also the spreadsheets that Herr Smith and Colonel Wood came up with. You can do the calculations with a slide rule, or even on paper if you're good enough at math. But you're safer with the spreadsheets."

"That was a good sale," Gemma said behind him, a few minutes later while Willem Krause was leaving with his books. Researchers got a ten percent commission on books sold and twenty-two fifty wasn't bad for a quarter hour's work.

Darius jumped a bit. "Jeez, Gemma. Where did you learn to sneak up on people like that?"

"Don't take the Lord's name in vain, Darius. Not even half the Lord's name. I don't understand why the good Lord sent a bunch of up-timers back to our time just so they could blaspheme."

"Maybe," Darius suggested, "it's because the good lord doesn't actually care that much about blaspheming. Maybe he cares more about what's in your heart than what comes out of your mouth."

"Maybe," Gemma agreed. "But I'm not going to risk centuries in purgatory on the chance." Then she smiled at him.

Darius' heart gave a little flutter. Gemma Bonono was pretty. Not pretty in a "oh my god, she's gorgeous" kind of way. Pretty in a "home-town girl" sort of way. If your hometown was in Italy in the seventeenth century, that is. Or at least so Darius imagined. Not that he'd ever been to Italy, not yet.

Gemma also worked in the library. She was more a translator than a researcher, since she spoke Italian, Latin and German. Her English was coming along, too.

"I gotta go, Gemma." Darius sighed. "I need to keep the commission from that sale, so I've gotta do some of the pro-bono questions."

"I'll help," Gemma said. "It'll be good practice."

They went back to the reference desk to pick up the next pro-bono question. As it happened, that question—like so many others—was one that had been asked and answered before, so they made a note to reference the number for the already researched answer and put it on the out-going stack, then went on to the next question. One of the many clerks would get in touch with the person who had asked the question, find out what kind of report they wanted, and either answer it verbally or, for a fee, have a written report made up and sent out. Some questions already had reports written up and ready to send out, but not all of them.

That part wasn't the researcher's problem. Darius and Gemma would mark down on their timesheets that they'd spent however many minutes answering the question. Enough hours of answering the pro bonos would pay their library fee, which is what they were after.

While they were doing this, Darius explained to Gemma that the sale had been to another aviation nut, and who knows, maybe he'd come back with questions. Most of the people who bought that book never returned. Darius wasn't sure if it was because the book answered all their questions or if it was because the answers in it scared them off.

Willem Krause bought both books and read them through, which took him almost two months. Partly because there was a lot of stuff in them, partly because they were in the up-timer typeface and he wasn't used to it. Partly because they were in English and he would have done better with either German or Latin. But mostly because they were poorly written. What they were, were articles copied out of various encyclopedias, periodicals, and bits of books, strung together with connecting paragraphs inserted to explain why they had chosen this article or this scene from a given book. There was an article about a plane that had tried to pull out of a dive too fast and had its wings come off. The accompanying paragraph pointed out that while lift increased by the square, stress on the wings increased by the cube, and then failed to explain what that meant.

Willem made a note of another question to ask the next time he went to the library and went back to reading.

This was a few paragraphs from a fiction book, describing how the hero took off from an aircraft carrier. And the connecting paragraph discussed preflight checklists. It was poorly organized minutia of aircraft design and flight, put together by people who, for the most part, had never been in a cockpit or drawn so much as a line of a design of an aircraft. The knowledge was there and some of it was sneaking past the poor authorship to present itself to him. And *that* was the two-hundred-dollar book. Willem wanted to throw it across the room. Or, better yet, at the pimple-faced teenager who had sold it to him. At the same time, he realized that it was absolutely the best book available down-time on the subject of powered flight.

Willem presented his list of questions to Darius, who examined them carefully then looked at him with considerably more respect. "Some of these are new."

"The questions that aren't new...why aren't they answered in the book?"

"Because they've come up since it was written. There is a second edition being worked on now, but it won't be out till the end of the year, if then. It should be better organized, though. By the way, if you agree that the answers we find for you can be included in the next edition, there is a discount."

"How much of a discount?"

"Well, they may not want the answers for the book, so it's only twenty percent. Or you can gamble and if they use it and you're the only one that asked it, they will refund half the research cost."

Willem knew a scam when he heard one. But the whole library worked on a pay-me-again system. Almost every question asked would have an answer that more than one person would want. So the rates they charged took into account the fact that they could probably sell the answer several times. And they always charged extra if the customer wanted their answers kept private. Even if you paid the extra, it didn't keep someone else from asking the same question and getting it answered. It just kept that researcher from selling the answer to the general pool of previously answered questions. By now a lot of questions were answered by typing the question into the list of previously asked questions and getting back a reference number to an already found, correlated and printed answer. So even if Willem didn't take the discount, it was just as likely that someone else would come along and ask the question, so the answer would show up in the next edition of the book anyway.

"I'll take the twenty percent discount." Willem shook his head, partly in admiration for a good scam but mostly in disgust that he was the one who was helping write the next edition of *Aeronautics 101*—and he was paying for the privilege.

"Hey, Gemma," Gemma heard Darius call. "You want to help me with this one? It's that airplane nut again."

"How can I help?" Gemma asked. "You know that airplanes are . . . how do you say . . . out of my league."

"He wants the answers in German if possible and he'll pay extra for it. So I'll look the stuff up and then we'll go over it together and you can translate it into German."

"I'm still not the best at German."

"Yeah, but you need the work as much as I do."

"No way to get a dowry built up if I don't," Gemma said.

"All you down-time girls are always worried about the dowry business. What ever happened to love?"

"Love is for those who can afford it," Gemma said, primly. "And I can't. Not yet. Not since we spent so much on the doctors for Mama. My sister's marriage took what was left, so Papa and I are starting over."

"You guys can't go back to Padua?"

"Matteo is in charge of the shop. Papa doesn't want to work for his son."

Willem spent months in the National Library, looking at plans and reading texts on air flight. And in the process, paid for the pimple-faced boy's junior prom. And more.

Increasingly, he found himself entranced by the delta-wing aircraft. He told himself that it was because they didn't stall out. Which was certainly true. A stall happens when the loss of lift causes the nose-heavy airplanes to go into a dive. A delta has its weight farther back, so it doesn't stall. It just sinks and its controls get mushy. He told himself that a delta-wing would be able to land in narrower spaces because its wingspan would not need to be as wide. Also, true lift is square feet of surface area. The greater the distance from the leading edge to the trailing edge of the wing, "the chord," the less the span, or the distance from wing tip to wing tip, needed to be for the same lift. Of course, there are always trade-offs. More chord means more drag. And he was told that by Herr Hal Smith, the up-timer expert on aircraft design.

Willem looked at the copy of a picture of the Convair Delta Dart and imagined. He roughed out a sketch based on the Dart, but with a propeller rather than a jet engine. The propeller was in the front, as it was in most airplanes. Just behind the propeller was the engine, even though he wasn't yet sure what sort of engine he could get. Behind the engine was the cockpit and behind that the fuel tank. This was a small plane, one person and some armaments, but small, a short wingspan. He ran some calculations using the new slide rule he had bought, pencil and paper. The wing span would be only thirty feet and the plane would be thirty-five feet long.

Willem was no great artist, but like most people of his station he had been taught the basics. His drawing wasn't good, but it was good enough to give a real artist the idea. He drew a wing section and made marks on his silhouette to indicate where the ribs of the airplane would be placed. Then he took another sip of beer and went back to his calculations.

Pierre Trovler was in Grantville for the movies, for the pictures, for the art that came from the future. He wasn't in the encyclopedia, he'd checked. There was no way for him to know why, and if Pierre had known, it's hard to tell if he would have been pleased.

For in that other history Pierre had died in 1632 of food poisoning. Without that bad bit of mutton, it's quite likely that Pierre would have made enough of a name for himself to have gained an entry in the encyclopedia. But Pierre didn't know that. No one on Earth, in either timeline, knew it. All he knew was that he had looked and found no entry for Pierre Trovler, born June 9th, 1604, outside Paris. That lack of such an entry had left him a bit—actually, rather a lot—more modest. He knew he was a good artist, but knowing that he wasn't in the history books and not knowing why had been a cold shower to his ego. It had needed one. He worked harder now. For instance, he worked on the rough sketches that Willem Krause had given him with care and practiced skill, using Herr Krause's notes as well as his sketches and the drafting course from the adult education class at Grantville's high school to make designs and even a perspective view of the aircraft. He worked well into the night using the Coleman lantern, had some of the fried chicken that he had bought that noon, then went to bed.

Pierre Trovler handed over the cardboard tube that held the plans. The tube, as it happened, was made down-time, a copy of examples that had come with the Ring of Fire.

Krause took it with a smile that was both very endearing and probably more than half real. "So how is it?" he asked as he removed the cardboard cap from the tube. "Did you manage to turn my scribbling and notes into something worth seeing, or were they too bad to even give you a starting point?"

Pierre grinned in spite of himself. "I persevered, Herr Krause. In fact, they weren't bad drawings. To be honest, they weren't professional, but the information was there." He started to add that he thought that Herr Krause would be pleased, but decided not to. He doubted the man would be influenced by such a claim and it might raise expectations.

By now Herr Krause had the papers out and was looking at the drawings and the neat, careful notes. "Marvelous. This actually looks like the design of an airplane."

They talked for some time. They talked about the shape of the wing, and of the three-wheeled under-carriage.

"How do you turn it?" Pierre asked.

"These here . . ." Herr Krause pointed at the trailing edge of the wing and the line that Pierre hadn't known the meaning of, ". . . are actually separate little wings. They move up and down and change the airflow over the wing so that one wing has more lift or so that the lift is more in the front of the wing or more in the back." He pointed at the tail fin. "That has a rudder that pushes from side to side."

"Those parts will need to be clearer and drawings made of the . . ." Pierre paused. He didn't know how or why little wings Herr Krause talked about moved up and down. ". . . of whatever it is that moves those little trailing wings up and down."

"They're called ailerons," his employer told him. "Or, more generally, control surfaces. And they are moved by a system of cables that are run inside the wing and body of the aircraft."

"Just as you say, sir, but they will need to be

drawn for the plans and I will need to know what they look like."

"More than that, the book, *Aerodynamics 101*, insists that a scale model should be made and tested in a wind tunnel," Herr Krause said. "I will not skimp on such a step because, as the up-timers say, it's my pale pink body that will be strapped into the thing when it flies." Then he grinned at Pierre again. "Do you happen to know a carpenter of skill that could help us first with making the model and later with making the airplane?"

"I may, sir. Giuseppe Bonono is certainly skilled enough," Pierre said. "He is from Padua and came to Grantville to see what new skills and tools of the carpenter's art might have been developed in the future."

It took a few days to arrange a meeting with the carpenter. In part that was because it wasn't, as it turned out, one man. Giuseppe Bonono, a widower and master carpenter from Padua, had on arrival in Grantville discovered Black & Decker power tools. Hand-cutting a hole in a piece of wood so that you might insert a dowel had never been one of Giuseppe's favorite occupations. Electric motors to do the grunt work so that the carpenter could concentrate on the art of carpentry had impressed him greatly. So had the advancements in treating wood. Not that the up-timers knew everything. Giuseppe had his own tricks of the carpenter's trade and thirty years of hands-on experience.

It was, by up-time standards, a small shop in Röttenbach, on the road from Grantville to Badenburg. By the standards of the seventeenth century, especially in terms of output, it was major industry. Still, while their bread and butter was the tables, chairs, and desks they produced, they were also very interested in prestige work.

Willem Krause's delta-wing airplane had the potential to be prestige work. The sort of work that they could advertise and that would bring in sales.

It only took convincing them of that.

Not that they were going to do it for free. Prestige work meant prestige prices, after all.

"Gentlemen and masters, I am on a budget," Willem complained pitifully.

"You do that very well, Herr Krause," Giuseppe complimented him.

"Yes, thank you, Master Bonono," Willem agreed immodestly. "I thought the squeak at the end was especially artful, as though you had just twisted the tongs in which you held my stones. Nonetheless, it is true. If we can't come to an equitable agreement, I will be forced to go elsewhere. I don't want to. Pierre tells me good things about you. But my backer is already concerned over the expense involved and he actually has access to tongs. Red hot tongs, if needed."

No one asked who his backer was. There was no law forbidding the building of aircraft for Louis of France or the Holy Roman Empire. But being able to say honestly "I had no idea who it was for" might prove useful. Besides, it wasn't their business.

Eventually they agreed on a price for the scale model. It was to be a one-twentieth-scale model which would make it a bit over a foot wide and a bit under two feet long. It would be much heavier for its volume than the full-size one would be, but the control surfaces would be adjustable so that the model could be tested in the wind tunnel with ailerons up and ailerons down so that the effect on drag lift and ground effect could be measured.

"Gemma," Master Bonono shouted. "Gemma, bring wine!"

"Yes, Papa," a girl's voice said.

The noise of the power tools was muted here and Willem was glad of it. His ears were still ringing a bit from the noise of the table saw.

A pretty young girl brought wine and Willem gave her an appreciative smile for the wine as his eyes took in her form. Nicely curved, firm, yet soft. He let her see that he had noticed, then went back to the discussion. "I'm told the model will need attachments where they attach little threads which are in turn attached to weights and scales and dials. One at the center of balance, one at the nose, one at the tail, and one on each wing."

The girl seemed to accept his appreciation as her due but showed more interest in the plans. "A delta wing?" she asked curiously.

"Yes!" Willem was suddenly more interested in the girl. "You know about delta wings?"

"Not really. But I was the German translator on your additional questions at the research center, so I had to read up on aircraft design. From what I read, delta wings are not particularly well thought of by Herr Smith."

"There are disadvantages but also advantages. For one, a delta wing doesn't need as much wing span for the same amount of lift. So a delta might be able to use a runway that a straight wing wouldn't."

"You know this man?" Master Bonono asked his daughter suspiciously.

The girl, Gemma, rolled her eyes as her papa went all fatherly on her and Willem hid his smile as the girl answered.

"I've never met him till today, Papa, but I have seen him at the research center, consulting with Darius."

"You watch out for that boy. He doesn't have two dollars to rub together, even if he is an up-timer."

"He's just a friend, Papa!" Gemma said with clearly strained patience and a face growing a bit pink.

When Willem first learned that the girl knew of his interest, he had had a moment of concern. But it was clear, after all, that all that had happened was a coincidence and perhaps a useful one. "So you have some familiarity with aircraft design?" he asked. "From your work in translating the questions?"

"A little," Gemma admitted, doubt clear in her posture. "I have a good idea what the words mean, anyway."

"So here," Willem said to Master Bonono while gesturing at the girl, "you have a consultant on the interpretation of the design in your own house. How convenient."

Making such a model is not the work of an hour or a day, but for a master like Giuseppe Bonono it wasn't the work of a lifetime, either. In a couple of months, there would be a one-twentieth-scale model, of the arrowhead plane, as Giuseppe called it. Ready for the wind tunnel test over at Smith Aeronautics.

Leaving the Bononos, father and daughter, to their work Willem went looking for flying lessons.

☆　　☆　　☆

"And this is realistic?" Willem didn't even try to hide his doubts.

The man shrugged. "It was my son's, and he mostly used it for gunfighting games. But it has the flight simulator on it. The ads say it's realistic, but I don't really know. It's fifty dollars an hour if you want to use it. If you don't, there's others who do."

Willem tried it and didn't know if it was realistic or not. It did let him get used to the idea of banking into a turn and a little bit familiar with the gradualness of flight. And, perhaps more importantly, the misleading nature of that gradualness. Planes do things slowly and smoothly... till they don't. The don't part is when they get close to the ground. Then things get fast. A crash at two hundred miles per hour is pretty sudden.

The second simulator was a thing of wood and canvas, controlled by men with ropes and poles. They rocked and tilted the mini-plane in three dimensions in response to Willem's manipulation of the controls. Again, it was far from perfect but it taught him something about flying. Well, reinforced something the flight game had shown him. If you bank the plane to the right then bring the stick back to neutral, you're still banked to the right. To get back to level flight, you have to move the stick not just back to neutral but beyond it, till you have reversed what you did to bank in the first place. And all the time you were banking to the left and un-banking, you were turning left. So, to turn left, you pushed the stick left, then back to center, held the stick as you made most of the turn, then pushed the stick right till you were out of the bank, then brought it back to center. And with each move it was easy to go too far or hold it too long, and it took practice to get it right.

That was what the low-tech simulators that had sprung up since the *Belle* had first flown were about, letting you practice before climbing into one of the still few planes that had been completed since the *Belle's* first flight. Flight time in those was very expensive. The *Belles* were unavailable, strictly for the military. Kelly Aviation usually had one plane running, well, sometimes. In general, Mr. Kelly would finish it, then a few days later take it apart for parts for the next one. But during those times when one of his planes was in fact flight-ready, you could take flights in it and even get flying lessons. For the paltry sum of *two hundred fifty* dollars an hour.

The Kitts had an airplane and mostly kept it running. It was a two-seater, front and back, and lessons were *three hundred* dollars an hour. Over the two months that Giuseppe and Gemma were occupied in building the model, Krause racked up over a hundred hours in various simulators, forty hours of ground school, reading maps from the air and such, and a grand total of seven and one quarter hours in the air. He thought he knew how to fly, not well perhaps, but well enough. Besides, he was spending a lot of money on flying lessons.

It was in the days before the model was ready for the wind tunnel that the secrecy, which had been more a matter of habit and general caution, became a matter of vital necessity. Hans Richter flew into history and John George into insanity within days. In response to the change from the CPE to the USE, John George and the elector of Brandenburg had withdrawn from the Swede's alliance. John George had never been the most popular neighbor to the up-timers, but now he was considered a traitor by the king of Sweden and at least a potential threat by the Americans. Building an airplane nominally for John George would be seen as an act as hostile as building the plane for Cardinal Richelieu. Possibly more hostile. After all, John George was closer. It made no real difference in Willem Krause's plans. He had always been careful about such things. Because if no one knew who was paying the bills, it would be harder for them to come in at the last minute and take away his airplane. Now, keeping them in ignorance would be essential to keeping the project going.

"I lost another commission today," Pierre Trovler told Willem dejectedly. "Because I'm French. I'm not a cardinal or a politician. I'm an artist."

"You have my sympathy, my friend," Willem told him. "As long as you don't expect me to express it too loudly. People are excited by boys at Wismar and incensed by the League. I suggest you don an appropriately patriotic mien. Perhaps a painting of the heroic outlaw driving into the enemy ship. Or, you could join the CoC. I'm just grateful no one is asking where I was born, since my family's estates are in the electorate of Brandenburg."

"I'm already a member of the CoC," Pierre told him. "I was before this happened."

"Really? I wouldn't have thought you were the sort. Didn't you just say you weren't political just after you disclaimed being a cardinal? Do you paint in red robes?"

"You don't have to be a cardinal to be Catholic and you don't have to be a politician to believe in liberty. I know you're of the nobility, but you're a regular guy, not like John George."

Willem gave no sign by word or action that anything had changed but something had. For while he was in no way John George and cordially despised the man, neither was he a regular guy. He was of the nobility and that made him different from peasants of any situation, no matter how grand their circumstance or how mean his. He was of the nobility. His genial manner was just that—a manner. He stepped down from his natural station to put people like Pierre at ease and get the best labor out of them, not because he thought them his equal. But here they thought they were—even normally sane people like Pierre. He would have to be more careful now.

Willem watched as the technician attached the thin steel wires to his model airplane. One from the top of the model, set at the center of gravity, went through the top of the wind tunnel, over and around a pulley, off to another pulley, then down the side to a weight and gauges for reading. The bottom center of gravity wire went down through the bottom of the wind tunnel to an adjustable spring.

There were similar sets of wires at the nose, center, tail, and wing tips. Together the wires and gauges would measure the lift and drag of the airfoil at varying wind speeds and at various flap and aileron settings.

Then they started the fan and the model *Arrow* was pushed back by the wind. The technician took measurements: lift at nose, lift at tail, drag—each measurement taken several times, once for each air speed. The process was repeated with smoke and more notes were taken, when the smoke started swirling and where on the wing. Then the fan was turned off and the flaps were adjusted, and the process started again. After they were done, they had the Reynolds number by working backwards from the point of non-laminar flow.

That, and a whole lot more data that could be fed into a computer spreadsheet program to give solid estimates of lift and drag over a range of speeds and angles of attack. They added weights to different points on the model, adjusting its center of gravity to include the weight of things like engine and pilot. Maneuverability, carrying capacity, takeoff speed, and more, were provided by the wind-tunnel tests of the model in combination with the knowledge bought by thousands of lives over a hundred years in that other timeline. It seemed to Willem complete, and offered a level of confidence that surpassed that even of shipwrights. And compared to what the Wright boys, Curtiss, Sikorsky, or even Douglas had had to work with, it was complete.

It took a few days to process the data. Well, it took a few days to get around to processing the data. It took a couple of hours to input the data and the computer took microseconds to do the calculations. And it didn't take Hal Smith much longer to interpret the results.

The faster the plane was going, the greater the lift. As was standard but, like the weight, the lift was centered well back on the plane. In fact, even at fairly low speed, the center of lift was farther back than the center of gravity, which meant that in flight the *Arrow* was going to be nose heavy. Because of ground effect, that was even more of a problem on takeoff and landing. Because the ailerons were actually elevons, combining the function of both elevators and ailerons in one control surface. And because it was a tailless delta, you couldn't go flaps-down for takeoff and landing. Not without shoving its nose into the ground. So they would need to shift as much of the heavy bits as they could toward the back of the aircraft.

He discussed his changed designs with the boy Darius because he had been the researcher for the whole project. "Herr Smith doesn't much care for the delta-wing design," Willem told Darius with another of his half-grins. He had just returned from a very expensive half-hour consultation with the only aeronautical engineer on earth. When not working for the State of Thuringia-Franconia Air Force, Hal Smith—for a piddling five hundred American dollars an hour—did consultations with prospective aircraft designers. And to spend that five hundred dollars an hour, you made an appointment and waited your turn.

"Well, he's probably right, sir," the youngster admitted. "I know they look cooler, but that doesn't necessarily mean they're better."

"I know, Darius, but 'cooler'—did you say?—looking airplanes may have a higher sales price because they look better, faster, or more dangerous," Willem said, "We aren't the only ones building aircraft and it's generally better to stand out from the crowd at least a little."

☆   ☆   ☆

Armed with the information from the wind tunnel tests and analysis, Willem didn't abandon the delta, but did adjust his design. He did several things to move weight toward the rear of the aircraft. The gas tank, storage and armaments were moved back, but he wanted the pilot as far forward as he could manage. That just left the engine, the heaviest single part of the aircraft. He considered the idea of a center-mounted engine and a long drive shaft, which might have worked, except that the drive shaft would then go right through the small of the pilot's back. And that left a pusher, a plane with the propeller in back. Well . . . why not? They were supposed to be quieter, anyway, not that Krause had ever been in a pusher, but that's what the books said. Besides, the *Dart*, even if its engines had been spread throughout the body of the plane, the thrust at least had gone out the back. The Krause *Arrow* would be a pusher. That simplified things greatly. The engine and prop would be right at the back, with the gas tank just in front of the engine. The cargo and/or weapons would be between the gas tank and the pilot. The pilot would be as far forward as he could be and still have room for the control runs. Then it was off to the carpenter's shop to turn the designs into an airplane.

"Plywood?" Willem asked.

"That's what the up-timers call it. Take a thin sheet of wood, not a lot thicker than a sheet of paper, then a thin layer of glue. Another thin sheet of wood laid out crosswise to the grain of the first sheet, more glue, another sheet, still more glue, still another sheet, constantly changing the direction of the grain. Then compress it all and let it dry. The up-timers call it plywood; we call it laminated wood and it's what the up-timers call a composite material. Whatever you call it, it gives you wood that won't split along the grain because the grain isn't all going one way. Wood that spreads the stresses placed upon it in ways that normal oak or ash can't."

"What about spruce?" Willem asked. "The books mention aircraft spruce."

"Yes, but what is aircraft spruce?" Giuseppe Bonono asked. "All I know is that the books talk about spruce in the Americas. I know there is spruce in Europe. It's light and fairly strong, easy to work. But I don't know if it is this airplane spruce that they are talking about. It's pretty clear that not all spruce is airplane spruce. But I know about laminated wood. I know things I can do to make sure that it's strong and light."

"All right. The Convair Delta Dart was made out of aluminum, after all, and we aren't going to get that."

They went on to talk about the structure of the wings and the internal supports of the fuselage. Where the control runs would go and how they would be attached. What kinds of glues would be used where.

"What about the skin? Laminated wood . . . even very thin it's going to be heavy," Giuseppe warned.

"Doped canvas," Willem told him. "I have Pierre Trovler working on finding the right canvas and doping agent. The book, *Aviation 101*, second edition, suggests that the frame be lacquered before the canvas is applied. Apparently raw wood and canvas aren't a good combination."

The *Arrow* wasn't the only work of the carpenters, nor of Pierre Trovler. They had chairs and desks to make and portraits and landscapes to paint, respectively, and Willem Krause wanted to see and understand everything that went into the construction and maintenance of his aircraft. To Giuseppe and Pierre, this seemed simply a reflection of Willem's obsession with aviation.

In part it was that, but Willem, having determined that he would find his home among the lords of France and Austria, not the peasants of the USE, intended that he would know all that was needed to see to any repair or even rebuild the *Arrow*. He noted the interest that Gemma showed in him, and in other circumstances he would have taken advantage of it. But not here. Not now. Not among peasants who thought themselves his equal. It was too risky. The girl would have to make do with a clumsy farm boy to lose her innocence.

Still, gradually, amid impatient letters from Saxony, the *Arrow* did come together and became an aircraft. In all considerations save one. It had no engine. Engines, even the heavy engines of pickup trucks and vans, could not be had for love or money. Half a dozen companies were making down-time produced engines and each and every one was sold before it was built.

A rich peasant could get an engine. A rich burgher from the Netherlands could arrange the creation of a company to make them for his airplanes. But a noble of Germany had to wait his turn. Money wasn't enough. You had to have connections.

The plane was finished. The months dragged on. No engine came to Willem Krause.

"Where is my airplane?" John George of Saxony demanded in the fall of 1634. "Krause has had over a year. There are dozens of airplanes by now and I don't have even one."

Karl Gottlieb knew better than to point out that he had harbored doubts about the project from the beginning. John George didn't care for "I told you so's." Instead he simply said, "I don't know. I could send someone to check up on Willem Krause."

"Send someone?" John George asked. "No! Go yourself. I want to know where my money is going. Gustav Adolf and that jumped-up peasant Stearns are pushing things in the CPE and I won't have the Swede as overlord of the Germanies."

Karl wasn't John George's spymaster, but he also wasn't a field agent. He was the assistant spymaster for Saxony and really too well-known to be sent to Grantville. But that was now beside the point. He had his orders and the elector had a whim of iron.

"Where, Willem Krause, is the elector's airplane?" Karl asked as Willem opened the door.

"What are you doing here?" Krause whispered harshly. Then with almost no pause, "Come inside, quickly."

Once Karl was inside and the door closed, he asked again, "Where is the elector's airplane?"

"It's sitting in a hanger at the Grantville airport, waiting for an engine," Krause said. "Just as I wrote in my last report. Do you want the airplane seized by the up-timers while they decide whether building a plane for John George is abetting treason against the USE? If I understand the laws correctly, I will be exonerated and the plane turned over but not, I am sure, before Gustav Adolf has the elector's head on a pike. Is that what you want?"

"What I want, Krause, is for you to deliver the aircraft that you promised over a year ago and stop being a drain on the elector's finances."

With some difficulty, Willem kept his temper. The fact that he and Karl Gottlieb had never cared for each other was beside the point. It was a safe bet that Gottlieb wasn't here because he wanted to be. "Then we are in accord. I also want the airplane finished. It is finished, so far as any parts that might be obtained or reasonably fabricated. The issue is engines. I have begged and bribed, but so far have been unable to obtain one."

"By this time you could have had one made by hand."

"Yes, I could have," Willem Krause acknowledged. "But that would have cost twice as much as the whole rest of the airplane. No. As I think about it, it would be closer to ten times the cost of the rest of the aircraft. Steel is not soft and its shaping is no mean endeavor. To get engines light enough in comparison to their power to allow them true utility in powering an airplane needs careful and skilled shaping so that the loss of weight does not also produce a loss of strength." Willem shook his head. "These things are not easily done. Every syllable in each report represents hours or days of labor and, yes, considerable outlay of silver. But look around you. Am I living in luxury?"

Willem waved and then watched without concern as Karl Gottlieb went through his room. For it was true. Willem had spent every pfennig—even every American cent—that was designated for the airplane on the airplane. His room was decent but not large, and located outside the Ring of Fire where the rents were cheaper. That his clothing was clean and of good quality was more a function of washing machines and sewing machines than of extravagance. Nor was the room filled with gewgaws and objets d'art. Instead, there were plans and the wind-tunnel model. Notes and requests for engines and letters of polite refusal, all of which assured him that he was on their list and they would get to him as soon as they possibly could.

It was a clearly irritated Karl Gottlieb who waved him back to his seat on the bed. "Oh, sit down. When can I see the plane?"

"Whenever you like," Willem said, then added with a certain malice in his tone, "And while I am sure that Stearns' Jew spymaster has agents at the airport, who knows? They may fail to recognize you . . . or fail to care."

Karl Gottlieb's lot, over the next couple of weeks, wasn't a happy one. He had had hopes on his trip from Dresden that he might find Willem Krause engaged in fraud. But the evidence was to the contrary, and while he was still convinced in his heart of hearts that Krause was somehow cheating the duke, there was no evidence to support that belief.

The one good thing about the trip was sitting in the cockpit of the *Arrow*. It was a tight fit, but comfortable and as Karl moved the stick he could look out the windows and see the way his actions moved the control surfaces. Finally, he was convinced. Given a power plant, this would fly and fly well. There was too much care in every detail, too much skill in every piece to allow any other outcome.

☆ . ☆ ☆

Regretting the necessity, Karl returned to Dresden with a completely favorable report. "If an engine can be procured, the plane will fly. Nor is Krause the only one who is having his plans delayed by this bottleneck. Engines are needed by everyone from the army and navy to every industry. Every engine produced by every manufacturer, no matter how poor its quality, has a dozen buyers," Karl Gottlieb explained to the elector. But he couldn't explain the why of it, because he didn't understand himself. The world had changed and with it the rules of commerce and needs of production. Those changes were apparent but unnatural to a man born and raised in a world without engines. "I see no way for us to acquire an engine and without one the *Arrow* is a useless shell."

"But I see a way to acquire an engine," John George informed him. "In fact, one is already in our city. One of our wealthy merchants bought a steam engine and several other machine tools in Magdeburg, then had them sent here over the last few months. He is now trying to put every craft hall in Dresden out of their livelihoods by underselling them. I have received complaints, but he has stayed barely within the law and he has friends." Then John George smiled, thrilled with his cleverness. "The emergency of military necessity will require the loan of his steam engine. Which, just by chance, will give my friends time to acquire their own engines and compete with him on a better footing.

"You, in the meantime, will see to the transport of the engine from Dresden to Grantville by secret means, so that it can be installed in my *Arrow*—so that a surprise for that arrogant Swede may come from my quiver—all unknown to him."

Arriving back in Grantville with a three-cylinder steam engine and several hundred pounds of boilers and condensers, Karl Gottlieb was subjected to complaints from Willem Krause.

"It's too heavy and not powerful enough. It has only twelve horsepower. I need at least fifty for the *Arrow* and a hundred would be better."

"Tell the elector," Karl returned. "I want to watch. It's his idea and our task to make it work, or at the very least make a good-faith effort to make it work."

"But . . ."

"So who can you talk to about steam?"

"I have no idea. The notion of using steam engines in aircraft has come up a few times, to the everlasting amusement of every up-timer in the Ring of Fire. But we can find out." It wasn't that easy. It seemed that every steam expert in the Ring of Fire had found lucrative employment elsewhere. Willem applied to Darius and Darius directed them to Vince Masaniello of the Steam Engine Corporation. They didn't, as it happened, talk to Vince.

Charles Anthony Masaniello looked at the engine and said, "That's one of the Schmidt boy's engines. Pretty good engines, well-enough made, too, if not up to our standards. Pretty good tolerances, too. What are you fellows after?"

"We wish to increase its horsepower, Herr Masaniello."

This wasn't the first time Charlie had heard that.

"Call me Charlie. Why do you want to up its horse-power?" Then he held up his hand. "I'm not trying to get into your business, but most of the time when folks want to up the horsepower it's because they think a steam engine is the same as an internal combustion engine. And they ain't." Charlie spoke Amideutsch fluently, but with a pronounced West Virginia accent, something he made no effort at all to curb. In fact, he emphasized it, because it made him seem even more up-timer and therefore more expert on steam engines. He was expert. He would have been considered an expert up-time; down-time he was the "pro from Dover" and knew it.

The guy who had introduced himself as Willem Krause was a little taken aback by the question and Charlie waited for him to decide if he was going to answer it.

Eventually, almost twenty seconds later, Herr Krause did answer his question. "We wish to use the engine as the power plant for an airplane."

Charlie grinned and almost laughed. He didn't because it was safe bet that they would misinterpret the laughter. Instead he said, "Dad would love this. He's been working on steam tugs for years. Look, it's not the horsepower. It's the torque. The . . . well, a big difference between steam and internal combustion is that steam has full torque at zero r-p-m. An internal combustion engine needs to wind up to get its full torque. Another difference is simply that by upping the pressure you can up the h-p, though in this case you may not need to. Just gearing the engine right might get you there. Your real issue is going to be the boiler and condenser, keeping their weight down enough to let you get off the ground. I can, for an agreed-on fee, draw up some specs that can let a good down-time smith take one of Adolf Schmidt's condensers and adapt it to an airplane. It's going to be heavy and it's going to cause some extra drag, and you're going to have to figure out how to feed and exhaust the boiler burner, but it should work. The fee for that will be considerable, but it will give you a power plant."

"Could we run without the condenser to test the airframe? Just to see if the airframe flies?"

"You could. At a guess, this engine would use about a quart of water a second. How many gallons do you think you can carry before the condenser is lighter? Figure six hundred pounds of water for a five minute takeoff and landing loop."

There was more negotiation but they paid. By now the pressure from John George would have turned coal into diamonds in hours not centuries. They really didn't have any choice.

Karl Gottlieb thought that he had figured out Willem's plan. Krause intended to steal the elector's airplane. And Karl intended to stop him. He would watch. And once the airplane was ready, he would take it back to the elector. Pursuant to that goal, he started taking flying lessons while Krause and his smiths reworked the condenser. It was slow handwork, using the machine-made pipes, but hand welding them together. It took weeks.

"It's ready," said Herr Krause with an intensity that Darius had seldom heard from him . . . or anyone else, for that matter.

Naturally, that night the snows came. Not for the first time that winter, but a major blizzard. All that could be done was steam tests and engine tests. So, steam tests and engine tests they did. The prop spun up with incredible speed starting at full torque, and simply adjusting a lever not only stopped the prop but reversed it. Which Willem found marvelous. The plane moved with ease and panache, and they got good reads on how much fuel they needed for how much flight time. The delay caused by the weather was irritating, not dangerous. The one thing that bothered Willem about the *Arrow*'s power plant was that it took over five minutes to build up a head of steam. There would be no jumping into this plane and being in flight less than a minute later.

The day finally came. They had done tests. The *Arrow* was as ready as they could make it. Willem sat in the cockpit, reclined not for comfort but to save space. He watched the steam gauge with care and waited with impatience for the pressure to reach the levels needed for sustained flight. When all was ready he dialed the throttle up to take off power then released the brakes. The *Arrow* was heavier than he would have preferred, especially with the weight of the boiler and condenser. But still, according to all their calculations, it should lift off about halfway down the runway. It started quickly and picked up speed slower than he would have liked, but it did pick up the speed. He wasn't quite sure how fast he was going when he reached halfway point on the runway. The *Arrow* wasn't equipped with a speedometer. It was a matter of estimation and he figured he was going fast enough.

He pulled back on the stick and nothing happened. The wheels stayed glued to the ground. He put the stick back to neutral and waited for more speed to build. It was harder to build up speed when the stick was back. He also dialed the throttle as high as it would go, full emergency power, as it were.

Two-thirds of the way down the field he was going faster and tried again. Something was wrong. He was going faster than he had ever gone before at takeoff in any plane, and he was still glued to the ground. He should be getting something by now.

He wondered if he should shut down and try again another day. He'd give it another few seconds. After all, he could reverse thrust to slow rapidly.

Seconds later he tried again. Now he was scared and angry. Too close to the end of the runway for comfort. Stick still back, he reversed thrust. The gearing took the strain, the prop and the shaft did not snap, and the prop bit into the air—backwards.

Suddenly, with no warning, he was airborne, the nose was coming up fast. And his mind was behind the plane still trying to slow it down. He pulled back on the stick and the nose lifted faster.

Willem had only a few hours of flight time. He had soloed once, for all of five minutes. Just enough to get his solo permit stamped. He had never been in a plane that moved like this one. No one had ever been in a plane that moved like this one. It wasn't that it was especially maneuverable, but it maneuvered differently than a more traditional airframe would. More of the lift, but also more of the weight, was toward the back of the aircraft. With the elevons flipped up and the prop reversed while still in the ground-effect range, it acted like a takeoff ramp made out of concrete. The nose flipped up like it was giving the world the finger and the *Arrow* shot into the sky at something over two g's change of vee.

It shot into the sky with its propeller spinning madly backwards. Momentum and air pressure got it into the sky, but there was nothing to keep it there. Still, it got almost fifty feet into the air. And all the way up—and all the way back down—it was flipping over backwards. For at the top of the arc, Willem pushed the stick all the way forward, just as his limited experience as a pilot told him to do. The tail hit the ground first but by then the *Arrow* was angled at forty-five degrees back toward the start of the field.

Willem had a few seconds, two, maybe three, to wonder what the fuck had happened before the canopy cracked into the runway and ended his capacity for questioning forever.

Hal Smith didn't need to be called in. First flights out of Grantville Airport weren't so common that he had to miss many of them, and first flights of delta-wing aircraft were even rarer. He had seen the takeoff run. He had seen the leap into the air. He had seen the crash.

And he knew exactly what had happened. Knew that he had told Willem Krause the right thing, but for the wrong reason. That he had never thought of the true reason that the centered prop was such a bad idea. Hal had never been a great fan of deltas. He'd never designed one and never flown one, so he had never thought about what would happen if you put a prop at the back of a delta wing with half its sucking power contained by the ground and the body of the plane.

To make a plane go forward, you push air backward. When you push air in one direction, you're pulling it in from all the other available directions. That mostly doesn't matter because it is *all* the other directions. There is no restriction on where the air comes from to replace the air your prop displaces. Not, however, when that flow of air is blocked by the body of the airplane above it and the ground below it. When that happens you get a vacuum.

Well, calling it a vacuum is overstating the case. The low-pressure zone produced is to a vacuum cleaner what a vacuum cleaner is to a vacuum tube. Not even in the same range. The pressure differential is only a few ounces per square inch, less even. But there are a lot of square inches on the undersurface of a delta wing thirty feet wide by thirty feet long.

The pressure differential is the same thing that lets planes fly, but in this case it glued the plane to the ground as long as the prop was pulling air out from between the wing and the ground. Hal Smith knew all that the moment the *Arrow* lifted off. He prayed in those moments that Willem Krause would push the thrust back to full forward. It hadn't happened and he couldn't blame Herr Krause for not realizing what had happened in time. The only person that Hal found to blame for the death of Willem Krause was Hal Smith. He fell back into his chair by the tower and felt the cold wind and every day of his seventy-one years.

There were too many gaps in the knowledge brought back, too many errors. Not from lack of knowledge but from lack of understanding of the knowledge they did have. He wanted to quit then as he had wanted to quit at each of the deaths that had, over the last year and more, followed the introduction of flight into this century. He knew he couldn't quit, for his quitting wouldn't prevent a single death. The young men and women who dreamed of flight and dared turn their dreams into reality wouldn't stop. Not if God Himself came down and told them to leave the heavens to him. They couldn't . . . and Hal couldn't blame them for that.

Epilogue

Darius stood next to Gemma as they watched the ceremony. Willem Krause had been buried three days before. This was different. A small plaque made of bronze with the name WILLEM KRAUSE engraved on it. Above the name were the wings of a pilot and a compass and a square on the right and left to symbolize an airplane designer. It looked like a Masonic symbol to Darius and he almost smiled at the thought that someday this would be taken as proof that the Masons, even in the seventeenth century, were secretly trying to introduce a new world order. Herr Krause would have laughed his ass off at that, Darius was sure.

That wouldn't stop the questions, though. Willem Krause's room had been cleared out the day he died, before anyone had thought to look. No one knew who was financing him. For all Darius knew, it was the Masons or the Illuminati, though they weren't even supposed to have started till next century.

It didn't matter. Willem Krause had built an airplane.

He had flown it, if only for a few seconds and had died providing a bit more understanding of what conquering the skies cost and how it was done. His wasn't the first name on the wall of the Grantville airport tower and it wouldn't be the last. But this was the first time that Darius or Gemma had known the person behind the name on the wall.

Darius held Gemma's hand and thought about flying. About how the *Arrow* might be modified and made to fly. It should be possible.

The Society of Saint Philip of the Screwdriver

Rick Boatright

Then the LORD God said, "Behold, the man has become like one of us, knowing good and evil; and now, lest he put forth his hand and take also of the tree of life, and eat, and live for ever"—therefore the LORD God sent him forth from the garden of Eden, to till the ground from which he was taken. He drove out the man; and at the east of the garden of Eden he placed the cherubim, and a flaming sword which turned every way, to guard the way to the tree of life.
—Genesis 3:22–24

Mankind had its chance to have a life without surprises, but chose the harder path—to be like God. Now, we get to deal with the complexities of the world, and with the embodiment of that complexity, the imp that is the personification of Murphy's Law.

Murphy's imp never gives you any warning

before things fall apart. You have to be ready. You have to think about failure in advance and prepare for it.

In the long run, ready never works out. No matter what you do, the imp always finds a way.

> *The Charter and By-Laws*
> *of the Society of Saint*
> *Philip of the Screwdriver*
> Father Nicholas Smithson

Grantville, September 1635

"Yuck. Six in the morning is too early for real life." Doris McIntire had just reached the main reference desk at the front of the SoTF State Library. She had the early shift this Wednesday, opening the library after the weekly closure for cleaning. Always a relief, Wednesday, she thought. The place got a bit rank between the thorough cleanings, but what could you do? The library was the best resource in the world.

But something was wrong. She looked over at the unmanned guard station by the door, and through the barred glass into the front hallway of the still empty high school. She did not see the guards who should come and open the doors. "Where the heck are the guards?"

Suddenly, a shape blurred past the window and the door banged open. A dirty, wild-haired man carrying a large bag burst in shouting unintelligibly. He looked from side to side, apparently seeking something. When his gaze settled on the ready reference shelves, he reared back, swinging the bag. The bag gurgled loudly.

There was no time to think, no time to call for help. Doris did the only thing she could do, the thing she had trained for month after month. She reached down to the holster under the reference desk, pulled the .38 revolver that was always there, and put three rounds in the wild man's center of mass. Then she ran around the end of the desk, grabbed the bag and flung it out through the open door down the wide hallway toward the front door of the high school. As it hit the metal doors it burst into flame.

"Oh, *und* here we go again," Maria Baumain said, grinning at Brother Bernard. "I'm making a cappuccino for a Capuchin, just like I do every morning!" She started steaming the milk, and grinned at the monk.

"*Ja, und* I'll have to go find you a real Capu—" Brother Bernard started to say.

God's own whistle tore into the ears of everyone in the shop. Maria screamed and dropped to the floor, clutching the side of her face. Some of the customers screamed even louder. Some reached for weapons. Some ran toward the injured girl and others ran away.

Cora was only steps away. She grabbed a bar towel to press onto Maria's cheek to stem the bleeding from the hole created by the impact from the steaming wand. Maria kept screaming at the pain from that and the burns over half her face. Then, as the whistle died down, the smell of hot metal wafted across the room. After a few moments of searching, the espresso maker's power was cut off. It made a "tinking" sound as it started to cool.

"Get me a bowl of ice water!" Cora called out. "Maria's scalded. We need to get it cooled down. Somebody call the ambulance."

"Already on the way," someone replied.

Cora got a cold compress over about half Maria's face, while still holding pressure on the cut. This wasn't going to be good.

Father Nicholas Smithson read the letter for the third time. It was unlikely that the content would change, but he felt that he had been waiting for a long time for this news. He looked across the table at his friend, Father Augustus Heinzerling, and smiled.

"That's it then?" Augustus asked.

"You would think, with the pope taken out of Rome, with the influence of Lawrence, Cardinal Mazzare, with the general hue and cry going on, that for a single simple priest to be released from his vows to the Society of Jesus and to enter the secular clergy would be a simple matter," Father Nicholas said.

"Simple? Ha! Where the pope is, the inquisition is. Someone must determine if it is in the best interest of the church for the author of one of the best-selling books in Europe to be released from his personal vows of loyalty to the pope," Augustus replied. "And as I think about it, I'm surprised the inquisition hasn't asked about *How Not to Think Like a Redneck* yet. Not to mention Saint Philip."

"Ignore him, Nicholas. He's just jealous," Father Christopher Schreiner said. "What does the letter say?"

Nick reached up to his breast pocket and removed the little yellow screwdriver he wore there. There was a similar one in Christopher's pocket. He twirled the screwdriver back and forth in his fingers. "Apparently my request got through during the confusion following the pope leaving Rome. It's yes. I am now officially a member of the secular clergy, reporting only to the bishop of my diocese, who is, of course, Larry. I am not sure how it got done without Father Vitelleschi's approval." Nick smiled. "But in any event, it's done."

"And so?" Augustus asked.

"And so, in the absence of white-robed Dominican inquisitors knocking at our door accusing me of Manichaeism, and with Cardinal-Protector Mazzare's permission to use Saint Philip Neri's name and image as the personification of the group, I think it's time," Nick said. "You both have read the bylaws for the Society of Saint Philip of the Screwdriver, as have Father Kircher, Cardinal Larry and John Grover."

The other two priests nodded and smiled.

"This is Grantville, not Rome. We're forming a society, not a prayer group, so it's not the Grantville Oratory." Nick paused. "I still wonder if Larry was wrong, and we would have been better off with Saint Vidicon, but never mind." Nick waved his hand pushing the thought away. "Never mind. It's too late to rethink that. It's time to move from the casual group to what we've talked about, and this release gives me the freedom to do that."

Nick took a moment to reflect. "You both know my dilemma."

"No one doubts your priestly vocation, Nicholas," Father Christopher said. "But your skills in the library do more than just bring in funds. You are contributing to the growth of a new culture."

"Then I have a duty to try to see to it that it's a *human* culture, not just a technological one. What use is wealth to a priest? And, despite our joking about the inquisitors, it can't be a purely Catholic culture, or a Catholic institution. Too many others are part of this community," Nick said.

"So, we get the minds together, we crush Murphy's imp, and you buy the beer. It works for me," Augustus said. "Speaking of beer, why don't we go celebrate your release? I understand there's a new lager at the Gardens." He pushed back from the table.

Nick smiled. "Of course, Augustus. And I'm sure that I'm buying."

Doris sat in the staff room of the State Library with her hands wrapped around a cup of some herbal tea Charlotte Kovar had handed to her. "Do we have any idea who he was?"

"No," Chelsea Perkins, the head of security for the library replied. "No note. The police will ask, but I doubt he's been around town. I suspect he came straight here."

"What do we do now?" Charlotte asked.

"I clean and reload the revolver. You take Doris home to rest and you go with her to see to it she does," Chelsea said. "All her family is out of town. Then, I go bang some heads in the guard room. I'll have to be ready for another attack, just like always. Doris, I'll need to go to the meeting tomorrow with you."

"Do we have to?" Doris asked, looking up.

"You helped write the policy. We go to the meeting, and you get counseling, need it or not," Chelsea said. "It's necessary."

"I suppose," Doris said. "But I'm going home now, and I'm going out the back door."

Cora sat in the waiting area outside the ER at Leahy Center waiting to hear from the doctors. Every time someone moved, she looked up. She sat there, staring at the blood-stained towel in her hands, doing nothing.

"Aunt Cora?" Nina Kindred burst through the doors into the waiting area. "Aunt Cora? Are you okay?"

Cora looked up. "Okay?"

"Are you okay? You've got blood all over you. I'm going to go get someone."

"No, no. It's not my blood, it's Maria's."

"Oh, thank God," Nina said. "Paul told me that there had been an explosion in the coffee shop, and that you had gone to the hospital, and..."

"Hush." Cora put her hand over Nina's. "You're not here for the paper, are you?"

"Oh God, no. I'm sure he'll send someone around to interview you but, for goodness sake, Aunt Cora, you're *family*."

"That's okay then. You can wait with me? It's hard just waiting."

"Of course. However long it takes," Nina said.

"I'm glad you're here. I didn't want to be alone," Cora said. "Someone has gone for Maria's family. Her dad works for Johnson's Grocery. They'll be along soon, but someone needs to be here for Maria."

"What happened?"

"The espresso machine blew up. That's all I know for sure. One minute Maria's frothing milk, the next minute she had a piece of steel sticking out of her face and steam was blowing everywhere."

"The espresso machine?" Nina asked. "But you only bought that one about a year ago!"

"Yes. The little one I had from home finally gave up the ghost, remember? So, I had Clarence Dobb's folks make us a new bigger one."

"Clarence Dobbs? But, he's a plumber!"

"Yes. He makes stoves, hot water heaters, pumps,

anything that deals with water. Who better to make me an espresso machine? He took the old ·one so he could copy the filter piece, and made us the new three-handle machine. I can't imagine what could have gone wrong. She was just frothing a cup of milk!" Cora looked down again at the bloody towel in her hands and the tears started anew.

"Come on, Aunt Cora," Phoebe said. "Let's go get you cleaned up, get rid of that towel and your apron, and get your face fixed and your dress clean."

They headed toward the ladies room.

Reverend Simon Jones walked into Clarence's Heating, Plumbing and Air Conditioning. "Afternoon, Bonnie."

"Afternoon, Reverend Jones."

"Clarence around?"

"He's over at the pump plant. They're working out some kinks in a new design."

"You heard about Cora's?"

"Yes. Just a bit ago. How is Maria?"

"I don't know yet. Mary Ellen's on her way out to the hospital," Simon said. "I'll pass along what she finds out, but I have another problem. Can you call over and ask Clarence to meet me at Cora's with whoever built that infernal device, say in about an hour?"

"Sure, Reverend Jones. I'll be happy to. Let's make it about an hour and a half. Two o'clock okay?"

"Two o'clock is fine. I'll be waiting."

Reverend Mary Ellen Jones arrived at Leahy Medical center just as Cora and Phoebe came out to the waiting area. "How are you holding up, dear?"

"Okay," Cora replied. "I'm waiting to hear, though, how Maria's going to be."

Lise Gebauer came through the door to the ER into the waiting area. "Cora. Maria's going to be okay." She sat down across from the three women. "The wand missed the major nerve cluster in her cheek and only chipped the cheek bone. We've stitched that up. There will be a scar. It punched out a piece of tissue too small to sew back in place, and there will be a pucker on her cheek, but it won't be horrible." Lise took a deep breath. "She was very lucky. The worst of the burns are second degree. Apparently she fell away from the steam and no part of her face was in it long enough to be cooked. There are a lot of blisters. It is going to hurt, but the steam missed her eye completely. We had to cut away a bit of hair on her right side above the cheek, but she'll recover. We should be able to send her home in the morning. Is her family here yet?"

"No," Cora said. "Her dad is out on a delivery run for the grocery. Her younger sister is in school, and you know her mom got that cough last winter and didn't make it."

Lise shuddered. "Too many didn't make it through the influenza. . . . We do what we can. Do you want to see her?"

"Of course!" Cora replied. "I'll sit with her at least until her father or sister gets here."

Chelsea Perkins came out of the staff lounge, and checked with the guard at the front entrance. "Anything else unusual, Otto?"

"No, Frau Perkins. All is quiet. People reading

books." Otto pointed to the floor where the body had lain. "The coroner has taken the body, and the janitors have finished cleaning the floor and wall. The front doors should be repainted by noon." Otto looked at Chelsea. "How did it happen?"

"Someone screwed up. Someone is not going to be happy." Chelsea walked off toward the security office.

"All right. Albrecht had the outside tour this morning." Chelsea looked at Albrecht and noticed the other guards in the room paying close attention. She knew that this was another test of her leadership. "You have your log book?"

The guard responsible for walking each circuit around the high school had to stop at a number of places where metal stamps had been placed in small boxes, and click the stamp onto a line of his log book. Before he left for the tour and upon his return, he clicked the log book into the time-clock. It wasn't as good a system as the up-time paper tape that showed *when* each location had been logged, but it at least proved that the route had been walked.

"I do, Frau Perkins. Here it is." Albrecht presented his log to Chelsea.

Chelsea flipped to the last page. "This says you finished at oh-six-thirty, half an hour after the shooting. How could you have accompanied the door guard if you weren't done?"

"I was almost done, Frau Perkins. I had reached the station outside the front door when I heard the shots. I tried the front door and it was unlocked, so I ran in and saw the intruder on the floor." Albrecht paused. "I assisted with the search and moving the body, and did not clock the round out until I was able to get away."

"The front door was unlocked? You are very sure of that?" Chelsea asked.

"Yes, Frau Perkins," Albrecht said.

Chelsea looked at the assignment sheet for the morning, then looked around the room. "Where is Francis?"

"Francis is at home with the influenza, Frau Perkins," Albrecht said. "He sent word yesterday that he would not be at work."

Chelsea turned to Karl Bauer, the watch supervisor for the night before. "Karl, why is this duty sheet not updated showing Francis is to be out?"

Karl smiled. "I could find no one to take Francis' shift, Frau Perkins. I stayed over the night. I did not need to write down my name to remind me that I was working."

"I see nothing to smile about, Karl. What happened this morning?" Chelsea asked very coldly.

"Tuesday, the library closes at ten at night, and reopens at six in the morning," Karl said.

Everyone nodded.

"The high school cleaning crew buffs the floors of the hallways during the night, and painting and other maintenance that is hard to do while people are working takes place," Karl continued.

Chelsea stared at him. "We all know that. What's the point?"

"There are only two guards overnight on Tuesday..." Karl started to say.

"Karl, I made up the schedule. I am the chief of security. You work for me. You don't need to explain the rules, I made them. You and Albrecht were here alone until the morning shift arrived. Now. No more excuses. What happened?" Chelsea said angrily.

"At six o'clock this morning, the morning shift had not yet arrived. Albrecht was being slow getting around the school, and had not yet returned. I was waiting in the reference area. I saw through the window a man walking down from the football field toward the school. You know how many people are upset that the library closes on Tuesday, and I thought that if the library was late opening, this man might be angry, so I went out and opened the door. He must have seen me open the door because he smiled. Then I went back to the security office to find Albrecht or someone to work the front security desk."

"So, you saw a total stranger outside, you didn't investigate him, you didn't check to see if he had a dangerous bag, you unlocked the door, and then you left the front of the library with no one guarding?"

Karl started to wave his hands and opened his mouth as though he was going to say something.

Chelsea interrupted. "Never mind. I don't care what possible excuse you have. Guards are supposed to *guard*, and there is nothing more important to guard than this library. Karl, you're fired. Give me your badge and belt right now."

Karl began to speak. Chelsea held up a hand, and Albrecht and two other guards closed in next to him. He shrugged, removed his badge and the leather Sam Browne belt that was the guard's uniform and handed them to Albrecht.

"You have five minutes to clean out your locker. I want you off the school grounds in no more than ten. Don't bother asking for a reference. Johann, Ester, you go with him and see him off the grounds." Chelsea stood, staring until Karl was gone from the room.

"I am *so* not looking forward to telling this story to the meeting tomorrow," she said to no one in particular.

Reverend Simon Jones was waiting at the coffee shop when Clarence Dobbs and a man Simon didn't recognize came in. The shop was open, and many people were looking at the espresso machine from a distance. Not only was Cora a member of his congregation at the Methodist church, but Simon was an accomplished mechanic and wanted to see for himself what had gone wrong.

"Simon, I don't think you've met Jonas Klein. Jonas works on our water heaters and worked on the espresso machine," Clarence said.

Simon shook Jonas' hand. "Sorry to meet you under these circumstances, Herr Klein."

"Yes, Pastor Jones. A sad day."

"Shall we take a look?"

The three men went behind the counter. The floor had been mopped, but the failure was clear. The fitting where the steaming wand screwed into the espresso machine was empty. With a heavy sigh, Jonas reached into his tool box and they began the task of disassembling the machine.

Cora came into the shop just as the men were finishing cleaning up.

"Well?" she asked.

"How's Maria?" Simon asked. Everyone in the shop turned toward her.

"She's going to be okay. A scar, and a long time healing from the burns, but okay," Cora replied. "Now, what happened?"

"It's complicated, Cora," Simon replied. "I think we need to go through it with the Saint Philip group. Can you come to the meeting tomorrow evening?"

"What meeting? What do you mean it's complicated? What happened?" Cora asked.

"The meeting at the parish hall at Saint Mary's. The part you want will start about seven and you need to be there. We'll go over the accident with everyone and figure it out. It's the group that Father Nick organized to do accident reviews for anyone who will participate. That way we have everyone's thoughts and everyone's ideas and everyone learns from each other's mistakes. This is complicated, Cora, and you should come. Jonas and Clarence and I will be there, and we all will talk through what happened. It was an accident, but it was an accident that could have been prevented. You should come. Please?"

"All right," Cora said. "I'll be there. Seven at the parish hall. But I still don't know what happened. What *happened*, Simon?"

"The boiler's pressure cut off didn't. It could have been a lot worse. This was almost the best possible outcome," Clarence said.

Cora looked from man to man. "You're not asking me to come to this meeting just so that some excuse can be cooked up, are you?"

"No, Cora. It's important. Please?" Simon said.

"Okay, okay. Seven at the parish hall. Got it. Now, let me talk to my staff and see to my business." With that, Cora turned away and went back to work.

Each Thursday, a diverse group would gather at St. Mary's for the meeting of the Society of Saint Philip of the Screwdriver. They came from every available faith. The group included engineers, but also included librarians, electricians, plumbers, bankers, lawyers, judges, gunsmiths, machinists, farmers, teachers, and clergy. What brought them together was an involvement with what could loosely be called "complexity."

The group was in some ways an outgrowth of John Grover's "Murphy Reports" from the VOA and the early electronics oversight group. The direct inspiration came from the joint minds of John, Father Athanasius Kircher and Father Nicholas Smithson. After reading the Wizard novels of Christopher Stasheff, Father Kircher and Nick had been enamored of the Order of Saint Vidicon of the Cathode. While they had been forbidden by Father—now Cardinal—Larry Mazzare from organizing a group around the fictional saint, they used his symbol, a small pocket Phillips screwdriver. Instead of Saint Vidicon, they instead chose as their patron a saint with a sense of humor, who himself spent many years attempting to prevent the works of Murphy's imp: Saint Philip Neri. The coincidence of the screwdriver was too good to pass up.

The group had grown casually. Its avowed purpose, to the extent it had one, was to reduce the inevitable cost that human error brought to any complex effort. If anyone asked, participants said that they weren't the Grantville Safety committee. They rejected that name and the responsibility. Still, the informal group quickly became the place to report and review accidents of all types. Industrial accidents, embezzlement, undetected frauds, losses to theft and waste, all were seen as manifestations of Murphy's imp, and all were subject to review and discussion by the group. They shared the thought that together they could reduce the butcher's bill that up-time knowledge would cost the world as the complexity of their civilization increased.

The group wasn't a confessional. Each case ended with one of two results. If they could propose a way to avoid similar incidents, someone wrote up a report and a checklist to help accomplish that. If not, they wrote a report asking for suggestions. One of the proposals in Nick's charter was that they begin distributing their reports more formally to libraries and centers of invention.

Someone had made a banner with an image of Saint Philip Neri. It was inspired by the image in the *Catholic Encyclopedia* but the saint was wearing half a beard, smiling broadly, holding a little yellow screwdriver, and standing with one foot crushing a green imp. Below the portrait was the legend: HOLY SAINT PHILIP, PROTECT US.

There were other banners. "Never attribute to evil that which can be explained by the perversity of the universe." "Even tragedy provides an opportunity for humor." "There are no silver linings without clouds." Another said "TANSTAAFL," with a line drawn through it and "Free Beer" written below. Finally, there was a banner, half filled with a field of green imps. Each imp had a red-circled X drawn over it.

John Grover and Father Nicholas looked at the group clustered around the folding tables serving as bar and sideboard.

"Are you sure you are ready to do this, Nick?" John asked.

"Yes. I've been ready for months. It's not like all of them don't already know what's coming," Nick said.

"Okay then. I'll see about herding the cats," John said. *"Settle down, folks!"*

Slowly the chatter lowered, the mugs and steins were refilled, and people found chairs around the room. John gestured to the chalkboard to one side which had a short list of names on it. "Anyone forget to sign up?"

A general murmur of negativity ran around the room.

"Okay. You all notice that Nick's name is at the top of that list, and he has an announcement and a proposal before we start the show and tell. Father Nick, the floor is yours."

John sat in a chair where he could see the room and Nick.

"Good evening, my friends," Nick said. "I do have an announcement. Today, with the consent of His Holiness Urban, I am released from my vows as a Jesuit and am returned to the secular clergy."

"'Bout damned time!" Simon Koudsi shouted.

"It's remarkably quick for such a request, Simon. But I agree, and that brings us to my second point." Nick pointed at the image of Saint Philip on the wall behind him, and brought out his screwdriver. "I certainly know you're not all Catholic."

"You got that right too!" Reverend Simon Jones said.

"Am I to continue to be interrupted by Simons, or should I simply continue?" Nick said. Through the resulting laughter, he continued: "That leads directly to my proposal. I believe it's time that we move from this casual group to something with more organization, which we can export to other communities. Therefore, in keeping with our principles, I propose the formal incorporation of the European Service Committee of the Society of Saint Philip of the Screwdriver. Copies of the proposed bylaws are on the table by the door. Please pick one up tonight as you leave. We will have a special meeting to discuss the organization soon. The committee's function will be to sponsor this and other meetings, to publish information gathered, and to evangelize what we've done here. I'm happy to take questions, but you should review the proposed bylaws first, I think."

"If this *committee* is to be the sponsor, does that mean that you still buy the beer, Nick?" Simon Jones asked.

"Yes, Simon. I will continue to buy the beer, and the pretzels and the coffee," Nick said.

"So the society is a Catholic order?" the Russian prince and envoy, Vladimir, asked.

"No! Although the suppression of Murphy's imp is Godly work, this group, and the committee, are not specifically related to any church. We use Saint Philip as our patron because his humor and joy are important tools in the face of the tragedies that Murphy brings us, and because having a face, an identity for the group is simpler than some formless up-time corporation. The best analogy I have is that the society is something similar to the intergroup committees of Alcoholics Anonymous or other such organizations. It's a way for the independent groups to coordinate their work on the nature and perversity of the universe and the application of humor to the banishment of Murphy's works from our works. Read the draft bylaws."

Vladimir nodded and smiled. "Good. The patriarch would have trouble with me joining a Catholic order!"

Nick looked around the room. "The work we do here is important." Most of the listeners nodded. "By bringing together our minds and our eyes, the imp can't hide. Together we can find a way to do as John says: Keep Murphy firmly in front of us where we can see him. We know he acts in the world, we know that God has a sense of humor that includes things which can, at best, be seen as perverse. Can there be any doubt that the God who arranged that the bread should fall butter side down seventy-five percent of the time has an odd sense of humor?" Nick paused. "But the fact that Murphy's imp acts in the world should not be a cause for depression. Remember Saint Philip Neri's saying: 'A joyful heart is more easily made perfect than a downcast one.' Joy is our servant and our protection. And with that, I'll end this intrusion into the evening. Look over the bylaws, and at the next meeting we'll discuss if we are agreed about doing this."

Nick looked at the chalkboard. "I am saddened to see the State Library on the list again, but I am particularly interested in hearing the details of yesterday's incident that has caused the proprietor of City Hall Café and Coffee Shop to put her name first on the list." Nick gestured to Cora. "The floor is yours."

"I don't want the floor. I'm not even sure why I'm here and I didn't write my name up there. I think Simon did it," Cora said.

"Cora, we all know about the accident at the shop yesterday, and we are happy that Maria will recover, but we would appreciate it if you would share your version of what happened. Just tell the story, and we'll listen. And there may be questions after," Nick said as he sat down.

"I still don't know why I'm here," Cora said. "I bought an espresso machine from Clarence about six months ago, and it blew up and nearly killed Maria!"

Father Nicholas stepped over to Cora on one side, and Reverend Jones on her other. Simon held her shoulder while Nick held her hand. "Cora, we're going to ask you to try to tell us what happened exactly. Just start slowly. How does the machine work?" Simon said.

"I don't know how it works inside, but outside, you put coffee in the filter and put it on the machine and sit a cup under it, then you pull down on the big lever, and espresso squirts out of the filter into the cup." Cora started to calm down.

"But that's not all, Cora," Nick said.

"No, it isn't. If someone wants steamed milk, you take the milk pitcher and put it under the steam wand and open the steam valve and steam comes out and heats up the milk, and froths it. That's all there is to it. It's really, really, simple."

"Then what happened?" Simon asked.

"Brother Bernard had ordered a cappuccino, and Maria was joking with him like she always does. She flirts with everyone, and she always said she was making a cappuccino for a Capuchin, and Brother Bernard always laughed and said that he was no Capuchin, he was the *Dominican* spy in Grantville. Anyway, Maria was starting to steam the milk and all of a sudden, the pipe the steam comes out of just blew out of the machine and hit Maria in the face. Then the steam hit her and burned her face."

"And then what?" Nick asked.

"Then we called the ambulance and took her to the hospital."

"Thanks, Cora. Why don't you sit down and listen now for a bit? People may have some questions, but there's no reason to stand here," Simon said. He and Nick took her to a chair, and Simon handed her a glass of water.

One of the people said, "I have a question. Cora, do you do any maintenance on the machine? How do you clean it? That sort of thing."

"I run a clean shop," Cora nearly shouted. "We clean it every night, and you have to clean out the filter between shots. Is that what you mean?"

"No. Do you do anything *inside* the machine? Do you clean the insides any?"

"No. I don't know anything about the insides."

"And with that," Simon said, "I think that it's Clarence, Jonas, and my turn."

Clarence and Jonas explained how they had built the machine, how the boiler operated with an electric coil on a thermostat and a water level sensor, how the steamer took steam off the top of the boiler through the wand with a simple valve and a fixed pipe, and how a pressure relief valve was on top of the boiler to keep it from blowing up. Questions arose to clarify the difference between this and Clarence's line of hot water heaters.

Then Simon explained what they had found when they took the machine apart, how more than half the boiler had filled with scale from the evaporating water, and how a piece of scale had broken off and had jammed the thermostat so that it didn't prevent overheating, and another piece of scale had blocked the steam pipe. That the pipe had worked loose over time, and finally one last time, the pipe had blocked off completely and the wand had flown out.

The questions went back and forth for a short time,

but the conclusion was clear. Clarence knew about scale buildup from hot water heaters, but hadn't thought through how much more scale would be deposited from the massive evaporation of the steam for the steam wand. He hadn't consulted with, or had Jonas consult with, the steam guys in Grantville. The steam heads were shaking their heads. When the discussion wound down, John Grover stood and looked around.

"I think we're done then," John said. "Let me summarize. The boiler needed a port to use to put vinegar or something in to clean scale on a regular basis. The wand needed to be tightened every night, and there needed to be an externally visible pressure and temperature gauge to track if problems arose. Are we agreed that we've got this?"

The room sounded with agreement.

"Then we've got enough to put this incident behind us, and to put the solution in front of us. Who wants to write the report and the new procedures?"

Jonas stood. "I built it. I will write the report. I may need help with the words."

"Help is available," John replied, then turned to Cora. "Cora, we know what happened, we know how to fix it, and we know how to prevent it from happening again. Jonas will write a complete report, and write a checklist for you for how to maintain the machine so that it is safe to use. We're convinced this was a true accident, another incident of Murphy's imp sneaking in when we weren't looking. Do you have any questions?"

"No, I don't think so. We can go back to making espresso then?" Cora asked.

"As soon as we fix the machine, and you have the checklist Jonas is going to write," Clarence said.

"Good!" Cora said.

John looked at the board. "We have only one other report tonight, and I propose we take a break first, then we'll pass the floor to Doris McIntire and Chelsea Perkins from the State Library... again."

"Everyone ready?" John looked around. "Okay, then. Doris, Chelsea, you have the floor."

Neither of them stood. Chelsea looked at Doris and said, "This one's on me, I think. One of my guards, and I'm not bothering with who just now—we've already dealt with that internally—but one of the guards opened the front door of the school and the door into the library this morning at six. He was alone, which is against policy, and he had not had a check-in from the guard detailed to do the outside walk-around before opening the door. As you all know from the last time, that's part of the procedure. The outside walk-around should finish, come in the employee door, check with the duty guard, and then the duty guard, with a second watcher, is supposed to open the outer doors and then the inner."

Chelsea took a deep breath. "Yesterday morning, neither of those things happened. The duty guard, who will *not* be guarding anything for the foreseeable future, skipped those steps, and at six o'clock, simply unlocked the inner door, went through it to the front door of the school, unlocked that, and just walked back to the ready room. He had no partner, and so no one stayed at the front desk. I offer no excuses. We had the policies in place, but they were not followed." She looked at Doris. "I can't tell any more, I wasn't there."

Doris patted Chelsea's hand. "I was there. I will never understand them, but I was there. I was coming out to the front desk. Apparently, the guard had already opened the door and there was no one at the security desk, so I didn't know the door was unlocked. I was thinking about Brother Johann's plan to try using the high school history classes to each sort a box of loose papers from the overflow storage." She took a deep breath. "I had my head down, and had just reached the front desk when I heard the school's front door bang open. Moments later, the library door burst open and that..." Doris hesitated, "...that *person* ran in carrying a bag. The bag was oil stained, and he was shouting. I'm still not sure what he was shouting. I'm honestly not certain of the language, but the hate seemed clear enough. It's the first time I've had to do this; the guards are supposed to check every bag and box that comes into the library, but I really didn't doubt that I was right. He sort of spun back as though he was going to fling the bag into the stacks. So, I pulled the front-desk gun and shot him."

Doris looked down, then she looked up and around the room. "The bag fell back and I grabbed it and threw it out the door toward the front doors. It burst into flames when it hit, so I knew I was right, but I will never, *ever*, understand why these people want to burn us out. They come from all over, you know. They seem to think that burning the library will undo us being here. You can't burn ideas. Are they stupid?"

Chelsea took over. "After the first shot, three guards and two librarians responded. The invader was down, and the high school staff responded to the fire at the front door. It was out within two minutes, from the ready hoses. We have no information on who the arsonist was. He had no documents on him at all, and Doris had put three hollow points, center of mass. After that, it was the usual clean up."

Simon Jones spoke, "Chelsea, how many does that make now?"

"Five we've had to shoot in the last four years. The security guards capture a bomb or flammables about once a month through the regular checks. The walk-around finds someone trying to break into the school or something occasionally," Chelsea said. "It's a much harder job than I expected when I took it."

Doris spoke, sounding tired. "Being a librarian in Grantville is sure different now. Who would have thought that librarian certification required monthly range time?"

The group spent a half hour asking questions, double-checking the procedures and considering what could be done differently. Despite the trouble it caused, the conclusion the group reached was to fall back to the "missile silo paradigm" and to require two keys to open the library's front door, each passed hand to hand from one duty guard to the next, so that no one could ever open the library alone again. Several people noted that in both the library and the coffee shop cases, the problem could be prevented by a change in procedure. The final conclusion was that once again the checklist stands as one of the most useful tools against the imp of the perverse.

John Grover stood. "Doris, the Grantville Society of Saint Philip of the Screwdriver offers you our formal thanks. You are welcome here any time, even if you haven't shot an idiot. Cora, thank you, too.

Your participation will help prevent other workers from being hurt or even killed by small boilers again. And so, for both of you, I have our thanks, and this talisman..." John handed each of the women a small, yellow-handled Phillips screwdriver. "In the hopes that it will help you to keep Murphy's imp before you, and joy and humor in your hearts."

The room echoed with, "Amen."

A man in overalls opened a bag by his seat and removed two jars and a paint brush, then went to the last banner. Soon it sported two more imps crushed under the cross of Saint Philip's Screwdriver.

Sometime later, after everyone else was gone, Nick looked around the room, knowing that the catering staff from the Gardens would soon have the tables down and the room cleared. He stared up into the eyes of the image of Saint Philip. "Of course, I buy the beer. I can't think of anything better to do with the money." He removed his rosary from his belt, and left the parish hall, heading for the church. "But I'm still a priest."

The Cartesian Way

Mark H. Huston

Spanish Netherlands,
Early October 1632

>   *René:*
>   *Within is the singularly most important paper on mathematics ever written. It is called the Crucibellus Manuscript, and it is only the first volume of several.*
>   *Digest the enclosed manuscript. This one was hand delivered to me by a man who got it from the writer in Grantville, supposedly a man of our time who accessed the substantial library there.*
>   *Mathematics, the sciences, and philosophy have taken a 350-year leap forward overnight!*
>

Your friend in knowledge
Fr. Marin Mersenne
>

René Descartes looked at the bundle that accompanied the letter. He had heard of the town from the future, who hadn't by now? But there were so many rumors, so many things that sounded too fantastic to be true. So, logically, they were not.

The church said the age of miracles was over. That was not true, because surely this was a miracle he held in his hands. Or at least the first evidence of a miracle. He cut the string with a small scissors and tore back the several layers of oiled paper from around the folio. Dropping the wrappings to the side he went to his desk, which overlooked the garden of the small house he was renting.

For the next two weeks, he studied the book. The little house was silent. His servant came in the morning, while he slept, and prepared his meals. Then she left him in solitude for the rest of the day. He studied, took notes, and studied more. He settled into a routine of reading a section of the work, taking notes, and then thinking solidly about it for a day or more. He scribbled questions in the margins of the book. And he thought.

And he thought some more.

The third week after receiving the manuscript, and having examined it from many perspectives, he flew into an uncontrollable rage. "It isn't fair!" He threw papers from his desk, tore up notes and letters, kicked furniture, and broke the door of a very sturdy Dutch armoire. He broke dishes, and raged at the great unfairness of it all. "This was mine! Mine! Mine to discover, mine to tell people how to find! My methods. My name. My legacy!" He broke the remaining plates and after exhausting himself, collapsed onto the floor in the small study, sobbing. "This was all to be mine, someday. It is what I've been working on for years. My Methods of Logic. How to think. This should be all mine."

After a while he drew himself up, and began to pick up the pieces of the manuscript. He stacked them carefully together, then set them on a table in front of him. He stood in front of the table, hands behind his back, peering at the neat but tattered stack. "These mathematics are understandable, reachable. And were reached with my methods. The book I am writing now. That I *was* writing now. That I am *no longer* writing. That I have *no need* to *ever* write."

He stared at the manuscript for an hour, standing in front of it. His mind quieted from the rage, and he began to think. It was what he did: think. To think. Thinking...

At the end of the hour, he began to chuckle, and after a moment he broke out into a peal of guffaws. He laughed so hard that he cried. He eventually found himself on the floor again, in front of the table, exhausted.

"Never let it be said that God doesn't have a sense of humor."

Paris, February 1633

"Did you know I had a child, Mersenne?" René Descartes rested the copy of an up-time book on the table in front of him, incredulous. "A child? Th-that's preposterous. A child." He shook his head, and ran the alien concept through his brain once again. He tossed it on the table, which was heaped with copies of up-time texts, including several biographies of himself. "When I went to Holland, I vowed to give up women. They are a distraction. A constant and nagging distraction. They make a man unreasonable, and he cannot concentrate." He began to pace in the long room, with tall windows on one side so the sun could stream in. "One tends to think with the wrong brain, the little one, when women are around."

Marin Mersenne looked up from his manuscript, and smiled. "Do I need to remind you, you are talking to a Minim friar, René? That little brain you speak of is why we take a vow of chastity, along with poverty, and obedience." He pulled up the sleeves of his coarse black wool habit, crossed his arms and leaned back in his chair, smiling broadly.

René paused, and then awkwardly guffawed. "Ha! I would suppose so, my friend." He paced again to the table, and spread his arms wide to lean on it. "Look at this. Three hundred years' worth of man's thought. Piled on a table in our brand new Académie Française. Just like that. Plop! And this is just the surface. It will take us years to assimilate all of them. The math, that is straightforward. We can follow nearly all of that. But the philosophy, Marin, that is what excites me."

Marin nodded. "I can see that, René. I can see your influence all over these books. In many ways, your math, and your methods, were the start of nearly all of this. You are the foundation, my friend, of modern thought. It says so, somewhere in this book, I think..." He held up another up-time copy.

René tried to suppress a giddy grin, and failed miserably. "Rather remarkable when you think on it, isn't it?" He straightened up from the table and once again failed to suppress a strutting walk toward the windows. "Did you read what it said about me, Marin?

About taking care of the woman, the one who bore my child? I provided for her even after my death."

Marin grew still for a moment, waiting for René's giddiness to pass. "It is too bad about the child, René."

René turned back from the window, toward Marin, and shrugged. "No need to mourn. I have left Holland. I will never meet this woman from Holland, never bed her, never have a child with her. And one needs to be born first, in order to die. Even Christ. There is no need to mourn for something that will never happen." He shrugged again. "Butterflies. The up-timers call it the butterfly effect. More poetic than their usual penchant for reducing everything to acronyms."

"It has been how long since they arrived? Eighteen months? Twenty?" Marin shuffled through the pile of papers in front of him.

René leaned against the windowsill. "Do you know what it means, Marin?"

Marin raised his eyebrows. He was a rather handsome man in his thirties. "I think it will take many years before we know what it all means, René. There are so many—"

"No, that isn't what I am talking about." René waved his arms about as if shooing flies out of the air. "I am talking about me. What it means to me, and how I should interpret my once future actions that will now never be."

"I am not sure I understand..."

René came back to the table and picked up the copy of his biography, and waved it at Marin. "I'm talking about this. The man described in these books." He used the first manuscript to shove others about on the table. "Me. You see, up until the moment when this version of the future somehow collided with our reality, I was the same man as described in these books. Maybe even a little while after, at least until I first heard about Grantville. At that point, I became a different man, and the one who wrote these books is forever dead. At least will never exist."

Marin nodded. "It was the same for everyone. We all were changed from what we would have been. Different choices. Different mistakes, different thoughts."

"But you agree that we are the same men, only changed by our knowledge. You and I are not some new creation."

"Yes. We are the same men, just changed in our paths for the last twenty months or so."

René smiled. "So we are the same men as in these books."

"Of course."

"A child," René said. "And a woman. Do you know what this means?"

Marin grinned. "I know it isn't usually in that order. A woman usually comes first."

René made a face at Marin. "Don't mock me, I'm serious here. We have known each other for, what? Ten years? And you know how I always felt about distractions. Women, chiefly. Terrible distractions. I hate distractions." He held up the manuscript. "But look at what I accomplished. Even with a distraction. This nameless Dutch servant girl, and a child. Do you know what this means?"

Marin thought for a moment. He looked at René, and the pile of manuscripts, and then back to René. Finally, he smiled. "I think I see, René. You learned to love someone. In spite of your work, in spite of your hatred for distractions, you learned to love."

René sat at the table across from his friend, serious and muted. "I never thought I could love someone. That I, René Descartes, the man who was—and is to create the new ways of looking at things, could discover love such as that."

"But you have always loved God. I see that from all of your correspondence from your works from the future. You were always scrupulous about staying within doctrine of the church. You clearly have a love of the Church and God."

"Of course. But that's different. Loving God is like loving your mother and respecting your father. It is simply something you do. Quite frankly, staying within doctrine is something you do in order to create—what did I read in one of these up-time political books? Ah, yes. Plausible deniability. Yes, that was it. One must always have plausible deniability when dealing with the inquisition. That's why Galileo wrote his book on planetary motion as taking place in a 'hypothetical' universe. Doesn't look like that was enough; they are still going to put him on trial, aren't they?"

"That will be a bit, well, awkward, I think." Mersenne frowned. "It's a great challenge for the Church to determine what this all means."

René came back to the table and sat across from his friend. "Awkward, yes. Something we scientists must watch with great interest. Church doctrine versus Galileo, and Galileo has the up-time science on his side." He pushed some books aside, and opened a copy of a third-grade science textbook. This was one of the few original texts they had, and in it was a two-page color drawing of the solar system. The sun was solidly in the middle. Exactly where Galileo had placed it.

Paris, May 1633

"Do you believe it? A woman is Crucibellus. A woman! Damned bluestocking. It sends one to thinking, doesn't it, René?" Étienne Pascal looked down the row of seats toward Descartes and smiled slyly.

The lecture was completed, and the crowd in the small drawing room was beginning to stand and move toward the doors. All around Descartes stood a group of men, and all had been taking copious notes. René Descartes looked back to Pascal, who sat next to him. "Why that smile, Étienne? What is it that you know that we do not?"

Pascal rose with Descartes and leaned in to speak quietly. "My son and daughter have been in the town of the future for several weeks now. I have letters. They say that men and women are equals there. It excites my daughter to no end."

"I have not had the honor of meeting them yet, Monsieur Pascal. Perhaps that can be arranged when I return," Colette Modi said quietly. Descartes turned to look into the eyes of the world-renowned Crucibellus. Her eyes were quite striking in a way he hadn't seen when she was at the podium. While she lectured on number theory today, the intelligence in her voice was clear. But her intense gaze, coupled with her voice, now struck him and his group as someone very special. Pascal recovered first.

"Madame Modi, it is a true joy to meet you in

person. We didn't think we would be able to have this time with you, after the lecture." Pascal's manner was smooth, as one who was a member of the *petite noblesse* should be, thought René a little jealously.

"The pleasure is mine, Monsieur Pascal." She curtsied as she returned the greeting.

Recovering, René bent into his own bow, and out of the corner of his eye he could see several other members of the Académie Française doing the same. "Madame Modi, it is truly a pleasure."

She focused on him directly once again. "René Descartes?"

He rose from his bow and nervously returned her gaze. "Yes, Madame. That is I."

"I imagine that you were well into writing *Le Monde* when my manuscript was sent to you? My apologies for the interruption. *Cogito, ergo sum* is a phrase that is known across the centuries. It is a pleasure to know one of France's most famous philosophers."

René felt his face flush, and he bowed again in thanks. "You do me an honor in saying so, Madame Modi. I must admit that the arrival of your manuscript was met by me with...uh...mixed emotions. So much of the work was based on the very things I was working on. I was, shall we say, cast adrift from my plans."

Madame Modi smiled and nodded to him, her eyes cast down in an apology. "You know we have something in common, Monsieur?"

"I-I am not sure I understand, Madame. Of course we both love the mathematics, and the pursuit of knowledge." René felt off balance as the woman looked directly at him.

"A dream. According to your biographers, you decided to become a philosopher when you were in Germany many years ago, on a winter campaign when you served with Duke Maximilian. In what was called a 'stove heated room.'"

René smiled. "Ah yes, my Day of Discoveries and Night of Dreams. I have read some of the future accounts of my past and my no-longer-possible future." He looked at her with gentle accusation. "There was much abbreviation I found. But on the whole, they seem to have gotten it right. There are a few items, but I won't quibble. But you are right, a dream is what sent me down the path. Or a series of dreams, rather. Did the same thing happen to you?"

"Somewhat the same thing. I had a dream where all of the great mathematicians faded into darkness after the Ring of Fire, unknown. I took as my task to make sure that wouldn't happen. Newton should not be overlooked."

René nodded quietly. "Nor should Sartre, or the Scotsman, Ferrier."

She looked at him, with a questioning gaze. "You have read much, I see. More than I, certainly. I have focused on the math, and left the philosophy to others." She straightened slightly. "But you, it makes sense. Your math was brilliant, but your philosophy is what helped change the world."

A big man, whose patience had run out waiting for a break in the conversation, joined them, large and loud. Pierre Fermat. "Oh good heavens, don't tell him that! He's already hard enough to put up with."

René was slightly relieved when the intense questioning gaze of the woman left him. He had always been awkward in the face of beauty, and while sequestered away in the Dutch countryside, he didn't think of women. It was a tremendous advantage to his work. But in Paris, things were very different. He smiled. The big man, Fermat, was speaking.

"I'm Pierre de Fermat, Madame. Allow me to make some further introductions." He pulled her by the hand without waiting for her approval. "As you know, the cardinal has started the Académie Française a few years early, and he has gathered many of us together. He had to haul Descartes out of the Netherlands to bring him here. I believe you have met Father Mersenne?"

Mersenne, wearing sandals and his only clothing of a severe black monk's robe tied with a cord of four knots, bowed to her. "I am honored to meet you, Madame. It was very kind of you to send me the original manuscript."

Fermat butted in. "Kindness had nothing to do with it. She knew you would send it to every mathematician in France the instant you read it. This is a shrewd young lady, indeed."

She turned and smiled at the Minim priest. "I hoped that was you in the audience, Friar. When I saw your robes, I assumed it was you. Thank you for coming to this small lecture."

"You must meet the rest of them, Madame." Fermat tugged at her arm. "Over here we have the Académie Française Moon Crater Club. According to the research and some of the maps we have seen, these fellows here are charter members. This is Peter Gassendi, who your up-time people will like. He has always been on the pragmatic side. He is very much a *smug* empiricist now. This young man is Jacques de Billy, whom we

dragged to Paris from Rheims, along with his friend
and mine, Claude Gaspard Bachet de Méziriac. Oh,
and let's not forget our Turk, Kâtip Çelebi, come to
hear you from Istanbul. He has no moon crater named
after him, at least that we know of."

The crowd began to ease away from René, flowing
along with Madame Modi. As they eased away from
him, he heard Madame Modi interrupt Fermat, asking
about some theorem. René felt relieved. The highly
social, and somewhat loud Fermat irritated him. As
he began to step backwards, away from the intensity
of the crowd, he felt himself stepping solidly on
someone's foot.

"Ouch." It was a quiet cry of pain, and an excla-
mation of suppressed surprise. René turned around
nearly in a panic, and opened his mouth to apologize.
But he was instantly struck dumb by the beauty with
which he was presented. In shock, all he could do is
blink into the face of the girl, whose own face was
forcing a smile over what appeared to be some level
of real pain. At the same time, her eyebrows were
questioning, expecting something as she shifted her
weight to her other foot...

He blinked at her twice more, his brain a jumble.
Finally, *"Apologize, you dolt!"*

"Umm. Uh. I'm sorry mademoiselle. I am a clumsy
mule. I did not look behind me. Please forgive me."
René shifted uneasily; he was still quite close to her.
"I didn't realize you were there, I-I apologize again."
He stepped back to bow to that beautiful face, and
promptly stumbled backwards into a chair, tried to keep
his balance, and ended up plopping down hard on the
seat. He could feel his face flush, and he looked around

to see if anyone noticed. It appeared all of the room's focus was on Madame Modi, and nobody had seen him. Except the woman on whom he had stomped. And she was now standing on one foot, and hiding her mouth with her hand as she giggled, pain under the giggle.

René wished he could melt into the floor. He made some mental calculations on how much heat that might take.

The woman, quite young by his measure, at least younger than him, hobbled to the seat next to him and took off her shoe. It was a flimsy affair, barely a slipper. He stared down at his own heavy boots. Still staring at his boots, he added lamely, "That must have hurt quite a lot. I am very sorry."

"I was too close to you, as I was trying to listen. I should have realized. It's my fault. My mother says I am too nosy. This will give her more reason to tell me not to come to lectures. Not that I am a nosy person, but I was just trying to listen to Madame Modi when you stepped back. Perfectly innocent, not nosy—Oh dear. I am rambling." She took a deep breath, and extended her hand. "Isabeau. Isabeau Montclair."

Gently taking her hand, almost if he were afraid he would break that too, he gathered from somewhere deep inside enough courage to look her in the eyes. "René. René Descartes. I am truly sorry for your foot, mademoiselle." She had dark eyes, with flecks of green and grey scattered about, dark hair, a youthful and innocent round shape to her face, and skin very smooth. No pox scars, pristine. It made her look very youthful.

"Think nothing of it, Monsieur Descartes. I am sure it will heal. Sometime." She smiled slyly at him.

"You are making fun of me now." Inside he felt relieved. *She can't be hurt too badly if she is joking with me*, he thought. But what to say next? What should he do? The pause stretched on. What should he say? Dammit. Why was he acting like a school-boy? He glanced at her, she was sitting demurely, and glanced at him. He broke eye contact and once again examined his boots. There was more awkward pause. The crowd started to thin. After an eternity, she finally put on her shoe and rose from the chair. He rose with her, and offered her his arm.

"Do you require assistance, mademoiselle?"

She gazed at him a moment, as if considering. "No, I think I am good. Nothing broken." She wriggled her foot to test it. "*Merci*."

René could feel his face fall. "But of course, whatever you wish, mademoiselle." He bowed and turned to go, this time avoiding the chair. Before he could take a step, he felt a hand on his shoulder.

"I have changed my mind, René Descartes. I think my foot hurts more than it should. Perhaps you should assist me to my carriage." She locked her arm around his in a movement that surprised and delighted him. He could feel the warmth of her arm, and the weight of her body against his. He caught his breath for a moment, felt his face flush slightly, and they eased carefully to the door.

Paris, October 1633

"Will he be here soon, Isabeau? I tire of waiting." Isabeau's mother, Angelique Montclair, was absently fluffing pillows in the ornate drawing room. Late afternoon light filtered in through the large multi-paned windows, while the fireplace at the other end of the room tried and failed to radiate its heat to where Isabeau sat.

Isabeau sighed. "Very soon, I am sure. He is terrible with time, you know Mama. Terrible. He forgets what hour it is. He forgets appointments because he doesn't keep a calendar. The cardinal actually gave him an up-time watch from Grantville so he would not be late. He forgets to put it on."

"An up-time watch? That's worth a fortune! Does it work? Or does it need those embattlements?"

"Embattlements?"

"Oh, I don't know what you call them? Fortifications?"

"Fortifications?" Isabeau furrowed her brow and struggled to understand her mother.

"They make the electricity-things."

"Oh! The batteries." Isabeau laughed "Yes. It has batteries."

"That makes it worth even more money."

"Mother, is that all you ever think about? Money? I know we have enough from before Father died. The farms in the country, his other interests. I have seen the letters, you know. We are secure."

Angelique stopped her fluffing, and looked at Isabeau with a single raised eyebrow. "A woman on her own in this world is never secure, Isabeau. We are *petite noblesse*, not some family whose fortune and lands have come down from the old days. The only thing we *have* is money, dear." She set the pillow down on the small couch and sat next to Isabeau. "The only reason we are accepted at all—that you are allowed to attend lectures and traipse across Paris like a princess and rub shoulders with real nobility—is *because* we have money. You may think they accept you because you know circles and rectangles and hypotenuse, but they wouldn't give you the time of day if it wasn't for the cash. I don't know a battery from a battlement, but I do know that."

"But, Mother..."

"No buts. That is why this match is so important. Personally, I think Descartes is crazy. But, fortunately you seem to truly like him, so that counts for something." She patted Isabeau's hand.

Isabeau turned and faced her mother. "But he isn't crazy, Mama. Not crazy at all. He is brilliant, more brilliant than this world can contain. There are times when observing his mind can be like staring into the sun. You cannot look directly at it. Remember when Gassendi demonstrated for us with paper and pinhole, how to observe the sun? You can't look at the sun directly or you will go blind. But if you look at it after it comes through a pin hole, and see it project itself onto a blank paper, then you can make out the details. That's what being around René is like. You cannot understand him if you look directly at him. He is too strong mentally, too overwhelming. But if you are patient, and do not stare, and wait for him to turn his thoughts into something the rest of us can understand, then you can really learn things. See things with a perception that comes from somewhere very special. He can help you to see things that you never, in your most amazing dreams, could possibly think of."

"The cardinal has said that he is a good catch too, you know. I corresponded with him just last week. He always asks about you and René. Do you know that he sends me a note nearly every week, inquiring about you and René?"

"And what do you tell him, mother?"

"That you are both good Catholics, and we are hopeful."

"*We* are hopeful?"

"I occasionally editorialize. The cardinal is always happy to hear of news about Monsieur Descartes and you."

"So you report to Cardinal Richelieu on our relationship?"

"No, my dear. It isn't anything like that. We just have a correspondence, that's all. He sends gifts on occasion. It's quite gratifying to someone like me to have a famous correspondent. You're not the only one in the family who can have a famous friend, you know. I do it for our family."

"Mother, you're a spy for the cardinal."

"No dear. Not a spy. Simply a proud mother who desires the best for her daughter. And as suitors go, Descartes is the best one I can see. Except he is crazy. And has a large nose, even by French standards."

Isabeau smiled at her, and extended her hand. "You know I would be bored out of my mind with any other suitors. Most of them are not bright enough to know when I insult them. I know math and sciences better than any of them—"

"I never understood that about you." Her mother interrupted. "Why you insisted on learning mathematics, learning about the sciences, attending lectures. 'Tis something you were born with, like your father. God rest his soul, he was the same way. Always scribbling, always thinking about triangles and odd circles.

It wasn't natural, and it isn't natural for you either. Especially as a woman."

"Mother. We have discussed this before. What is and isn't natural for a woman is changing. Slowly here in France, faster elsewhere. But it is changing. Look at Madame Modi when she was here in the spring. She had hundreds of the most brilliant minds in France falling at her feet, hanging on her every word. To be part of that is—is indescribable. Beyond imagination."

Angelique looked at her with another raised eyebrow. "Sane men do not cut apart people and animals of all sorts and study them. What he does isn't normal." She extracted her hands from Isabeau's grip. "He spends half of his time cutting up hanged criminals, and half of his time figuring out how to blow people up, or shoot down airplanes or fly airplanes, or drill through a mountain—"

"Did I tell you he showed me how you can drink the air?"

"That's what I mean. People do not drink the air!"

"He showed it to me in the summer. There was a device they made, like two hollow cannonballs and pipe between them. He heated it, and then one end became very cold. He put a cup under the cold end, and in a few moments pure water was formed out of the air, and dripped into a cup. Enough to take a sip of cold water. That was in July, when it was so hot."

"You drank water! That will kill you, or make you sick enough that you wished you were dead. You should stick with wine. For someone so smart, you're very stupid sometimes."

"Mother..."

"...And another thing, he has changed lately, don't

think I haven't noticed. He seems even more brooding lately, darker. Have you noticed?"

"Mother, please," Isabeau said firmly. "He has many things on his mind. The Académie Française, his experiments, and all of the up-time reading he is doing. It is very tiring for him. Is that something you put into your letter to the cardinal?"

"I'm not that stupid, dear. The cardinal only gets sunshine and roses from me."

They were interrupted by a knock on the door. Both of them turned to it, and then back to each other.

Isabeau smoothed her dress in front of her and made a face at her mother. "You can go now, Mother. Please?"

"Very well. But I will be right next door."

"Listening," Isabeau admonished.

"Of course, dear. You don't think I would leave you alone with that madman, do you?" With that, she turned and left the room through a door near the fireplace. There was another polite knock.

"Come." The door opened and the footman ushered in René Descartes. His square frame stumped into the room, and he flung his cloak off his shoulders, handing it off to the footman in one motion.

"How late am I, Isabeau?"

"No more than usual, René." She sighed.

"My misery continues. I argued with Fermat at the Académie Française again today. Long and loud. I don't know if I can keep this up much longer." He continued to stump across the room, agitated, at the same pace as when he entered. "I cannot think like this. I cannot fit into their laboratories or factories and their meetings of—of nothing! Deadlines. They want deadlines for things that have never been invented before, things that are little more than rumors or shadows or outlines on the papers they bring from Grantville."

"René, calm down. It isn't necessary for you to shout. Please." She crossed her arms and looked at him. He ignored her.

"These things must be thought about, they must be explored. One cannot snap ones fingers and create a flying machine..." He continued to pace, almost frantically now. Isabeau stood and intercepted him as he crossed by, snatching his arm.

"René! Please. This is as bad as I have ever seen you about Fermat and the Académie Française." He paused and looked at her for a moment, and then continued to pace without registering that he heard her. "You know this is for the good of France—"

"Do not tell me of the good of France, the glory of France, the future of France, the greatness of France, the everlasting peace of France, the greater glory of God and France, or of France showing God's way to the lesser nations!" He was now waving his hands about as he started pacing again. "I am sick to death of France, sick to death of Paris. I cannot concentrate here. I simply cannot. There are too many meetings, too many people, too many demands..." he trailed off, seeming to realize where he was. He immediately looked sheepish, and his ears turned pink. "Damn."

Isabeau flashed him her patient smile.

"Sorry." He gracefully went to her, and kissed her hand. "I am sorry, Isabeau. You are the only thing that keeps me sane, in what has become an insane world. More insane by the day. Your presence is enough to soothe me."

"Thank you, René." She paused a moment and looked into his eyes. They were dark, intense and overwhelming. He seemed to catch her gaze as well, and his full intensity focused on her. She felt her diaphragm tighten, like it did the day she met him, when she latched onto his arm. She pulled him close. He bent to her compliantly, still smelling of the coolness from the street, and the chemicals of the Académie Française. "My mother is a spy for the cardinal. We must be discreet."

His hand went around her waist. "Does this mean I cannot complain about that idiot Fermat in front of her?" He whispered back to her.

Her hands went to his shoulders, and she tilted her head back to continue gazing into his eyes. "That might be foolish, she would notice the difference if suddenly you stopped. So would the cardinal for that matter."

He bent to her a little further, and touched his nose to her forehead, and then down her nose. Their lips brushed. "I thought we were quite good at keeping quiet, so no one could hear us."

She leaned slightly forward with her body, and pulled her head back. "You are incorrigible," she whispered.

"You made me that way, Isabeau." He kissed her, gently at first, then as her passion rose, she responded. They kissed. After a long moment, René broke the kiss. "She spies for the cardinal?"

"Not in so many words, but yes." She smiled coyly and played with his jacket button. "Not out of malice, but out of her love." Isabeau didn't add more to the statement, to do so would be unfair to her mother. They pressed their foreheads together gently. "Did you tell Fermat about the paper? What you want to write?"

He sighed deeply, paused, and broke the embrace. He looked at her a moment, then turned away and stepped to one of the windows. The brilliant spring day was fading, but the traffic in the city below looked as if it were trying to hold on to the sunshine, bustling toward the light as it drained out the long city boulevards, wanting to hold onto this day a bit longer, before the chill of a spring night returned. René understood their hope. Understood the cool night would be returning. He turned back to her. "Not yet, Isabeau. I'm not ready. It's inevitable. The thought of these philosophers must come out into the open. Spinoza, Rousseau, Kierkegaard, Nietzsche, Russell, the list goes on. Just the acceptance of the concept of natural rights of man destroys the last thousand years of thought. And that is only one thing. It is so much, so fast. It means so much, asks so many bold questions. Questions I dare not have asked in this age. Grantville has unleashed a force that is too great to stop."

"You used to say that God unleashed Grantville on us."

"I'm not too sure anymore. About God—"

"René!"

"I have read things, Isabeau! As much as I possibly could. And then I thought. I thought long and hard on things by the greatest minds from the future. Men who took my work and built on it. My work, Isabeau. Great philosophers who grew up with the sun in the center of their solar system, and their solar system one of billions in a galaxy, and that galaxy one of an infinite number of other galaxies in the universe. That changes the way a man looks at the world. I was taught as a child, with absolute certainty that the heavens were a fixed dome, and the sun revolved around the earth. The Jesuits taught me this as a truth. But they were wrong. There is where I started." He began to pace again. "Do you understand, Isabeau? A philosopher that knows about the construction of the universe as a *truth* from since he was a child, what kind of a *difference* that makes on his mind? How he views God? How he views man in relation to God? How he views the existence of God? Just that single lesson is enough to change your view of this planet, and where it sits in the greater scheme. Just that single lesson."

"René. The cardinal must not know of these things. How you feel about this. He has stated what he thinks of Vatican Two reforms that have been passed around—"

"Which I have read," he interrupted firmly. "And studied. They are fascinating and speak to the changes that are coming. That *must* come, and inevitably will come to France. Whether Richelieu wants them to or not."

"I see." Isabeau sighed and pulled René to the couch, and they sat. She turned to him, worried. "René, do you speak of this to anyone? Anyone besides me?"

He snorted a suppressed laugh at her. "Somewhat with Mersenne, but I can trust him. I am not a fool, my dear. That sort of thing can get one in the deepest sort of trouble. And yet..." His voice trailed off in thought, and his eyes glazed over as he stared at the fireplace along the far wall.

Isabeau had seen this sort of thing from him before, and she waited patiently for a minute while he thought. There were times he could do this for hours.

"What should we do, René?"

He stood up and away from her, and then looked at her strangely, seriously, but in a way that she had not seen before. He took a step toward her, and she involuntarily shrank away. "Do you mean that, Isabeau?" His intensity could be mercurial.

"Mean what?" She was confused. This was one of those times when his mind was elsewhere, working on a level she didn't fully comprehend.

"Did you mean that?"

"I-I don't understand. Mean what?"

"What should we do? You asked, what *we* should do?"

She shook her head trying to gain focus, and smiled. "Yes. I asked what should *we* do." She began to feel uncomfortable as he took another step closer. "Simple enough question."

He stopped and looked at her with a curious gaze. "Do you know you are the smartest woman I have ever met?"

She felt her face flush. "René—"

"You see, Isabeau, you didn't ask what *I* should do. You asked what *we* should do. *We*. So there is only one thing *we* can do."

"What is it?"

"One question first. Are you with me in this? The philosophers of the future? The advancement of human thought?"

She answered without hesitation. "Of course. How could I not be?"

He reached out and held her hand, smiled warmly, and then knelt in front of her. "We must marry."

The Library at the Académie Française, after Galileo's trial, July 1634

Marin Mersenne slammed his palm onto the library table with a great deal of frustration. "It is a matter of doctrine, René! You are more aware than anyone I have ever worked with—and I have worked with every scientist in France who is worth his salt—that Church doctrine determines how we study the sciences. The natural philosophy of the future is diametrically opposed to present Church doctrine. It's heresy, pure and simple."

René had his back to Mersenne, and was gazing out the massive windows of the library. René wasn't looking at anything particular. And at the moment he was quite irritated with Mersenne. "I will write my summary. And publish it."

Mersenne's voice softened, trying a new argument. "You have read your future works. You were always scrupulous to maintain adherence to the teachings of the Church. Your letters are full of conversations addressing the very issue. That history must mean something to you, René."

René continued to stare out the window. "My desire was to have my book on philosophical method, my *Le Monde*, be the accepted text of the Jesuits, the only education worth a damn in this world. I wanted my book accepted as a canonical text, and have my methods taught at the highest levels by the best teachers." He turned from the windows and faced the friar. "Don't forget plausible deniability. That's why Galileo wrote his book on planetary motion as taking place in a 'hypothetical' universe. Fat lot of good that did him with the Inquisition."

"René, do you mean you do not have faith in God and

the Church as you professed? That all of your entreaties to me about staying faithful to doctrine were false? I don't believe it, René. You were practical, cautious, but I have never doubted your faith in the Church. Ever."

René tossed the book on the table and again turned to the window. "In the other time line, I completed *Le Monde*, but abandoned it after four years of work. Do you know why?"

Mersenne sighed. "Galileo."

René spun around, glaring at Mersenne. "Yes. Because of Galileo, that idiot, and the Inquisition, who are even bigger idiots. They attacked him, they attacked the Copernican system, and they attacked everything that was scientific progress!"

"They were only following Church doctrine." Mersenne returned the glare with a challenge.

René met his gaze. "Then I spent my years kowtowing to a false doctrine, Friar."

René watched Mersenne's face turn from frustration to a look of pain. "You do not know that, René. We do not know that. The Church does not know if the Ring of Fire is an act of God, or a temptation of Satan. Uptimers barely believe in Satan, while in our world we battle him every day. Satan is as real to us as the ground beneath our feet." He paused, thinking. "Let me ask you a question, René. And I want you to answer it as honestly as possible. Can you state the truth of the Ring of Fire with all certainty? Satan or God? The Church is struggling to determine what this all means. And to handle it poorly could lead to schisms and further fractioning of the true Church. I urge you to please reconsider publishing the paper, René. Please."

"I will publish this paper. It will not be controversial.

It will be a summation of up-time thought and philosophy. It has taken me months to write, and I have much more to do. I am doing nothing different than Crucibellus did with mathematics. She took the up-time concept and made it accessible to the down-time mind. I am doing the same with philosophy. And I am not the only one who feels this way. There are others here, but they push me to take the reins. I am taking the thoughts that started with me, the Father of Modern Thought, and tracing it all the way through modern up-time philosophers. It is a direct lineage. No one is better equipped to write it than I."

"Listen to yourself, René. You are talking like a demigod of some kind."

"Perhaps I am, Marin. Some of the books on this table speak of me in those terms."

Mersenne threw up his hands in disgust, shaking his head. After a moment, he shuffled through the pile of books on the table, finally unearthing what he was looking for, a copy of the Catholic Bible. He held it up. "René, as of this moment in time, the Church's official position is the earth is in the center of the universe as Ptolemy, Aristotle, and God through his scriptures have placed it. Despite the outcome of Galileo's trial and despite the attempt on the life of the pope. It is still official Church doctrine. It has not yet changed."

It was René's turn to look disgusted. "You have a mind, Marin, use it. You reviewed Copernicus' calculations yourself. He adhered to doctrine by telling everyone his calculations were merely 'aberrations that one must compensate for.' He knew we were not the center of the universe. The math proves it. Galileo's observations prove it."

"Don't you think that I know that, René? I am not a fool. Galileo is right! We are not the center of the universe. But the Church still says so. Doctrine says so. And Church doctrine is what determines your soul's relationship with God. That has been an accepted truth for a thousand years! We must take this one step at a time. A gradual change. This Ring of Fire is a damned thing. It's trying to force change on an institution that can trace its lineage all the way back to Christ himself. You wonder why people think the Ring of Fire might be the work of Satan? You are the fool who isn't facing reality."

"You are a magnificent defender of orthodoxy, Marin." There was no sarcasm in René's voice, merely a statement of fact and respect.

"I am a man of faith, René. Who understands the thing with which you gamble."

"And what is that?" René was puzzled.

"Your soul."

"My soul is my business," he snapped back.

"Then I will fear for it, even if you will not. You are destroying the Aristotelian model. Calling it moribund. Not worth our time. So be it. But in the reality-that-might-have-been, it took over one hundred years for this new system to fully take root. And you expect acceptance to happen the day you publish, because you said so? Without schism? Without violence? Without a fight? Understand this. I must defend doctrine. If you publish, I will attack your ideas."

"As you did with Flood and the Rosicrucians?"

"Yes. My arguments were impeccable and you know it."

"Yes. They were. While so many chose ad hominem

attacks, you clearly demonstrated the new age Rosicrucian nonsense of expecting scientific solutions from the invocation of supernatural agencies. Observation and fact was your argument. I will have no such weaknesses when I complete the writing."

"Is there anything I can do to talk you out of this, René?"

"It's not your choice to allow, or not. It's mine. We cannot call ourselves men of science unless we divorce doctrine from discovery."

"The two are inseparable!"

"The two are choking each other! And neither will grow until they are separate! As long as doctrine holds over science, we do not honor our God-given intelligence. When doctrine is wrong, as proven by science, the doctrine must change. If it does not, then the doctrine is the fool, and destined for the fool's path. Prayer doesn't hold up an airplane wing. It's air pressure."

Mersenne sighed. "You always were stubborn, René. And from our future readings, you grew more so as confidence in your thinking grew." He paused and once again focused on René. "You are certain about this path, my friend?"

"More than I have ever been about anything." René tried not to let belligerence creep into his voice. He wasn't sure if he succeeded.

Mersenne leaned forward in his chair and once again challenged René, this time gently. "And your wife? How is she with this choice of yours?"

He could feel his voice weaken slightly. "She supports me, and our joint desire to bring these discussions out into the open. She supports me absolutely."

Mersenne rose from his seat at the table, and embraced his friend. At first, René stood still, arms limp at his sides. After a moment he returned the embrace. Mersenne then stepped back and looked René in the eyes. "We part as friends, René. But we must part. It is my duty to destroy your arguments. But you know I will never attack the man."

René nodded in the affirmative.

Mersenne's voice grew even more serious. "Are you ready for what is to come?"

René nodded again, slower this time.

Mersenne smiled at him. "Will you tell Director Fermat that you intend to publish, or should I?"

René perked up, all signs of pain gone from his face, and he smiled back, broadly. "I will. I enjoy pissing him off."

October 1634

Isabeau watched René as he stepped through the open doorway to their home. He handed his cloak, blade, and broad-brimmed hat to his servant. Another servant closed the door behind him. Isabeau was standing in the doorway of a small room, off the main hallway that served as his office. It had thick doors and walls so that his solitude could be complete. She watched him carefully, trying to gauge his mood. He seemed neutral, not happy, not sad, not elated, just flat. Drained. Guarded. As he glanced down the hall toward his office, he caught her eye. She smiled at him, and he merely nodded. No change in expression. He mumbled acknowledgement to the servants, an up-time habit they adopted, and walked slowly to her. The servants melted away. She embraced him, and he returned the embrace. Lightly at first, and then gradually over a minute, his embrace became so tight that she could barely breathe. It was a desperate embrace, an embrace of a man who needed a rock of strength in a turbulent sea. He hung on to her for a while longer, and then stepped away.

She questioned him with her eyes.

He sighed slowly and deeply, just shaking his head. He abruptly stepped into his office, and she followed, closing the door behind them. He settled into his usual chair, she onto a couch. She waited patiently for him to speak. Isabeau knew it would take some time for her husband to gather his thoughts. The more agitated and emotional he was, the longer it took him.

She took a moment to glance around the small room. It was a high and ornate ceiling, decorated with a fresco of Odysseus sailing for home on the dome, with ornate cherubs and plaster floral decorations around it. His writing desk was in the corner, and around it were stacks and stacks of manuscripts. Some were handwritten by him, others had copious notes in the margins. Except for the fireplace, the rest of the room was bookshelves with only a high window for natural light. A clock on the mantel tocked loudly, drawing attention to itself in the silence. Isabeau tucked her feet under her dress and waited.

René was staring at the bookshelves next to the door, forefinger and thumb framing his jaw at one side of his face. With his other hand, he slowly drummed his fingers on the arm of the upholstered chair.

Finally he spoke. "Ridicule." He looked at her for the first time since they had entered his office. "I suffered ridicule." He grew quiet again.

Isabeau decided it was time for him to talk. Her feet came from under her dress, and she straightened her posture on the couch. "Tell me what happened at the lecture."

He just looked off into the bookcase again.

"René, tell me what happened. You presented the paper, didn't you? René?"

He turned to her slowly, and nodded in the affirmative.

"To the members of the Académie Française?"

He again nodded.

"This was a private presentation?"

He shrugged. "There were some others there I didn't recognize, only a few."

"And how was it received? René, answer me. I know the difference between sulking and thinking. You are sulking."

"I am also thinking."

"How was it received?"

"I think 'poorly' would be a good descriptor." He nodded. "Yes, poorly would just about do it."

"You knew there would be resistance. We spoke of it often."

"Spectacularly poorly. That might be better."

"René, tell me."

He took a deep breath, and sighed.

"René! Did you begin with the Aristotelian review, and how it didn't properly fit with the world, and then how the Platonic view tried and failed to make sense of the Christian world?" She motioned to him expectantly, trying to get him to pick up the conversation. "How did that go?"

He nodded and smiled ever so slightly at her encouragement. "That part went quite well. I was speaking their language, they understood the two models, and how philosophy had followed those two paths." He nodded again. "Quite well."

"Then I reviewed my work, not only what I was working on before the Ring of Fire, but also the impact that Galileo's trial had on my work. Went over several other examples of my writings very briefly, and then began to touch on the work of others who came after me. Just outlines. My book will be over a thousand pages when I am done, and there is no way I could possibly touch on everything in this first lecture. But I wanted to move forward. I've been reading and thinking for so long, it was time to *do* something."

"So what did you do?"

"I went over my Rationalist movement. They understood it. I've been talking about it for two years now, and it wasn't anything totally new to most of them." He turned to her, his excitement building. "Did you know that Baruch Spinoza is being raised by the Stearns family?"

"I know that, yes." She impatiently waived her arm. "But you went over the Rationalists to the Empiricists?"

"Yes." He grew quiet again. "That's when some of them began to walk out. Not all at once, but in steady stream from that point forward."

"They walked out of your lecture?"

"Yes!" He hit the arm of the chair with his fist. "The audacity of these men to walk out on René Descartes! I am the world's greatest living philosopher, one of the greatest the world has ever known, and they simply began to walk away from my lecture. One by one, they walked out."

"René, you didn't speak of yourself in those terms,

did you? You know what that does to Fermat when you say such things."

"No, I didn't. But that doesn't mean it isn't true."

She sighed, exasperated. That argument could happen on another day. Again. "What happened next?"

"I began to talk about the Existentialists."

"And then?"

"Nietzsche."

"I see."

"I only told them what *he* said, and why *he* said it. *Gott ist tot*. God is dead."

"Did they understand?"

René snorted. "Did they understand that what Nietzsche meant was that the Christian God as a moral compass was no longer the only source of morality? Was part of his argument that moral people can exist without the Christian God? No, Isabeau. And if they did, they didn't acknowledge it."

"And then?"

"And then, I was in an almost empty lecture hall, with only one person still sitting in their seat. Just one."

"Who? Fermat? Someone from the Inquisition?"

He shook his head. "Mersenne. He sat in the front row, in the center, and had tears streaming down his face."

Isabeau grew concerned, but she stayed silent, letting him gather his thoughts again.

"Mersenne stood up, and told me he would always pray for me, no matter what. In the middle of an empty lecture hall, his quiet and strong voice told me he would always pray for me." René's eyes began to tear up, and his jaw took a hard set. "I didn't realize this would be so hard, Isabeau. I thought...Well, I

knew it would be challenging, and that we would
have difficulty, and that many would not understand.
But..." His voice trailed off.

"Come here," she said, after a moment. She patted
the couch next to her.

He wiped his eyes with the back of his hand and
swallowed hard. "Why?"

"Just—come here. Sit."

He rose out of his chair and sat next to her. She
gently took him by the shoulders and turned him,
and then laid him so that his head was resting on
her lap. She began to stroke his forehead. "Better?"

"Always."

She watched his eyes slowly close as she gently drew
her fingers across his forehead. "I have something to
tell you, René."

"Mmmm?" One of his eyebrows arched quizzically,
eyes still closed.

"I am pregnant."

"Mmmm—*what*?" His eyes bulged open, and his
face burst into instant illumination like an up-time
lightbulb. He sat up next to her, and stared at her
like a schoolboy. She couldn't help but giggle. "You—
You're sure?"

She nodded.

"When will he-she-it be born?"

She laughed, feeling happier than she had in weeks.
While he was working on his lecture the house was
quiet, even glum at times. When she finally was certain
of the pregnancy, she was bursting to tell him. Her
mother had cautioned her against getting his—and
her—hopes up too soon. "These things are uncertain,"
her mother said, "and dangerous. But the women in

our family are strong, and have borne many children without a great deal of fuss. I'm hopeful you will be just fine."

"Isabeau, this is wonderful news, on what's been a less than wonderful day! It makes the pain go away like nothing else." He leaned away from her suspiciously. "Did you plan this? Telling me today?"

"Yes. I did plan to tell you today. I wasn't surprised you received the reception at the Académie Française you did. And the child should come in the spring, according to Mother, if all goes well."

He grew pensive for a moment, and then put his hand on her stomach. She reclined, and he gently put his head on her lap. "Can I hear anything yet?"

"Soon, I am told." She stroked his ear gently, knowing that pleased him. Smiling mischievously, she used his ear to pull his face to hers. They kissed, deeply. She eased closer to him, pressing her body to his in a way she knew would get his attention.

He unexpectedly pulled away. "This won't hurt the baby, will it? Or you?"

She laughed and pulled him toward her.

The next week

Henri de Champs was a very pious man. He was also intelligent, thoughtful, loved his family, his king, and owned a successful cloth business. A few years ago his wife passed away after a short illness, and he now lived with his daughter and her husband and children. He could afford a place of his own quite easily, but it was far better to be near the children and eating homemade food than eating a lonely meal indifferently prepared for him by servants. He was a quiet man who never made a fuss about anything.

There was a new parish priest, a young man who told Henri about the philosopher Descartes. In a sermon, he was described as the man who wanted to kill God himself. Descartes taught that morality was not the province of the church, or even of God, but with man himself. Henri had heard of Descartes, of course. Who in Paris had not? Two years ago, he was hailed as one of France's greatest minds, along with Fermat and others who started the Académie Française, with the support of the king and Cardinal Richelieu.

But now, the man Descartes had overstepped his bounds. Descartes was clearly not pious; he was an elitist, and arrogant to boot. The Inquisition had done nothing, it seemed to Henri. The authorities, nothing. The cardinal did nothing. Someone had to do something. This sort of talk, these teachings of heresy were not to be tolerated.

Henri went to the young priest to see what the church was going to do about this man, this heretic who was worse than a Huguenot, worse than a murderer, and surely a mouthpiece of the Devil himself. The priest too, was a very pious man, who preached against the Huguenot, against Descartes, and against all heresy, including the Ring of Fire. "That very name," he thundered from the pulpit, "that very name tells us that these people from the future are agents of the Devil. Is not Hell a place of fire? Is not Hell a place of rings of suffering, ever increasing suffering? Surely something called the Ring of Fire is born of Hell, a spawn of the Devil."

The priest told Henri that Descartes was likely

possessed, and that his intelligence and his mind overcame his heart. His ego made him weak, and his elitist thinking made him stupid, ignorant, and a blasphemer. The priest told Henri confidently that this man would be struck from the face of the earth by God.

Henri agreed, and thanked the priest profusely.

That night, as Henri slept, after a wonderful meal made by his daughter from the same recipe his wife used years ago, he had a dream. God came to him, and told him that he must be the one to kill René Descartes.

Two weeks later

Armand D'Abo, the head of security of the Académie Française, handed Pierre Fermat, the Director of the Académie Française, a tattered pamphlet. The pamphlet was taken from one of the protestors that were now in the street outside the Académie. D'Abo watched as Fermat read the pamphlet for the second time. D'Abo had seen Fermat angry before, but never like this. Clearly he was trying to contain his fury.

"Dammit. Dammit to Hell! I never should've given permission to Descartes to lecture on up-time philosophy. Never!" He held the proof in his hand up for D'Abo to see. "Obviously, someone attended the lecture, took notes, and published them. This was supposed to be only an academic discussion on something that stupid bastard Descartes insisted on pushing on the Académie, and now it's circulating on the streets of Paris. Likely in the hands of the Inquisition." His face paled. "In the hands of the king!" His face paled more. "And in the hands of Richelieu." He paused for a moment to collect his thoughts. "*Merde!*" He angrily balled the paper into a wad and tossed it to his desk. "There is so much at stake, the fate of France, of the Catholic church, of our very civilization! And Descartes wants to lecture on philosophy, the idiot. Why couldn't he just take an interest in designing airplane wings, or material sciences, or something practical?"

D'Abo wisely assumed it was a rhetorical question, and remained silent. Fermat continued. "His mathematics are superb, his work on optics was revolutionary, but that was before. Now, all he wants to do is read philosophy from the future, and write. And lecture on the convoluted points of logic and religion that are simply not important. I don't understand why Descartes can't see the needs in front of him. The terribly important needs of the country. He is one of the most stubborn men I have ever met! *Mon Dieu!*"

D'Abo felt he could comment on this aspect of Fermat's dialog. "*Oui*, Director Fermat. He is very stubborn."

Fermat shook his head. "It was supposed to be a closed session, D'Abo, but somehow, details of his lecture leaked out. I want to know the source of the leak, D'Abo. Track them down, and make sure that they never set foot in the Académie again."

"*Oui*, Director Fermat." D'Abo felt a little bolder. "But it seems the damage is already done. People are gathering in the street in front of the Académie."

Fermat turned on him. "Funding. Funding could be a problem if this becomes too big of an issue. The support of the king and Cardinal Richelieu are key to keeping the Académie operating. If Descartes keeps stirring up shit like this lecture, I figure I will have to take action and have Descartes tossed out on his ear. There is just too much at stake."

D'Abo watched as Fermat tried to calm himself. Pacing, he went to the window. The second-floor office overlooked the street below, and he leaned on the windowsill and absentmindedly peered down into the street, trying to gauge the crowd. Fermat barely had time to flinch out of the way as a rock was hurled at him, crashing through the window and landing on his office floor.

"Director Fermat, are you all right?"

Fermat stepped back from the window and brushed glass from his jacket. "Yes. What the hell is going on down there?"

D'Abo pulled Fermat back from the windows. "Extinguish the candles, Director. So they cannot see us inside."

As Fermat went to his desk to snuff out the candles, D'Abo went carefully to the windows. The shorter days of fall meant dusk came early. Keeping a practical distance from the windows so those below couldn't see him, he peered up and down the street. He could see torches approaching from both directions. Another rock hit the window, and bounced off. Someone else managed to hurl a cobblestone through another. There was a knock on the door.

"Come!"

Sergeant Maurice, D'Abo's assistant chief of security, entered the room hastily. "Director Fermat, are you all right? Officer D'Abo?"

"We're uninjured," Fermat answered for both of them "Have you sent a runner to the guard?"

"*Oui*, Director. But I think it wise the members leave the building while we can. The crowd is increasing, and it seems they are looking to riot. I don't want to take any chances." Maurice gave a quick glance to D'Abo for approval, and D'Abo nodded back.

"There are more on the way, Sergeant Maurice. You can see from here."

Fermat continued, "Then I don't want to take any chances with the building. There are too many experiments, too much work here to allow a mob to ruin any of it. What we do here is too important. Send another runner, and tell the Guard to break this up immediately. The Académie Française must be protected. Send cavalry immediately."

Captain of the Guard Louis Gerard de Montpassant laughed at the message. It was now completely dark, and there was no way he was risking mounted troops and horses through the narrow and uneven medieval streets. He would kill three or four of his men and probably a dozen horses before he reached the Académie Française. This was not the Paris of the future, with broad boulevards and open squares. This was still the Paris of the 1400s. Streets were crooked paths and haphazard mazes that took knowledge to navigate. De Montpassant had seen the layouts of the future Paris, and he very much liked it. The broad boulevards provided excellent fields of fire for dealing with unruly crowds. Cannon stationed at public squares could cover multiple directions at once. It was an excellent design. *Ah well, pikes would do just as well. They will get there a little slower, but at least they would get there.*

Dinner was about to be served, and the men would not have time to eat before they mustered out. De Montpassant felt a little badly for the rioters. His men were going to be very unhappy after double-time marching on an empty stomach for two miles. They were going to take it out on someone.

"How many were killed, Mersenne?" René asked dejectedly. Isabeau and Mersenne were sitting with René in his office.

"I was told eighteen bodies were found in the street. We don't know how many people crawled away, or were taken away by other survivors. Surely several more. It was very dark during the riot. It wasn't until daylight that you could see the bodies. Captain D'Abo and his men were able to prevent any of the rioters from getting into the Académie itself. But it was a near thing. Many of them were injured, including Captain D'Abo."

"This is terrible," said Isabeau. "Mersenne, how bad is Captain D'Abo?"

"Little is certain, Isabeau. But he is at his family home recovering. If there is no infection, he should recover. It's in God's hands now." Mersenne gave a sidelong glance at René, who steadfastly ignored his subtle dig.

Isabeau turned to her husband. "I think we should do something, René. It is obvious that people blame you for what happened—"

"*Me!* What did I do? Did I create that pamphlet? Did I rage from the pulpits? Did I prey on the ignorance of others and drive them into a deadly frenzy?"

"No, of course not, dear. But the blamed person, you shall be. It was your lecture—"

"I only lectured on what others had said, not what I believe."

Mersenne jumped in. "That distinction of logic is doing you about as much good as it did Galileo when he set his book in a 'fictional universe.' Don't try to play that game with me, René. I have known you and your mind for too long. Once you started reading the philosophy from the future, you were lost to us. Your mind couldn't reconcile the ideas of the future and still accept the past and our present. Your stubbornness is only surpassed by your brilliance. I have fought you at every turn. But with logic and respect. Not respect for the ideas, you know my feelings on those, but respect for the man. Whoever published this pamphlet for the public like this clearly had no respect for the man or the science." Mersenne stopped for air, and looked at René. "No matter what, this riot is on your hands, René."

"I refuse to accept the responsibility for the deeds of others. I had no direct control—"

"Bullshit!"

Both men stared at Isabeau with slack jaws.

"An up-time phrase I learned a few weeks ago. Very fitting for this occasion." She turned to her husband. "We talked about this many times. You knew there would be consequences. Certainly not this soon, certainly not this severe, but we knew there would be a toll to pay. Denying that toll now is the worst you can do. You must accept responsibility for what happened, apologize to everyone starting with the king and ending with the families of those injured. 'Damage control' is another up-time phrase that comes to mind. And while we may speak of the elegance of the French language as the highest ideal for political communication, we need to 'manage the spin' of this debacle, if I may be so inelegant. That is, if you want to remain in France, and out of the clutches of the cardinal, and the Inquisition, and the king. Because they are three distinct and independent enemies. And you have made enemies this month, to be sure."

René rose from his seat, and shouted. "This is not my fault! I did not do this thing."

Isabeau looked imploringly to Mersenne. *Do something, please,* she thought at him, hoping he would understand.

He caught her look, and nodded. He stood in front of René. "René. Listen to me. We are not saying you did it." He looked sideways at Isabeau. "But this is the perception people will have." He nodded to Isabeau, who nodded back. "I have an idea. I think we should go and visit Captain D'Abo. That will at least show support for those at the Académie Française who were wounded." He glanced at Isabeau, non-verbally urging her to take up the argument.

"He's right, René. That's a start. At least a public start. His home is less than a half mile from here, we can walk there in a few moments." Isabeau joined Mersenne standing in front of René, who reluctantly met their gaze. He stared at them for a moment.

"Very well. But this is to support the captain. That is all. I still don't believe I hold responsibility for the actions of ignorant priests."

"Let's go now," urged Isabeau. "We can make it there and back before dinner."

Within moments, they were out the door and making their way through the streets of Paris toward the home of Captain D'Abo. It was a blustery and raw late November day and Isabeau and René were bundled into their heaviest cloaks, Isabeau with hers hooding her head, René with his bundled around his body, his large brimmed hat pulled low on his face. Mersenne, as always, was wearing open sandals, and clad only in his coarse woolen friar's robes. It always amazed Isabeau how the man managed not to freeze to death in the winter.

They had gone only a short distance when they were approached by a well-dressed man. Isabeau looked at him and smiled. Middle-aged, graying hair neat and clean, fine gloves of lambskin. He came directly to her husband, who was to her right. Mersenne walked to her left. With her hood on, and a gust of wind, she couldn't hear the man's voice clearly. But it sounded like he was asking René if he was Descartes, the philosopher.

"Yes, that is I. But I don't have time to speak to anyone right now..."

As René answered, the man casually pulled open his cloak, and gently, almost delicately, pulled a dagger from his belt. His relaxed motion had put René and Isabeau off their guard, and Isabeau could see that her husband had already dismissed the man. He was looking down the street and past the man. He didn't see the knife.

Isabeau screamed. Her husband started to turn toward her, and finally saw the blade. With his hands inside his cloak, and his cloak drawn tight around him, the only thing he could do was try and protect himself from the inevitable blow. He raised his arms inside the cloak, and Isabeau lost track of the blade in the whirl of heavy cloth, his hat, and her arms instinctively reaching for where she thought the knife would be. She succeeded in finding the assailant's wrist, and she held it as the dagger plunged into her husband. Still trying to hold it, she felt the man twist his wrist and pull the knife back for another blow. She could feel the scrape of bone as it slid out of her husband.

The assailant took a step back and they locked eyes, she hanging onto his wrist. He had no expression, Isabeau could see, and a part of her mind felt even more afraid as she saw the deadness of his eyes. With his other hand, he deliberately and firmly pushed her back, while twisting his wrist in her grip to free his weapon. She stumbled away toward Mersenne. The man turned away from her, and back to René.

René had stumbled backwards, clutching his left shoulder, Isabeau saw. He must have deflected the first blow with his cloak and forearm. He then started an attempt to strip his cloak away, so that he could get to his blade. The cloak became tangled and caught on the hilt of the sword, and his broad hat fell into his face. The assailant moved in again. Isabeau found herself rooted to the spot. Out of the corner of her eye, she saw Mersenne move, and then place himself between René and the assailant. The assailant stopped at the sight of the friar's robes, and took a step to one side to go around him. Mersenne moved to block him. Mersenne simply stood there. He didn't take a defensive posture; his arms were at their sides. It was almost like he had bumped into the man on the street, and they were trying to find a way past each other. The man moved to the left, and Mersenne countered, then to the right with the same result.

Mersenne started to say something to the man, in his clear and strong voice, and the man made a waving motion with his hand, and sliced Mersenne's throat. Isabeau felt a warm spray hit her face. Mersenne stood there for only a second, tried to reach for his throat, then collapsed to the dirty street in a heap. Isabeau watched as the assailant calmly stepped over the body.

By now, René had dropped his cloak and hat. As the cloak dropped it was still caught on the hilt of his sword. He grabbed the hilt and the cloak in one motion, and pulled them together. He now had his blade in front of him, but he was tripping over the cloak as he held both. The man continued to advance. René lunged. Isabeau saw her husband's blade strike the man in the chest. It stayed there, only stuck into him by the tip, the cloak restricting the range of motion.

The assailant screamed in pain and surprise, and stumbled back. With his motion, the cloak finally fell away, pulling the tip of the sword out of the assailant. The sword landed at René's feet. He picked it up by the blade and retreated as he fumbled for the grip. The assailant continued to advance. Isabeau could see her husband slip to one knee on the blood-covered cobblestones. The man was now between her and her husband, she couldn't see . . .

The assailant suddenly stopped. She watched him from the back as he staggered, bent at the middle. He then began to swipe back and forth with his blade, like a child playing with toy swords. She heard her husband scream. His cry broke her paralysis, and she found herself able to move again.

The two men were locked together. René had plunged his blade deep into the assailant's chest.

Kneeling, he held the man at bay, impaled on his sword. The blade was very deep, and the man close enough, that the wild swinging of his blade connected with René's face and forearms. The assailant weakened, and René was covered with blood and slashes. The man collapsed and fell on top of her husband. As he rolled to the side, Isabeau could see that his expression had not changed. Her husband lay motionless in the street.

She started screaming. She remembered screaming for a long, long time.

April 1635

Pierre Fermat stood in front of the Paris town home of René Descartes. Over his shoulder was a portfolio of contracts and paperwork, and under his arm was tucked a small gift for Marie Descartes, the infant daughter born two weeks ago. Much was made of the fact that the mother had taken the infant for her baptism shortly after the birth, and that the father was not present.

Wishing he were elsewhere, he rapped on the thick door. It was immediately opened by a burly servant, and he was carefully and quite impolitely scrutinized. "Pierre Fermat for Monsieur and Madame Descartes, please."

The servant grunted an acknowledgement and motioned him into the hallway. He was flanked by two other servants. He recognized one of them as a former student at the Académie. Fermat knew that Descartes still had many friends in the academic world, and his followers were all students of up-time philosophy, the study of which Fermat had banned at the Académie. He was ushered upstairs into a small vestibule where he was allowed to stand by himself for a few moments.

Finally, a door opened, and he stepped into the room to meet René Descartes, who was sitting upright in a chair, with his wife at his side. It was the first time that Fermat had seen Descartes since the assassination attempt, and considering what he had gone through, he really didn't look that bad. His face was lightly scarred, his nose was missing a chunk on the left side, and his right eye looked like it drooped slightly. He was recovering, from what Fermat could tell, which agreed with the reports.

"Pierre," began Descartes.

"Isabeau, René." After a formal bow to each of them, he produced the gift. "Something for the baby. I understand she is doing well, as is her mother?"

Isabeau stood and accepted the gift from him. "Yes, thank you, Director Fermat. Marie is sleeping now."

"Ah. Just as well, I've never been good with babies. Babies or puppies." He laughed, internally fighting the tension within him. He glanced around the room, and saw another chair. "Do you mind if I sit?"

Isabeau nodded, and he sat, drawing the chair closer to them.

"Well," Fermat said nervously.

"Indeed," replied Descartes.

Fermat cleared his throat. "This is something I've been putting off for a while, René. As I am sure you know."

"Indeed," said Descartes again.

Fermat was a brilliant man. He knew that about

himself, he had accepted it a long time ago. He knew the people he was lucky enough to work with were all savants in some field or another. But none could be as frustrating as the man who sat across from him. A remarkable man. A pain in his ass. He took a breath and started to speak. "René, I—"

"Do you have the papers?"

Fermat stopped. *He knows what all this is for.* He then smiled, and pulled a stack of paper from his satchel. "Indeed."

"Where do I sign?"

"It's all marked out on the contracts, René. I can leave them with you and you can have your lawyers look it over—"

"I will sign them now, and you can take them back with you. I wish this to be our last meeting."

"Indeed," replied Fermat. While Descartes read and signed the various documents, Fermat felt his usual need to fill the silence. "Do you know where you will go? What you will do? We all assume you will go to the Netherlands again. After all that is where you did most of your writing."

Descartes replied with only a raised eyebrow. He continued reading and signing.

Fermat plowed onward. "I see that your hands have healed. I heard that you had several tendons severed in your left hand. Can you still use it?" In response, Descartes lifted his left arm and flexed his fingers. Clearly only the thumb and the middle finger still functioned properly. The rest were frozen in place. He dropped his left hand, and continued shuffling the papers with his right hand.

Fermat nodded. "At least you can still write." Fermat

leaned forward toward the pile of paper in front of Descartes. "There are a couple of release forms there, and some contractual documents that forbid you discussing with anyone what we have worked on, or what you may have seen while at the Académie."

"I was stabbed in the shoulder, face and arms, Pierre. None of those affected my ability to read."

"Indeed." Fermat could feel himself nodding in agreement. "I suppose that time you spent in the army with Maximilian and the Prince of Orange came in handy. Never thought of you as one who was handy with a blade. And the killer was someone who was never any trouble, a good man by all accounts." Once again, Fermat received an eyebrow for his trouble. He waited for the last document to be signed and handed back to him.

Fermat stood and stuffed the papers into his folio. "Thank you." He then looked at the couple. "I know others have said this, but I wanted to add my official condolences for our mutual loss of Marin Mersenne. He had a strong mind, and was responsible for so many advances. He was taken from us too soon."

Descartes stood quickly, and Isabeau went to his side, steadying him. He seemed to fight off dizziness. "Marin Mersenne was far more than a strong mind, Fermat. He was a man of deep faith. And his faith..." Descartes' voice trailed off, and he looked distant.

A puzzled Fermat prompted Descartes. "His faith...?"

"Indeed," replied Descartes.

It's Just a Dog

Walt Boyes

Weimar, June 1633

When Adolf Graube entered his mother and father's house, he always stopped in the doorway and breathed deeply. It was a scent that brought back the feelings of his childhood. His mother was in the kitchen. She turned when he entered, and hugged him. He was taller, so she had to reach up to put her arms around him.

"*Ach, mein Bube,*" she said, "it is wonderful to see you! You don't come home enough. Does the duke really keep you so busy you can't come see your poor old mother and father every so often? Are the hunting dogs really more important than us?"

Adolf took off his coat and hat and hung them at the door. His mother bustled into the kitchen and his father led him into the main room where the table had been set for dinner.

"Sit, sit," his father said, and Adolf sat in the place he used to use when he was a boy. "Tell me how things are at the Schloss, *mein Herr Hundeabrichter*." His father grinned.

"I am not a master dog trainer yet, and you know it, Papa, just a regular worker with the dogs. Someday, maybe," Adolf said. "Well anyway, we are getting the deerhounds ready for the fall hunt, and that takes time," Adolf began. "And we have just had a new litter in the kennel. One of the *Hubertushund* bitches. I sort of like the new name *Bluthund* that the Americans call them."

Dinner went well. As they were relaxing over a beer, Adolf's mother cleared her throat.

"Adolf, you are twenty-five years old, and you have a good job. It is time to start thinking about getting married."

"*Ach, Mama,*" Adolf said, ducking his head. "I am not yet ready to marry. I want to be the *jagdmeister* before I marry. As a simple dog trainer I am not ready. I do not have a house, and I cannot afford to buy one."

"But the wife will bring enough dowry to afford a house, perhaps," his father said.

"And I have some very nice girls I want to have you meet," his mother declared.

Adolf sighed. There was a small silence.

"Well, then," his mother said, "will you be able to come for dinner again next Sunday?"

"I think so, maybe," Adolf said.

"Good. I will invite a young lady from a good family and her parents."

"Oh, Mama!" Adolf groaned. "I have to get back to my dogs."

"We will see you next Sunday," his mother said, sweetly, savoring her victory.

Weimar, August 1633

"Ein feste Berg ist unser Gott!"

Adolf sang lustily, but not, he knew, well. His voice was loud but he had difficulty carrying the tune. So he sang the first verse with everyone else as loud as he could, and much more quietly during the remaining verses.

This had been the first Sunday in several weeks that he had been able to attend church with his mother and father. He had gone to services near the duke's house because he needed to be near the dogs. Now that the bitch he was working with had whelped, he didn't have to be there all the time.

On the way out of the church, after the service, Adolf's mother steered him to a family standing in the nave.

"I want you to meet this girl, Adolf," his mother said in his ear. "All you have to do is to say hello."

The young woman turned around. She was blonde, well-built and very pretty. She smiled nervously. Adolf smiled back, and nodded his head.

"Adolf, this is Gertrude Schmidt, and her parents, Herr Schmidt and Frau Schmidt." German women didn't take their husband's last name, Adolf mused, so her family must also have been Schmidt. Adolf shook his head and brought his mind firmly back to the present, and to Gertrude.

"I am pleased to meet you all," Adolf said. He was staring at Gertrude, and she was staring right back.

"Um," Adolf said, "may I walk you home from church? If that is all right with your parents, of course."

"I would like that," Gertrude said, as her father nodded. "And please call me Trude."

"Trude. I like that," Adolf said, with a big stupid grin on his face, offering her his arm.

The parents, both sets, stood watching them as they walked down the hill toward the Schmidt house.

Frau Schmidt smiled. "I think this will work out nicely," she said to Adolf's mother. "Nicely."

Weimar, November 1633

Adolf looked at the calendar Duke Albrecht had brought back from Grantville. He was almost afraid to touch it. The pictures were so very real. Not like woodcuts or etchings, or the paintings in the duke's house here in Weimar.

Duke Albrecht lived relatively simply in a townhouse because the schloss had burned down several years before and was being slowly rebuilt as the Wettin family could afford to do more work. But there were still enough beautiful things in the duke's house to make a poor young man wide-eyed and amazed.

It was also amazing what changes the Ring of Fire had made in just a few short years. Duke Wilhelm had abdicated, for heaven's sake, and was now something called the "leader of the opposition" in the *Reichstag* of a brand-new empire, run by the king of Sweden, also for heaven's sake. Duke Bernhard was off probably fighting against the empire that his brother was probably going to be prime minister of. Duke Ernst was governor of a "state" not a duchy. And Duke Albrecht kept saying he was "ceo" of the Wettin companies. Whatever a ceo was. Adolf had heard it pronounced "see-ee-oh" but he didn't think it was quite right.

Adolf always said his head began to hurt when

he thought about those things. Adolf knew dogs. In fact, he had just gotten promoted. He was now one of the dog masters at the Schloss. For years now, he'd helped keep the ducal hunting dogs. There were many different kinds of dogs in the ducal pack, depending on the kind of hunting they were expected to be part of. Adolf was mainly in charge of the large game-hunting dogs. These were the dogs that the Wettin family and their guests took hunting boar and deer and even a bear once in a while. It was easier to think about the dogs, and how to care for them, how to breed them for better hunters, and what was for dinner that night.

Practical, dogs were, Adolf knew. Dinner, sleep, fun, companionship. That was what was important to the dogs. It wasn't a bad way of looking at things, Adolf often said, both to himself and to the dog masters.

Duke Albrecht had come back from Grantville with a calendar. It didn't look a lot like any calendar Adolf had ever seen, and it was for a year that hadn't happened yet. The duke had given it to Adolf and said, "The Grantvillers have books on dogs, and the many breeds of dog that have been made in the future. But there is only one dog I am very interested in. It is named the Weimaraner, the Weimar dog."

The duke went on, "It would be excellent to have a Weimaraner dog, but there were none in Grantville when the Ring of Fire happened. I couldn't get the Grantville Library to let me have the book I saw, but I found somebody who had saved a calendar of pictures of up-time Weimaraner dogs. So I've brought you the calendar so you can see what they looked like. Do you think we could breed them up ourselves?"

Adolf looked at the pictures. The calendar had pictures of ghost gray dogs forming the letters of the alphabet. On the cover was a wide-eyed hound balancing three children's blocks, A, B and C, on his head.

He looked at Duke Albrecht. "They look something like a cross between a Saint Hubertus hound, what the Americans call *bluthund*, bloodhound, and that dog that is coming out of Hungary. What is its name? The Vizsla, yes, that's it. Let me think on it, Highness, for a few days."

Duke Albrecht nodded. "Here, keep the calendar until you are finished with it. You will need the pictures, yes?"

"*Sicher*, Your Highness." Adolf bowed. "Of course. I will take as good care of them as I do the dogs."

The duke laughed. "In that case, Adolf, I know this project is in good hands."

Adolf took the calendar to his room in the kennels. He sat on his bed, turning the pages and turning over what the duke wanted in his head.

He got up, and went to the dog run. He called his favorite bloodhound out of the run. "Hilde, *komm her!*" As the bitch ambled over to the gate of the run, he looked at her. She had the mark of the hound. She was mostly grizzled with black, white and gray coat, and brown patches barely visible through the coat. She was tall and fit, with a muscular deep chest that just screamed, "I can run all day!" He let her out of the run, and she leaned on him, as hounds do. Adolf scratched behind her ears and she made a deep rumbling noise that he often thought was what a huge cat might make, purring. If, that is, the cat was a dog.

Weimar, November 1633

Adolf went to see the chief huntsman, and showed him the calendar the duke had given him.

"Where can I find a Vizsla?"

"What's a Vizsla?" Gerhard, the *jagdmeister*, asked.

"You know, the brown hound that comes from Hungary."

"*Ach, so*," Gerhard said. "Why do you care?"

"Duke Albrecht showed me a book he got from Grantville, that shows dogs called Weimaraners. He gave me the copy he had made for him there. We don't have a dog like them. He says he wants us to breed him some."

"Is the Vizsla for this?"

"Yes. The dogs in the pictures look a lot like a stockier, taller Vizsla. I've seen a couple of them, but I don't know where to buy one," Adolf said. "And they are gray."

"Who? The Vizsla? I thought you said they were brown."

"No, no, hunt master, the Weimar dogs in the book. They are gray, like they were ghost dogs."

"Well, I will see what I can do. Do you want a dog or a bitch?"

Adolf thought. "I think I want a dog. Two if I can get them so I can pick the best of the two for stud."

"You don't ask for much," Gerhard grumbled.

"It isn't me," Adolf said, a little defensively. "It's the duke."

"I don't know what we can do. Aren't we at war with Austria?"

"I think so," Adolf said.

Gerhard pressed on. "Isn't Hungary part of Austria?"

"Yes, I think so," Adolf said. "But isn't part of it conquered by the Turk?"

"*Ja*. So?" Gerhard was being unhelpful. "Do you see the problem?"

"Yes, but I have to have an answer for the duke! Can we make this Weimaraner dog or not?"

"Well," Gerhard finally harrumphed. "I will see what I can find out."

Max, who was responsible for the pack dogs, the fox hunting dogs, and the rabbit dogs stepped into Gerhard's little office. "I couldn't help overhearing. The duke wants his own Weimaraner dog, eh?"

"*Ja, das ist richtig*," Adolf said. "That's right."

"Well, if you can't get a Vizsla, why don't you think about using a Chien-gris?"

"What, you mean the dog from the French king's kennels?" Adolf said. "Don't you think we might have the same problem as with the Vizsla? We're at war with the French too, nitwit." He play-punched Max on the shoulder.

"Yes, but perhaps my lord Bernhard might be able to help us there," Max said. "You could see if Duke Albrecht would write him and ask him."

"Fine. That's what we do, then," Gerhard stood, signaling an end to the discussion. "I'll see if I know anybody who might be able to get us a Vizsla dog. Adolf, you talk to the duke and see if he will write to his brother. And we will see if we can make us a real Weimar dog."

Weimar, November 1633

Adolf found himself thinking about Trude. He thought about her a lot. He was fascinated by her smile, her laugh, and her eyes that always seemed interested in him. He continued to be surprised that she liked him, but he was getting to accept it as a gift from God to an unworthy man.

He'd invited Trude to come and visit the kennels and meet some of his favorite dogs. He was hoping that she'd like them, and what he did for the duke. And he'd been right.

Trude sat happily on the floor of the kennel, with wriggling little balls of fur with feet in her arms, in her lap, and on the floor around her. As one of the little puppies licked her nose, she giggled.

"Do you like my dogs, then?" Adolf asked.

"Oh, yes, I do!" Trude said, smiling widely. "And these little things came from that big one there?" She pointed vaguely at Adolf's favorite bitch, Hilde, who raised her head and stared at her. Trude looked away.

"Yes, they are hers," Adolf said, rubbing behind Hilde's ears. "They are just a day old and I thought you'd like to see them."

"Oh, my," Trude said, and then stopped. "You must think me a very silly girl to be gushing like this over just a dog."

"Trude, there is no such thing as 'just a dog,'" Adolf said, sliding over to her on the floor and taking her hand. "Dogs are wonderful parts of God's creation. They give love unconditionally, and all they want is love and food in return."

Trude nuzzled the little brindled puppy she was holding. "All you want is love, eh? I bet you want your dam's milk too." She rose to her knees and handed the puppy off to Adolf, who set it at Hilde's teats. The little puppy latched on easily even though it didn't have its eyes open yet, and began to eat.

Trude gazed at Adolf with a speculative look in her eyes.

Weimar, Mid-November 1633

"Come, my sweet, we have thinking to do."

Adolf unlatched the kennel and let Hilde out into the kennel yard. He headed toward the gate, the big bloodhound at his heels. "And we are going visiting," Adolf said. Hilde woofed softly.

It was a crisp, cold day as Adolf and Hilde walked down the hill from the duke's hunting lodge where the kennels were. They crossed the plaza and turned into the street where Herr Schmidt had his shop and home. Adolf knocked, and Frau Schmidt came to the door.

"*Guten Abend,*" Adolf said. "*Ist Trude zu Hause?*"

"Yes, she's here. Wait," Frau Schmidt said. "I'd invite you in, but you have that huge hound with you!"

"It's all right, Mama," Trude's voice came from the stairs. "We are going for a walk. The dog doesn't have to come in."

Frau Schmidt grumbled. "I don't know why that huge thing has to go around with you, Adolf. After all, it's just a dog!"

Trude pulled on her wrap, and she and Adolf laughed as they started off down the street, Hilde on the outside, guarding the pair. "Just a dog! Imagine that, Hilde!" Trude said.

Hilde woofed.

"Where are we going?"

"To the kennels. I have something I want to show you."

"What?"

"A booklet from the future! It is a calendar," Adolf said.

"From the future? Oh, you mean from Grantville! I haven't ever seen a book from Grantville. What does it look like?" Trude said.

Trude sat on the floor of Adolf's room with Hilde's head in her lap as he paged back and forth through the copy of the calendar from the future that Duke Albrecht had given him. He paused on each page so he could show her the things that made these dogs different from all the downtime dogs he'd ever seen. The calendar had enough pictures, twenty-six of them to be exact, two on each page and one on the cover and back, and several different Weimaraner dogs in each one.

Adolf thought there were four of them, two dogs and two bitches. He went through the calendar's months from A to Z quickly and then he slowly went through each page. As he did, Hilde's tail thumped contentedly on the floor. Trude watched him quietly, as she stroked Hilde's head.

"These are photographs?" Trude asked. "They are marvelously detailed, even better than stone lithographs!"

"Yes," Adolf said, turning a page. "According to the duke, the man who took the photographs is a—was a—famous artist in the up-time. Wilhelm, no, *William*, Wegman, his name was."

"They are beautiful, absolutely beautiful dogs," Trude said. "Look at their faces. You'd think they could speak."

"Yes, they look very intelligent. And those light eyes. I wonder how I will find a dog like that to breed to," Adolf said.

"Doesn't the duke have any dogs with light eyes?" Trude was surprised.

"No, it isn't usual. Most dogs have the brown eyes, like Hilde here." Hilde thumped her tail, pleased to be talked about.

"But I have heard of a dog that comes out of Hungary that has the short and shiny coat like in these pictures, and the Chien-gris dog from France sometimes is light-eyed. The Hungarian dog is supposed to be a very old breed, too. They call them Vizsla."

He scooted nearer to Trude on the floor, so that their heads touched as they pored over the pictures. Trude smiled. Hilde's tail thumped, and she woofed softly.

Weimar, April 1634

"So," Adolf's father said, "Have you decided that you want to marry Trude? You have been stepping out for several months now."

Adolf tried to change the subject. "I've been given a project by Duke Albrecht himself," he said. "I've been working on breeding a new kind of dog. It was bred by the up-timers in the Weimar of the eighteenth century, for one of Duke Albrecht's descendants. The duke says he wants to make a real Weimar dog now. A real Weimaraner."

"What is the dog supposed to look like?" his father asked.

"They are gray, almost like a ghost, and they have light eyes."

"Well, we've always had gray dogs!"

"Yes, Papa, but they don't look exactly like the Weimaraner from the future. The duke wants a pack of those."

"What are you getting for this project?" his father said. "Surely the duke promised you a reward."

"Nothing other than my wages, Father," Adolf said.

"You should go to the duke and ask for a reward, Adolf. You will never get anywhere unless you put yourself forward!" His father slapped the table to emphasize the point. It was an argument that was old and well worn.

"It will be a long while before I can present the duke his new dog breed," Adolf said. "I will have to give him something before I can ask for a reward, Papa." Adolf's answer never varied.

"And I don't know about marrying Trude, either!"

Weimar, Late April 1634

Adolf, Max and *Jagdmeister* Gerhard sat looking at the duke's calendar from Grantville for the umpteenth time. "Well, it's got the shape of a Vizsla," Gerhard said, "but it looks much larger."

Max pointed to one of the pictures. "It's got the head of a Vizsla, though. Look at the difference between these pictures and the Saint Hubertus dogs, even the ones we get that are occasionally gray."

Adolf thought. "One thing we know, though. We have to breed two grays together to get grays. Otherwise we might get lucky, or we'll just get brown puppies."

"What you're saying, then," Max said, "is that we need to breed the Vizsla in, but select for the Vizsla head and a coat that is very smooth and shiny like the Vizsla's but a gray coat. That's going to take some time."

"Well, we have a couple of those French bitches, the Chien-gris. We get mostly gray puppies from them. There's a male from one of those litters that is just about ready to breed by now."

"And look at the eyes in the pictures. They aren't brown! How are we going to breed that in? Do we even have a light-eyed dog?" Max wondered.

"That I don't know yet," Adolf said. He turned to Gerhard. "How are we coming with getting a Vizsla? It sounds like we really need a male, maybe two."

"I have asked Duke Albrecht to write to a man he knows in Austria, Janos Drugeth, who is from Hungary and who is powerful in the court of the emperor. We have not heard back from him, yet," Gerhard said. "But you know how the nobles are—they trade dogs back and forth all the time. They all seem to be looking for the perfect hunting dog."

"And we don't?" Adolf shot back.

"*Ja, ja, ja!* Sure we do. *Nicht wahr?*" Gerhard nodded.

"While we're waiting, I want to see what we can do with the stock we have," Adolf said.

Weimar, May 1634

"Come on, girl. You can do it!" Adolf coached his beloved Hilde as she delivered her litter of pups. Adolf had bred her to a Chien-gris dog who had a very gray coat. So far, she had delivered five pups, and three of them were mostly gray. There was a male and two females in the litter. "Good girl, Hilde!"

The puppies looked a lot like the pictures in the up-time book, except they had brown eyes and a slightly rougher coat. Their heads were more like the bloodhounds and they had the "mark of the hound" in their coats, too. The undercoat had some brown in it on the three gray ones.

As usual, Trude had come to the kennel to meet the new puppies.

"See, Trude," Adolf said, handing her a puppy. "This is what I am trying to make for Duke Albrecht. This is as close as we can breed yet to the up-time Weimar dog."

"A real Weimaraner," she said.

"Yes. That's what they will be."

Trude held the little gray puppy close. The tiny bitch puppy had just opened her eyes, and she looked at Gertrude with her big, brown eyes.

Adolf fetched the book they'd pored over together before. "This is what they are supposed to look like," he said, pointing to the cover, with the wide-eyed gray dog balancing three alphabet blocks on his head. "I still have to figure out how to get the light eyes."

"What are you thinking?" Trude asked. She seemed very interested. Adolf wondered if she was interested in what he was doing, or just interested in him. It really didn't matter. He liked Trude a lot. More than he liked Hilde, which was saying a lot. He thought Trude liked him back. He hoped she did. He prayed she did.

"I'm thinking we should give Hilde back her puppy, and go. I can walk you home."

Trude bent and laid the puppy back in the whelping box, where she immediately sought and found her dinner. Trude straightened, and smiled at Adolf. "I'd like that," she said.

The couple walked arm in arm out of the kennel and down the cobblestoned street. The street was very narrow, in some places almost too narrow for two people to walk abreast. The street smelled.

"It will truly be nice," Trude said, "when they get the new sewer finished."

"Oh, yes. And it will make the stables and the dog runs smell better, too, when we get the pressurized water hoses the duke's engineers are making."

Adolf and Trude had been stepping out now for about eight months. Adolf sucked up his courage.

"You know that I like you very much, Trude," he began.

"Yes, and I like you too."

"Do you think it could be more than 'like'?"

Trude turned to face him, taking both his hands. "Yes, it could. In fact it is. Silly man. I've been waiting for you to make up your mind."

"I don't have a lot of money. I don't know how I could support you."

"I have a decent dowry," she said. "That will help. We can get a house together."

"Will you marry me?"

"Of course, silly man," she said.

He bent his head and kissed her to seal the proposal.

They walked arm in arm to her parents' house. She invited him in. Adolf swallowed hard, sucked up his chest like a soldier, and prepared to meet the firing squad. Well, at least her father.

Trude's mother hustled her away, as soon as they entered the house. Her father motioned Adolf into the kitchen.

"*Sitz,*" he said. Like a good dog, Adolf sat.

"So, young man, what are your intentions toward my daughter?"

"Herr Schmidt, my intention is to marry your daughter, if you will give me permission. We care for each other, and we think we could be a good match. I have prospects. One of these days, Gerhard is going to retire as *Jagdmeister*, and I think I will be able to get the job." Adolf stopped because he knew he was babbling.

Schmidt sat there looking at him. He didn't say anything for a while. Adolf felt like trying to melt through the floor.

Finally, Schmidt said, "Well then. I should speak to your father about posting the banns."

Adolf found that he'd been holding his breath. He let it out in a huge sigh.

"Now it is late, *mein Sohn*," Schmidt said, "and you should take yourself off to your bed."

"*Danke schön*," Adolf said as he went out the door. "*Gute Nacht!*"

Gyulafehérvár, Transylvania, July 1634

George I Rákóczi crumpled the letter in his fist. The prince of Transylvania sat back in his chair and tapped the table with the fingers of the hand that was not clenching the paper.

"So, they don't want to concede to me my title or the lands they've stolen, but they think I will do them favors?" He cursed the Habsburgs, as he regularly cursed them. Not that his curses appeared to have any effect.

"What do they want, Lord?" his secretary asked.

"The so-called emperor of Austria and Hungary, which territory includes, he claims, the land of Transylvania, damn his eyes! He would like to have me gift some of my dogs to a damn German duke, who isn't even a subject of his!" Prince George pulled his beard several times as he often did while thinking hard.

"Fine. I daren't refuse the request, since it is reasonable, and might put the emperor ever so slightly in my debt. But here's what we are going to do. Istvan, I'm putting you in charge of this," he said to his secretary. "Get the huntmaster to pick the Vizslas to send, and have him pick the scrawniest, most pitiful two dogs in our entire kennel. Send those to this Duke Albrecht of Saxe-Weimar. We will see what he does with them."

"Yes, Lord," Istvan bowed and started to leave the room.

"Wait."

"Yes, Lord."

"At least Albrecht is a Protestant. That's one saving grace. But by the time Ferdinand finds out, if he

ever does, that the dogs were wrecks, we will have
been able to say we complied with the request of
our brother monarch. There's one in the eye for him!
Write the letter for me to sign, Istvan!"

"Yes, Lord."

Istvan left and went out to the stables. He found
the huntmaster at work training a dog.

"The prince wants two of your poorest specimens
of Vizsla dogs to go to some princeling or other in
the Germanies. Pick the two worst and let me know
when you are ready to ship them and I will arrange
it," Istvan said.

"Hmmm. I have just the ones. They are from a
litter of only two, and they are very strange looking.
They have the eyes of the Devil—they are blue and
very light, not the warm brown of our good dogs. We
can send them tomorrow."

Istvan said, "I will have shipping papers drawn
up. Build them traveling crates and put some food
together for them. It will be a long trip to Weimar."

Weimar, April 1635

Hilde's little gray puppy wasn't either little or a puppy
any longer. She was curled around the legs of the
cradle that Adolf and Trude's brand new son, Gerhard,
was in. Trude said that the gray bitch had appointed
herself assistant mother to their son.

Adolf came in the door, stamping the snow off his
shoes as he entered. Gretchen raised her head and
thumped her tail two or three times on the floor in
welcome. Adolf had named her after the famous *richterin*, the head of the Committees of Correspondence.

Adolf and Trude both belonged to the Weimar branch. Duke Albrecht didn't seem to mind, especially since his brother Ernst and *die richterin* were, if not friends, then respectful acquaintances.

Trude turned from the cutting board to her husband's hug and kiss. "You'll never guess what happened today," Adolf said.

"No, I probably won't," Trude said, irritated. "And I won't know until I hear it, silly man. So what?"

"We got a shipment of two Vizsla dogs from Hungary, actually Transylvania, today. They are a miserable pair, though. They are a little short, and they both are scrawny and undergrown. One has an undescended testicle, so he's probably useless. But they both have the light eyes I've been looking for."

"So what is next?"

"I think that Gretchen is about to have a boyfriend," Adolf said. "She should come into her heat next month, and I will breed her to the Vizsla that has two balls. His name is Béla."

"Will that give you the dog you are trying for?"

"Maybe, but probably not. The heads are still not quite right, and those light eyes—" Adolf moved closer to his wife.

"You will not get what *you* are trying for," Trude said, laughing and fending him off, "until after dinner and *der Bube* sleeps. So save your ardor!"

Weimar, late August 1635

Gretchen panted. Adolf stroked her head. "You are doing fine, little girl. Any minute now, and they will come out. I think I feel four or five little ones in there, girl. So let's get busy and get them out here where we can see them."

Gretchen pushed and the first puppy emerged. She licked it clean, and ate the afterbirth, as the second pup made its appearance. Soon all five puppies were nursing, their little eyes screwed shut.

"Trude, look!" Adolf shouted, as he saw Trude and Gerhard coming into the kennel yard. Gerhard was just toddling, and Trude hoisted him into her arm while she held a basket in the other. "Five of them! Five! Three boys and two girls. And they are all gray!"

"They are beautiful," Trude said. "Look at their coats, how shiny and smooth!" she went on, as she let Gerhard down. He toddled purposefully over to Gretchen, and patted her on the head.

"Good job, Gretchen," the toddler said. "Lunch now, Mama?"

Adolf picked him up and swung him onto his shoulders. "Lunch now," he said, as he and Trude made for a trestle table and benches in the kennel yard. Trude unpacked the basket.

"So," Trude said as she poured the small beer into two stoneware mugs, "how close will these dogs be to the magical 'Weimaraner'?"

"Pretty close, I think. It depends on what the eyes look like when they open them. The pups have finer heads than I was expecting, and they should have the large chest but lean flanks that Béla has, and be a little shorter than Gretchen," Adolf said, between bites of the meat on a slab of bread concoction that people were beginning to call 'sandwich' in Amideutsch. "If the eyes are light, like his, we will have our first generation we can call Weimaraners."

December 1636

Duke Albrecht swung down from his horse in the kennel yard. "Gerhard said you have something to show me?" he said to Adolf.

"Yes, Highness, I do. If Your Highness will please wait right here," Adolf said, and bowing, turned and began to go into the kennel building. A sound from the duke stopped him.

"Highness?" Adolf said.

"It is cold and it is starting to snow," the duke said. "Couldn't this wait for a nicer day?"

"I will be but a minute, Highness," Adolf said, ducking into the kennel.

He came back leading five gray dogs, with light yellow eyes.

"Highness," Adolf said, "your Weimaraner dogs." He took each dog in turn and walked them around the kennel yard, showing the duke what they looked like.

Duke Albrecht stood there, his eyes wide, the cold and the snow completely forgotten.

"And they seem to have the personality that the up-timer duke bred for, too?" the duke asked.

"*Jawohl, Hoheit*," Adolf said. "They are people-dogs, but they are hunters too. No cat is safe in this yard." His gesture took in the snow-covered kennel yard and the road as well.

Bystanders had gathered now, to see the duke's reaction to Adolf's work.

Duke Albrecht said, "I like them. How old are they? What have you named them?"

Adolf said, "They are eight months, *Hoheit*. I named

them from the calendar, Highness. This one is Ahh, this one is Bay, this one is Cee and those are Day and Ey."

The crowd laughed, as did the duke. "I think I shall take Ahh with me for a while, then. Come, boy."

He mounted his horse and turned it around in the kennel yard. Adolf took off "A's" leash and "A" seemed to understand as he moved to stand just behind the duke's left stirrup. The others sat when Adolf told them to, watching.

"Let's go, boy!" The duke prodded his horse into motion, and he and the Weimaraner headed down the snowy hill to the house.

He stopped just as he was about to pass through the kennel gate. "Adolf," he called.

"Yes, Highness," Adolf said, noncommittally.

"Gerhard is retiring in six months, and he has asked that I make you his successor as *Jagdmeister*. Is that acceptable to you?"

"Oh, yes!" the new Huntmaster of Weimar replied. To himself, he said, "It's *not* just a dog."

St. George Does It Again

Kerryn Offord

June 1635, Grantville

Svetlana Anderovna was caught up in a most delight-
ful dream. Yesterday she'd married the man she loved
and they'd spent the night making love. She snuggled
up to her lover.

Suddenly she was totally awake. Yes there was a
naked body in bed with her, but it wasn't, couldn't
be, Jabe McDougal. Terrified of what she'd see she
slipped gently away from the warm naked male body
she'd been all but wrapped around. From six feet
away, with one hand on her dressing table and the
other grasping her hair brush as a weapon, she was
able to identify the man—John Felix Trelli.

The same John Trelli who'd been her escort to
Jabe's wedding. The same John Trelli she'd been trailing along behind for months while he helped sell war
bonds. The same John Trelli who'd never even tried
to flirt with her. She dressed quickly and retreated to
the door, her eyes never moving from the pulse she

could see beating at his throat at less than a third of her own heartbeat. He had to still be sleeping. Nobody could fake that low heart rate. In the near silence of the room she could hear the gentle rumble of a cat purring. But that was impossible. There was no cat in the room, just the slumbering form of John Trelli, known to some as Puss.

Svetlana carefully closed the door and walked off. Hopefully John would take the hint and remove himself before she returned. She shook herself. How could she have been so foolish as to make love to John, a virtual stranger? She'd been distraught, but surely not that distraught? Unfortunate memories of the previous evening flashed past her eyes. Someone she didn't know had thrown herself at John, and he had taken advantage of her distraught state. Svetlana nodded. Yes, it was all John Trelli's fault.

July 1635, Grantville

Sveta swung her head to see how the new hairstyle moved. Not sure what she thought about what she was seeing in the mirror, she turned to the three girls who'd dragged her to the beauty salon. "What do you think?"

"Katy's done a great job," Janie Abodeely said, referring to the beautician who'd been working on Sveta's face and hair for most of the morning. "You look absolutely scrumptious." Julia O'Reilly and Diana Cheng nodded their agreement.

Sveta badly wanted to believe her friends, but the way she'd been brought up, without a woman's influence, meant she'd never learned how to be a woman.

In the mirror, she compared her appearance against her friends. She decided that she looked quite passable. She wasn't as beautiful as Julia, who was an acknowledged beauty, but she was at least as good-looking as Janie and Diana. She sighed. She'd love to be exotic looking like Diana, or at least have hair that same beautiful raven-black color, instead of the sort-of-pale-honey color she was cursed with.

She leaned closer to the mirror, to better inspect Katy's handiwork. The eyebrow plucking had been painful, but nowhere near as painful as having her body waxed had been. However, she couldn't complain about the results. She reached out for Katy and hugged the tiny—at least compared to her—beautician. "Thank you, Katy."

"It was fun," Katy said.

"Like exploring uncharted territory," Diana suggested.

Katy giggled. "Now remember, Sveta, you need to take proper care of your skin and hair."

Sveta sighed. This new look was going to be expensive to maintain. Maybe she could . . .

"Don't even think about it," Julia said. "Just pay the nice lady so we can find you some clothes to match your new look."

The "nice lady" was Frau Trelli, the owner of Carole's Beauty Salon. It had been Frau Trelli, John Trelli's aunt, who'd first introduced Sveta to his cousins Julia and Janie. Sveta couldn't understand why Frau Trelli was being so nice to her. If there was anybody who knew that the supposed relationship between her and her nephew was nothing more than a face-saving exercise, it was Frau Trelli. She had barely had anything to do with John since Jabe McDougal's wedding to Prudentia Gentileschi. For a moment—a very brief moment—Sveta felt guilty about that. John had been the perfect camouflage for her distress when the man she loved married *That Female*. But it was only a brief moment. Then the memory of how he'd taken advantage of her when, distraught that Jabe was forever denied her, she threw herself at him surfaced, and she was able to firmly suppress the guilt.

"I bet she's thinking about Puss," Julia said.

Sveta looked at her friend. Why was Julia thinking that she'd waste a moment thinking about John Trelli? She knew there was nothing going on between them.

"Okay, okay, George then," Julia said, holding her hands up defensively.

The reminder that she'd jokingly said her pet name for John would be "George" lifted her spirits. She wondered how he was enjoying *that* nickname.

Magdeburg

"You got yourself your own pet, George?"

Puss looked away from his horse, who was thoroughly enjoying his dust bath, to the source of the comment. The speaker was another sergeant in his platoon, and the smirk on his face told Puss that the story had made its way to Magdeburg. Not that he was surprised. It had been too good to expect his family to keep it to themselves.

His Aunt Carole had delegated him to act as the absolutely gorgeous, as opposed to merely sensationally beautiful, Corporal Svetlana Anderovna's escort to a wedding, and she'd objected to using his nickname. Instead, she'd insisted that her pet name for him would be George. That wouldn't have been a problem. He'd been called worse things. However, her comment—some might even call it a joke, but in his experience, Corporal Anderovna didn't do jokes—neatly paraphrased the Abominable Snowman character from the Bugs Bunny video she'd just been watching with Aunt Carole's daughters. Anybody familiar with the video, and his cousins had made sure plenty of people were made familiar with it, could easily make the connection between Corporal Anderovna's throwaway comment and the Abominable Snowman's speech. That had been the source of a lot of male envy. Most guys would be happy to have Corporal Anderovna pet and hug them.

What most of them probably wouldn't know was the source material for that cartoon was John Steinbeck's *Of Mice and Men,* and any pet falling into the character Lennie's hands tended to be petted and hugged to death. He hadn't bothered to bring that up, because he knew the response would have been "but what a way to go."

For a brief moment the memory of the wedding night surfaced. That had been great. Waking up alone in Svetlana's bed the next morning hadn't been. Not that he'd been surprised that she'd left. She'd probably been too embarrassed to talk to him. She'd certainly done her best to avoid being alone with him for the rest of his leave. Ah, well, he'd never really believed such a gorgeous girl could really be interested in him.

August 1635, Grantville

Sveta lay on her bed in her tiny room in the woman's quarters and waited for the nausea to fade. When it did, she carefully slid off her bed. She was supposed to be meeting her friends after work, but the way she felt, she'd rather not. Unfortunately, if she didn't turn up they'd come looking for her. Even a locked door wouldn't stop them—Diana had demonstrated how insecure her room was just last week by picking the lock in less than a minute.

When she joined her friends, Julia swept Sveta into her arms and hugged her. "You look like death warmed up," Julia said.

"Julia," Janie protested.

Sveta savored the comfort of the hug, something else that had been lacking in her life until . . . okay, she admitted it to herself, until she met John Trelli and his family. She gently pushed Julia away so she could greet Janie and Diana. "I almost didn't come, I felt so sick after work."

"You really don't look too good," Janie said.

Julia pouted. "That's what I said."

"Have you vomited at all?" Diana asked.

Diana was on the medical program, training to eventually become a doctor, so Sveta forgave her the technical language. "No, I haven't puked. I just don't feel well. It's probably something I ate."

"I guess that means no night on the town, so how about coffee and a roll at Cora's?" Julia asked.

Sveta was all for that. "I'm sorry I'm such a party poofter."

"Pooper," Janie corrected. "It's party pooper, and you aren't. You can't help it if you don't feel well."

Sveta let Julia drag her back for another hug before they joined Janie and Diana on the short walk to Cora's.

She managed one step into Cora's before the smell hit her. Diana guided her into an alleyway where she puked up her guts.

"Is she all right?" a breathless Julia asked.

"It depends on what you mean by all right," Janie said. "What was it, Sveta, the smell of the coffee?"

"Coffee with milk," Sveta said. Even the memory of the smell had her trying to puke again.

"What's the matter with Sveta," Julia demanded.

"This is purely a guess mind you," Diana said, "but, I suspect Sveta is suffering NVP."

"What the heck's NVP?" Julia asked.

"Nausea and vomiting with pregnancy," Diana explained. "It's not something you're likely to meet in your veterinarian training."

"Morning sickness? You're saying Sveta's pregnant?" Julia asked.

"In the balance of probabilities, it is a definite possibility." Diana put an arm around Sveta and hugged her. "Could you be pregnant?"

Sveta swallowed. Yes, it was possible. She nodded.

"Do you know who the father is?" Julia asked.

Sveta's head shot up. "How dare you . . ."

"I'll take that as a yes, then. Next question, is it Jabe?"

Sveta glared at Julia. She, like the other two girls, knew Jabe was the man she loved. But Julia's face only showed sympathy. She ducked her head. "No."

"If Jabe's not the father, then who is?" Julia asked.

Sveta kept her head bowed. She didn't want to admit anything about that night.

"Come on, it has to be someone," Janie muttered. "Oh, hell . . ."

Sveta met Janie's eyes. Why was she looking at her like that?

"Puss?" Janie choked out.

"Puss? You think Sveta did it with Puss?" Julia demanded.

"You did it with Puss? Why?" Janie asked Sveta. "You told us you barely know him."

"After the wedding. I was upset, and John escorted me home."

"And you made love with Puss?" Julia demanded. "Even though you were in love with another man? How could you do that to him?"

Sveta didn't like the accusing looks being sent her way. "He was the one who took advantage of me. I didn't know what I was doing." She all but shouted the last sentence.

"Are you feeling better now?" Diana asked.

The voice of reason penetrated, and Sveta relaxed. She did feel better. "Yes."

"Then I suggest we move this little discussion to somewhere other than right outside Cora's."

That was an exaggeration, they were actually in the alleyway beside the café that was the gossip capital of Grantville, but Diana's point was well made. Sveta knew there was going to be enough talk about how she bolted after putting one foot across the threshold. "Where?"

"Lacking the other interested party, I think we should drop in on Auntie Sue," Janie said.

"John's mother?" Sveta shuddered. Frau Trelli knew her story. She knew that being escorted to Jabe's wedding by John had been a face-saving exercise. What was she going to think of her?

Janie nodded. "His mom and dad are going to have to be told at some stage, unless you intend getting a termination..."

It took a few seconds for Sveta to mentally translate the meaning of the English word. She looked at Janie aghast. "I'm not a baby killer."

"Then we go to Auntie Sue's."

Sveta slumped, defeated. "Very well."

"Hey, it's not as if you're going to your funeral. It's just bad luck that you got pregnant. You must be a real Fertile Myrtle to conceive first time," Julia said.

"Julia!" both Diana and Janie cried.

"Well, it is unlucky," Julia protested.

Sveta made eye contact with Janie for a moment, then dropped her head. It was as if the other girl was reading her innermost secrets.

"On the other hand, if they did it more than once, without contraception, they were playing with fire," Janie said.

Sveta ran her tongue over suddenly dry lips. She couldn't bring herself to say the words, so she gave a single nod.

"Was he any good?" Julia asked.

The eager curiosity in Julia's voice shocked Sveta. How could she ask such a question at a time like this?

"Julia O'Reilly, how could you ask such a question?" Janie demanded.

"You want to know if he learned anything from Donetta, just as much as I do."

"Still, you shouldn't ask Sveta a question like that!"

"All right then, how would you ask her?"

Sveta stared at the squabbling girls. Who was Donetta, and what was her relationship to John?

On the Saxon Plain, somewhere near Zwenkau

Puss was feeling particularly unloved. His patrol had been assigned to directing incoming troops to their forming-up areas for the battle everyone knew would happen tomorrow. It had been a long and dusty day as thousands of men and horses kicked up the dust as they walked past his checkpoint.

He stepped away to let a wagon proceed and fumbled for his water bottle. He shook it gently as he pulled it from his belt webbing—about a third full.

The first mouthful was used to rinse away the dust. Then he drained the bottle. He wiped the moisture from his lips with the sleeve of his combat jacket while he fumbled the canteen back into its pouch. "What a lousy day."

"Just think of what tomorrow'll be like, Sarge," Corporal Lenhard Poppler said.

Puss scanned the landscape. If it wasn't for the crushed grain, trampled down by thousands of men and horses, it would be a beautiful scene. By this time tomorrow it would be completely different.

Grantville

"Surely I should wait until I'm sure?" Sveta protested as Julia hammered on the door of John's parents' home.

"You've showing the same symptoms Alice and Judy did when they were at about the same stages of their pregnancies," Janie said, naming her sister and sister-in-law.

"Besides, Diana says you're pregnant," Julia said.

Sveta was about to question the logic behind that statement when the door opened.

"Hello, girls. What brings you round this way?" Suzanne Trelli asked.

A strong hand grabbed Sveta's wrist and dragged her up the steps. "Sveta's got something to tell you, Auntie Sue," Julia said.

"Then you'd better all come in. I'll just put the kettle on."

"No coffee," Julia called out to Suzanne's back.

"No coffee it is," Suzanne called over her shoulder before hurrying off.

"Why did you have to say that?" Sveta demanded of Julia.

"Do you want a repeat of what happened at Cora's?" Julia asked. "You know, throwing up at the smell of coffee."

She shuddered at that memory. "No, but what is Frau Trelli going to think?" Sveta asked, wringing her hands.

"Under the circumstances, Sveta, I think Auntie Sue might just think that you're pregnant," Janie said.

"You really should thank Julia for preparing the ground for you," Diana added.

She was hustled into the house and along to the kitchen where she was seated between Julia and Janie.

Suzanne placed a plate of dry crackers in front of Sveta. "Try some of these, you might find that they help."

Sveta stared blankly at Frau Trelli. How were dry crackers supposed to help her? She glanced around at her friends. As she made eye contact with them, each in turn smiled and nodded. Unfortunately, Sveta had no idea what message they were trying to communicate to her.

"I'll make it easy for you. You, or at least our budding doctors, think you're pregnant."

Sveta swallowed. Guilt had her starting to blush. She dropped her head in shame.

Suzanne lifted Sveta's head so their eyes met. "And the reason you want to tell me you're pregnant is because John is the father, yes?"

She didn't actually want to tell Frau Trelli that, it was more a matter of having to.

"Oh, you poor thing." Suzanne reached down and pulled Sveta into her arms. "And John so far away when you need him."

It was too much. Sveta burst into tears in Frau Trelli's arms. Later, when she emerged from her crying jag, she discovered she'd been abandoned by her friends.

"I sent them home. It's not as if you need their moral support anymore."

Sveta dipped her head back into Frau Trelli's shoulder. This time she felt the damp and backed away. "Oh, I've made you all wet."

"I won't rust," Suzanne said, pulling Sveta back into her arms. "Let's make ourselves a nice cup of catnip tea and find somewhere comfortable to sit and chat."

That sounded good to Sveta. *A chat* sounded a lot friendlier than *a talk*. She helped Frau Trelli load a tray with a teapot, some cups, saucers and spoons, and the plate of dry crackers, and then followed her into the living room.

Somewhere near Zwenkau

Puss snuggled inside his sleeping bag, inside his bivy bag, under the star filled sky. Beside him, Corporal Michael Cleesattel was snoring quietly under a couple of military issue blankets.

Puss was having trouble getting to sleep. Everybody believed there was going to be a great battle tomorrow, and you could write a book about all the battles he'd managed to miss for one reason or another.

He hadn't graduated until 1632, so he missed everything before that. When he tried to enlist to fight he'd been given some rubbish about the needs of the service, and sent to train as a military policeman. Okay, so at nearly six foot, he was significantly taller than most down-timers, and he had earned a junior black belt from the martial arts school in Fairmont where Sensei Karickhoff—the then head instructor of the army's unarmed combat school—had taught, and he could ride a horse, and he was a pretty good shot with a hand gun and rifle, but they weren't good reasons for assigning him to the military police.

To make matters worse, he'd graduated from training and immediately been posted to Erfurt, just in time to miss the Croat raid on Grantville. All around him people were getting combat experience and being promoted because of it. Heck, he'd even managed to miss the big battle at Ahrensbök because he'd been posted to the backwater that was the Wietze oil facility, and then he'd been away escorting an oil shipment to Magdeburg when the French raided the place.

With his luck, he was likely to miss tomorrow's battle as well, although he didn't know how Murphy was going to arrange that, not with them being so close to the front line.

Grantville

Sveta snuggled under the covers of her bed in the women's quarters and let her hands drift down to her belly. Was it really possible that a new life was growing there? That she was really pregnant? If she was, there would finally be someone of her own to love and be loved by. She'd never again be alone and unloved.

The crack of dawn the next day, somewhere near Zwenkau

Puss walked out of the briefing tent ready to swear and curse. He held on to his disappointment until he joined his patrol. "We're assigned to road watch around the field hospital."

Corporal Lenhard Poppler looked westward, toward the area where the field hospital was still being set up. "That's what, two miles behind the lines."

"About that," Puss confirmed.

"Great move, Sarge. How'd you manage to score us that assignment?"

"Just lucky, I guess."

"I like your luck, Sarge," Michael said. "Long may it last."

With the rest of his patrol nodding their heads in agreement, Puss chose not to voice his opinion of his luck. Murphy had struck again.

Grantville

Sveta was dragged out of a deep sleep by someone knocking on her door. It was way too early to be her wake-up call. Then she realized it wasn't the manager's voice asking if she was awake, it was John's mother. "Coming," she called as she slid out of bed and grabbed a bathrobe. She was still fumbling with the waist tie when she opened the door.

"Oh, good, you're awake," Suzanne said as she pushed past Sveta into her room.

Suzanne's husband leaned against the door frame and smiled sympathetically at Sveta.

"You can't stay here," Suzanne announced. "Felix, why are you standing at the door? Put the cases on the bed."

"Suzanne's decided that you should move into John's old room," he explained to a confused Sveta.

Suzanne looked around Sveta's room before turning to her husband. "If you'll wait outside, I'll pack Sveta's things while she dresses."

The door closed behind Felix and before she knew it, Frau Trelli had splashed some water into the washing bowl and was pushing Sveta towards it.

"Now you just follow your usual routine, and we'll have everything packed in no time."

"But you don't want me to move into John's old room," Sveta protested.

Suzanne rested her hands on her hips. "You really think I'd make the effort to drag Felix here at this hour of the morning if I didn't want you to live with us?"

Herr Trelli had seemed very relaxed about being

dragged about at this time of the morning. From her limited knowledge of family life, the mothers of illegitimate progeny of the household's male members weren't exactly welcome in the family home. Frau Trelli, however, took her silence as agreement.

"Right, so what's your problem?"

Sveta tried to blink away the tears that were starting to form in her eyes. "John and I aren't together."

"You're having John's baby. You can't get any more together than that." Suzanne reached out and dragged Sveta into an embrace. "There, there, it's not so bad. John'll do the right thing by you."

The "right thing" was marriage. Sveta knew that. But she didn't want to marry a man she didn't love. She wanted to marry Jabe. But that wasn't going to happen. She wanted to try and explain how she felt, but Frau Trelli's kind eyes stopped her.

Suzanne pulled Sveta close, and she buried her face in Suzanne's shoulder. A hand held the back of her head while another patted her gently on the back. "Come on, we have to finish your packing before Felix gets tired of waiting, and you still need to get dressed."

Later that day, somewhere near Zwenkau

Puss took off his wide-brimmed hat and wiped the sweat from his brow with his sleeve before replacing it. Then he took off his dark glasses and admired the dust that had collected on them since he last cleaned them. He'd long since stopped cursing his luck, and moved on to thanking whatever entity was responsible for keeping him away from the battlefield. The sight of wagon after wagon of wounded men rumbling past had cured him of ever wanting to be caught up in a battle.

A medevac wagon was approaching from the hospital. Puss put his glasses back on and stepped out onto the road to stop the traffic so it could join the flow of vehicles heading for the front. As it rumbled away, Corporal Thomas Klein handed him a mug.

"Fresh brew, Sarge, you drink that while I take a turn."

Puss was happy to step off the road and savor his mug of coffee without too much dust getting mixed with it. His eyes followed the long column of vehicles threading into the distance. It was a pity he wasn't an artist, because that long column of vehicles approaching the field hospital under a red sky would make a brilliant memorial to the battle.

Grantville

Sveta sat cross-legged on the bed in the bedroom of her child's father, hugging the large, well-loved teddy bear that had been sitting on the bed. Frau Trelli had taken her to see Dr. Shipley for a pregnancy test. The test would take a few days to give a result, but the doctor had indicated that everything pointed to her being pregnant, and that, if Sveta was sure about the date of conception, could expect to deliver in March of next year.

She snorted. As if she was going to forget the day the man she loved married another. Still, she had a letter she had to write. She slid off the bed and carried the teddy bear to the desk where John must have sat to do his homework in times past. Together they wrote a letter to John.

A few days later, outside Leipzig

Puss was lying comfortably on the ground, his back supported by his saddle, and the brim of his hat pulled over his eyes. His personal kit was laid out beside him, ready to be loaded at a moment's notice onto Thunder, who was lazily picking at the pile of hay cut from one of the trampled fields.

"Mail for Behrns, Cleesattel, Klein, and Trelli."

Puss tipped back his hat and searched for the source of the call. Seeing the company clerk, he did up his webbing and picked up his rifle before walking over to the mail cart.

There was the usual CARE package from his family, and a single letter. He accepted them and returned to his kit, where the vultures were already circling.

Puss attempted to ignore them. Instead of opening the CARE package, which was what Corporals Klein, Poppler, Cleesattel, and Behrns were interested in, he studied the letter. Normally the family included their letters in the packages, so who was writing to him? A quick glance on the back only added to his confusion. The return address was his parents' house in Grantville. Well, there was one sure way to learn who the letter was from. He used the blade of his clasp knife to break the seal.

He didn't read far before he froze in abject terror. He blinked a few times before rereading the first sentence.

"Something wrong, Sarge?" Michael asked.

Puss folded the letter so Thomas couldn't read it over his shoulder. "Sveta"—it felt funny using Corporal Anderovna's nickname—"is pregnant."

"Oh, like, wow. How'd you manage that?" Lenhard asked.

There was a yip of pain from Lenhard as Michael clipped him across the ear. "The usual way, dummy."

"But he's not even betrothed to the girl," Lenhard said. "Are you?" he asked Puss.

"No." From the cultural awareness module of his military police training, Puss knew that a certain amount of latitude was permitted to betrothed couples. However, good girls did not let things go too far until they were betrothed.

He read the rest of the letter. Sveta certainly hadn't wasted any words. She'd said what she had to say, and then asked him what he intended doing. There was nothing about how worried she was about the situation, but she had to be. Babies were expensive, and a single mother had a lot of obstacles in her way. Well, he knew what he had to do, and he didn't need the fact that she had moved in with his parents to tell him what it was. "Looks like I better ask for leave so I can get home and marry Sveta as soon as possible."

"Don't like your chances," Hermann Behrns said. He glanced around. "Anybody here like the Sarge's chances?"

Three shaking heads told Puss that none of them liked his chances of getting leave. He folded the letter and tucked it away. If he couldn't go to her, maybe there was an alternative. "Then I better have a few words with the chaplain."

"He won't be able to get you leave, Sarge," Hermann called to his back.

Grantville

Felix gave Sveta a sympathetic shake of the head as he laid the mail on the table in front of his wife.

Suzanne quickly sorted out the mail, sliding letters across the table to the down-time sisters who were more daughter substitutes than boarders, and her husband. There was nothing for Sveta.

She hadn't expected anything either. Who would write to her here? Certainly not John. Not yet, anyway. She knew from her job with the Joint Armed Services Press Division that it could take a week just for her letter to get to him.

"You're looking happy, Elisabeth," Frau—call me Sue—Trelli said to the eldest of the boarders.

Elisabeth Müller held up her letter. "My book has done better than expected, and Frau Fröbel says they are planning a second printing."

Suzanne clapped her hands. "Congratulations." She hurried around the table to give Elisabeth a hug.

Sveta felt a stab of jealousy watching the easy affection between Frau Trelli and the older girl. She wished she could reach out to Frau Trelli like Elisabeth, but she felt too embarrassed, guilty, and a bit of a fraud. It wasn't as if she was in love with John. She was just pregnant with his child.

Then Suzanne opened the letter from John and read aloud what he had got up to since he last wrote.

Even Sveta managed to smile at some of the things he and his men got up to, although, if one was to believe John, it was mostly his men getting into trouble and him getting them out of it. The letter opened a window on the world of Sergeant John Trelli, soldier, and introduced her to someone completely different from the man she'd shepherded around war bond rallies.

Sveta received a reply to her letter three days later. She retired to her room where she cuddled the teddy bear while she prepared herself for the recriminations she was sure were to be heaped upon her.

Tears began to trail down her cheeks as she read the letter. John was being so understanding. He was even willing to marry her, if that was what she wanted. After talking to Janie and Julia, she'd been almost hoping that he would insist on them marrying. At least that would indicate some interest in her as something other than his child's mother, but there was nothing to suggest that he might love, or even care for her. She buried her face in the worn fur of the teddy bear and cried.

Eventually the tears stopped, and she was able to return to John's letter. There were promises of financial support, and that he wouldn't pressure her to make a decision. There was also a separate piece of paper a lot smaller than the main letter. Sveta cracked a smile after reading it. It certainly deserved its "destroy after reading" heading. John's mother—and he freely admitted it—would surely be tempted to kill him if she ever saw what he'd written about her. She hid that page in her Bible and prepared to share the rest of John's letter with his parents.

"It's only what I expected of John," John's mother said as she passed the letter onto her husband.

John's father took the letter and read it. "I'm sure he does want to marry you, Sveta."

"It's good of you to say that, Herr Trelli. But we

all know that the only reason we're talking about marriage is because I'm pregnant."

"We'd be happy for you to marry John even if you weren't pregnant," Suzanne said.

A week later a package in heavy bond paper was delivered to the Trelli residence. Sveta waited for Máma, as she now called John's mother, to open it, but instead she slid it across the table to her. She accepted the letter knife from Máma and broke open the heavy wax seal.

There was a covering letter from a lawyer in Leipzig, a copy of John's will, and two copies of a marriage contract. She passed them all over to John's father, whom she'd started calling Pápa.

"John has made arrangements for the pair of you to marry by proxy," Felix said.

"Is that legal?" Suzanne asked.

John's father nodded. "According to John's lawyer, all we need is for Sveta to sign the contracts before witnesses, and exchange vows with John's stand-in."

Sveta bit her lip. "I will need my father's permission."

"Where does he live?" Felix asked.

"He lives in Savonia, near the fortress of Olavinlinna, in Finland."

"That doesn't exactly sound like we'd be able to send him a letter and get a reply in a few days' time."

"No." Sveta knew exactly how long it could take to get news in and out of Savonia, except in winter, when the lakes and rivers froze, making travel so much easier. She'd made the trip herself on her way to Grantville. "At this time of year, it could take four weeks just to get to the fortress from Borgå."

"And Borgå is where?" Felix asked.

"It's a port on the Gulf of Finland, about thirty miles east of Helsinki, the modern capital of Finland." Before Pápa could ask the usual question, Sveta continued. "Helsinki's a lot smaller than Borgå. King Gustav I created the town nearly a hundred years ago in an attempt to challenge the Hanseatic city of Reval, and it hasn't done very well."

Suzanne ran a hand through her hair. "You could send him a letter, but, if it's going to take over three months to hear back..."

Sveta saw where Máma was looking. Her hands fell protectively over her belly. John's mother's meaning was obvious. She'd certainly be showing in three months' time.

"Is your father likely to raise any objections to you marrying John?" Felix asked.

Sveta shook her head. John's family was Catholic, but her father wasn't sufficiently interested in her to care about that.

"Right then. Sveta, you write your father asking his permission, and thanking him nicely for giving it. We'll post that off and set about posting the banns."

"And I'll start planning the wedding," Suzanne said.

Later that evening Sveta entered the kitchen with the letter for her father. It'd been a surprisingly easy letter to write, but while she'd chewed over how to explain becoming pregnant to a man she wasn't even betrothed to, she'd been reminded of something Julia had said.

She walked over to the table where Máma had spread out the contents of a large cardboard box, and sat opposite her. "Máma."

Suzanne looked up. "Yes, dear?"

"Who is Donetta?" Sveta didn't like the look that flashed across Máma's face. It looked too much like she'd bitten into something sour.

"Where did you hear that name, dear?"

Sveta recognized evasion when she heard it. Did that mean Donetta had been someone important in John's life? "Julia was asking me what it was like making love with John, and Janie was telling her to stop embarrassing me, but Julia said Janie wanted to know if he'd learned anything from Donetta just as much as she did."

Suzanne stared at Sveta, her eyes opened wide for a moment before she blinked and shaking her head. "No, they couldn't have, neither of them would have been more than thirteen or fourteen." She smiled ruefully at Sveta. "Sorry, ignore what I just said. Madam Donetta Leasure née Frost had an affair with John right under her fiancé's nose a few months before they were due to marry. Things got a bit messy when her fiancé realized what was going on, and we had to ship John out of town until after the wedding for his own safety."

Sveta couldn't imagine a man marrying a woman who had a relationship with another man while they were betrothed, not unless there was a good reason. "Was her family very rich?"

"Donetta's parents? They run the tack shop in town."

So, if her family wasn't rich, that only left one reason why the man had married her. "Was she very beautiful?"

"She certainly thought so," Suzanne snorted. "You don't need to feel jealous of Madam, dear. She and her fool of a husband were left up-time."

Sveta wanted to protest that she wasn't jealous, she was just curious. She was left wondering what John had felt for Donetta. "Thank you for telling me. What is it you're doing?"

Back in her room Sveta pulled out her Bible and searched for the "destroy after reading" letter. When she'd first read it, she'd thought John was just making jokes at his mother's expense, but now she realized that John just knew his mother.

She glanced down at the list again. After two hours spent flicking through the wedding file Máma had been putting together ever since the birth of her first daughter, Sveta now understood his warning that his mother would insist on a "white wedding with all the trimmings."

September, somewhere en route to Poland

Puss sat in his tent looking at the photographs of the wedding. Sveta looked beautiful. The white princess-style off-the-shoulder dress suited her and he was glad that she'd let his mother have the wedding she'd dreamed of giving his sisters. Losing both of them left up-time had hit his mother hard, which was one reason he'd been sure she'd willingly accept Sveta. That Sveta was carrying her first grandchild had just been the icing on the cake.

And speaking of icing on cake, Mom had sent him a piece of the wedding cake. He savored it as he bit into it. It was a proper fruitcake, and mom had remembered to cut him a piece with plenty of marzipan. While he let the almond flavored icing dissolve in his mouth he checked the rest of the photos. His old friend from school, James Warren, was there with his wife Kelli, and their new baby. He was glad James had accepted his request to be his stand-in; there was nobody he trusted more, and if James had so much as thought about giving Sveta more than a peck on the cheek, Kelli would have decked him.

The thought made him smile. He was getting very possessive about his Sveta. It'd just be nice if he could believe she felt the same about him. But he knew she had only married him for the sake of the baby.

Two weeks later, outside Świebodzin, Poland

Puss took advantage of the short break to sort through the latest package from home. There was the usual resupply of the essentials—cake, coffee, cookies, sugar, hard candy, and toilet paper—as well as some writing paper, pens and ink. But more importantly, there were letters from home. Puss distributed everything else amongst his belt webbing and saddlebags, but kept the letters separate. He selected Sveta's and pushed the rest into a jacket pocket.

Breaking the seal he was soon back in Grantville watching the movie made from a screenplay he'd written while he was on the war bonds treadmill. According to Sveta, and she would know, as she'd had the task of typing up his hand-written drafts, they'd actually followed his final screenplay relatively closely. Even to the extent of actually filming the finale at the very castle he'd used as his model. He just wished he'd been there with Sveta to see it.

"Trelli, get your men together."

The sudden thump on his back brought Puss back to the present. "What's happening?" he asked as he hastily folded Sveta's letter and put it safely away.

"Some of the auxiliaries and men of the Gray Adder have run amok and are sacking the town." Sergeant Johannes Cöper, the platoon sergeant, didn't seem too concerned that the Finnish auxiliary cavalry attached to 3rd Division had run amok, but he was clearly upset that proper USE soldiers had joined them. "The general has ordered the division in to deal with them."

Puss glanced in the direction of Świebodzin. It wasn't as if there had been a long siege or anything that would normally justify sacking the place. He turned to ask Sergeant Cöper some more questions, but he'd already moved on, which meant he'd better get a move on himself. "Behrns, Cleesattel, Klein, Poppler, get your gear together and saddle up."

They entered Świebodzin behind the division's own cavalry. The MPs didn't do any fighting; the cavalry did all of it. They just got to pick up the pieces.

Puss badly wanted to throw up, but he had nothing left in his stomach. The dead adults had been bad enough, but the children had been much worse. Why would anybody want to bayonet a baby? He rewrapped the baby in its swaddling and placed it beside what he assumed was his mother, who'd been raped and murdered. He stepped back, and as he looked down upon the dead mother and son, he thought of Sveta and their baby, and he wanted to kill those responsible.

But that wasn't the worst. That came when he found a girl who couldn't have been more than eight. She was naked, battered and bruised, bleeding from both the vagina and anus, and white with shock. He'd carried her shivering body to the first aid station the medics had set up in the town square. She didn't make a sound the whole time. He wasn't even sure she knew what was happening to her.

Puss hadn't felt anything when he helped lead the twenty, mostly still drunk, rioters who'd been caught in the act to the fence line in a pasture just outside Świebodzin. There, he'd helped tie the prisoners to the wooden fence before retiring behind the firing line. From there he'd watched the executions by volley gun before advancing to supervise men of the Gray Adder regiment as they collected the shredded remains of their former colleagues and dumped them into the mass grave they'd dug earlier.

It was different when it came to the officers. For a start, they were to be executed by a regular firing squad made up of members of the volley-gun batteries.

Ex-Captains Hermann auf der Mauer and Traugott Nachtigall were lined up either side of their commanding officer, ex-Major Johannes Dietrich.

"How can you allow this travesty?" Johannes Dietrich demanded as Puss checked the bindings holding him against the wood support. "We did nothing wrong."

"The men went mad when a sniper murdered Colonel Küster," Hermann auf der Mauer said.

Puss ignored the comments, but Traugott Nachtigall took offence at his silence. "You rear-end mother-fucker, what do you know of war? I bet you've never even been in combat. What right do you have to judge us?"

For a moment he saw that eight-year-old girl again.

He looked at the ex-captain, and then to his own officer. "The prisoners are secure, sir."

"Very good, Sergeant. Retire your men behind the line."

Spittle from ex-captain Nachtigall struck Puss and mingled with the blood of an eight-year-old Pole. He looked up at Nachtigall, who seemed proud of his small victory. Puss gestured for his men to leave before following them.

Grantville

In the glory days of 1633 and 1634, the Grantville office of the Joint Armed Services Press Division had boasted over a dozen staff members, but those days were long gone. Now, the permanent staff consisted of Lieutenant Johann Dauth, the three radio operators who maintained a 24/7 radio watch, and three enlisted women who rotated the position of front desk receptionist while doing their real job of composing press releases and running them off on the duplicator machine for distribution to the local media.

There was some kind of bug going around, and the office was down to a skeleton staff, meaning, instead of getting out of the office over lunch, Sveta had to stay in the office. She'd just settled her mug of hot soup on her desk and sat down when Lieutenant Dauth burst out of the radio room waving a printout.

"Magdeburg's just passed on a story from Scoop claiming USE troops are sacking a surrendered town in Poland."

"Scoop" was the nickname of twenty-year-old Ambrosius Weineck. He had made every effort since joining the Fightin' Flacks (as some called the reporters of the military's press office) to portray himself as the next Ernest Hemingway. He'd earned the nickname for producing a rather long list of "scoops" that weren't.

Her lunch forgotten, Sveta reached for the paper Johann held. A quick skim—and it was a very quick skim—Scoop must have outdone himself in the brevity of the story he filed with headquarters in Magdeburg. "It's a little light on any details. Have headquarters heard from Dirk and Werner?" she asked, naming the two competent reporters the department had with the 3rd Division.

"Not a whisper."

Johann looked ready to pull his hair out, and Sveta couldn't blame him. Either Dirk and Werner hadn't filed anything because there wasn't anything to report, or they were in the thick of it, getting the real story. There was, however, another possible source of information. "What are the *Times* and *Daily News* getting?"

In theory, the press office shouldn't know what was in the stories the reporters working for the two main Grantville papers were sending over the radio; however, the office had the use of a computer, and the geek responsible for maintaining their computer system had cracked the newspapers' codes. With their computer and their own radios monitored 24/7, the press office was able to read the stories the reporters were filing well before the papers' editors did.

"They haven't sent anything yet," Johann said.

"So either Scoop's gone off half-cocked again, or they're busy chasing the story."

Johann nodded. "I'm sure the boss has already ordered Scoop to get some details."

"What do you want me to do with this?" She waved the printout.

Dauth sighed. "Try and work your usual magic on it so we've got something for a press release."

It was a tall order, but Sveta rolled a fresh stencil blank into her typewriter, and after reading the cable again, started typing.

Over the course of the day reports reached the office that confirmed Scoop's original story, and then some. Sveta was typing out yet another update press release when Johann walked quietly up to her desk. This was unusual, as throughout the day he'd announced each new development as he bounced out of the communications room.

She reached up for the papers he held, but Johann pulled them away. "Dirk's filed an interview with your husband. It's pretty graphic."

Having given her a warning, Johann obviously felt free to let her read the story. At first sight, it was a mass of red pencil where parts he didn't want her to include in the press release were marked. Naturally, she started to read those areas first. She bolted for the bathroom.

"Can you write it up, or do you want me to do it?" Johann asked from the bathroom door.

Sveta rinsed her mouth to get rid of the bile taste and splashed her face with water. "I can do it, but can I call John's family first to let them know he's okay?"

"Sure, make your calls, but keep them short. We may need to keep the phone free."

She asked the Fluharty Middle School secretary to pass on the message to Máma that she'd heard that

John was okay after the recent fighting in Świebodzin. She did much the same with the secretary at the SoTF State Technical College, where she left the same message for Pápa. Then she settled down to work the terse filed cables from Werner and Dirk into press releases.

The standard press releases were easy to write, but translating the interview with John into something for general consumption was difficult, as she kept visualizing what John must have seen.

October 1635, the south bank of the Odra river, near Zielona Góra

Puss was, as usual since Świebodzin, keeping a watchful eye on the remnants of the Gray Adder regiment. He had been thinking about what happened. Not so much the actual rape, loot, murder and burn that the men had engaged in, but more the message General Stearns' reaction would be sending to them.

"Lieutenant, I've been wondering if the general did the right thing at Świebodzin by punishing the officers."

"I wouldn't worry about them, Trelli. They had it coming," Lieutenant Heinrich Diefenthaler said.

"I wasn't thinking of the officers, sir. I was thinking of the men who weren't caught in the act. Shouldn't we be trying to bring them to justice?"

"To what purpose, Trelli? By his actions, General Stearns has ensured that such an event won't occur again."

"Why not?" To Puss the problem was obvious, but then, he'd read all of his sisters' college psychology textbooks and anything else he could find to try and understand Donetta Frost's motivations for the affair she had with him.

"I'm sure every officer in the 3rd Division is now planning on imposing stiff discipline so that their men don't run amok and get them strung up in front of a firing squad. But what about the common soldiers? All they've learned is that as long as they don't get caught, they can get away with murder. Heck, they could take advantage of the precedent, and use it to get rid of unpopular officers."

"Trelli, you have a nasty mind," Lieutenant Diefenthaler said. "A very nasty mind. It could become a downward spiral. The officers make themselves unpopular by imposing stricter discipline, so the troops retaliate by going crazy."

Puss nodded. That's exactly what he'd been thinking. "So, do we start searching out the instigators and bring them to justice?"

"I'll pass your concerns on to Captain von Frankenberg, Trelli."

"Thank you, sir." After Lieutenant Diefenthaler walked off, Puss returned to watching the men from the Gray Adder. The regiment was largely recruited from Mecklenburg, where the CoC columns had been involved in some pretty nasty fighting during Operation Kristallnacht. One could almost suggest that they had been predisposed to running amok and committing atrocities even before Świebodzin. There had certainly been enough of that from both sides in Mecklenburg. All they'd needed was a trigger—like the death of their commander at the hands of a sniper—to send them over the edge.

Grantville

Sveta's friends came bearing gifts. She met them at the door and shepherded them along to her room.

"How's the baby?" Janie asked.

Sveta patted her bump. "It's started to move." She was reminded of the first time she felt her baby move a couple of weeks ago. Until then she'd been on tenterhooks. Too many well-meaning (or maybe, just mean) people had talked about the risk of losing a baby before the second trimester. Apparently, once a baby started to move, you were less likely to miscarry. Although, having sent that reassuring signal, it would have been nice if it could stop kicking every time she managed to drop off to sleep.

"Is it moving now?" Julia asked.

Sveta reached out and pressed Julia's hand against her abdomen.

"Oh, it kicked. That's so cool. Diana, you have to feel Sveta's baby moving."

"How are you feeling, Sveta?" Diana asked, letting Julia guide her hand.

"Remarkably well, much to the disappointment of the doomsayers."

"Mom was like that," Janie said. "A bit of morning sickness early on, then nothing for months." She sent Sveta a wry grin. "But I don't think you'll be able to avoid backache as you near term."

"How did your mother cope with that?" Sveta asked.

"She had Dad to give her massages. Oh, I'm sorry, Sveta."

Sveta waved away Janie's concern. She had a husband, but would he even want to touch her? She sighed and picked at one of Diana's cookies. "John's feeling overly concerned about money again." Sveta shook her head. "So what if we can't afford our own home? Lots of children continue to live with their parents after marriage."

"Not Americans," Julia said. "They want their own space, away from their parents."

"Space? Always this need for more space. What about the support of your family?" Sveta shook her head. "And anyway, why is John so worried? With the price people are paying for up-time guns, he's got a small fortune in this room."

"You haven't suggested Puss sell some of his guns?" Julia demanded.

"Not yet." Then she noticed the horrified looks on her friends' faces. "What did I say?"

"Blasphemy!" Julia said.

"Double blasphemy," Janie agreed.

"Sveta, a West Virginian's guns are sacrosanct. Some of them are family heirlooms," Diana explained.

"There are families in Grantville where their guns are worth more than their houses, but they would never sell them," Janie said.

"So, no selling his guns?" Sveta asked.

"Not unless you want to really make Puss angry," Julia said.

"Or you're really desperate for money," Diana added.

Zielona Góra

Street fighting sucked. Puss sat with his back against the wall of a building and checked his weapons. He had a service issue Sharps carbine clone, and a pair of stainless steel Ruger Vaquero Cowboy Action revolvers in .45 Colt he'd owned for years, a copy of a Gurkha Kukri knife one of his dad's friends had made out of an old leaf spring, and a bag of grenades. The rest of his patrol was similarly armed, but with their own choice of fighting knife, and a pair of the service issue cap-and-ball revolvers in place of the Rugers.

The grenades had proved a godsend in the battle so far. They were modeled more on the World War II German "potato masher" than the American "pineapple" grenades, but they were miles ahead of whatever the Poles were using—probably the old spherical ball type where you had to physically light the fuse before using. At least the USE grenades could be ignited with a simple pull of a string.

Puss saw the signal from the captain of the company his patrol had been attached to as a sort of fire-support team. That meant they were ready to enter the street. He slung his carbine and raised his head to check on the target. It was less than thirty feet to the building. "Grenades."

Five men pulled grenades from the sacks each of them carried. Almost as one they checked the target, pulled the friction-igniter strings, and with covering fire from Captain Casper Havemann's rifle company, lobbed their grenades toward the target, before dropping behind cover.

Seconds later, the air full of dust and smoke, Puss and his patrol went over the wall they'd been hiding behind and, with more covering fire, ran for the building.

Puss was the first to reach the building. He dropped his shoulder to barge open the shattered door, and he was in the house. With a Ruger held before him in a two-handed grip, Puss advanced into the building. This was the part of street fighting he really didn't like. The enemy could be anywhere, and a grenade dropped from above was almost impossible to avoid.

They cleared the ground floor first, stopping only to tear down the smoldering drapes to prevent a fire. Then, with the rest of his patrol providing backup, Puss advanced up the narrow staircase. It was a bit like playing paintball back up-time, except hits were likely to hurt a heck of a lot more. At the top of the stairs he lobbed in a grenade—no sense taking risks. He followed up the blast, to find the space empty.

Puss smothered the smoking embers before they could catch anything alight while the rest of the patrol checked the other rooms. Other than the men on the ground floor, this house had been empty.

With the first house secure, a section from the infantry company flooded in and started to tear an opening in the attic space's dividing wall. When they broke through Puss lobbed a grenade through the opening, and quickly followed the blast. With the top floor cleared the infantry followed a constant flow of grenades down the building until it was clear. In this way they made it to the end of the street without exposing themselves to fire from snipers.

The other side of the street had been taken out by another platoon of Captain Havemann's company, making the road in between relatively safe. Puss and his patrol sat on the steps of one of the row of houses they'd taken and took the opportunity to reload their revolvers and have a drink. They watched Captain Havemann lead his headquarters section to the rubble at the end of the street, where he could plan the next step of their street-clearance operation.

BOOOM! BOOOM! BOOOM!

All hell broke loose as the Poles fired a massive artillery barrage along most of the front. Cannon balls tore into buildings and rubble began to fall from the damaged walls. Debris from a critically damaged building fell onto the headquarters section. Two survivors of the collapse started pulling away at the rubble. One fell to sniper fire, but the other managed to pull Captain Havemann from the rubble and drag him to cover.

"Shit! Shit! Shit!" Puss could already sense the company wavering around him. Havemann was a man with a towering presence. Just having him walk along the line gave his men confidence. Unfortunately, the reverse applied if something happened to him.

"Take this and give me covering fire."

"What the hell?" Lenhard Poppler started to ask as Puss thrust his carbine at him. "You goddamned idiot!" he shouted as Puss sprinted toward the fallen officer.

Puss used a feet-first baseball slide to take cover beside Captain Havemann and the man who'd dragged him to cover. A quick glance at the size of the lumps of masonry covering the rest of the headquarters section told him that these two were likely to be the only survivors. The private was a weed of a man. How he'd managed to drag the captain, who was easily twice his weight, to cover was anybody's guess. The man was still bleeding, but he'd done his best to staunch the flow from the captain's injuries.

The Poles were intensifying their fire around where Puss was huddled, but contrary to what Corporal

Poppler thought, he wasn't a complete idiot. He emptied out his bag of grenades and started lobbing them over the rubble. For a few seconds he had a screen of white smoke from the black powder grenades. "Go!" he screamed at the private, while he dragged Captain Havemann over his shoulder in a fireman's lift and sprinted back to Corporal Poppler.

Eager hands relieved Puss of his load, and he took his carbine back. "Who's in charge?"

Hermann pointed to a lieutenant taking cover in a doorway. The man was signaling everyone to pull back. Unfortunately, most of the men weren't taking any notice. They were looking at Puss. Right now, he was the person they were most likely to take orders from. Puss took his lead from the lieutenant and signaled them back. Over the next hour the company made a fighting withdrawal, until they were back where they'd started that morning.

Grantville

The knock on the door was a bit more impetuous than most callers to the Trelli residence used. Except of course, when the call was urgent. The household froze, knives and forks poised in the air. Slowly all eyes congregated onto Pápa, who smiled ruefully around the table and laid his knife and fork on his barely started dinner.

"I'd better see who that is," he said as he pushed back his chair and headed for the door.

The rest of the household was silent. Sveta could almost feel covert glances in her direction. An unexpected caller at this hour could only be bad news, and the most likely bad news was that something had happened to John. A sudden burst of activity from her baby just reinforced her concern.

Pápa appeared at the dining room door. "It's Ernst Schreiber, from the *Grantville Times*, with a photographer. John's okay, but he's been a bit heroic, again."

Sveta looked past Pápa. She knew Herr Schreiber from her work. She also knew what not a lot of people didn't—that Ernst Schreiber wrote the *Times'* famous—no, make that infamous—Rodger Rude column. "What do you want?"

"Sveta!"

"Sorry, Máma." She pointedly didn't include Ernst Schreiber in her apology.

"Just a few photographs of Sergeant Trelli's family and maybe a few words..."

Whatever Ernst had intended saying was lost in the ringing of the phone. Felix, already on his feet, answered it. "We know. Herr Schreiber, from the *Times* has just shown up—what was that? We should expect to hear from the *Daily News* as well? Thank you."

Felix Trelli hung up the phone. "That was your office, Sveta. Lieutenant Dauth wanted to warn you that Scoop has filed a story about John."

"Scoop!" All the terror she felt when Ernst knocked on the door found an outlet in that scornful word. She turned on Ernst. "You're trusting something Scoop filed?"

Ernst shrugged. "It's a good human-interest story. Local boy hauls officer from the jaws of death, then leads the officer's command in a fighting withdrawal. The press office in Magdeburg has confirmed enough of it that we intend on running the story."

If the press office in Magdeburg was confirming anything Scoop filed . . . Sveta swallowed bile at what that suggested. Suddenly there was a brilliant flash of light. Blinking furiously, Sveta tried to focus on Ernst's photographer. "Did you just take a photograph?" she demanded.

It was a bit of a redundant question, as Jacob Fiedler was already swapping out the spent bulb in the flash unit he'd just used. He nodded anyway.

"Don't even think about doing that again."

"That's not very nice, Frau Anderovna. Jacob's just doing his job. We just want a bit of human interest to accompany the main story."

"What is the main story, Herr Schreiber?" Felix asked.

Next day

"ST. GEORGE DOES IT AGAIN!" The headline in the *Grantville Times* blared out in seventy-two-point letters.

Sveta stared at the photograph under the headline. Whoever it was who said a picture was worth a thousand words had something like that photograph in mind. Even after being screened so it could be printed in the paper, you could sense the urgency as the man ran out of the cloud of smoke carrying a man over his shoulders while helping another limp to safety. It was bad enough he'd earned a St. George Medal saving some people from a rabid dog, now he had to risk enemy fire to rescue some soldiers as well.

"Why would he risk his life like that?" she asked Máma.

"Because that's the kind of person John is."

Sveta was close to tears. She was learning to admire the man she was married to, and the silly fool seemed intent on getting himself killed. "I wish he would stop. He's going to get himself killed if he keeps this up."

"Have you ever thought that maybe John doesn't think he deserves you, and that if he proves he's a good soldier, he might be more worthy of you?"

Sveta was stunned by the suggestion, and burst into tears. "But he's given me a family."

Suzanne reached out and stroked Sveta's hair. "I don't think John knows how important a real family is to you, Sveta. I'm reminded of something Betty told me John said back in June, when he first took you around to her place. Do you remember what he said when she suggested that he escort you to Jabe McDougal's wedding?"

Sveta tried to remember back to that horrible day. Slowly the words came back to her. "That a girl with my looks could have anybody she wanted."

"Have you ever wondered what John might have been thinking when he said that?"

Sveta had totally forgotten that conversation. She thought about it now, and came to a surprising conclusion. "John thinks I'm pretty?"

Suzanne grinned. "A bit more than pretty. You're a very beautiful girl."

Sveta thought of the most beautiful girl she knew. "As beautiful as Julia?"

"At least as beautiful as Julia."

"Oh!" Sveta had never really seen herself as being beautiful. She knew she was better than passable, but beautiful was always what other people were called, never her. "More beautiful than Donetta?"

Immediately Sveta wished the name unsaid. She glanced at Máma. There was moment of shock, and then a smug smile appeared on Máma's face.

"Madam's beauty was barely skin deep, Sveta. Your beauty runs deeper, and will last longer." Then Máma enveloped Sveta in a massive hug. "Don't worry, darling, everything's going to turn out all right."

Sveta luxuriated in Máma's embrace. She was happy Máma had accepted her. And even happier that her baby would be born into this wonderful family. Now, if only this war would end...

The Maltese Crux

Alistair Kimble

"Jean, I have need of your assistance." Grand Master Antoine de Paule, Prince of the Church and decreed cardinal by Pope Urban VIII, gestured at a stack of missives on the worn and gnarled table. "An investigation of sorts."

Jean Baptiste Lascaris de Castellar, second in command of the Knights of Malta, had been summoned to Valetta, Malta. He had been attending to his duties as pillar of the Langue of Provence in France.

"I am at your service." Jean bowed slightly. "As always, but shall I address you as Your Most High Eminence, or something to that effect?"

"You are in the service of the Lord and the Church as well," de Paule said, wagging a finger. "Do not ever forget. And please dispense with such formalities as Eminence, Prince and so forth. I'm only interested in using those titles, and the powers conferred upon me by His Holiness, to secure the Church's assistance for our humble order."

"Of course. How may I be of assistance?" Jean

glanced at the stack, but gleaned nothing and eased onto the wooden chair.

De Paule insisted on a hard chair for those summoned to his private chamber, probably as a means of control or power. Jean employed the method himself back home, but now on the receiving end the imposition seemed a petty gesture.

De Paule crossed the room, white and crimson robes hanging loose. He'd traded his traditional knight's garb for those of a churchman, as if adopting all the affectations of a cardinal. Or perhaps de Paule's body succumbed to frailty or softness, and the drapery hid the decline.

Jean, during his time in Provence, dispensed with the frilly collars and puffed shoulders adorning most knights, preferring a simple slashed doublet and plain, high-collared shirt beneath. Baggy breeches eased movement, but his old boots remained—tall, wide, and frayed about the edges, but cradling his feet without peer.

De Paule paused before a selection of wines and sighed.

"Where is your cup bearer?" Jean asked.

"This conversation is between us, and us alone."

"I understand," Jean said. "At least we aren't having this discussion in the council chamber. I find some of the tapestries there rather bland, and—"

"I'm not sure you *do* understand." De Paule pulled the stopper from an opaque glass decanter. "We have serious work ahead."

Jean straightened and shifted, a minor relief, but more importantly, providing the appearance of attentiveness.

De Paule shook his reddening head, lending the wispy white hairs a pinkish hue.

"What is it?"

"One of those letters," de Paule pointed, "suggests the Knights of Malta's best days are long past, and all we'll become is a bawdy and lecherous band of pirates with no credibility or usefulness."

"Ridiculous."

De Paule grabbed the decanter and goblet and brought them back to his table, but remained standing. "I've read detailed accounts, and studied a list of the grand masters and their contributions."

"May I ask from whom you received these letters?" Jean asked.

"Cardinal Richelieu." De Paule shook his head. "Sadly, a few years back and certainly brimming with motives assuredly stale due to his political failures. I should have taken the documents and reports regarding Grantville more seriously—especially when our German commanderies corroborated much of Richelieu's information."

"So, I deduce from your reaction your contributions to the order are lacking," Jean said, "or less than you expected."

"You're overly blunt, Jean," de Paule said.

"My apologies, Grand Master."

"While the list is occasionally impressive, my tenure as grand master resulted in a new residence and some plans for fortifications, but no glory." De Paule lifted a sheet from the stack. "And your tenure, well—"

"My tenure? Me?" Jean's eye widened, his forehead wrinkling. De Paule had known of this for some time and was only just now telling him. "A grand master?"

"Yes, and your tenure is less impressive than mine save one dubious distinction." De Paule raised an eyebrow.

Jean cocked his head.

"The dates of death are also included, and while I'm due to expire sometime in 1636, I am choosing to ignore that piece of the future." A faint smile touched de Paule's lips and faded. "You however, will, according to history, succeed me as grand master and live into your late nineties. But my point is that our tenures are unimportant. We contribute no significant actions or decisions to elevate our legacies."

"Me, a grand master? *Late* nineties? I feel robust now in my seventies," Jean straightened and shifted; the movement provided minor relief. "But it's beyond belief, and a position for which I never aspired. If charged so, I would serve with honor and devotion."

"I know you would," de Paule said. "You're a loyal knight, but you'll have a long wait." He smiled with his eyes, though sadly. "I've yet to request last rites and refuse to bow to what the up-time histories portend."

"Of course, Grand Master. I'd never presume, I—"

"That's enough, Jean," de Paule said, and stiffened, as had his speech. He turned, decanter gripped tightly. "I'm more concerned about the order's legacy. *Our* legacy." He tilted the container over his cup but hesitated; his nostrils flared and he threw the decanter....

The heavy glass struck the wall, smashing against the stone and splintering. Jean flinched, but more for the fine French wine now trickling in dark trails down the stone.

Jean held his tongue, but concern crept into his

heart; he rarely witnessed de Paule lose his temper or shift his emotions so swiftly.

De Paule's face flushed, but he moved on, not lingering on what he'd done to the poor vintage. "I will not allow the order's decline to begin with us. The Knights of Malta's best days are ahead. We have to make certain." He glanced at the wall, and his shoulders slumped. "We were important once—"

"Pardon, Grand Master, but we are still important. Look at the gift we've been given by those *Americans*," Jean said, "the foresight and knowledge of what comes next."

"Ah, ever hopeful, but have you not read any of this drivel?" De Paule crumpled the papers in his hand. "The rubbish recounted in these reports Richelieu sent?" He tossed the paper on the floor.

"There are many who would name as heretics those who believe in this future—despite the proof laid before them."

"Are you among them?" de Paule asked.

"Of course not. I'm a practical knight." Jean bent over, stretched his back, smoothed his breeches, and grabbed de Paule's discarded paper. "But shouldn't our concern rest with conflicts occurring in Christendom as we speak?" He smoothed the crinkles and scrutinized the words. "These events have not even happened, but apparently everything we'll ever do is compared with the Great Siege."

"I *am* concerned with Christendom, and Christians killing Christians: a rotten affair," de Paule said, "but our mandate is quite clear."

"Yes, neutrality when Christians war with fellow Christians."

"A much greater threat lurks." De Paule faced the window, and the gray sea beyond. Peeps and whines of flitting gulls wafted through with the cool winter breeze, a respite from arid summer winds, freshening the room with notes of brine. Jean flared his nostrils and took in the sea-salted air.

De Paule grabbed another decanter . . . "The Ottomans." . . . and poured another red. "They are our enemies, not our fellow Christians."

"Agreed," Jean said, "but you should have broken *that* decanter, I think. A much better wine for staining the walls."

"Enough." De Paule sipped. He shook his head, lips puckering, and swallowed. "You are correct. I *should* have broken this one."

"The world has changed," Jean said, "and who can say with any certainty what the future holds now that these Americans are here."

De Paule nodded. "Yes. Not to mention their odd customs and casual blasphemies—" he waved a hand at the letters "—but these documents copied from this so-called Grantville Library are troubling."

Jean smiled, hoping to lift the old man's spirits. "Though one thing is certain."

De Paule raised an eyebrow.

"We were given this island and have protected our charge with honor," Jean said. "You are the near-equal to cardinals thanks to His Holiness, so why not use your newfound influence?"

"No doubt the purple was conferred upon me as a token gesture by His Holiness, but this is why I've summoned you, Jean. You've been away from Malta long enough that I believe you will be unbiased in executing your duties. I trusted in others recently and have found that trust misplaced." De Paule sipped, obviously forgetting the wine's foul qualities. His face scrunched, and he shoved the wine aside. "We have responsibilities beyond Malta, and stand as a gateway, a stepping-stone to Europe. From Malta the Ottomans could stage, and sweep into Italy. This island rests too near the northern parts of Africa—and I needn't remind you of all the problems there." His fist pounded the thick wood. "I have taken action, but need your help."

"I am here to serve."

De Paule nodded. "The order was to present a falcon each year on All Souls' Day, correct?"

"Yes," Jean said, "to the Viceroy of Sicily, and onward to the emperor, but during these troubling times I don't see how that helps our cause."

"Along with the troubling reports, Cardinal Richelieu sent me a curious manuscript, *The Maltese Falcon*. He's quite a collector of manuscripts and his machinations are well known, and that brought to me a line of thinking I'd normally never arrive at on my own."

"Now I'm very curious," Jean said.

"I must admit the narrative was somewhat perplexing and nigh unreadable." De Paule's smile elevated the tips of his thin, gray mustache. "However, I managed to glean the meaning behind the story."

Jean sat, and with genuine interest leaned forward.

De Paule lowered himself onto his oversized chair, probably stuffed with thousands of feathers to cradle his old bones. "A Maltese Falcon is the crux of the story—specifically the search for the figurine and the greed of horrible people to acquire the jewels adorning its surface. There are betrayals, romantic interests and so forth, but I found the manuscript a bore."

"An intriguing notion, reading such a story," Jean said, "but what purpose did it serve? His Eminence, Cardinal Richelieu, is quite fond of our methods and use of naval assets. Do you believe he intended to incite you to some sort of action upon your receipt of his reports a couple years back?"

"I'm never certain of Richelieu's motives, but I also received word His Holiness, Pope Urban VIII, read parts of the up-time future, and is concerned over the direction of the church. The order *will* assist His Holiness in righting the church, and at the same time, guarantee our continued relevance."

"How?"

"Patience, brother." De Paule moved a stack of papers on the table, revealing a book. "I commissioned a Maltese Falcon figurine as a token of the order's commitment to the church."

Jean stroked his pointy beard, staring; the possibilities overwhelmed.

"A small gift, yes. However, there has been a complication." De Paule rested an elbow on the table and rubbed his forehead. "The figurine went missing."

"Tell me it wasn't encrusted in jewels."

De Paule's eyes met Jean's.

"Oh, God." Jean sat back. "You want me to find this figurine, this Maltese Falcon."

"Yes, and I need the Falcon before I depart for my audience with His Holiness."

"What of Vice Chancellor Abela? He's a full score my junior." Jean nodded, as if the motion would sway de Paule, but he knew better. "Abela can hunt for the figurine."

De Paule shook his head. "Normally I'd acquiesce, but I trust you, and after all, we're both of the Langue of Provence. No, Abela is both priest and student of the law. I fear he won't do in this affair."

"Forget I mentioned Abela," Jean said. "We are forewarned and can change the future, even if it's supposedly preordained. Surely His Holiness is aware of the danger the Ottomans pose."

"The Ottomans will soon take Crete." De Paule gestured at the papers. "It has been recorded, and my greatest fears are coming true—an Ottoman siege is imminent."

Jean's nose and ears felt cold, and his hands chilled.

"Ah, now you see." De Paule nodded. "We sit here, our legacy and reputation built upon a siege that occurred in the last century. Our Christian brothers in Europe hack each other to pieces, and our fight against the Ottomans is forgotten." De Paule grabbed the shoved-aside wine and downed the rest. "*We* are forgotten, however, *they*—" he gestured eastward "—the true enemy, have not forgotten the vicious defeat handed them by our fore-brothers."

Jean rubbed his hands together, erasing the chill. "But shouldn't this knowledge be used to change events for the good of not only us, but our enemies as well?"

"Would the Ottomans feel such concern for us?"

"War does not have to visit Malta and expose the innocents here to possible death," Jean said. "Or worse, slavery."

"We'd only be shoring up our defenses. When I present the Falcon, His Holiness will be moved to assist his greatest knights against the Ottoman threat that *will* arrive on our doorstep."

Jean folded his arms. "We should prepare, but I'm not sure this is our best course."

"Can't you see? Knights resplendent in the best armor and weapons man the battlements, while white and crimson banners bearing our eight-pointed cross wave?"

Jean entertained thoughts of rallying knights and peasants manning the walls in defiance of the Ottomans, but shivered at the loss of life a siege would levy.

"You doubt my plan?" de Paule asked.

"Not exactly, Grand Master, but—"

De Paule gestured toward the door. "Find my falcon."

"And where do you propose I begin?"

"The sculptor. He was last in possession of the figurine." De Paule pushed to his feet. "I'll be touring Malta the next few days. See you have the falcon when I return."

Discretion was paramount, and Jean, an aging man, was in the awkward position of locating the figurine by himself. As soon as de Paule departed, Jean entered the grand master's quarters hoping a clue beyond the name and address of the sculptor would present itself.

A peek at the papers littering the table revealed the manuscript, its frayed corners catching his attention. The words Hammett, and *The Maltese Falcon* ran down the spine, and within he found a rendering of the figurine. He grabbed the manuscript, hoping the sketch would aid his investigation.

Jean would have preferred more men at his side, but

given the implied secrecy, he'd suffer with a simple man-at-arms for the visit to the sculptor's. Since he'd been away from Malta for so long, Jean was at a disadvantage as most of the men-at-arms were unfamiliar. He did, however, recognize a dark-skinned man, Bekir—one of the few Turks indentured to the order. He'd likely prove more useful as a porter than in a scuffle.

Jean and Bekir descended into town from the square, entering the maze of whitewashed and beige buildings with cobblestoned, narrow walkways and grooved paths. The breeze shifted, carrying the heady scent of saltwater tinged with pungent human waste like that of a salty soft cheese gone rotten.

The address given Jean was near the waterfront, where the homes and shops rested atop one another and the rot of dead fish filled the air. He swallowed his disgust and pressed a handkerchief to his nose. Bekir, however, seemed to relish the air outside the confines of the citadel.

They turned up the alley where the sculptor's shop should be. Decaying parched wood exteriors mixed with cracked stone facades were out of place with what Jean was accustomed to, though he'd always known people lived and died in places such as this. He didn't need reminding that being born with title and privilege was a blessing.

All the signs had caked white with salt and had faded from the ceaseless sun and salt-laden air. He counted up from where he turned, and yes, fourth on the right, a rundown hovel at home with the rest of the interconnected buildings.

Jean rapped on the splintered door with a gloved hand, the wood giving under the light pressure.

Rustling followed by a muffled shout came from within. Jean hammered the door with his fist, cracking the wood. He glanced over his shoulder at Bekir.

The porter shrugged.

A scream like a cat being eviscerated pierced the door. Jean motioned at the door; Bekir took one step forward, kicked the cracked and weathered wood off its hinges, and stepped inside.

"Very effective." Jean drew a four-edged rondel—a family heirloom from the last century. He carried it for close-in fighting, and admired the threatening cruciform appearance it had when viewed from the point.

He followed the porter into the opening and was met with outlines and vague shapes. Most of the light came from the doorway, casting a rectangle deep into the room. An opening leading to another room at the rear lit a small square poking into the front room. A shadow moved from one side of the square to the other and back, reversed direction, and repeated the journey.

Bekir took position off to one side, impassive but alert. A thick coating of dust, presumably from sculpting, covered the floor and what little furnishings adorned the room. Those furnishings featured broken legs and arms, or filthy upholstery riddled with rips and tears. Lime, chalk and mustiness permeated the room, spiced with wafts of excrement.

The crack of a chair toppling followed by a metallic clank came from the adjoining room. Jean nodded at Bekir who took up position to one side of the rear opening.

Jean took the lead this time, and with his blade ready, edged through the opening. A woman rested there on her knees, hands to her face, sobbing. Beside her lay a wet-tipped stiletto. Motion above the woman caught Jean's eye.

Bekir entered and stood beside Jean, keeping silent.

A man swung by the neck from an exposed beam. Blood soaked the cloth above the man's hip and trickled from the dead man's toes, painting crimson lines in the dusty stone floor as the body gently swayed back and forth in slow, easy circles. Light from a hole in the ceiling that probably once held glass illuminated the dead man as he swung.

"Antonius, I presume?"

The woman jumped, sucking in a quick gasp. "Who are *you*?"

Jean dropped the rondel into its scabbard, a small piece of leather that did nothing to cover the blade. He grabbed her under the arms and lifted. The solid clunk of a heavy object hitting the floor sounded.

He shoved her aside for a view of the floor. There, lying askew was a black sculpture of a falcon. The hanged man no longer held his interest, not with the flat black bird staring up at him—he'd found the figurine.

It was much larger than expected, roughly the length of a human head, but not quite as wide, and with a sizable square base covered on one side with the falcon's tail feathers.

"Cut him down?" Bekir's accent was thick, but in small doses, palatable. He positioned himself between Jean and the woman.

"Not yet."

Bekir nodded.

An overturned chair lay ten feet from the swinging man and the stiletto lay beneath him. The chair had to have been used to aid the hanging, and the wet tip made the blade's part obvious. The rest of the room was much like the front room—covered in dust and broken-down furniture. A rickety bench toward the back of the room held an unfinished bust and was littered with chisels and hammers. A large crack in the rear wall opened on a gloomy alleyway.

"Who are you?" The woman's voice was husky and shared Bekir's accent: two Turks in one day. How interesting.

Jean turned his attention to the woman. She was young, perhaps in her early twenties. A layer of white powder covered an olive complexion and permeated her black hair. Dark, red-rimmed eyes studied him as a single thick eyebrow arched, looking like a black caterpillar rearing up to sample a leaf.

"I know what he is." She nodded at Bekir.

"Oh?" Jean asked.

"A slave. Much like I was."

"You were Antonius' slave?" Jean asked the woman, and turned to Bekir. "Cut him down."

Bekir nodded.

"I asked who you were." She clapped her hands together; white dust puffed in a cloud around them. Jean covered his nose and mouth with a gloved hand.

Bekir paused and turned, facing Jean and the woman.

Jean shook his head. "I'm afraid I'll be asking the questions. You're not in a position to demand anything from a knight of the order. I came here to ask Antonius a few questions, and he's answered one of them."

"And who was going to ask him these questions Antonius answered from the end of a rope?"

The young woman certainly had an easy way about

her, despite addressing a man, a knight, someone clearly of higher station. Foreigners, and, furthermore, Turks on Malta never spoke to knights in this fashion.

Jean sighed. "I'm a knight."

"Yes?"

Jean's fist clenched, and he took a deep breath. This woman, this Turk, tested his patience—a virtue of his, one well known throughout the order.

"This one is a filthy animal, a gypsy," Bekir said. "Do not trust her." He spat on the ground at her feet and turned his attentions to Antonius.

She lunged, but Jean stepped in front of her and shoved her to the ground. "That will be enough."

She rubbed the small of her back and remained on the floor. She fussed with her hair; the nervous action gave rise to another white cloud.

"You screamed earlier," Jean said, "but now you do not seem so upset over his death. I've a mind to arrest you."

She wiped her cheek, leaving trails amidst the other lines of dust and tears crisscrossing her face. "I was his apprentice, Petek." She sneered. "But he treated me like a slave."

"An apprentice, not a slave. Isn't that unusual? I must say it's rather odd finding a Turkish gypsy apprenticed to an Italian on Malta."

"And what are you? Frenchman? Spaniard? This isn't your country either."

"French, and on the contrary, His Holiness has granted the order dominion over Malta." Jean stood over her, and behind he heard a snap and a thump as Antonius hit the floor. "Now, I'm known for my patience," he said, "and tolerance, both of which you are testing. For a woman, a Turk, and a gypsy, you are taking great pains to insult the order. You're a guest here, an apprentice learning a trade, and you'd do right by yourself to still your caustic tongue." Jean raised a hand and waved for Bekir. "Other knights would have been less lenient I'm afraid—"

"Yes, I'm sure." Anger flashed in her eyes.

Bekir stepped past Jean, leaned over, and back-handed Petek across the face. She crumpled to the ground. A fresh course of sobs followed.

"That will do, I'm sure." Jean remained calm, but was mildly surprised at the casual violence. "Petek has this day been witness to the unspeakable."

Bekir moved to stand behind Petek.

Jean scraped a rickety wooden chair, its white paint peeling, over the rough floor. The knight thanked the Lord he'd not worn armor today. He sat on the edge, ready if the wood gave way. "Tell me what happened."

Her eyes narrowed, drawing her single, long eyebrow into the shape of a black chevron. "He hanged himself and robbed me of an apprenticeship. He was impossible and crude and abusive, and treated me like an animal." She peered up at Jean from under the thick eyebrow, eyes wet. "He was the only one to recognize my talent and the only one who would agree to take a Turkish gypsy as an apprentice." She stared at Antonius, reduced to a pile of robes on the floor, and spit. "He was a pig, and I stuck him like one."

"So you murdered him?" Jean asked.

"No. I stabbed him *because* he's dead. He abandoned me. I stabbed him because he treated me like an animal, but I did not murder him. He hanged himself, or maybe someone else snuck in here."

"I believe you may be a fine actor given your background, but the scream sounded genuine, and your explanation of the stabbing is quite plausible. But tell me," Jean said, "why would he hang himself?"

She turned her gaze on Jean, "Maybe it has to do with the falcon he sculpted," and shrugged.

"I will think on that, but the reason for my visit was to make an inquiry regarding a figurine and my quest appears complete." He flipped open the Hammett book and showed Petek the image of the Maltese Falcon.

"The one over there is a fake." Petek laughed, albeit with a nervous edge.

"Bekir," Jean said, "the figurine. Bring it to me." Despite its size, the Falcon was lighter than expected.

"You don't understand," Petek said.

"Then tell me."

"Can't we leave this room? That body?" Petek's gaze shifted from Jean to the pile of robes and back to Jean. "I have superstitions about such things."

Jean pulled Petek to the other room and sat her on the ripped and torn sofa, but he remained standing, cradling the figurine in his left hand. It bore a remarkable resemblance to the one in de Paule's book.

"Very interesting." He turned over the figurine and examined its features. "Now, tell me everything. About this—" He faced the figurine toward her. "—and about Antonius." He nodded toward the back room.

"I didn't kill him."

"That much I do believe. However, you expect me to believe you knew nothing of it? How could you not hear someone being murdered or being hanged? You would have heard someone shuffling about back there, even if you were sculpting in the front room."

She shook her head. "There is much noise here, certainly you know this much. I didn't hear you before you spoke."

"Let's say for the moment you're telling the truth," Jean said. "Why would he hang himself? Or, if he didn't commit that sin against God, be the victim of another sin against God, murder?" He held the figurine before her.

"For the figurine, the falcon, but not the one you hold."

"Speak plainly."

"You're holding a copy."

Jean examined the figurine closely: along the left wing ran a thin, deep, incision. A damaged figurine as a gift to the Pope? Not likely. Perhaps this woman spoke the truth.

"There is another figurine," she said, "but I know little of it, only that unlike the one in your hands, Antonius set many jewels in it."

"That would explain his murder."

She nodded, the black hair hanging before her face was matted with dirt and dust, creating a mushy paste of sweat and tears. "We both made a figurine based on the drawing in your book."

Jean hefted the falcon, "So, this figurine may be a fake. Much depends on whether or not Antonius was murdered. If he was, then the murderer either knew this one for a fake, as you assert, or simply thought it was not worth stealing."

"But—"

"Yes?"

Petek fumbled for words. "Antonius—he drank a lot, and told everyone he was sculpting an item teeming with jewels, commissioned by the pope."

"Your explanation lends itself nicely to the theory he was murdered, but you would want me to believe some outsider murdered him, wouldn't you? I'm not so sure. How would anyone know this one was the fake?"

"I know it is."

"That's because you supposedly sculpted this one." Jean tapped the falcon. "No. I'll be taking it back to the citadel." He watched her face for a reaction: any sign of weakness or deception, but was met with only a blank stare.

For a woman, Petek displayed an even temper and recovered quickly from seeing her master swinging, and that concerned Jean. He sensed a deeper plot in motion, and suspected a read of Hammett's book prudent before taking further action. Answers were needed before de Paule returned, and presenting a fake to the grand master would be a failure.

"I'm ordering you to the citadel two mornings hence. I'll leave word at the main entrance in the square for you to be allowed entry," Jean said. He'd also send word to prohibit her departure from Malta in case she decided to run.

Petek's expression, though shielded with hair and covered with a dusty pallor, projected uncertainty and fear.

"You weren't planning on leaving Malta anytime soon were you?" Jean asked.

"I've nowhere else to go. But may I have your name?"

"Jean de Castellar. The guardsmen will certainly know it."

"I'll just ask for the patient and tolerant knight." She smiled, splitting her bottom lip. A red slit shot across her dusty white lips.

"You could try that, though dour is becoming more and more appropriate."

Jean, with Bekir trailing, departed the hovel with more questions than he'd brought. At least he retrieved a figurine, if not *the* Maltese Falcon de Paule coveted.

The sun brushed the edge of the sea, casting the alleyway in darkness. Having much to think on, the dimly lit pathways and long walk were welcome so long as Jean and Bekir could find their way back to the citadel.

Jean examined the figurine for a few minutes of the trek before handing the responsibility over to Bekir.

Petek claimed more than one figurine had been crafted, but the fact one rested before her while Antonius swung above puzzled Jean. It wasn't plausible that she grabbed the figurine and *then* found Antonius swinging. No, more than likely the figurine was already at the dead man's feet, but what did that mean?

Jean and Bekir reached an incline and climbed for the citadel's gates.

A man lunged from a doorway. Jean's hand flew to his rondel, but the lunge was not meant for him. Bekir gasped, and the figurine slid from his hands, and clunked against the cobblestoned walkway. The Turk went limp and toppled; his head bounced off a cobblestone, but that mattered little as blood sheeted down and off his side, gathering between the stones before trickling down the hill like red rainwater.

With his rondel readied, Jean circled away keeping Bekir's body between him and the attacker. Jean's only other weapon, Bekir's blade, now rested beneath the dying man.

If the attacker was a common cutpurse, confronting so obvious a knight and his man-at-arms would mean death, but this man had dispatched Bekir with ease. No, the attack was about the figurine.

"Where is the figurine, the falcon?" the attacker asked. He wore all black from head to toe, with no hint of a white-collared shirt beneath. The attacker's eyes sparked a hint of recognition, but the droopy mustache and long bead-strewn hair lent him a silly countenance Jean couldn't place.

"You've mortally wounded a man in my service," Jean said.

"A Turk, nothing more." The attacker shrugged. He carried a long slender blade not unlike Jean's rondel, but the man used his precisely—he'd downed Bekir with a single thrust. Jean was no novice with a blade, but in a fight with a far younger man and so obviously skilled, well, he understood his limitations in age and skill.

"There's no need for further bloodshed," Jean said, rondel readied.

A torch from above flickered in the attacker's eyes, and as if in agreement, he pulled out a cloth and wiped the blade of Bekir's blood. "I know who you are, knight, and I also know you're a better swordsman than you're letting on."

"But I'm old, and I'm afraid you have me at a disadvantage," Jean said, one hand palm up and placating, the other grasping the rondel.

"I did, but no longer. I did not expect you to have Bekir with you," the man said.

"I thought you a pirate, but you're a man-at-arms?" Jean asked. The attacker's familiarity with people from the citadel was at odds with his pirate-like appearance.

The man stiffened. "I've sinned, and yes, stooped to piracy, but I'm no man-at-arms." He sniffed. "Enough, now where is it?"

Jean nodded at the falcon lying on the cobblestones.

"Not that one." The man chuckled. "No. One that is more, let's say, valuable."

"So, you're the one responsible for Antonius?"

"Another death of no consequence," the one-time pirate said. "Now where is the figurine?"

"Why did you leave this one?"

The attacker huffed. "It's quite clearly a fake."

"And you thought Antonius knew where the so-called real one was? Tell me, what makes this figurine the fake, and why would you believe I have any idea where the jeweled one is?" Jean asked.

"Antonius crafted one as well as that Turk, Petek. Hers was not adorned with jewels, but Antonius' was." The man squinted and stepped back toward the doorway. "The fate of not only Malta, but Christendom is contained under the jewels and within the figurine Antonius crafted. It's obvious to me now you know nothing of this and retrieved the wrong figurine. Thank you."

Jean leaped over Bekir's body toward the doorway, rondel ready. "You'll need to come with me to the citadel."

The attacker's eyes widened at Jean's sudden charge. The attacker stepped inside the doorway and shoved the thick wooden door closed as Jean hit the threshold with his right side. The knight cried out, thinking perhaps a rib or three had cracked, now regretting his lack of armor. His numbed fingers opened, releasing the rondel, which clanked against the stone entryway.

"Damn." Time away from Malta apparently dulled his judgment. The weight on the door eased—the attacker must have fled. Jean drove his shoulder against the wood. Something hard smacked him on the head and he fell.

Jean awoke to watered wine splashing his face. Relief followed the shock when he recognized the pourer as a knight of the order. He sat up and briefly explained what had happened to his brother knight, who was clearly surprised over finding Jean, the seneschal of the order.

Jean caressed the tender spot left by the head blow, wishing he'd stopped the familiar attacker and one-time pirate. He'd fully intended on taking the man with him to exact judgment for Bekir's murder. But now, with the man besting him and slipping away, and with night quickly coming, he decided the best course was returning to the citadel to study the figurine and read *The Maltese Falcon*.

The knight, assuring Jean that Bekir would be seen to, escorted Jean and the falcon to the citadel.

Jean found Hammett's story compelling, despite odd word choices and quite a few he either misunderstood or had little or no context to interpret properly. He discovered a few curious links to present circumstances, and a few ideas regarding his next course of action.

He snuffed out the lamp and stared at the darker shadow of the figurine, its outline a convincing representation of the bird of prey. As he lay in bed, he muttered a quick prayer for Bekir, but doubted his appeal would do the Turk any good upon meeting Saint Peter.

From there, the falcon dominated his thoughts. Based on his reading of *The Maltese Falcon*, he became certain the falcon in his possession was not a copy, but the only figurine, as in the outcome of the book. Now, Jean only needed to determine the parts each person played: the Turkish gypsy Petek, the mysterious pirate-like attacker, and de Paule's ultimate goal.

He broke his fast the next morning in his chambers with the figurine for company. The falcon in Hammett's book had been a fake, but people schemed, offered currency, killed, and even pretended love for a chance to uncover the treasure hidden beneath its veneer. In the book there had been no treasure, and knowing de Paule had read the manuscript, that was probably true with this figurine.

He'd taken his morning meal rather late, and the sun now pierced the window above, directly lighting the black bird. The incision running along the wing he'd noted the day before had both widened and deepened from hitting the cobblestones when Bekir dropped it. Jean peered more closely at the crack. Tucked within was a thinly folded paper.

"What the—"

Jean sat back, working his thin, short beard to a point. He snapped his fingers.

A toothpick.

Using the slender gold implement in this manner pained him, but proved effective. He poked the tip deep within the figurine, pierced the paper, and pulled it free.

"Oh, Lord." Jean sat back, stomach roiling.

He held in his hands folded vellum with a red wax seal depicting a bas-relief of a man in a boat with a net—the Ring of the Fisherman. The man in the boat was Saint Peter. URBAN VIII PONT MAX arced across the seal's upper rim.

The room's heat intensified and Jean's hands shook. His chest tightened as he traced the seal with his finger, studying the impression's features, searching for any hint of forgery. He breathed deeply and using the toothpick lifted the seal carefully to keep the wax mostly unharmed.

He unfolded the vellum and there was no doubt he held in his hands a papal brief—it was far too small and plain to be a papal bull.

The inscribed Latin commanded the Knights of Malta to spearhead a naval offensive against the Ottomans. Jean studied everything from the seal to the language as well as dates and the quality of the vellum, searching for evidence of forgery, but found nothing.

He sat back and rubbed his eyes. He absently stroked his beard and realized most of the day had passed during his hours of study.

The attacker from last night was mostly correct in his assessment: the fate of Malta and Christendom was indeed contained within a figurine. The belief that Christendom's fate rested within a *jeweled* figurine was the attacker's only mistake. Jean was in possession of the important figurine after all.

De Paule returned late on the day Jean discovered the papal brief and requested his presence the next morning in the council chamber for a full recounting.

Jean left word at the gate for the woman, Petek, to be brought up to the council chamber just before noon. He had arrived thirty minutes prior, and exchanged pleasantries with a dozen of his brother knights, all adorned in their council dress while Jean wore plain but comfortable breeches and a doublet, long blade and rondel at his hip.

Why take the report before a group of high-ranking knights? De Paule must believe he knew the outcome and wanted witnesses. The grand master would have been better off meeting Jean privately if the discussion veered embarrassingly.

Petek arrived as expected, but the presence of her companion—the same man who murdered Bekir and confronted Jean in the alley two evenings prior, surprised him. Two guards in full armor accompanied them. He noted, with some satisfaction, both Petek and the man were bound.

"This is a surprise." Jean looked at Petek and tilted his head toward the man. "He has a name?"

"I do," the man said, "but *I* brought her here, caught her on the docks, leaving, and now *I'm* treated like a criminal along with her. Wait 'til the grand master—"

"You murdered my man-at-arms."

"A filthy Turk," the man snapped. "Our true enemies."

A common sentiment throughout Christendom— and generally true. Individual Turks, however, were another matter—Bekir had competently and quietly served the order, his death unnecessary.

"I expected her today." Jean glanced at Petek; she'd cleaned up and wore a loose, black covering knotted at one shoulder and a baggy white shirt underneath. Jean turned his stare on the man. "But not you. How friendly of you to turn yourself in."

The man scowled.

"So, your name?" Jean leaned close to the man, and saw past the droopy black mustache and the beads tied in his hair. "Wait. Now I remember, you're the exile, formerly Sir Rodrik. A brother. In the failing light the other evening I'd only a hint."

The young man's face reddened.

"Now this is extremely interesting," Jean said.

The chamber doors swung open and the chatter within fell to whispers. Jean studied Petek and Rodrik, but spoke to the guards. "Bring them in upon my summons only."

Jean paused beside an ornate table positioned before the chamber door and grabbed the cloth-draped figurine he'd placed there.

The council chamber was a long, narrow rectangle with rows of semi-cushioned chairs fronting a few rows of hard benches in the rear. A modest dais held the grand master's seat at the head of the room. High walls led to a gold-painted ceiling with rows of exposed beams across its width. Thin ornamental slats of wood fitted between the beams completed the coffered appearance. The air within was still and reeked of sweaty men and unlaundered clothing.

De Paule, seated upon a thick red-cushioned miniature throne, nodded at Jean.

"Your Most High Eminence," Jean said, and de Paule nodded in assent. "I have news of the investigation you so cleverly charged me with, and I must say, I am most disappointed in its outcome."

De Paule's face was grave, but he displayed no outward signs of disappointment. "I see. You had no luck in retrieving the figurine. But what is beneath the cloth?"

"What lies beneath the cloth is the possible destruction of Christendom." Jean rested his hand atop the covering.

De Paule's hands gripped the arms of his chair, and he pulled himself forward on the cushion. "Explain yourself, knight. What sort of evil have you brought before us? I do not understand."

"You will," Jean said, "once I explain."

De Paule rose to his feet. "Guards, reveal to us what our brother knight refuses to."

Two grim-faced guards approached the table, ornamental armor clanking and rattling.

"I beg of you, Grand Master."

De Paule sighed. "Tread lightly."

"Your Most High Eminence, please indulge me a moment." Jean gripped the figurine.

De Paule waved off the guards. "Hurry to your point."

"I found a figurine, but this one," Jean patted its top, "is a fake."

The grand master sat back in his chair and puffed. He looked old, the lines on his face running deep with fatigue. "I thought for a moment you'd brought an artifact of evil before us." De Paule brought a hand to the ornate crucifix dangling at his chest.

Jean nodded. "Nothing quite so spectacular as that, you have my assurances."

"Then you did not locate the original?" de Paule asked. "But what am I to bear as a token of our order's devotion to His Holiness, Urban VIII?"

"I'd think a gift secondary, considering the evil plot I've thwarted," Jean said.

"Oh? You apprehended a thief, but recovering the falcon and its jewels was beyond you?"

"I caught a woman, Petek, a Turkish gypsy. I found her kneeling at the feet of the man you sent me to question, Antonius. He'd been hanged, but also perforated by a narrow, pointed blade."

"Excellent work, brother." De Paule smiled. "We cannot allow murderers to propagate on Malta, they are but another step toward the piracy in our future I so despise."

"My heart is lightened to hear your view on murder. But there is more."

"Yes?"

"I have in custody an exiled knight, Rodrik," Jean said. "He is responsible for the murder of my man-at-arms, Bekir. He's also admitted to acts of piracy."

De Paule shifted in his chair, knuckles white from choking the throne's arms. "And where are these criminals?"

"One moment, Grand Master," Jean said, "I said earlier I found a figurine—"

"Yes, and apparently it's under the cloth." De Paule pointed at the covered object beside Jean.

Jean took a deep breath and prayed, hoping his next ruse of a second figurine would draw a reaction. "No, this one is the fake." He patted the figurine. "The jeweled figurine is under the protection of my personal guard and on a ship to His Holiness. The jewels, however, must be hidden beneath a black veneer. I dared not disturb the veneer for fear of delivering a damaged figurine to His Holiness. But you have nothing to fear; His Holiness will receive your message, and your intentions will be quite clear." Jean nodded toward the door at the rear and returned his gaze to de Paule.

"Clear the chamber," de Paule said, surging from the throne. "Guards, clear everyone, save Jean."

Jean's ruse had indeed drawn a reaction.

Whispers blossomed as the door at the rear opened. Those whispers became mutters of discontent as perplexed knights exited the four side doors, boots scuffing the floor as guards ushered them out.

Jean's eyes fixed on de Paule's as the shuffling and clanking of the prisoners approached from behind.

The grand master's face turned white, then sallow and sickly; he dropped into his chair. "What in the Lord's name is happening? Rodrik? And the gypsy you mentioned?" De Paule studied them, but finally rested on Jean. "You overstepped your mandate."

"Pardon me, Your Most High Eminence, of what are you speaking?" Jean asked. "I followed your directive, and now His Holiness will understand your devotion—the order's devotion, will he not?"

"You—" de Paule pointed at Rodrik "—how did you let this happen?" De Paule turned his attention back to Jean. "Yes, I originally entrusted Rodrik with arranging the falcon's creation and with the hiring of a suitable craftsman as atonement for his sins, but he obviously failed."

"You entrusted an exile turned pirate with such a delicate matter?" Jean asked.

"He begged me for reinstatement," de Paule said, "and I would acquiesce under the condition he complete a task for me. I never condoned murder."

Rodrik's face flushed. He lifted a hand as if to protest, chains clanking, but his bonds prevented the action.

Petek remained silent.

"Your Most High Eminence," Jean said. "Grand Master, are you saying Rodrik is in your employ, and then ensnared you in some plot?" Jean prayed the grand master had been coerced or compelled, or that one of the prisoners would stumble, but so far, only de Paule showed signs of deception.

De Paule cupped his head in his hands. "Jean, you have erred. The falcon you sent back to His Holiness contained a private message. It was meant to—"

"—embroil us in war," Jean said, finishing de Paule's statement. He lifted the cloth from the figurine.

De Paule's head snapped up. "You recovered the falcon? The message is not sent?"

Jean nodded, knowing he was taking a chance and that de Paule could still deny accusations. With hope that the grand master was still an honorable man with the good of the order guiding him.

Jean withdrew the paper poking from the wing and held the letter aloft. "This letter was meant to antagonize the Ottomans."

"His Holiness has seen fit to engage the Ottomans," de Paule said. "You've defiled a private message from His Holiness, Pope Urban VIII, meant solely for me."

"No. I don't believe so," Jean said.

"Do not question me, knight," de Paule said. "You forget your place, your station."

"I'm afraid the forger made a grievous error," Jean said. "The letter is not authentic, however, I'm certain the Ottomans would have overlooked that part." Jean looked at the ceiling, praying he was right about the forgery. Another thought entered his mind—Richelieu. Perhaps de Paule and Richelieu conspired—a dangerous contemplation, and even though Richelieu's power was thoroughly diminished, perhaps he conspired to reclaim his former prominence.

De Paule's face was flat and without passion, as if resigned, but still Jean saw no clear evidence of de Paule's wrongdoing.

Jean poked a little further. "You were using His Holiness as the instigator, and then, once the Ottomans attacked, the pope would be forced to send assistance."

De Paule sat in silence, revealing nothing.

Jean pushed on. "And is it chance His Eminence, Cardinal Richelieu, sent you the manuscript and the reports foretelling the order's bleak future?"

"I've not the energy for Cardinal Richelieu's failed schemes," de Paule said.

"But this one *is* a fake," Petek said, ruining Jean's momentum, "I swear there were two. Antonius and I both sculpted one. His had jewels."

Rodrik, the exiled knight turned pirate, laughed, as if he finally understood, and glanced at Petek. "You're a fool, but I'm much more of one. The jeweled falcon never existed, only the imperfect scarred figurine Jean found in Antonius' residence."

"So, I was correct in my assessment," Jean said, "there was only one figurine all along."

Rodrik nodded. "Antonius lied, he merely told everyone, including Petek, he had crafted a jeweled figurine."

Petek bit her lip. "My master was a lazy man of little ambition. I often performed his work. I'm not sure why I believed him this time, only that he spoke constantly of the falcon and its worth."

Jean paced, hands clasped behind his back. "Did your master perform any work on the figurine?"

Chains clanked as Petek pointed. "The only bit of work he performed was to teach me the veneering. The cut along the wing I took as a sloppy finish for my sloppy work."

Jean nodded. There was merit to Petek's explanation. "Perhaps Antonius was murdered after all, especially if he espoused to all who would listen about the value of his non-existent figurine." Jean ceased pacing, and faced de Paule. "Though I'm of the belief he hanged himself."

"But you mentioned Antonius had been stabbed," de Paule said.

"Yes," Jean said, "but based on Petek's story, she stabbed Antonius after the hanging. Once we're through here we should release Petek and find her a new master."

De Paule nodded. "I concur. Luckily the murderer is here." His gaze shifted once more upon Rodrik.

Rodrik huffed. "Believing the falcon you have there to be a fake, I left it beneath Antonius' swinging body. Had I known, this falcon and its message would be on its way to Murad and the Ottomans." He sneered. "De Paule's intention was to—"

"Be silent!" de Paule's hands shook.

"You never intended me to find the falcon." Jean crinkled the brief. "You used me to distract from your true purpose. My unsuccessful investigation would have allowed you to prove to His Holiness you intended the stolen figurine to be a gift if you were ever questioned."

"Of what are you speaking? The idea is preposterous. I've not the imagination of Richelieu or cunning of Gaston," de Paule said.

"Was I to be the scapegoat for the forgery as well?" Jean asked.

De Paule's eyes twitched. "No, I never..." And he wiped his face with trembling hands.

"The grand master's intention was to incite the enemy." Rodrik's voice rose; one of the guards pushed him to his knees. "I am not alone in this," Rodrik said, "I was acting under orders and I am not responsible for Antonius' death."

De Paule shot from the throne again and pointed at Rodrik. "No, but you are a murderer, and will be judged, even if the victim was a Turk. I decree on this day, the twenty-fifth of—"

"Wait!" Jean studied the papal brief once more. The date was the mistake, specifically the twenty-fifth.

"I will not be interrupted," de Paule said. "On this day—"

"Silence." Jean commanded, and blinked when no one spoke or moved. "This letter is a forgery and you have borne false witness, Grand Master."

"How dare you? I am a cardinal, a prince of the Church, and your grand master. You will be silent."

"No. My apologies, Grand Master, but you lied. This brief is not from His Holiness," Jean said. "The date on this brief uses the year of the incarnation, counted from March twenty-fifth and is used exclusively on papal bulls. A papal brief uses either the year of the Nativity, beginning the twenty-fifth of December, or—"

"—standard years beginning the first of January." de Paule fell back on his throne. His crimson visage faded to a deathly white.

De Paule motioned the guardsmen to escort the prisoners from the chamber.

"Jean," de Paule said. "Be reasonable. The good of the order depends on decisions we make right now.

My time is limited. Richelieu made sure I knew my death was imminent by sending me the letters and manuscripts."

"No," Jean said, "not all of what you read will come to pass. I think he meant to incite you to action, even if that was before his fall."

"I'm tired. Plots and machinations are for younger, healthier men. I desire to finish as grand master. Die as grand master." De Paule shifted on the throne.

Jean stepped forward and placed a foot on the edge of the dais. "Tell me you were forced into this course of action."

De Paule sagged. "Yes, Rodrik came to me with messages from Cardinal Richelieu, prodding me to action. Richelieu offered recompense and support for the order."

Jean sighed in relief. "We must inform His Holiness at once. We cannot allow Richelieu to use the order for such purposes. I can deliver the message myself."

"Very good," de Paule said, but his eyes flitted back and forth and a fresh sheen of sweat coated his face.

"Grand Master?" Jean asked. "All is well, you've been coerced have you not?"

De Paule rocked to his feet, forcing the withdrawal of Jean's foot from the dais.

"I cannot let you deliver any messages to His Holiness," de Paule said. "I've been summoned for other matters and will inform him myself."

"Thank you, Grand Master. I prayed for such an outcome, and must admit I believed the worst for a few moments," Jean said. "I believe the order will thrive and under your leadership will flourish."

De Paule stumbled backward landing on the throne.

"I cannot do this any longer. Perhaps in my youth I'd have gone along with this. But Rodrik followed my commands and I should have known the plan would go awry."

Oh, God. He is guilty after all. But Jean still hoped some coercion existed.

"I was only trying to ensure our legacy," de Paule said.

"You mean *your* legacy." Jean fought to tamp down his anger. "You were willing to forfeit the lives of others." Jean turned his back on de Paule and wanted nothing more than to leave the council chamber, but paused and took a deep breath. "Remember this: For the wisdom of the world is folly to God. He traps the crafty in the snare of their own cunning."

"An epistle of Saint Paul to the Corinthians." De Paule's shoulders drooped. "I will resign. Like I said before, I've not the energy for machinations, or cleverness. Perhaps my time has come to an end and your tenure as grand master is upon us, unless the up-time histories are in error. But you'll lead with honor, of that I'm positive."

"No," Jean said, "we should seek the guidance of His Holiness before proceeding. However, you'll be confined until then."

The sovereign council reconvened and sat for hours, and assured Jean he'd be named grand master once de Paule faced the papacy's judgment.

Afterward, Jean sat in silence, thinking. One fact was clear: investigations were a younger man's game and not for someone of Jean's age and station. No, he required an adjutant. Perhaps young Rodrik deserved redemption and another chance to serve the order, but first he'd suffer penance as a jailer at Château d'If... six months would suffice. Surely Jean could secure such arrangements.

Jean's gaze fell once more upon the table. Only the simple black cloth remained atop its surface.

The Maltese falcon had been stolen. "So Hammett's story now has some truth behind it after all. The figurine is lost."

Jean often reread not only Hammett's story, but de Paule's forged papal brief that had nearly brought ruin upon the Knights of Malta. Jean, the order's new grand master, took to heart the threat the Ottomans posed, but would prepare for a siege, not instigate one.

NEXT STOP? THE WILD, HAUNTED WORLD OF

TIM POWERS

DON'T MISS YOUR EXIT

An ex-Secret Servant agent. A woman haunted by the ghosts of California's highways. And the government conspiracy that ties them all together.

ALTERNATE ROUTES

HC: 978-1-4814-8340-7 • $25.00 US / $34.00 CAN
PB: 978-1-4814-8427-5 • $7.99 US / $10.99 CAN

A fast-paced supernatural adventure story that sweeps from the sun-blinded streets of LA to the horrifying labyrinth of Greek mythology. Sebastian Vickery and Ingrid Castine must learn to abandon old loyalties and learn loyalty to each other if they hope to survive in a world gone mad.

FORCED PERSPECTIVES

HC: 978-1-9821-2440-3 • $25.00 US / $34.00 CAN

Pursued by a Silicon Valley giant hungry for their souls, fugitive ex-Secret Service agent Sebastian Vickery and his companion Ingrid Castine throw themselves deep into the haunted world that lurks just beneath the surface of sunny California.

"Powers writes in a clean, elegant style that illuminates without slowing down the tale.... [He] promises marvels and horrors, and delivers them all." —Orson Scott Card

"Other writers tell tales of magic in the twentieth century, but no one does it like Powers." —*The Orlando Sentinel*